Improving Instruction Through Supervision, Evaluation, and Professional Development

Improving Instruction Through Supervision, Evaluation, and Professional Development

by

Michael F. DiPaola
The College of William & Mary

and

Wayne K. Hoy
Ohio State University

Information Age Publishing, Inc.
Charlotte, North Carolina • www.infoagepub.com

Library of Congress Cataloging-in-Publication Data

DiPaola, Michael F., 1947-
Improving instruction through supervision, evaluation, and professional
development / by Michael F. DiPaola, the College of William & Mary and Wayne
K. Hoy, the Pennsylvania State University.
pages cm
Updated revision of Principals Improving Instruction, 2008--Ecip galley.
Includes bibliographical references.
ISBN 978-1-62396-478-8 (paperback.) -- ISBN 978-1-62396-479-5 (hardcover) --
ISBN 978-1-62396-480-1 (ebook) 1. School supervision--United States. 2.
School principals--United States. I. Hoy, Wayne K. II. DiPaola, Michael F.,
1947- Principals improving instruction. III. Title.
LB2806.4.D56 2014
371.2'03--dc23

2013037691

Printed in the United States of America

CONTENTS

PREFACE

Improving Instruction Through Supervision, Evaluation, and Professional Development is an updated revision of *Principals Improving Instruction*. It reflects what we've learned from working with both teachers and administrators who have implemented our supervisory model in efforts to improve both teaching and learning. We've maintained the conceptual framework while updating sections on what we've learned about high yield instructional strategies from John Hattie's work. Of course the impact of Common Core Content Standards is embedded throughout. Finally, we included the link to a website that contains all the observation tools in electronic format so that observers can have the opportunity to collect data on a tablet or laptop, save it as a PDF file and e-mail it to the teacher observed. We continue to believe that teachers and principals need to work together to improve instruction in schools. This new book recognizes the reality that all principals are responsible for supervision, evaluation, and professional development of their teachers—tasks that are neither simple nor without conflict. The primary audience of this text is aspiring and practicing principals. We hope to help them understand both the theory and practice of supervision, evaluation, and professional development. Observing instruction, collecting data for reflection, and having conversations about teaching, however, are not the sole provinces of principals. Master teachers, teacher leaders, and teacher colleagues can also benefit from the supervisory sections of the book, especially the chapters on high-quality instruction, improving instruction, and the classroom data collecting tools.

Improving Instruction Through Supervision, Evaluation, and Professional Development, pp. vii–x
Copyright © 2014 by Information Age Publishing
All rights of reproduction in any form reserved.

We don't believe that teaching and learning will improve unless principals and teachers work together as a team. Principals and teacher colleagues have the responsibility of helping teachers become more effective, and by that we mean improving student learning. Increased teacher effectiveness occurs through the professional development of teachers, which is embedded in the informal, formative process of supervision.

CONTENTS OF THE BOOK

The text addresses the critical aspects principals need to improve instruction:

- *Instructional Leadership*—The principal is responsible for defining and communicating shared goals, monitoring and providing feedback about teaching and learning, and promoting school-wide professional development. Teachers and administrators must learn to work together in ways that increase student achievement.
- *Improving the School Context*—Principals are critical in developing the culture and climate of schools such that improvement of instruction is central and supported.
- *Supervising*—We distinguish between helping teachers be better teachers and evaluating their competence. Supervision is the collegial and informal process of helping teachers improve their teaching.
- *Evaluating*—Assessing overall teacher performance is a formal role mandated by the state and district. Principals must make the hard decision of recommending lifetime employment for teachers and ensuring quality of instruction.
- *Professional Development*—Lifelong learning is a salient aspect of the professional lives of teachers. In the supervision and evaluation of teachers, the principal is responsible for identifying and providing resources that ensure continued professional growth. The goal of job-embedded professional development is the improvement of teaching and learning.
- *Integration*—Supervision, evaluation, and professional development are integral and complementary aspects of the role of the principal as instructional leader. It is counterproductive to attempt any one in isolation.
- *Improving Instruction*—Systematically evaluating, supervising, and developing teachers' abilities is a pathway to increased student learning, which is the focus of this text.

- *Applying Theory to Practice*—Principals must be able to translate good theory and research into sound practice. We provide hands-on and authentic applications of the concepts and principles of supervision, evaluation, and professional development.

We hope you will find this a stimulating and useful book—one that guides your thoughts and actions about teaching, learning, supervising, evaluating, and developing professionally—all of which will help you become an instructional leader.

ACKNOWLEDGMENTS

Our colleagues in the field and at universities are important sources of ideas and criticism. First, we would like to extend our thanks to Professor Patrick Forsyth at the University of Oklahoma who coauthored *Effective Supervision: Theory into Practice*, which was the original source of many of the conceptual underpinnings of our work. We also thank Professor Anita Woolfolk Hoy for her advice and intellectual contributions to this project. Professor John Tarter was a constant source of encouragement and a sounding board for many of our ideas.

Conceptualizing a research-based, practical method of collecting class-room data that observers could collect easily and that teachers could understand, analyze, and reflect upon was no small undertaking. It required not only practical experience in classroom observation and an understanding of high-yield instructional strategies, but also creativity in designing observation tools that were clear and user-friendly. We are indebted to Valerie DiPaola, a master teacher and school administrator par excellence, who brought her wealth of experience in the classroom, as a master teacher, supervisor, and director of instruction to bear on the creation and design of many of the data collection tools and observation guidelines presented here.

We would be remiss not to acknowledge our practitioner colleagues who provided the cases, reactions, and criticism that grounded this book in practice. The following principals generously shared their experiences and expertise: Stephanie Guy, Randi Riesbeck, Jennifer Parish, Amy Colley, Lucia Sebastian, Chuck Wagner, John Caggiano, and Tony Vladu.

The following successful superintendents provided a reality check that anchored our work in the day-to-day administrative practice of schools: Harry Galinsky, John Hannum, Judith Wilson, Robert Rimmer, Thomas Morton, Jonathan Lewis, Patrick Russo, Steve Staples, Tom Reed, and Frank Walter.

Finally, but certainly not the least, we thank Leslie Bohon-Atkinson for her commitment and diligent assistance in the preparation of all phases of this work. Her attention to detail and constructive suggestions were invaluable.

FEATURES OF THE BOOK

Each chapter is grounded in the latest research and theory and provides specific suggestions for applying that knowledge to practice. Throughout the text, you will find numerous tools specifically designed to collect a variety of data in classrooms to improve instruction. Embedded in each chapter are exercises that require you to apply Theory into Practice by responding to a set of questions posed by the key issues of the chapter. After the explication and illustration of the key concepts and principles of the chapter, we provide an actual Instructional Leadership Challenge as described by a successful practicing principal. We challenge you in Reflective Practice to compare the actions of these expert principals with theory, research, and the best practices summarized in the chapter. We also invite you to Develop a Portfolio exhibit based on your learning and experience. If you create at least one exhibit for your portfolio from each chapter, by the end of the course you will have a comprehensive and useful set of personal plans for implementing an instructional improvement strategy in your school.

We also challenge you with a Communication Exercise in each chapter to practice and model effective techniques for conveying information while fine-tuning your interpersonal skills. After providing a brief set of suggested Readings to complement the content of the chapter, we conclude by examining What Do Superintendents Say? about a particularly difficult issue. Throughout the text in our Theory into Practice exercises, we connect and highlight the activities, tasks, and events with the appropriate ISLLC Standards. The Appendices provide a set of valuable tools: a sample evaluation instrument, forms, observation guides, and helpful websites for principals.

Michael F. DiPaola
Williamsburg, Virginia

Wayne K. Hoy
Columbus, Ohio

CHAPTER 1

INSTRUCTIONAL LEADERSHIP

The contemporary role of the principal has evolved into one that is multidimensional, but primarily focused on instructional leadership. The increasing global emphasis on accountability reinforces the instructional leadership dimension of the role of the principal (Hallinger, 2005). The core tasks of instructional leadership are supervision of instruction, evaluation of instruction, and professional development of teachers. We propose a useful model that develops and integrates these three essential tasks of instructional leadership.

The adoption of the Common Core State Standards (CCSS) (National Governors Association Center for Best Practices, Council of Chief State School Officers, 2010) presents a paradigm shift in how we operationalize teaching and learning. This shift requires significant changes in *how* teachers teach Common Core curriculum and what they do in the classroom to foster higher-order cognitive skills. School leaders are being challenged to align the vision of their schools to meet the shift embedded in Common Core State Standards.

In everyday practice, principals are required to supervise and evaluate both new and experienced teachers. The new teacher evaluation systems accompanying the Common Core State Standards require the school principal to systematically and periodically evaluate teachers and to make recommendations for retention and tenure. Although the professional development of teachers is typically neither mandated by the state nor

Improving Instruction Through Supervision, Evaluation, and Professional Development, pp. 1–24

required by the district, principals will need to provide teachers with training to meet the challenges in teaching higher-order cognitive skills. In fact, it is impossible for principals to supervise and evaluate teachers fairly without providing a professional development program to help teachers be successful and improve their teaching.

The principal's role as an instructional leader is to supervise, to evaluate, and to guide the professional development of their teachers—the core tasks of instructional leadership. The entire process is about improving teaching and learning. It is student learning that is the ultimate test of the effectiveness of teachers, principals, and schools.

ROLE OF THE PRINCIPAL

The job of the principal has been described in many ways. Traditionally, the role involved tasks such as setting clear goals, allocating resources to instruction, managing the curriculum, monitoring lesson plans, and evaluating teachers. Today, it includes much deeper involvement in the "core technology" of teaching and learning, carries more sophisticated views of professional development, and emphasizes the use of data to make decisions (King, 2002). Habegger (2008) describes successful principals as those who assure instruction is aligned with academic content standards, set a goal of continuous improvement in the building, design instruction for student success, develop partnerships with parents and the community, and nurture a culture where each individual feels valued. Bottoms and O'Neill (2001) characterize the principal as the "chief learning officer" who is ultimately responsible for the success or failure of a school.

For more than 30 years, the principal has been described in the literature as the instructional leader of the school. Hanny (1987) argued that "effective principals are expected to be effective instructional leaders.... [T]he principal must be knowledgeable about curriculum development, teacher and instructional effectiveness, clinical supervision, staff development and teacher evaluation" (p. 209). Fullan (1991) elaborates on this definition of principal leadership, calling for an active, collaborative form of leadership in which the principal works "with teachers to shape the school as a workplace in relation to shared goals, teacher collaboration, teacher learning opportunities, teacher certainty, teacher commitment, and student learning" (p. 161).

There is a universal call for instructional leadership by principals. The National Association of Elementary School Principals (NAESP, 2001), in defining standards for principals, emphasizes the role of instructional leader, while state legislatures across the nation have mandated that principals are to be leaders for learning. The research on effective schools makes a compelling argument that strong administrative leadership is required for the disparate elements of good schooling to be brought together and kept together (Lezotte, 1997).

Although the link between instructional leadership and student learning may be indirect, an extensive review of the research led to the conclusion that instructional leadership is second only to classroom instruction among school-related factors that influence student outcomes (Leithwood, Louis, Anderson, & Wahlstrom, 2004). More recently, proponents of value-added, outcomes-based education have redefined instructional leadership, moving from leader of a professional community with a focus on teaching to leader of a professional community with a focus on learning. One of the basic standards of the NAESP (2001) insists that principals put student and adult learning at the center of their leadership as well as serve as the lead learner.

In 2008, the Interstate School Leaders Licensure Consortium (ISLLC) revised six policy standards for school leaders to promote the success for all students.

Educational leaders promote the success of every student by:

1. facilitating the development, articulation, implementation, and stewardship of a vision of learning that is shared and supported by all stakeholders

2. advocating, nurturing, and sustaining a school culture and instructional program conducive to student learning and staff professional growth

3. managing the organization, operation, and resources for a safe, efficient, and effective learning environment

4. collaborating with faculty and community members, responding to diverse community interests and needs, and mobilizing community resources

5. acting with integrity, with fairness, and in an ethical manner

6. understanding, responding to, and influencing the political, social, economic, legal, and cultural context (Council of Chief State School Officers, 2008, pp. 14-15).

We will link many of the exercises and questions in this book with these leadership standards.

Although definitions of the principal's instructional leadership vary in the details, most include leadership behaviors focused on the goal of improving student achievement (Copland, 2002; Leithwood, Harris, & Hopkins, 2008; McEwan, 2003; Reeves, 2003; Supovitz & Poglinco, 2001; Waters, Marzano, & McNulty, 2003). Instructional leadership has been succinctly defined as "direct and indirect behaviors that significantly affect teacher instruction and, as a result, student learning" (Daresh & Playko, 1995, p. 33). With the adoption of the Common Core State Standards, instructional leaders must not only help their teachers master the content and pedagogical changes in the standards, but they must also anticipate the impact of the CCSS on other organizational procedures and practices and provide leadership in modifying such things as student scheduling, grading practices, and school class schedules.

As a consequence of the expanding responsibilities, a growing number of researchers maintain that instructional leadership should be distributed across the school community, with principals, superintendents, teachers, and policymakers having complementary responsibilities (Elmore, 2000; King, 2002; Spillane, Halverson, & Diamond, 2000).

MODELS OF INSTRUCTIONAL LEADERSHIP

Most researchers agree that instructional leadership is composed of key elements fundamental to improving teaching and learning. Yet, many models of instructional leadership have evolved during the past two decades. To sketch the evolution of instructional leadership during this period, we focus on four models of leadership that are prominent in the literature.

Hallinger and Murphy's Model (1985)

Hallinger and Murphy (1985) developed their model of instructional management based on two major sources: an extensive review of the literature on school effectiveness and the examination of actual behaviors of elementary principals. From their empirical and theoretical analyses, they developed a framework of instructional management with three functions composed of a myriad of specific descriptors. They identified three major functions of instructional leadership:

- defining the school mission—framing and communicating goals
- managing the instructional program—supervising and evaluating instruction, coordinating curriculum, and monitoring student progress
- promoting a positive school climate—protecting instructional time, promoting professional development, maintaining high visibility, providing teaching incentives, enforcing high academic standards, and providing incentives for students.

Murphy's Model (1990)

Using a comprehensive review and integration of the research from the literature on effective schools, school improvement, staff development, and organizational change, Murphy (1990) refined and elaborated the earlier Hallinger and Murphy Model (1985). He elaborated an instructional leadership framework that consisted of four basic dimensions of instructional leadership:

- developing mission and goals
- promoting quality instruction and monitoring student progress
- creating an academic learning climate
- developing a supportive work environment.

Patterson's Model (1993)

Patterson (1993) recognized the importance of student learning as the ultimate outcome of instructional leadership. The basic behaviors of his model include:

- providing a sense of vision to their schools—articulating a shared vision of improving student learning through more effective teaching
- engaging in participatory management—empowering others by involving them
- supporting instruction—recognizing instruction as the key to learning
- monitoring instruction—knowing what is happening in the classroom and providing feedback
- facilitating the achievement of learning goals.

Weber's Model (1996)

Weber (1996) examined the school's organizational structure and concluded that even if an instructional leader were not the principal, such a leader was imperative. After an extensive review of the research, he concluded: "The leaderless-team approach to a school's instructional program has powerful appeal, but a large group of professionals still needs a single point of contact and an active advocate for teaching and learning"

(p. 254). This single point of contact is typically the building principal who provides instructional leadership by:

- defining the school's mission
- managing curriculum and instruction
- promoting a positive learning climate
- observing and improving instruction
- assessing the instructional program.

Alig-Mielcarek and Hoy (2005)

Alig-Mielcarek and Hoy (2005) reviewed the research on instructional leadership, including the previous models, and developed a model of instructional leadership with three core functions that incorporate the fundamental properties of the earlier models. Instructional leadership has three basic functions (see Figure 1.1):

- defining and communicating shared goals
- monitoring and providing feedback on the teaching and learning process
- promoting school-wide professional development.

In defining and communicating shared goals, instructional leaders work collaboratively with staff to identify, communicate, and use the shared goals of the school. These goals focus the staff on a common mission—increasing student learning by improving instruction. The leader uses goals in making organizational decisions, aligning instructional practice, purchasing curricular materials, and providing targets for progress. The key is that achieving the vision of increased student learning drives all decisions.

In monitoring and providing feedback on the teaching and learning process, instructional leaders build their daily routines around supporting teachers and students. They are visible throughout the school and interact freely with students and teachers. They provide praise and feedback to teachers, students, and the community on academic performances. Finally, they ensure that the instructional time of the school is focused, meaningful, and uninterrupted.

In promoting school-wide professional development, instructional leaders become teachers of teachers. They facilitate lifelong learning by helping teachers to identify meaningful and relevant learning opportunities. They help teachers develop individualized professional development plans. They encourage teachers to learn more about student achievement

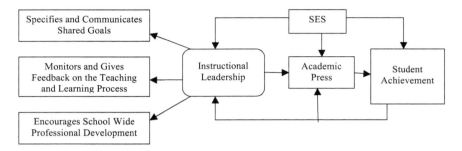

Figure 1.1. A simplified model of Instructional Leadership.

by analyzing appropriate data and making decisions based on the out-comes. They provide support and resources to teachers that enable them to become more effective in the classroom.

Educational research has revealed other malleable conditions of schooling that have a significant impact on student achievement (Barth et al., 1999; Erbe, 2000; Hoy & Hannum, 1997; Hoy & Sabo, 1998; Hoy, Tarter, & Kottkamp, 1991). The Coleman Report (Coleman et al., 1966) formed the cornerstone of this tradition concluding that socioeconomic status (SES) is the single most dominant predictor of student achieve-ment. In response to that finding, school effectiveness research flourished and became more sophisticated in the types of data used and the statisti-cal techniques applied (Goldstein & Woodhouse, 2000).

In sum, the research suggests a contingency model of instructional leadership in which leadership works through the climate and culture of the school. To be effective, the instructional leader must create an organi-zational setting conducive to student learning. For example, a climate with a strong emphasis on academics seems essential in promoting high student achievement. Figure 1.1 provides a simplified model of the path of successful instructional leadership. Note that instructional leadership works indirectly through academic press, also called academic emphasis, to promote student achievement; leadership is not directly related to school performance, but together leadership and academic emphasis can be effective regardless of the socioeconomic level of the school (SES).

Contemporary Model of Instructional Leadership: A Synthesis and Expansion

Although academic emphasis is pivotal in facilitating effective instruc-tional leadership (Alig-Mielcarek & Hoy, 2005; Forsyth, Adams, & Hoy, 2011; Hoy & Sabo, 1998), a number of other school properties are also instrumental in helping principals enable teachers to guide students to academic success. Faculty trust and collective efficacy are two other important features of the school that are critical in student achievement.

Faculty Trust

Trust is another aspect of school culture that is critical in developing high student performance. All trust relationships are built on interdependence, especially when the interests of one party cannot be achieved without reliance on the other. In schools, there are reciprocal trust needs; teachers depend on students and parents, and similarly, parents and students depend on teachers. Collective faculty trust is the teachers' willingness to be dependent on others based on the confidence that the other party is benevolent, reliable, competent, honest, and open; the trusted party can be relied upon to help and do no harm.

There are two independent streams of research that demonstrate the importance of collective trust in generating high student performance: The University of Chicago studies by Bryk and Schneider (2002) and their associates (Bryk, Gomez, & Grunow, 2011) and the Ohio State Studies by Hoy and his colleagues (Forsyth et al., 2011; Goddard, Tschannen-Moran, & Hoy, 2001; Hoy, 2002; Hoy & Tschannen-Moran, 1999, 2003; Tschannen-Moran, 2004) both demonstrated the importance of collective trust in promoting student achievement. These research findings show a strong link between faculty trust in students and parents and student achievement—even after controlling for the socioeconomic status and other demographic variables, the relationship is robust (Bryk & Schneider, 2002; Forsyth et al., 2011; Goddard et al., 2001; Hoy, 2002; Hoy & Miskel, 2013).

For example, although Bryk and Schneider (2002) did not start out to study trust in their study of the Chicago public schools, they found that trust was pivotal in the improvement in mathematics and reading performance. In fact, they found, "Schools reporting strong positive trust levels in 1991 were three times more likely to be categorized eventually as improving in mathematics and reading than those with very weak trust reports" (p. 111). These findings persisted even after controlling for teacher background, student demographics, and other school context factors. Increasingly, evidence is mounting that trusting relations among teachers, parents, and students promote student achievement and improvement. This is an important finding because changing the trust relations among teachers, parents, and students, although not easy, is much more manageable than changing the socioeconomic status of parents. Skilled principals can improve student achievement by developing school faculties with high collective trust for students and parents.

Collective Efficacy

Bandura (1997) was first to develop the construct of collective efficacy, which evolved naturally form his work on individual sense of teacher efficacy. Collective efficacy is the shared perceptions of teachers in a school that the efforts of the faculty as a whole can have a positive effect on students (Hoy & Miskel, 2013). At the collective level, the efficacy beliefs of the faculty are strengthened rather than depleted through their use, and the shared efficacy beliefs of the teachers gives the school a distinctive identity, which we call a culture of efficacy.

Like the research for academic emphasis and collective trust, collective efficacy is positively related to student achievement even controlling for SES, previous achievement, and other demographic variables; in fact, in initial studies by both Bandura (1993) and Goddard, Hoy, and Woolfolk Hoy (2000, 2004), the relationship between collective efficacy and student achievement was stronger than the SES-achievement relation. That is, collective efficacy of a school can be a stronger predictor of achievement than socioeconomic conditions. This positive relation has been replicated in numerous studies at both the high school and elementary levels (Goddard, 2001, 2002; Goddard, Hoy, & LoGerfo, 2003; Goddard, LoGerfo, & Hoy, 2004; Goddard, Sweetland, & Hoy, 2000a, 2000b). In brief, developing a culture of school efficacy provides the school setting with the capacity to improve school performance regardless of the SES of the school.

Thus far, we have identified three school properties that are important in facilitating strong student achievement in spite of the socioeconomic conditions of the school and parents: academic emphasis, faculty trust, and collective efficacy. It seems clear that instructional leaders should develop school cultures imbued with these three properties because they provide a culture that aids learning. Not surprisingly, these three concepts are highly correlated with each other, which raises the question: What is the common property undergirding academic emphasis, trust, and efficacy?

Academic Optimism

One is struck by the optimistic nature of both collective trust, which requires a leap of faith in others, and collective efficacy, which is also embedded in a positive perspective. Academic emphasis gives both collective efficacy and trust a positive focus on academics. Thus, academic optimism seems to be an abstract property that captures and integrates all three of these variables (academic emphasis, collective efficacy, and trust) into a single integrated construct. Actually, the theory of academic optimism as a latent variable composed of academic emphasis, collective trust in students and parents, and collective efficacy was confirmed in a rigorous empirical study by Hoy and his colleagues (Hoy, Tarter, & Woolfolk Hoy, 2006).

Academic optimism unites academic emphasis, faculty trust, and collective efficacy because each implies a sense of hope and the possible. Collective efficacy is the belief that the faculty can make a positive difference in student performance; the faculty believes in itself. Faculty trust in students and parents is the belief that teachers, parents, and students can improve learning; the faculty trusts its students. Academic emphasis is the enacted behavior generated by the trust and efficacy beliefs; the focus is on academic success. A school with a culture of academic optimism is one in which the faculty shares the belief that it can make a positive difference, that all students can learn and succeed, and that high academic performance can be achieved regardless of the SES of the school and parents (Hoy, 2012; Hoy & Miskel, 2013).

What is the instructional leader's role in improving instruction? Major effort should be focused on developing a school culture of academic optimism because it provides the organizational context to improve the academic performance of students. Building upon the model of instructional leadership proposed in Figure 1.1, the new model in Figure 1.2 is enhanced by adding the concepts of collective efficacy and collective trust to an emphasis on academics, producing a culture of academic optimism. The leader defines and communicates shared goals that are anchored in efficacy, trust, and academics. Then the leader monitors and provides feedback on the teaching and learning process. Finally, the leader promotes school-wide professional development activities to create collective trust, collective efficacy, and an emphasis on high academic performance. This three-pronged approach to instructional leadership creates a culture of academic optimism, which leads to high student achievement for all students regardless of SES. Hence, effective instructional leadership works through the academic optimism of the teachers, students, and parents of the school (see Figure 1.2).

FINDING TIME FOR INSTRUCTIONAL LEADERSHIP

Three primary roles have traditionally constituted the job of school principals (Cuban, 1998). First, principals have a managerial role. Second, they have a political role—a communicator, negotiator, and facilitator with parents, central office personnel, and other constituencies. Third, they have an instructional role—a teacher of teachers. Unfortunately, the managerial and political roles, not the instructional one, historically dominate the lives of principals as they react to the constant crises that seemingly arise on an

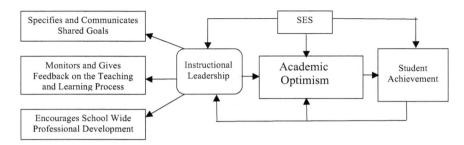

Figure 1.2. Contemporary model of Instructional Leadership: Leaders creating a culture of academic optimism.

THEORY INTO PRACTICE

ISLLC Leadership Standards 1 & 5

Describe the characteristics of your principal that best demonstrates her or his instructional leadership. How does your principal communicate a vision for student learning? Describe the way your principal provides feedback on your successes and failures in the classroom? Is it fair? Why/Why not? How does your principal help you become a better teacher? What advice do you have to help your principal become a better leader of learning?

---

hourly basis. Thus, too many principals conceive and construct their roles largely as managers of their schools.

In order to be successful in the Common Core, principals must preserve time for instructional leadership by making hard choices about their priorities. Given the conflicting demands of daily events, principals must be organized, purposive, and deliberate in their planning. Principals who aspire to be successful as instructional leaders must preserve a substantial portion of time and energy for supervision and support of teaching and student learning. They must not get distracted by the persistent focus on testing and hone in on teaching and learning in their schools. Instructional leaders must fulfill the managerial and political aspects of their job. They must keep their finger on the pulse of their managerial and political responsibilities but at the same time be directly engaged in their instructional responsibilities.

Effective instructional leaders rearrange priorities to reinforce their emphases on academic performance and instructional improvement. They spend more time in classrooms observing instruction and learning. They effectively manage their own time around instruction. They develop their own pedagogical and content knowledge. They reconceptualize their primary role as helping teachers acquire the requisite pedagogical and content knowledge necessary for success. Finally, they recognize that instruction is the primary means to student learning; thus, they define their role as a service provider for teachers (Supovitz & Poglinco, 2001).

The primary function of schooling is learning. In order to facilitate learning, principals must devote the majority of their time to instructional processes. They cannot complain that they do not have time for instruction, because that is their primary job. If quality teaching is to occur in the building, the principal has to lead this effort. Success for all students through instructional improvement is the prime focus in the lives of effective principals, and their decisions and priorities reflect their commitment. Increased learning for all students and instructional improvement are the hallmarks of effective schools.

EFFECTIVE INSTRUCTIONAL LEADERS

There is a substantial relationship between effective principal leadership and student learning (Waters et al., 2003). Hattie (2009) defines instructional leadership as "principals who have their major focus on creating a learning climate free of disruption, a system of clear teaching objectives, and high teacher expectations for teachers and students" (p. 83). His meta-analysis of the influence of principals on their students found that "principals who promote challenging goals, and then establish safe environments for teachers to critique, question, and support other teachers to reach those goals together have the most effect on student outcomes" (Hattie, 2009, p. 83). Principals who focus on students' learning and instructional strategies are the most effective (Hallinger & Murphy, 1986; Henchey, 2001). Other researchers use the term "learning-centered leadership" to describe leadership practices that involve the planning, evaluation, coordination, and improvement of teaching and learning (Goldring, Porter, Murphy, Elliott, & Cravens, 2009). A meta-analysis of the literature identified the relative effects of five leadership dimensions:

1. leading through promoting and participating in teacher learning and development
2. establishing goals and expectations
3. planning, coordinating, and evaluating teaching and the curriculum
4. strategic resourcing
5. ensuring an orderly and supportive environment.

The authors concluded that the more leaders focus their relationships, their work, and their learning on the core business of teaching and learning, the greater their influence on student outcomes will be (Robinson, Lloyd, & Rowe, 2008).

But principal influence is indirect; that is, it occurs through others who have frequent, direct contact with students during the learning process (Hallinger & Heck, 1996). Research evidence suggests the indirect influence of school leadership on student outcomes can be considerable depending on how principals behave (Leithwood et al., 2008; Robinson et al., 2008). Instructional leaders must recognize that there are neither quick fixes nor easy answers to the improvement of the teaching and learning process. Wang, Haertel, and Walberg (1993, 1997) performed a meta-analysis of more than 10,000 statistical findings on the significant influences on learning. Their results should not be surprising. In general, direct influences have a greater impact on student learning than indirect ones. The key to improving student learning rests within the classroom. Effective instructional leadership, therefore, involves influencing school processes that are directly linked to student learning (Hallinger & Heck, 1996).

Stein and Spillane (2003) identified leadership content knowledge based on how teachers and principals work together to deliver effective instruction. Effective instructional leaders know and understand how teachers influence student academic growth. In particular, they:

- know strong instruction when they see it
- know how to encourage it when it is absent
- know how to set the conditions for continuous academic learning among their teachers

A study of effective urban principals revealed nine strategies they employed to improve their schools. These principals:

1. set high expectations for all students
2. shared leadership and stayed engaged
3. encouraged collaboration among staff
4. used assessment data to support student success
5. kept the focus on students
6. addressed barriers to learning
7. reinforced classroom learning at home
8. employed systems for identifying interventions
9. defined special education as the path to success in the general education program (Council of Chief School Officers, 2002, p. 8).

A comparison of effective and ineffective schools revealed three primary differences. The effective schools had:

- student achievement as a major focus
- teachers and staff who expected all students to learn
- principals who did not tolerate ineffective teachers (Mendro, 1998, p. 264).

Instructional leaders also focus the extent to which students are achieving the intended outcomes of each course and the steps principals can take to give both students and teachers the additional time and support they need to improve learning (DuFour, 2002). Robinson (2010) conducted a meta-analysis that revealed three broad competencies of effective instructional leadership. Effective instructional leadership requires leaders who:

- align administrative procedures and processes with important learning goals
- solve the plethora of problems that arise in the course of improving learning and teaching in their schools
- use their knowledge, their problem solving ability, and their interpersonal skills to create a culture of trust and optimism.

She concluded that competent instructional leadership involves the integration of knowledge and relationships in a context of school-based problem solving (Robinson, 2010).

The pedagogical and content knowledge required to improve learning and teaching is so vast that it cannot be mastered by an individual instructional leader or leadership team (Spillane, Halverson, & Diamond, 2004). There is an obvious need to create the appropriate institutional and external conditions for instructional leaders to develop the competencies required for them to be successful. Equally important is the development of research-based tools and associated practices that scaffold the work of instructional leadership.

DISTRIBUTIVE LEADERSHIP

Spillane, Halverson, and Diamond (2001) argue that it is more legitimate to examine school leadership as the cumulative activities of a broader set of leaders, both formal and informal, within a school rather than as the work of one individual. This perspective shifts the focus from individual principals to the joint interactions of formal leaders, informal leaders, and other teachers in their unique school contexts (Spillane, 2006). Achieving increased student learning through others is the essence of effective instructional leadership (Hallinger & Heck, 1996, p. 39). Effective instructional leaders recognize the talents and expertise of others in their schools, provide opportunities for leadership development in others, and create a broad leadership base in their schools. Principals may be leaders among leaders, but it serves both their own and their schools' interests to develop broad-based leadership in their schools. The development of other school leaders serves many purposes. For example, it expands expertise across the faculty, thereby deepening efforts for instructional improvement and increasing the likelihood that these efforts will be sustained over time.

Instructional leaders need baseline expectations for all members of their school. Teachers should be given choices but be expected to strive toward these expectations daily. These expectations create a standard for instruction that, over time, can change the way that instruction occurs across the classrooms in the school. This means suspending preconceived beliefs about the differences and limitations of students. Instructional leadership, not just by the principal but by a wider cast of individuals in both formal and informal leadership roles, plays a central role in shifting school activities more directly to instructional improvements that lead to enhanced student learning and performance.

Distributing leadership responsibilities across the staff of a school is a necessity for principals who want to share as well as protect a portion of their time for instructional leadership. Principals who are instructional leaders purposefully delegate their management responsibilities across formal school leader positions. However, these principals are also cognizant that they should not just shift all of their management responsibilities to their assistant principals. Assistant principals also need the time to make regular classroom visits and have instructional experiences in order to participate in the conversations about instruction that contribute to the decisions and guide the direction of the school.

When quality instruction becomes the central focus in a school, those who are effective teachers become increasingly valued. In fact, often they become important informal leaders in schools, colleagues with expertise who are willing and able to help and share with their peers. The principal turns to effective teachers to become leaders in the school, and their colleagues recognize and respond to their expertise.

STANDARDS AND ACCOUNTABILITY

The passage of the Goals 2000 legislation in 1994 resulted in the vast majority of states adopting standards and developing assessments to determine

---

THEORY INTO PRACTICE
ISLLC Leadership Standard 1
What is your view of distributed leadership? How does your principal
provide opportunities for teachers to improve instruction? Do you
believe that most teachers know enough to take the leadership initiative
to help colleagues improve their teaching? Think of a teacher in your
school who is an instructional leader. What attitudes, skills, and
knowledge does she or he possess? As a teacher, are you ready to become
an instructional leader?

---

student success. The No Child Left Behind Act (NCLB) in 2001 established
ambitious goals and high-stakes consequences, including school accreditation and school choice, determined by standardized test scores. NCLB supported standards-based education reform based on the premise that setting
high standards and establishing measurable goals can improve learning for
all students. NCLB required states to develop assessments in basic skills and
administer these assessments to all students at select grade levels in order
to receive federal school funding. Consequently, since the enactment of
NCLB, curriculum and instruction have been driven by the assessments
much more than the state standards themselves.

Although some progress was made in closing the achievement gaps for
some groups of students, by 2009 a movement toward nationwide curriculum standards was initiated by the National Governors' Association and
the Council of Chief State School Officers, with support from the Gates
Foundation. By the end of 2012, the resulting Common Core State Standards (CCSS) were adopted by the vast majority of states. The wide adoption of the CCSS, coupled with College and Career Readiness initiatives,
creates a shift to more skills-based, higher-level thinking standards that
cannot necessarily be demonstrated on an objective assessment. Two
national assessment consortia (the Smarter Balanced Assessment Consortium and the Partnership for Assessment of Readiness for College and
Careers) are developing computer-based testing for a scheduled implementation in 2014–2015 (Burris & Garrity, 2012).

The implementation of the Common Core State Standards (CCSS) and
the accompanying assessments will largely determine the CCSS's impact.
However, implementation will be impossible without accompanying commitment and resource support of federal and state governments. Principals
and teachers need both professional support and resources to implement
Common Core State Standards with fidelity (Mathis, 2012).

CCSS and high-stakes testing require principals to be much more skilled
than ever before. Sternberg (2004) argues that successful leaders need "creativity to generate good ideas, academic intelligence to ascertain whether

those ideas are good, practical intelligence to know how to persuade other people, and wisdom to make the ideas work for everyone's benefit" (p. 113). He contends that if even one of these elements is missing, the effectiveness of the leader is diminished.

As pressure for improving student performance in this standards-based, assessment-driven environment swells and test results are increasingly scrutinized, school principals are being urged to focus their efforts on the core business of schooling—student learning. By concentrating on teaching, the instructional leader of the past emphasized the inputs of the learning process. By concentrating on learning, today's school leaders shift both their own focus and that of the school community from inputs to outcomes and from intentions to results.

Powerful instructional leadership involves more than just a general focus on increased learning and improving the quality of instruction, but that is a good start. Principals who increase their schools' focus on student learning and quality instruction will increase time on task and improve their students' performance. However, the real value of instructional leadership comes from the systemic connection of an intense focus on instructional improvement with a clear vision of instructional quality. A concrete vision of instructional quality provides a tangible representation of effective instruction planning and delivery. Teachers need prototypes they can work toward, and instructional leaders need ways to measure the extent to which teachers are successful.

Common Core State Standards, both as a concrete set of goals for student knowledge and as an abstract expression of uniform expectations for staff, provide a framework for instructional leaders for evaluation. Standards-based accountability challenges traditional assumptions. Instead of simply encouraging teachers' efforts, principals now must help teachers produce tangible results as they strive for ambitious academic goals. Such action requires not just innovative practices but also a different mindset (Elmore, 2000; Jamentz, 2002).

Several implications are apparent. First, given the numerous and often conflicting demands for reform, leaders must create coherence in improvement efforts (Supovitz & Poglinco, 2001). A principal may have a vision of how it will occur, but that vision must be communicated so that members of the school community understand there is a common goal to which everyone is committed and accountable. Policies, practices, and resources must then be aligned with that common goal. Instructional leadership is the "organizational glue" that keeps things on track (Elmore, 2000). By articulating a coherent vision of instruction, one that teachers can envision and embrace, principals take the first step in marshalling efforts for increasing student learning. They must also encourage and support consistent implementation of the vision both within and across classrooms.

Second, the distributed nature of leadership requires principals to find and execute the right combination of mandate and empowerment. On the one hand, they must make it clear that change is not optional and that common goals may require teachers to give up or defer some individual preferences. These principals lead the faculty in developing a set of non-negotiable expectations for effort and practice for everyone. On the other hand, principals must recognize that they cannot simply impose the expectations without including teachers in the process and assuring them of support and sufficient resources. A safe environment for teachers, using dialogue rather than dictates, keeps the focus on core instructional issues (Supovitz & Poglinco, 2001).

Finally, instructional leaders must model learning. Principals must be able to recognize the alignment of lessons with the CCSS, know what research-based, pedagogical practices look like in a classroom, assess the alignment of classroom assessments with those standards, and evaluate student work for evidence that standards have been achieved. Principals' knowledge should be deep enough to let them coach teachers using explanations, practical examples, modeling, and demonstrations. Just as important, leaders must demonstrate the same learning characteristics that they expect in teachers: openness to new ideas, willingness to be driven by results, willingness to risk failure, persistence, and resilience in the face of difficulty. In the era of accountability, simply observing a teacher's classroom three times a year is not enough. With standards comes accountability, and with accountability comes the need to understand and apply data to make decisions about instruction.

Uniform expectations do not always sit well with faculty. There are always recalcitrant teachers who refuse to budge from their longstanding practices. Principals cannot tolerate for long those who refuse to participate in the process of continuous improvement. They must act decisively and employ a variety of strategies to sway, disband, or dispel such opposition. They must work to make their vision of instruction the norm throughout the school and develop instructional expectations for each classroom. They must protect instructional time from a variety of intrusions. Such protection must extend outside the classroom as well. For example, band practice, pep rallies, athletic events, special assemblies, and intercom announcements are just some of the distractions that can disrupt the instructional routine of schools.

Skillful principals do not confuse consistency with conformity. They understand that teachers have a variety of valuable individual experiences, pedagogical techniques, and personal strengths that can contribute to their individual effectiveness in the classroom. The goal is to achieve a balance between a strong leadership role and autonomy for teachers. Effective principals convey high expectations for students and staff. They have well-defined and well-communicated policies. They make frequent classroom visits and are highly visible and available to students and staff. They are adept at parent and community relations (Cawelti, 1999; Robinson 1985). And, above all, they take every opportunity to support teachers in their work and enhance teachers' skills to improve student learning.

Principals' support for teachers manifests in a variety of ways including praise, encouragement, protection, counsel, and provision of resources. The kind of support depends on the personality and style of the principal, the specific needs of teachers, and the climate of the school. Taken together, these efforts subtly change the principal's role into that of a service provider of the work of teachers.

The shift from a focus on teaching to a focus on learning reflects the contemporary emphasis on outcomes. When learning becomes the heart of the school, when all of the school's educators examine their efforts and the initiatives of the school through the lens of their impact on learning, the structure and culture of the school begin to change in substantive ways. Principals foster this structural and cultural transformation when they shift their emphasis from helping individual teachers improve instruction to helping teams of teachers ensure that students achieve the intended outcomes of their schooling. More succinctly, teachers and students benefit when principals function as leaders of learning rather than merely leaders of instruction. They can accomplish this by employing several strategies. They organize their schools around an emphasis on instructional improvement that is supported by a distinct vision of instructional quality. They cultivate a community of instructional practice in their schools by creating safe and collaborative environments for teachers to engage in their work and by drawing upon a wide network of individuals to deepen the work. They also reorganize their own professional time and prioritize support for increased learning through instructional improvement—they walk the talk!

THEORY INTO PRACTICE
ISLLC Leadership Standards 3 & 4

What is your reaction to the implementation of Common Core State Standards? Has your classroom instructional practice changed? How? Have your principal's supervisory and/or evaluation procedures changed? How? Assess the merit of these changes. How has the community reacted to the legislation and subsequent changes? Have the changes produced a more efficient and effective learning environment? If so, how? If not, why?

SUMMARY

An essential role for all principals is that of instructional leader. We are not suggesting that the principal alone is responsible for instructional leadership. That simply is not the case. Leadership in instructional matters should emerge freely from both the principal and teachers. Leadership is a distributed resource, not a scarce one; hence, principals must find ways to tap the creative abilities and initiative of their teachers. In the final analysis, teachers deliver instruction in the classroom; they have expertise and experience in curriculum and teaching; and they have mastered a substantial body of content and pedagogical knowledge. Nonetheless, it is the principal's responsibility to develop a school that incorporates the best instructional practices. Hence, the principal should forge a partnership with teachers with the primary goal of improving teaching and learning. But how?

The principal must communicate a clear vision of instructional excellence, provide feedback to teachers through both the informal and formal processes of supervision and evaluation, and, finally, ensure continuous professional development consistent with the goal of high student achievement for all students. In brief, the model of instructional leadership we advocate in this text calls for (1) sharing a vision of instructional excellence and high student performance, (2) monitoring and providing constructive feedback to teachers through informal supervision and formal evaluation, and (3) supporting instructional excellence and academic achievement through appropriate professional development of teachers.

A PRINCIPAL'S INSTRUCTIONAL LEADERSHIP CHALLENGE

Instructions—Read the following account provided by a principal, reflect on her practice, and perform a case analysis.

I have been the assistant principal of Jefferson, a large suburban high school, for several months. This is my first administrative job after spending nine years as a social studies teacher in one of the district's middle schools, where I had a reputation for effectively working with students who were very challenging.

Jefferson has veteran administrators who are supportive but expect me to carry my own weight. I have been observing classroom instruction through informal, drop-in visits during the first two months of school, primarily of 10th grade teachers, since that is the grade I have been assigned to handle student discipline issues. During my short classroom visits, I see a great variety of teaching styles as well as variation in teachers' expectations of their students.

I noted that the majority of student discipline referrals have been coming from a small minority of teachers. In visiting the classrooms of those teachers I decided to focus on their classroom management practices. I've had several follow-up conversations with these teachers, both novice and veteran, specifically focusing on their management techniques. During those discussions I gave constructive suggestions, jointly developed specific plans of action, and attempted to assist them in improving their classroom management. All of the teachers have been fairly receptive, and I observed several of them implementing the suggestions.

At this morning's administrative team meeting, the principal reminded me and the other assistant principals that she expects, during both informal and formal classroom visits, that we will be monitoring instruction and providing specific feedback to teachers. She reinforced the district's focus on research-based instructional strategies linked to student achievement and asked us each to visit, by the end of the month, all the teachers' classrooms we have been assigned to evaluate this year. During these informal observations, we must create a prioritized list placing at the top those teachers we believe need the most assistance with instructional strategies, and specify what strategies need attention.

When I return to my office and review the list of teachers I have been assigned to evaluate, they range from calculus teachers to ninth grade basic skills teachers. The majority of them are veteran teachers, since the principal and senior assistant principal always evaluate the nontenured teachers. The assigned task seems daunting. I have expertise in the field of social studies, not in the sciences, foreign languages, math, or other subjects most of them teach.

REFLECTIVE PRACTICE

Place yourself in the shoes of this assistant principal. Has this AP been effective thus far? Why? If you were the new assistant principal of this school:

- How would you respond to the charge of your principal?
- Where should you begin?
- What should you be looking for during your classroom visits?
- How can you assess these strategies across disciplines and grade levels?
- How will you determine who needs most assistance?
- After you create a list, then what?

- What do you think about suggesting a division of labor in which you work with all the teachers on classroom management, and the others work on content issues?

Sketch your plan of action. Be sure to address the questions raised above and any other critical issues that you identify.

DEVELOP YOUR PORTFOLIO

Portfolios are being increasingly used for the purposes of licensing, hiring, and evaluation. In this text we have two major objectives for your portfolio development: first, to demonstrate your personal reflection and professional growth; and second, to provide evidence of expertise for external audiences such as licensure boards and prospective employers. Thus, at the conclusion of each chapter in this book you will be asked to develop an entry for your professional portfolio: for example, create a product that incorporates knowledge from the chapter into an action plan, a position statement, a newsletter, a presentation, or a policy statement. Potential sources of portfolio entries include communication exercises and skill development exercises. For this chapter, we begin with the following communication exercise.

COMMUNICATION EXERCISE

You have been appointed as new principal of Proctor Elementary School, an urban school of 435 students with 12 teachers. The PTA has organized a reception to welcome you and get acquainted with the parents and teachers of Proctor Elementary. The president of the PTA has asked you to make a brief 10-minute speech on your plan for instructional leadership of Proctor. Prepare a 10-minute speech using a Power-Point format.

READINGS

Cawelti, G. (2006). The side effects of NCLB. *Educational Leadership, 64*(3), 64–68.

Daresh, J. C. (2002). *What it means to be a principal: Your guide to leadership*. Thousand Oaks, CA: Corwin Press.

Daresh, J. C. (2006). *Beginning the principalship* (3rd ed.). Thousand Oaks, CA: Corwin Press.

Good, T. L., & Brophy, J. E. (2007). *Looking in classrooms* (10th ed.). Boston, MA: Allyn & Bacon/Longman.

Leithwood, K., Seashore, L. K., Anderson, S., & Wahlstrom, K. (2004). *How leadership influences student learning*. Ontario, Canada: Center for Applied Research and Educational Improvement.

Slavin, R. E., & Olatokunbo, S. F. (1998). *Show me the evidence: Proven and promising programs for American's schools.* Thousand Oaks, CA: Corwin Press.

Wallace Foundation. (2013). *The school principal as leader: Guiding schools to better teaching and learning.* Washington, DC: Wallace Foundation.

Woolfolk Hoy, A. W., & Hoy, W. K (2013). *Instructional leadership: A learning-centered guide* (4th ed.). Boston, MA: Allyn & Bacon.

PORTFOLIO DEVELOPMENT RESOURCES

Barrett, H. C. (1999). *Electronic teaching portfolios.* ERIC/AE, Washington, DC. (ERIC Document Reproduction Service No. ED 432 265).

Burke, K. (1997). *Designing professional portfolios for change.* Arlington Heights, IL: IRI/Skylight Training.

Burke, K., Fogarty, R., & Belgrad, S. (1994). *The portfolio connection.* Arlington Heights, IL: IRI/Skylight Training.

Campbell, D. M., Cignetti, P. B., Melenyzer, B. J., Nettles, D. H., & Wyman, R. M. (1997). *How to develop a professional portfolio.* Boston, MA: Allyn & Bacon.

Dietz, M. E. (2001). *Designing the school leader's portfolio.* Arlington Heights, IL: Skylight Professional Development.

Seldin, P. (2000). Portfolios: A positive appraisal. *Academe, (86)*1, 36–44.

Tuttle, H. G. (1997, January/February). Electronic portfolios. *Multimedia Schools.* 33–37.

WHAT DO SUPERINTENDENTS SAY?

What is most important to you in selecting a principal who will be an instructional leader?

Superintendent 1: Past performance as a teacher and in other roles they have held reflects a strong belief that the driving force in a school is all students learning.

Superintendent 2: The successful candidate must go beyond the rhetoric of instructional leadership and demonstrate the process with concrete examples.

Superintendent 3: Finding an individual who articulates and exhibits an understanding of Common Core Content Standards and effective assessment strategies at the individual, classroom, and building level.

Superintendent 4: Select an individual who will be viewed by the staff as a credible instructional leader based on his/her pedagogical and content knowledge, skills, and track record.

Superintendent 5: The candidate must be able to articulate a clear understanding of the critical role of the principal in the ongoing process of reviewing and improving the delivery of instruction.

Superintendent 6: A principal must understand and model a variety of instructional approaches and strategies that positively impact student learning. The effective principal must then demonstrate the skills needed to direct the faculty to focus on instructional issues and motivate staff members to improve their own skills to achieve school-based goals.

Superintendent 7: He or she must recognize that excellence in every facet of the school program, particularly instruction, never occurs by accident, only by design. The principal must work with teachers to set specific, measurable goals for student outcomes, and then plan and implement data-driven programs to improve student achievement.

Superintendent 8: The ability to build and sustain professional relationships in a teaching/learning community is critical. Those relationships and inherent mutual respect allow school communities to focus on instruction and to maintain that focus throughout the many distractions and detractors we face daily in schools.

CHAPTER 2

AN INTEGRATED MODEL OF INSTRUCTIONAL LEADERSHIP

Supervision, Evaluation, and Professional Development

Effective supervision in public schools is an elusive but fascinating activity, and much confusion and misapprehension surround the word "supervision" itself. "Evaluation," "rating," "assessment," and "appraisal" are all used to describe what supervisors do, yet none of these labels accurately reflects the process of supervision of instruction. In fact, such terms are in large part a source of suspicion, fear, and misunderstanding among teachers.

In this era of high-stakes testing and accountability, the quality of principals, teachers, and schools is judged by student performance on standardized tests. In this context, the supervision of instruction is viewed as a "quality control" process concerned with improving teaching in order to get better results for students. The process has little to do with the control of teachers. It does, however, create a compact of accountability. Supervisors create a collegial professional climate and culture, provide adequate resources and assistance in the instructional process, and make expectations clear. They encourage and support teacher growth and development that leads to increased student learning.

Improving Instruction Through Supervision, Evaluation, and Professional Development, pp. 25–41
Copyright © 2014 by Information Age Publishing

Teachers and principals are held accountable for the success of their students and their own professional growth. Consequently, supervision in schools becomes a collaborative professional process. Principals see their responsibility as helping teachers assist diverse learners and contributing to teachers' professional growth and development. To achieve these goals, principals not only identify potential areas for growth, but also provide assistance, resources, and opportunities for professional development. Finally, principals can neither ignore nor neglect their formal responsibility of evaluation. Hence, the process of instructional leadership bridges the traditional definition of supervision to include the professional development of teachers as well as evaluation of their performance. Supervision is the informal process of aiding teachers to become more effective in helping students. Evaluation, on the other hand, is a formal process in which judgments about the quality of performance are made. Through the process of evaluation, principals also hold those accountable who do not participate professionally during the informal supervisory process.

Although this integrated model of supervision, professional development, and evaluation may appear to be fraught with contradictions, we believe it realistically captures the day-to-day expectations of instructional leadership in schools. Our model is a real-world, pragmatic guide to improve instruction and consequently student learning in our schools. It is also how instructional leaders can hold accountable the small minority of teachers who are "going through the motions" and not taking responsibility for student learning. Our model of supervision, professional development, and evaluation is the integrating framework for the book.

SUPERVISION

In stark contrast to the industrial notion of overseeing, directing, and controlling workers, we see supervision as a collaborative effort. Supervision of instruction is the set of activities designed to improve the teaching-learning process. The purpose of supervision is neither to make judgments about the competence of teachers nor to control them but rather to work informally and cooperatively to improve their teaching. Although assessment of teacher effectiveness is necessary, it is not supervision of instruction. Evaluation is the formal process through which the quality of teacher performance is assessed. In sum, supervision is an informal, cooperative relationship between the principal and teachers, whereas evaluation is a formal hierarchical process between the principal and individual teachers.

A number of other assumptions need to be stated explicitly before we proceed to develop our model. The following propositions are the basis of a theory and practice of instructional leadership:

1. The only one who can improve instruction is the teacher him- or herself.
2. Teachers need the freedom to develop their own unique teaching styles.
3. Any changes in teaching behaviors require social support as well as professional and intellectual stimulation.
4. A consistent pattern of close supervision and coercion is unlikely to succeed in improving teaching.
5. Improvement of instruction is likely to be accomplished in a non-threatening situation, by working with colleagues and by fostering in teachers a sense of inquiry and experimentation.
6. Evaluation of the effectiveness of teaching is a necessary feature of instructional leadership, one that can complement informal supervision and professional development.
7. The principal-teacher collaboration is the key to an effective program of instructional leadership.
8. Positive organizational climate and culture are prerequisites for an effective program of instructional leadership and climate and culture are in large part a function of the leadership of the principal.
9. The principal must have the skills to navigate the three competing and complementary roles of supervision, evaluation, and professional development.
10. In the final analysis, the effectiveness of the teachers, principal, and the school is determined by the achievement of the students.

THEORY INTO PRACTICE
ISLLC Leadership Standards 2 & 3

Describe your principal as a supervisor. How often does she or he observe your classroom? What is the routine when a visit is made? To what extent do you receive data about your teaching? Your classroom management? The achievement level of your students? Student learning? The opportunity to reflect on your practice? Plans to improve what is happening in your classroom? To what extent is the visitation ritual? How helpful is your supervisor? Give some examples of help. If you were the principal, what would you emulate and what would you do differently?

TRADITIONAL CONFLICT BETWEEN SUPERVISION AND EVALUATION ROLES

In traditional school settings, there is often conflict between line and staff personnel; they compete for respect and authority from teachers. Principals dislike the meddling of support staff, especially those housed in the central office. Support staff (supervisors, curriculum specialists, professional development specialists) resent the interference of principals in curricular and instructional matters. The source of the conflict is often not so much a result of self-interest or a clash in personal values as of basic differences in priorities and the perceptions of the roles of the two kinds of personnel.

But instructional leadership is a team effort. Principals are responsible for the smooth functioning of the entire school operation. The challenges presented in implementing the Common Core State Standards (CCSS) (National Governors Association Center for Best Practices, Council of Chief State School Officers, 2010) and their related assessments are daunting. Teachers need support to learn and incorporate research-based instructional strategies that help students develop the high-level thinking skills embedded in the CCSS. Principals must recognize that they alone cannot meet these responsibilities and provide instructional leadership. They must work with support staff and teachers in making decisions to improve instruction. Hand in hand, they must work with teacher colleagues in a supportive and helpful manner. Members of the instructional team should be guided by their technical competence and expertise in specialized areas. All have the responsibility of improving teaching and learning in the classroom, a complex task that is planned and conceived in terms of months and years.

As instructional leaders, principals have to wear both hats—that is, deal with the practical problems of managing a school while being concerned with the more theoretical issues of improving instruction. They must be "tuned in" to research-based classroom practices to improve instruction. Instructional leaders must be change agents. Innovation is the expectation; improvement is the goal. New ways to teach, to structure classrooms, to motivate students, to set the stage for learning are major concerns of all instructional leaders.

THE ORGANIZATIONAL CONTEXT

The principal has another important administrative function. An effective program for the improvement of teaching and learning is doomed without the support, understanding, and cooperation of teachers. Principals must build an organizational climate and culture in which administrators, supervisors, and teachers understand and respect each other's roles. The principal is the single most important individual in setting the tone or atmosphere of a school; hence, the leadership styles of principals are crucial for the development of contexts in which teachers, supervisors, and administrators interact openly and authentically. Principals need to lead by example and by not asking teachers to do anything that they themselves would not do.

The climate and culture needed to implement the kind of integrated model of supervision, professional development, and evaluation we are proposing are characterized by the following relationships:

- *Open, authentic interactions among administrators and teachers.* Such interactions should increase accuracy of communication by limiting distortions due to status distinctions, and they should provide a climate in which individuals can agree to disagree. In students and teachers alike, authenticity tends to produce more commitment to the school (Goddard, Hoy, & Woolfolk-Hoy, 2000; Hoy & Hoy, 2013; Zepada, 2003).

- *Professional autonomy.* Teachers and supervisors need considerable autonomy to make changes in instruction; in fact, more effective schools grant teachers considerable classroom autonomy (Blase & Blase, 2001; Cheng & Couture, 2000; Dzubay, 2001; Eden, 2001; Rallis & Goldring, 2000).

- *Orderly teaching environment.* The school must be a place conducive to learning, one free from major disciplinary problems and vandalism. An orderly atmosphere is likely to be a necessary *means* for effective teaching and learning (Barker & Robinson, 2001; Clayton, 2001; McCloud, 2005).

- *High performance and achievement standards.* Principals need to hold high performance and achievement expectations for teachers, and teachers need to expect that all students can achieve. More successful schools stress high achievement standards (American Federation of Teachers, 2003; Fullan, 2003; Lee, 2003; Levine, 2002).

- *Participative and supportive leadership.* Warm, supportive relationships between principals and teachers not only enhance cooperation and respect but also, in combination with high performance standards and a well-structured organization, produce better student achievement levels (Fleming, 1999; Richards, 2003).

- *Shared decision-making and high motivation.* Supportive leadership and highly motivated teachers and supervisors who share in the decision-making process create the atmosphere necessary to generate cooperation and harmony between the technical and managerial levels of organization (Brost, 2000; Lange, 1993).

- *Colleague control.* Although principals are responsible to their superiors for management decisions, the development and improvement of instruction must be controlled primarily by professional colleagues—supervisors and teachers (Fullan, 2005; Lambert, 2005).

- *High morale.* A healthy organizational climate exists when teachers and principals feel that their social needs are being satisfied and that they are simultaneously enjoying a sense of task accomplishment in their jobs (Evans, 1997; Thompson, McNamara, & Hoyle, 1997).

- *Security.* If innovation and experimentation are to characterize classroom instruction, principals, supervisors, and teachers all need to be secure in their positions. Short-term thinking and the public demands for quick results often create an atmosphere of high stress in which principals and classroom teachers alike feel that their only security is in getting results. The focus should be on continuous improvement, and as long as that occurs, principals should not be "looking over their shoulders." Teachers also need to be secure enough to turn to their supervisor and colleagues for assistance as they all strive for continuous improvement (Cotton, 2003; Gullatt & Lofton, 1996; Owen & Davies, 2003).

- *Trust.* The proposed model can only work if principals, supervisors, and teachers develop mutual trust and understanding as they perform their different yet complementary roles. The coordination of individual efforts performed in an ethos of trust, subtlety, and intimacy is likely to result in a more effective organization (Forsyth, Adams, & Hoy, 2011; Fullan, Bertani, & Quinn, 2004).

- *Academic optimism.* Ultimately, supervisors must create a culture of optimism, which directly influences student achievement. Academic optimism is the collective view of teachers that all students can learn; that teachers, parents, and students can cooperate to improve student learning; and that high academic performance can be achieved (Hoy, 2012; Hoy, Tarter, & Woolfolk Hoy, 2006).

Current research suggests that principals should be instructional leaders: helpers, colleagues, and champions of ideas; they should be open, optimistic, and democratic innovators who share their knowledge, are concerned with individual growth, and are engaged in long-term thinking. They should know how to use data and help teachers interpret data in order to make sound instructional decisions.

> **THEORY INTO PRACTICE**
> *ISLLC Leadership Standard 2*
> The climate of a school is a primary responsibility of the principal. How does your principal build a positive school climate? Select three words that describe the atmosphere or climate of your school. Now, develop three paragraphs that illustrate the veracity of the words you've selected to describe your school. If you were appointed principal, how would you improve and manage the climate of your school during the first two months? During the first year? During the next three years? What kind of school climate best supports an effective program of instructional leadership?

ELEMENTS OF AN INSTRUCTIONAL LEADERSHIP MODEL

Some of the elements of a model for increasing student learning have been sketched. We now turn to the development of the relationships among those components. In specifying the relationships, remember that the proposed model is an ideal type, an analytic abstraction that may or may not exist in the real world. Nonetheless, the conceptual scheme should highlight the key ingredients of supervision of instruction, professional development, and evaluation in schools as well as providing a framework for analysis and practice.

The discussion thus far suggests that there may be an inherent tension between the supervisory and evaluative roles of the principal; however, our model views these two processes as basically complementary with some tension. Although the functions and responsibilities of supervisors and evaluators are qualitatively different (formative versus summative) and have different authority relations (informal versus formal), they both work toward the same goals of improving instruction and student learning. Finally, the responsibility for identifying, planning, and providing professional growth and development, a critical element linking supervision and evaluation, has often been ignored; its role is critical to instructional improvement.

Supervision Role

Supervisors are expected to provide advice and support to colleagues. Teachers must have confidence in those to whom they turn for help. Formal authority and status can produce tension for principals as they seek to establish collegial relationships. If teachers are successful in helping students achieve, so too is the principal. In the final analysis, only the teacher has a direct connection to student learning; the principal's influence on learning is indirect by the very nature of the structural arrangement of teaching. In the end, the principal's success depends on the teacher.

Unless teachers truly accept supervisors as colleagues, they are unlikely to experience the trust, support, and intellectual stimulation essential for fostering a sense of inquiry and experimentation. The improvement of instruction is a long-term, continuous process that is ideally achieved through skillful supervision. However, in reality, the formal process of evaluation is required for all and necessary for some.

The goal of the supervisor is not simply to identify immediate problems. The identification of such problems is a first step. Working with teachers to develop strategies to solve such problems, providing support and encouragement, and following up with suggestions for professional development are all components of supervision. Supervisors study the processes of teaching and learning as part of an ongoing system of assessment and experimentation. Diagnosis, analysis, problem solving, innovation, and change are supervisory imperatives. Although supervision can be broadly conceived as any set of activities planned to improve teaching, it is basically a cycle of systematic planning, frequent observation, analysis of the teaching-learning process, and the assessment of student outcomes.

After a culture of academic optimism (trust, efficacy, and academic emphasis) is developed in the school, five additional steps are required: (1) meeting with teachers prior to observations to make expectations clear and to explain the goals of the process, (2) conducting frequent classroom observations, (3) collecting systematic data for joint reflection, (4) arranging post-observation conferences for joint analysis of the teaching and learning, and (5) planning for growth and development. The final phase is also the beginning of a new cycle of analysis and improvement.

Our supervisory process varies significantly from the traditional clinical model in two ways. First, observations are more frequent. Although both the supervisor and teacher have the option of arranging to meet following any observation, meetings usually occur after several observations. Assessment data are analyzed frequently and are used to modify instruction for individuals or the entire class, when necessary. Next, there is an expectation that teachers and supervisors jointly identify areas for professional growth and development. Planning how, where, and when that professional growth will occur is an integral part of this process. All too often, supervisors identify individual needs but do not follow through and provide support and mechanisms for them to be met. The supervisory process will be explored in greater detail in Chapters 4, 5, and 6.

Evaluation Role

Administrators articulate the official organization goals, objectives, and values. They occupy a formal position of authority and power. Although principals may be supportive and helpful to teachers, they also have the burden of making organizational decisions about competence. State and district policy mandates formal evaluations of personnel. The principal is the individual who is given the responsibility of disciplining faculty and imposing formal sanctions when such action is in order. Thus, the administrative role is an evaluative one that prevents some teachers from being completely candid with principals about classroom problems. Principals execute the organizational policy of the school system in each building; they must make hard management decisions about the competence of all teachers and the retention of nontenured teachers.

Principals' primary orientation is to the entire school. They are responsible for discipline and compliance within the school, coordination of all the school activities, the solution of immediate problems, holding people accountable, and in general, the smooth functioning of the school. The principal is the individual directly involved in virtually all the day-to-day problems; hence, it should come as no surprise that the principal's perspective is very often more pragmatic, systemic, and evaluative than teachers' views.

Principals must be aware of the potential conflict between the roles of supervision and evaluation. This role conflict requires a very deliberate effort on the part of principals as they attempt to fulfill their obligation of improving instruction. Recognition of this potential conflict has led to experiments in restructuring school administration, such as creating roles of "instructional principal" and "operations principal" or associate principals with very specific distinct roles in the school—one for the instruction and the other for management. In large school organizations, it may be possible to separate the administrative and supervisory roles. In such cases, master teachers and other specialists with instructional expertise are welcome additions to the supervisory team. In most schools, however, the principal is required to both help teachers improve (supervision) and to assess their competence (evaluation), which are major challenges. The evaluation process will be explored in greater detail in Chapters 8 and 9.

THEORY INTO PRACTICE
ISLLC Leadership Standards 3 & 5

How often does your principal visit your classroom with the expressed purpose of rating your competence as a teacher? How are you graded? Does the grade mean anything? Grading and rating are evaluation, not supervision. Do you see connections between the informal process of supervision and the formal process of evaluation? If so, what are they? Are the criteria used to evaluate your performance clear? Do you believe that the process is fair? Has the process of evaluation been useful to you in becoming a better teacher? If so, how? If not, why not? How can the evaluation process be improved?

Professional Development Role

Instructional leaders also have the responsibility of helping their teachers grow and develop professionally. In fact, the processes of supervision and evaluation are incomplete because professional development is integral to both. Identifying specific areas for instructional improvement is only the first step in both supervision and evaluation; teachers, with the support of their principals, must engage in appropriate professional activities that help them increase their classroom effectiveness. Principals employ a number of strategies to promote teachers' professional growth. Consider the following:

- emphasizing the study of teaching and learning
- supporting collaboration among teams of teachers
- developing coaching relationships among educators
- redesigning and aligning curricula to both state and CCSS
- providing professional development activities appropriate for adult learners.

Principals who are initiating professional development opportunities should integrate reflection and personal growth to build a school culture in which individuals are reflective, trusting, efficacious, and self-regulating. Principals can enhance the process of professional development by acknowledging the difficulties of growing and changing, and recognizing that change is a journey of learning and risk taking. They should demonstrate fundamental respect for the knowledge and abilities of their teachers as they view the teachers as intellectuals rather than technicians. Principals need to speak openly and frequently with teachers about instruction, give suggestions and feedback, and solicit teachers' professional advice and opinions about classroom instruction. One key is to develop cooperative, nonthreatening partnerships with teachers that are characterized by trust, openness, and the freedom to make mistakes as they attempt novel teaching approaches. The process of professional development will be explored in greater detail in Chapter 7.

THEORY INTO PRACTICE

ISLLC Leadership Standards 1 & 2

How does your principal provide professional development? Is it worthwhile? Why or why not? Does your professional development evolve from specific classroom interests or problems? Give some examples. To what extent is professional development a ritual? You know the phrases—"professional growth," "individualized or customized professional development," "in-service education." Do these words mean anything in your school or are they just professional rhetoric? If you were the principal, how would you make professional development activities useful?

SUMMARY: AN INTEGRATED MODEL

Thus far we have developed the elements of our model. Now we turn to an examination of the entire framework. Effective instructional leadership can only occur in a school context that is nonthreatening, professional, and innovative. Hence, the principal must develop a school culture and climate conducive to serious examination of teaching and learning without fear of retribution for mistakes—a learning environment for professional educators. In the next chapter, we develop the specific characteristics of school climate and culture required for successful instructional leadership. Suffice it to say, climate and culture are critical ingredients of any attempt to develop a systemic program of instructional excellence.

The principal's instructional leadership is a function of three core processes: supervision, evaluation, and professional development. The focus of supervision is informal, supportive, collegial, and driven by the goal of improvement of teaching and learning. In some contrast, evaluation is formal, judgmental, hierarchical, yet driven by the same objective—to improve teaching and learning. Supervision and evaluation, however, are both wedded to professional development—a key mechanism through which teachers improve their instruction and ultimately increase student learning. Supervision, evaluation, and professional development are the three interactive elements through which principals develop a successful program of instructional leadership. In our model, instructional leadership means something specific—the dynamic interaction of supervision, evaluation, and professional development.

The goal of instructional leadership is specific and clear—student achievement. Increased student learning is produced by more effective classroom instruction by teachers. Although improving instruction is critical, it is student achievement that is the ultimate goal. This integrated model of instructional leadership that produces increased student learning is pictorially summarized in Figure 2.1 and serves as outline for the rest of this text.

A PRINCIPAL'S SUPERVISORY CHALLENGE

Instructions—Read the following account provided by a principal, reflect on her practice, and perform a case analysis.

I am the principal of Morgan High School, a comprehensive high school with 1,400 students. During the summer of 2001, Charles Garrett was hired to teach mathematics. He had three years of prior teaching experience, one at the middle school level and the other two at the high school level. His teaching assignments at Morgan included classes in Algebra I and Algebra II. During classroom observations both Jan, his department

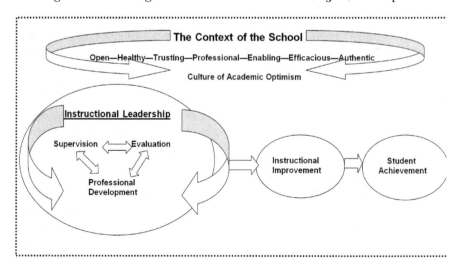

Figure 2.1.   An integrated model of Instructional Leadership.

supervisor and master teacher with no administrative authority, and I noted that he was well planned, organized, and had adequate content knowledge. However, his pedagogy consisted primarily of lectures.

It didn't take too many classroom visits to recognize that his daily routine was consistent: work through several example problems at the board and then assign sample problems for the students to complete—checks for student understanding were infrequent. Students sometimes appeared confused as they worked on their independent assignments. Mr. Garrett would respond to their questions by reviewing the example that he previously worked through on the board. During initial informal post-observation discussions with Charles, we focused most of the dialogue on his instructional techniques. We posed most of our concerns as questions, giving him the opportunity to reflect on his practice and discuss with us how he planned to modify his routine to enhance his instruction. On several different occasions, we volunteered some constructive suggestions and Jan offered assistance, but he expressed confidence that he understood our concerns and could address them satisfactorily. I provided Mr. Garrett the opportunity to observe master teachers at Morgan, both within and outside his department. He was given the names of several teachers and assured that he would be provided release time from his duty period to complete the observations.

We continued to drop in to see how Charles was doing, but didn't see anything changing. Consequently, I asked Jan to initiate a series of informal meetings and informally assist him in a more directive fashion. By early March, Jan reported that Charles was telling her what he knew she wanted to hear, but we saw no modifications in his classroom practice. I met with Mr. Garrett and urged him to involve the students more directly in learning activities. Specifically, I asked that he call on students to participate as he worked through each step of the demonstration problems, directly respond to student questions, and provide students the opportunity to work through several sample problems in pairs or small groups prior to working independently. Additionally, he needed to check for understanding frequently, asking specific questions to ensure that students clearly understood the concept being taught. I made it clear that I planned to observe a complete lesson in a couple of weeks and expected to see him attempting to implement my suggestions.

During my observation of an entire class period, Charles seemed to be making some effort to modify his practice in ways I suggested. It was apparent that he was uncomfortable during that class session and students seemed a bit confused by the way he was conducting the lesson. In a discussion that followed, I offered further assistance by recommending that one of his peers in the department model a lesson with one of his classes. Charles explained that Jan had already done that several times and it "undermined" his authority with his students. I also offered Mr. Garrett the opportunity to participate in an upcoming summer professional development program that focused on developing algebraic thinking and the use of Algeblocks and graphing calculators. He declined to participate, citing other summer commitments. His summative evaluation that year specified our concerns and his lack of progress. It contained a formal plan for improvement to be implemented at the beginning of the next school year.

In his second year at Morgan High School, things in his classroom seemed to get worse instead of better. Instructional problems that were observed in the first year continued into the second. And, although it was rare to see significant behavioral problems during an observation, students and parents were beginning to grumble about Mr. Garrett's classroom management style. Students complained that when they asked questions he responded, "You should have learned how to do that in elementary school." He frequently yelled at the class, told them to "shut up," and made comments about failing everyone. If they asked any questions, he complained that they should have been paying attention and responded in a negative tone.

In response to my observations and these complaints, I scheduled a conference with Mr. Garrett in mid-October. Mr. Garrett confirmed some of the student complaints and denied others. He shared that he had some very difficult students in his Algebra I class and that he believed the interaction between two students in particular was causing much of his frustration. I informed him that the student complaints came from several different classes. I suggested that he survey his classes to discern whether these were concerns shared by a vocal few or whether it was a much broader issue. I provided him with a copy of a survey form to do just that. Additionally, we focused on continuing instructional concerns. We discussed the relationship between effective instruction, student engagement, and classroom management. I gave him a copy of *Classroom Instruction that Works* by Marzano, Pickering, and Pollock (2001) and shared a few highlights. I told him we would have a second conference in mid-November after he had had a chance to complete the survey and read the book.

By early November, my frequent observations confirmed that the explanations he provided during his lecture were clear, the examples he presented focused on real-life problems, and most students were attentive. But, he continued to complete the majority of the problems and had limited dialogue with the students. During our next conference, I reiterated the need to increase student engagement. We discussed several high-yield instructional strategies specified in Hattie's (2009) book *Visible Learning*. I reminded him of the improvement plan, provided him with the names of several other effective teachers, and directed him to observe at least one teacher each week, focusing on student-teacher interactions and student engagement. I asked him if he had surveyed his students, and he stated that he had not yet gotten around to it. I directed him to complete the survey within the next two weeks.

In January, student and parent concerns resurfaced. Parents and students complained that Mr. Garrett taught to those "who understood" while the rest of the class was "invisible." Students shared that he rarely asked questions and he answered their questions depending on his mood. They were unsure when it was acceptable to ask a question and when it wasn't. In late January, I met with Mr. Garrett formally to discuss these concerns. He shared that he didn't have time to review mathematics that students should already have learned, it was not his job, and he would not do it. He also did not believe he could modify his style of instruction to conform to my suggestions. I shared with Mr. Garrett that we would not be renewing his contract. He submitted his letter of resignation the following week.

REFLECTIVE PRACTICE

Assess the effectiveness of this principal by reflecting on her practice. What strategies were effective? Why? Which would you change? Why?

If you were confronted by the challenge of working with this teacher, what would you have done? Be sure to consider the following:

- How much time and leeway do you provide to an experienced teacher who comes to work in your school? To an inexperienced teacher?
- How can you determine the causes of the poor performance?
- How much credibility do you give to student and parent complaints about a teacher?
- In this case, what kind of professional development is needed?
- When does the informal process of supervision end and the formal process of evaluation begin?

DEVELOP YOUR PORTFOLIO

The goal of all instructional leadership programs is to increase student learning. At first blush, the goal seems simple and straightforward. But what does it really mean? Higher performance in standardized tests? Solving real-world problems? Getting better grades? There are no simple answers. As an educational leader, what is your position on testing students for achievement results? Do you subscribe to standardized tests or are so- called authentic assessments the way to go? As a new principal, develop a short position paper on testing students to determine their levels of achievement. Be sure to address the arguments for traditional testing and for authentic assessment. A good place to begin is by reading Chapter 1 in Hoy and Hoy's *Instructional Leadership* (2013). The chapter contains a point/counterpoint discussion on the topic "Which are better: traditional tests or authentic assessments?"

COMMUNICATION EXERCISE

You have been appointed as new principal of Wilson Senior High School, a suburban school of 1,600 students with 115 teachers. This year for the first time students who do not pass the state standardized exams cannot graduate. The school has been working with teachers and students during the past two years anticipating this dramatic change in practice. After only a month on the job, you have just received the final test results from the state, and 27 of your seniors will not graduate in June. Although you clearly are not to blame personally, your superintendent has asked you to draft a two-page press release that explains the dilemma and proposes steps that will be taken to prevent failure of future students.

READINGS

Cawelti, G. (1997). Improving student achievement. *American School Board Journal, 186*(7), 34–37.

Good, T. L., & Brophy, J. E. (2007). *Looking in classrooms* (10th ed.). Boston, MA: Allyn & Bacon/Longman.

Goodwin, B. (2000). *Raising the achievement of low performing schools.* Aurora, CO: Mid-Continent Research for Education and Learning.

Hallinger, P., & Heck, R. H. (1996). Instructional leadership and the school principal: A passing fancy that refused to fad away. *Leadership and Policy in Schools, 4*(3), 231–239.

Hoy, A. W., & Hoy, W. K. (2013). *Instructional leadership: A learning-centered guide* (4nd ed.). Boston, MA: Allyn & Bacon.

WHAT DO SUPERINTENDENTS SAY?

Is the principal ultimately accountable for student performance on high-stakes tests, even though principals do not teach students?

Superintendent 1: Accountability begins with clearly articulated expectations, and clearly articulated expectations begin with the principal.

Superintendent 2: Principals are ultimately responsible for the comprehensive school improvement plan and its implementation/support. Each component of the improvement plan must directly impact student achievement.

Superintendent 3: No. "Ultimate accountability" in schools cannot rest with any one individual because studies of student achievement show performance is a multivariate phenomenon. The evidence suggests accountability for student performance on high stakes tests is distributed (but not evenly) among the teachers, parents, and to a lesser degree, the principal.

Superintendent 4: Yes. The principal is ultimately accountable for student performance even on high-stakes tests because no one else has the opportunity to motivate, train, and direct teacher performance on a daily basis.

Superintendent 5: The principal plays a prominent role in terms of the variables that impact student achievement (i.e., quality of the instruction, health of the climate, rigor of the curriculum). Therefore as the instructional leader, he/she certainly bears direct, albeit shared, responsibility for the overall performance of students.

Superintendent 6: Principals must accept ultimate responsibility for everything that goes on in their schools, including the results of high-stakes tests. Once you accept the role of principal, you accept the responsibility to be the instructional leader of the building. That means the ultimate outcome, student learning, is your first and most important responsibility.

CHAPTER 3

CREATING A SCHOOL CONTEXT TO IMPROVE STUDENT LEARNING

Although teaching in most public schools still occurs largely within the confines of the classroom, it is influenced by the broader school context. If we are to develop a comprehensive view for improving instruction and enhancing student performance, we must understand the organizational opportunities and constraints on teaching and learning. It is unlikely that any program of supervision, evaluation, and professional development can be successful if the school workplace is not conducive and supportive of such efforts.

The principal is the formal leader of the school and as such he or she has been given the formal obligation to show the way, and effective principals do just that—they lead. They initiate structure, maintain solid interpersonal relations among teachers, forge a vision with teachers for the school, and are a catalyst for change and improvement. They also are responsible for ensuring the cooperative and harmonious internal operations of the school. Finally, it is the principal who is in charge of the instructional program and answerable for the achievement of students. Improving teaching and learning are the ultimate goals of the school leader.

Improving Instruction Through Supervision, Evaluation, and Professional Development, pp. 43–72
Copyright © 2014 by Information Age Publishing

More than any other person, the principal creates and cultivates the nature and character of the school workplace. A collective sense of identity emerges in schools as principals and teachers interact and transform the workplace into a distinctive institution. There are many common terms used to refer to this indigenous feel of the school—ecology, milieu, setting, tone, field, character, atmosphere, culture, and climate. All are used to refer to the internal quality of the organization as experienced by its members. In this chapter, we will explore the social context of the school workplace by examining its structure, its climate, and its culture. In each case, our attempt is to understand the context so that principals can grapple with and improve the school milieu in ways that lead to improved teaching and learning. To that end, we supply the conceptual capital and empirical tools for the principal's success.

All organizations, including schools, have structures designed to help the institution coordinate its activities and run smoothly; in fact, all organizations have two structures—one formal and the other informal. To be sure, there is only one organization, but it is useful to understand these two important structural faces. Some school structures facilitate teaching and learning whereas others hinder the processes. What kind of school structure is best for promoting a context for effective teaching and student learning? What is the principal's role in promoting such structures? How can principals create structures that are functional and avoid those that are not? We turn to these questions.

FORMAL STRUCTURE

The formal structure of an organization is its attempt to make behavior more predictable and rational by standardizing and regulating activities. Frequently the term "bureaucracy" is used as an epithet to describe an organizational structure characterized by slowness, rigidity, red tape, and inefficiency. Because of its negative connotations, we will avoid using the term, yet we acknowledge that all organizations of any size have many "bureaucratic" features, which are not bad in and of themselves; in fact, it is difficult to conceive of formal organizations without rules, regulations, policies, standards, managers, supervisors, and specialists.

Formal structure is the way an institution organizes itself to accomplish its basic tasks. In particular, we will examine school structure in terms of division of labor, specialization, impersonality, hierarchy of authority, and formalization—the basic elements of school structure.

Division of Labor

A good many organizational tasks are simply too complex to be performed by one individual. Teaching is no exception. Division of labor leads to specialization. Most teachers cannot teach all the subjects of math, science, English, history, and a modern foreign language. Hence, the teaching is divided into subject specialties and levels so that we have math, science, English, and history teachers as well as elementary and secondary teachers. That is, the labor is divided according to one's expertise, and the regular activities of teaching are distributed into formal roles and positions.

Specialization

Division of labor is not only a useful and rational way to organize the tasks at hand, it also leads to specialization. Teachers specialize in a defined area such as reading, mathematics, or Spanish. In the process of specialization, the teachers develop increased expertise in their specialties; that is, specialization enhances expertise in both content and pedagogical knowledge in a given area. Specialization poses a real challenge to those teachers who teach multiple subjects—to be effective they must master both the content and pedagogical knowledge in each subject taught. As the organization becomes more complex, specialization increases; hence, high schools are more likely to have more specialization than elementary schools. Some elementary teachers teach all subjects, but not high school teachers.

Impersonality

Weber (1947) argued that the working atmosphere of an organization should reflect "the dominance of a spirit of formalistic impersonality, 'sine ira et studio,' without hatred or passion, and hence without affection or enthusiasm" (p. 331). Teachers and principals are expected to make decisions on the basis of facts, and not simply their feelings. Such a view should foster impartiality and promote objectivity. For rationality to prevail, personal considerations must give way to relevant data. Impersonality on the part of principals and teachers therefore enhances equitable treatment of individuals and promotes rational organizational thought and action. Principals are expected to be objective and fair in their treatment of colleagues and students but, we hasten to add, not cold and indifferent to them. Impersonality enhances rationality.

Hierarchy of Authority

Schools, like all organizations, have an authority structure. Positions and roles are arranged hierarchically such that each level in the organization is under the control of a higher one. For example, in schools, the hierarchy of authority runs from the principal to the assistant principal, to department heads or team leaders or grade level leaders, to teachers, and to students, with each role responsible to the one above it. Hierarchy is probably the most pervasive attribute of modern organizations and perhaps the most vilified. Almost without exception, however, large organizations develop a well-established system of authority and the disciplined compliance to directives from superiors. That is, hierarchy of authority promotes disciplined compliance.

When the authority is concentrated at the top level, the organization is centralized and we have a top-down structure; but if authority is diffuse, then the organization is decentralized and decision making is shared. Schools vary greatly in terms of the structure of authority, with some highly centralized and others decentralized with shared authority structures.

Formalization

Most organizations have a consistent system of abstract rules, regulations, and policies, which have been intentionally established to guide behavior; that is, the organization has been formalized to insure a consistent response to routine issues. The system of formalization covers the rights and duties inherent in each position and helps employees better understand their roles. Formalization promotes not only behavioral consistency, but also a continuity of operations, especially when there are changes in personnel. Thus, formalization ensures uniformity and stability of actions. All schools have a formalized system of rules, regulations, and policies, but the degree of formalization varies greatly among schools.

Efficiency

What kind of structure maximizes rational decision making and administrative efficiency? How should the formal organization be structured? Max Weber (1947) suggests the following analysis of formal organizations: Division of labor and specialization produce experts, and experts with an impersonal orientation make technically correct, rational decisions based on facts. Once rational decisions have been made, the hierarchy of authority ensures disciplined compliance with directives and, along with rules and regulations, a well-coordinated system of implementation, uniformity, and stability in the operation of the organization. In other words, each of these formal properties makes a positive contribution and functions to maximize administrative efficiency because committed experts make rational decisions that are executed and coordinated in a disciplined way.

Problems With Structure

Everything does not always work the way it is designed to function. Each of the basic elements we have described above has a positive impact on the organization, but actual life is more complicated. In fact, for each of the positive outcomes described above, there is a corresponding possible negative consequence.

Although division of labor can produce specialization, specialization sometimes produces boredom. The literature is filled with instances where such boredom engenders lower levels of productivity or produces employees who search for ways to make their work life more interesting (Hoy & Miskel, 2013).

Specialization can produce expertise, but expertise can create narrowness and tunnel vision so that at times, the ends of the organization are lost because of an undue emphasis on a specialty. Narrow specialization can cause boredom; in fact, job enlargement and enrichment are frequently used to combat monotony by making the work more challenging and providing employees with more autonomy and responsibility.

Impersonality can improve rationality in decision making, but it can also produce a machine-like environment in which people feel unable to interact as unique individuals fulfilling their needs. Such an environment often produces low morale, which in turn impedes organizational efficiency.

Hierarchy of authority enhances coordination, but often at the expense of communication. Every level in the hierarchy produces a potential communication block and the possibility for distortion. Teachers are reluctant to communicate to their principals information that will make them look bad; in fact, their inclination is to communicate only good things or things they think the boss wants to hear (Blau & Scott, 1962/2003). Formalization (rules, regulations, and policies) provides stability and coordination; however, it also often produces rigidity and goal displacement. Teachers and administrators can become so rule-oriented that they forget that rules and regulations are means, not ends in themselves. Such formalism and rigidity interfere with goal achievement. For example, rules provide teachers with simple solutions to problems. Unfortunately, teachers may become so rule-oriented that they look to rules to solve complex problems, an approach that ignores individual differences, decreases the search for viable alternatives, and produces an over-reliance on formal procedures. When principals provide a rigid system of rules for teachers, teachers often devise their own regulations for students. The result may be a rigidity of behavior that is unresponsive to the unique needs of individuals—be they teachers or students—and a mentality that there must be a rule or regulation for all occasions.

These potential dysfunctional consequences of each organizational characteristic are often overlooked. Figure 3.1 depicts the possible negative as well as positive functions of formal structure. The question for thoughtful principals is: Under what conditions does each characteristic lead to functional but not dysfunctional consequences? In other words, the administrative challenge is to structure the organization to capture the positive outcomes and avoid the negative ones.

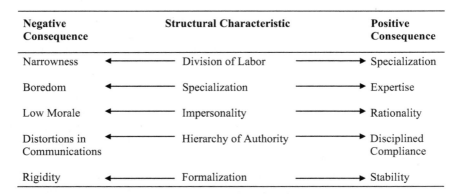

Negative Consequence	Structural Characteristic	Positive Consequence
Narrowness ←	Division of Labor	→ Specialization
Boredom ←	Specialization	→ Expertise
Low Morale ←	Impersonality	→ Rationality
Distortions in Communications ←	Hierarchy of Authority	→ Disciplined Compliance
Rigidity ←	Formalization	→ Stability

Figure 3.1. Positive and Negative Consequences of Structure.

THEORY INTO PRACTICE
ISLLC Standards 1, 2, 3, 5

Evaluate your school in terms of the five structural elements just described. What is the dominant structural element of your school? Which elements work the way they should? Which elements cause problems for a positive program of supervision and evaluation? What steps would you take as principal to create a school context to improve teaching and learning? Just how important is structure in the scheme of developing a productive workplace?

TWO CONTRASTING SCHOOL STRUCTURES

The structure of schools can either hinder or enable the effective operation of schools. Although the bureaucratic structure of schools is often dis-
paraged, research paints two contrasting pictures of organizational
structures (Adler, 1999; Adler & Borys, 1996; Hoy & Sweetland, 2000,
2001)—one bleak but the other bright. The negative side reveals school
structures that alienate, breed dissatisfaction, hinder creativity, and dis-
courage employees. The contrasting positive view shows school structures
that guide behavior, clarify responsibility, reduce stress, and enable individuals to feel and be more effective (Adler, 1999; Adler & Borys, 1996;
Hoy & Sweetland, 2001). Two classic aspects of all organizational structures, including schools, are formalization (formal rules and procedures)
and centralization (hierarchy of formal authority). We examine each
property in an attempt to identify those features that capture positive outcomes of school structure while avoiding negative ones (Sinden, Hoy, &
Sweetland, 2004).

Enabling Formalization

Formalization can be viewed along a continuum from enabling at one
extreme to coercive at the other (Adler, 1999; Adler & Borys, 1996; Hoy &
Sweetland, 2000, 2001). Recall that formalization refers to the rules, regulations, policies, and formal procedures of the organization.

Enabling formalization helps individuals solve work problems because
the rules, policies, and procedures are flexible guides that reflect "best
practices" and help organizational participants deal with difficulties and
dilemmas (Adler & Borys, 1996). Decision making and problem solving
are not improved by blind obedience to rules and regulations; in fact,
effective problem solving requires flexibility to substitute judgment for
rules. There is no best set of rules and regulations because situations are
dynamic; as events change, so should the rules and procedures (Langer,
1989). Flexibility is a hallmark of enabling formalization and is critical
for effective organizations—that is, ones that anticipate mistakes, engage
in open communication, and have the resilience to respond successfully
to unexpected negative surprises and problems (Weick & Sutcliffe, 2001).

Coercive formalization refers to rules, regulations, policies, and
procedures that are used to punish subordinates when they do not comply
with the organizations; such rules tend to hinder productive work
practices and more often than not alienate organizational participants.
Instead of promoting organizational learning, coercive procedures force
compliance, and in schools the results are higher levels of dissatisfaction

(Isherwood & Hoy, 1973; Hoy & Sweetland, 2000) and greater alienation of teachers (Hoy, Blazovsky & Newland, 1983; Sweetland & Hoy, 2000). Instead of giving teachers access to best practices, coercive procedures are rigid and designed to force compliance from recalcitrant teachers.

Enabling Centralization

Similar to formalization, centralization can be viewed along a continuum from enabling to hindering, each with a distinct authority structure. Centralization is the locus of authority for decision making—that is, the hierarchy of authority of the school. Schools with a high degree of centralization concentrate decision making at the top in the hands of a few; directives from superiors are to be followed without question to ensure disciplined compliance.

Enabling centralization is an administrative structure that helps teachers solve problems rather than getting in the way. The principal facilitates work across recognized authority boundaries while retaining their distinctive roles (Hirschhorn, 1997). Expertise is valued more than status or position, and teachers are able to exercise professional judgment. Enabling centralization is flexible, cooperative, and collaborative rather than rigid, autocratic, and controlling. Principals in such structures use their power and authority to help teachers by designing structures that facilitate teaching and learning; in brief, principals empower their teachers.

Hindering centralization refers to an administrative hierarchy that impedes rather than helps problem solving. Principals use their formal authority to control and discipline. The consequence is often alienation and hostility because teachers are forced to satisfy artificial standards rather than serve the needs of their students (Hoy et al., 1983; Sinden et al., 2004). Unfortunately, hindering structures often respond to pressures in dysfunctional ways such as increasing close supervision, over-standardizing work, and standardizing outputs (Mintzberg, 1979, 1989), all of which can hinder the effective operation of the organization.

Enabling and Hindering School Structures

It should not be surprising that in schools there is a close relationship between formalization (systems of rules, regulations, policies, and procedures) and centralization (hierarchy of authority): that is, when the formalization is enabling, so is centralization and vice versa. Thus school structures can be described along a continuum from enabling to hindering.

An *enabling school structure* is a hierarchy that helps rather than hinders and a system of rules, regulations, policies, and procedures that guides problem solving rather than punishes failure. In enabling school structures, principals and teachers work cooperatively across recognized authority boundaries. Similarly, rules and regulations are flexible guides for problem solving rather than constraints that create problems. Both hierarchy and rules are mechanisms to support teachers rather than vehicles to enhance principal power. The focus is on fairness, shared power, and rational decision making. There is great effort to match tasks with expertise and create opportunities for collaboration.

A *hindering school structure*, in contrast, is a structure that impedes and a system of rules and procedures that is coercive. The clear objective of the school structure is disciplined compliance of teachers. Teachers are subordinates to be managed and strictly controlled. Both the formal rules and the office of the principal are used to gain control and conformity. The structure is used to insure that reluctant, incompetent, and irresponsible teachers do what the principal decides. The authority of the principal is enhanced, and the power of the teachers is diminished. The structure fosters an impersonal climate that creates distance and coldness and reduces *esprit de corps* among teachers. Specialization builds barriers and restricts cooperation.

The contrasts between these two school structures are stark. Enabling structures call for flexibility, professional judgments, joint teacher-principal problem solving, fairness, expertise, and collaboration. Hindering structures are typically rigid, rule-oriented, authoritarian, narrow, and restrictive. Figure 3.2 summarizes the differences more fully.

The principal in an enabling school is one who finds ways to help teachers succeed rather than one who focuses on teacher compliance to directives and rules. Let's take one concrete example of enabling structure in terms of the principal's behavior. Consider the principal in one school who was under tremendous pressure to get student proficiency tests above the state average. The principal had an open door. She cared and supported her teachers and respected their professional judgments. She was unwilling to simply order teachers to get the scores up, and instead she saw herself as a colleague working with them on this difficult problem. One indicator of her supportive behavior was that she was always in her office every Saturday from nine to noon. There was no press for teachers to work on Saturdays, but everyone knew that the principal was available and ready to talk either on the phone or in person on Saturday mornings. She enabled. No secretaries, no students, no guidance counselors, no assistant administrators; she alone was there every Saturday. Leading by

	Features of Enabling School Structures	Features of Hindering School Structures
Formalization	•Promotes flexible rules and procedures •Views problems as opportunities •Values diversity of opinions •Encourages initiative •Fosters trust	•Enforces rigid rules and procedures •Views problems as constraints •Demands consensus •Punishes mistakes •Generates suspicion
Centralization	•Facilitates problem solving •Promotes cooperation •Encourages openness •Protects teachers •Seeks novelty and innovation •Encourages collaboration	•Demands compliance and obedience •Enhances control •Fosters mistrust •Punishes teachers •Discourages change •Rules autocratically
Impersonality	•Fosters fairness •Promotes rationality	•Creates distance and coldness •Reduces *esprit de corps*
Division of Labor	•Matches tasks and expertise	•Promotes narrowness
Specialization	•Increases expertise •Creates opportunities for collaboration	•Creates boredom •Restricts cooperation

Figure 3.2.   Contrasting types of school structure: Enabling and hindering.

example was evident; her high standards for her own behavior were clearly more stringent than those she held for her teachers, and teachers respected her for it (Hoy & Sweetland, 2001).

In brief, enabling and hindering school structures, as experienced by teachers, have different structural features and have different consequences for the teaching–learning context. The framework provides an explanation for the conflicting findings regarding the impact of structure on teachers— namely, that it is the kind (enabling or hindering) and not the amount of structure that explains the negative effects. Enabling school structures produce positive outcomes; hindering structures yield negative outcomes. If principals want school structures that are positive, they must develop ones that are flexible, open, fair, cooperative, professional, receptive to change, and trustworthy, and avoid structures that are rigid, authoritarian, suspicious, punishment-oriented, narrow, and restrictive.

THEORY INTO PRACTICE

ISLLC Standards 1, 2, 3, 5

To what extent is the structure of your school enabling rather than hindering? Develop a profile of your school structure using the elements described in Figure 3.2. Now check to compare how your school compares with a representative sample of schools by administering and scoring the Enabling School Structure (ESS) Form found at www.coe.ohio-state.edu/whoy. If you were the principal of your school, what would be your strategy to make the structure more enabling and less hindering?

INFORMAL STRUCTURE

As we suggested earlier, the school structure has an informal face as well as a formal one, and to neglect either is a mistake. The informal organization is the interpersonal side of the school. It is the system that is not included in the official blueprint or organizational chart. As administrators and teachers spontaneously interact on the job, they create networks of informal relations, which include unofficial roles, norms, values, cliques, communication channels, and teacher leaders.

Informal structure is built on sentiments and personal likes, and not on official roles and duties. Given a choice, teachers interact with people they like and avoid those they dislike. These informal social exchanges produce differences in interactions among individuals and groups. For example, a teacher's informal status in a school depends upon the frequency, duration, and nature of interactions with colleagues. Some teachers are actively sought and others are avoided; some are respected and admired, others are not; some teachers become leaders and others are followers. Finally, most teachers become part of the teacher group, but some are isolates.

Think of your school. Who are the informal teacher leaders? Why? What are the subgroups or cliques of teachers in your school? What do these cliques stand for? Which are the dominant cliques? Who eats with whom in the cafeteria and who sits together in faculty meetings? Who is the teacher spokesperson in faculty meetings? Who leads each clique? How do the cliques and their leaders get along? An observant teacher can map the informal organization of the school by simply being perceptive and answering the kinds of questions posed above.

Also important is the set of informal norms that emerge to guide teacher behavior. As teachers interact, they develop social norms, unofficial expectations that prescribe what they should and should not do in various situations. Informal norms are a powerful source for providing direction. Violation of important informal norms of their school can mean informal sanctions and ostracism from colleagues. "Handle your own discipline problems," "Don't criticize colleagues in front of students or parents," and "Support your principal" are examples of norms. Finally, sets of informal expectations are defined according to such roles as "task master," "comedian," or "spokesperson."

Sometimes the informal organization is at odds with the formal organization and there is conflict, friction, and game playing. Destructive politics becomes the norm in such schools, pitting teachers against the principal and one teacher group against another. At other times, the two structures are relatively harmonious and cooperative. Differences between groups of teachers and the principal enrich the workplace environment. In all cases, the informal structure arises within the formal organization and reacts to it; the formal, in turn responds to the informal. For example, proximity and mobility of teachers are formal assignments that influence the formation of informal relations in much the same way as strong, cohesive views by the informal leaders affect the view of the principal. The informal organization can be thought of as the "shadow" of the formal, albeit organized on the basis of sentiments and personal concerns rather than official roles and obligations. Let's briefly consider this shadow structure.

We have talked about formal hierarchy of authority. There is also an informal authority structure based on personal likes and dislikes. Groups of teachers emerge, coalesce, and form cliques. Some of these groups have more status and influence than others, and an informal status structure emerges; that is, a hierarchy of cliques develops.

Just as labor is divided in the formal structure, teacher cliques are divided in the informal structure based on social and personal interests. The cliques of the informal organization tend to be based on friendship and personal interests; that is, there is a division into cliques in the informal organization.

In the formal organization, expertise is specialized by task areas. But in the informal, specialization is based on relations and informal knowledge. To be sure, there is expertise, but it is less formally organized and more open. The organization is formalized by it rules, regulations, policies, and procedures, but the informal structure is guided by its system of informal norms and procedures. The norms are often quite different than the official rules; in fact, they can either support or undermine them. The formal structure is founded on the principle of impersonality and rationality, whereas the informal is built on personal relations and friendships. Personality and social relations are the hallmark of the informal structure.

The school has its system of formal communications and official memos, but the informal organization also has an informal communication network—the grapevine. Frequently, the grapevine is more efficient and faster than the formal.

Finally, schools have formal leaders such as the principal and vice principal, but it also has informal teacher leaders who often wield significant power. In brief, for every aspect of the formal structure, there is a corresponding shadow element in the informal structure. In Figure 3.3, we contrast and summarize these elements and suggest the dynamic interplay between formal structure and informal organization.

Thus, there are two important faces to school structure—the formal and the informal. An effective program of supervision, evaluation, and development requires complementary support from and between both. The formal structure organizes the official roles, tasks, and procedures, whereas the informal protects the integrity, self-respect, and independence of teachers, enhances the cohesiveness of teachers' groups, and improves authentic communication, especially when there are formal communication blocks (Barnard, 1938). Wherever there is a formal organization, there is also an informal one. The wise principal knows that informal structure is not the enemy to be suppressed, but rather it is another a useful device to improve the efficiency and effectiveness of schools.

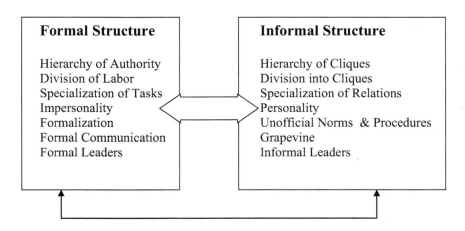

Figure 3.3.   Elements of the formal and informal structure and their interplay.

> **THEORY INTO PRACTICE**
> *ISLLC Standards 1, 2, 3, 5*
> Map the informal organization of your school by sketching the
> elements of informal structure found in Figure 3.4. How much friction
> exists between the formal and informal? What is the source of friction?
> How can it be eliminated? How well does the principal get along with
> the informal leader of the school? Who is the informal leader? Why this
> person? How supportive is the informal structure of the principal's
> supervision? Is the supervision authentic or a ritual?

School Climate

Another aspect of the school context that sets the scene for effective
instructional leadership is organizational climate. Teachers' performances
in schools are in part determined by the school climate in which they
work. Organizational climate refers to teachers' perceptions of the
school's work environment; it is affected by the formal organization,
informal organization, and politics, all of which, including climate, affect
the motivations and behavior of teachers. Simply stated, the set of internal behavioral characteristics that distinguishes one school from another
and influences the behavior of its members is the organizational climate
of the school. More specifically, climate is a relatively enduring quality of
the school environment that is experienced by teachers, influences their
behavior, and is based on their collective perceptions (Hoy & Miskel,
2005). There are a number of ways to conceive of the climate of the
schools, but we will briefly examine two of the most useful and well-known
frameworks and then turn to a synthesis of the two.

Organizational Climate: Open to Closed

Schools differ dramatically in their tone. In one school, the teachers
and the principal are zestful and exude confidence. They find pleasure in
working with each other; they cooperate and are open with each other. In
a second school, the brooding discontentment of teachers is blatant; the
principal rules with an iron fist and the teachers are suspicious and often
hostile. The psychological condition of such a faculty spills over to students who, in their own frustration, feed back to teachers alternating
moods of hostility and indifference. A third school is marked by neither
pleasure nor despair, but by a hollow ritual that reveals a pervasive phoni-
ness (Halpin & Croft, 1962).

These stark differences in the feel of schools led Halpin and Croft (1962) to a systematic attempt to conceptualize and measure school climate. They viewed the climate of the school in terms of its personality—that is, just as individuals have personalities, schools have organizational climates. The work of Halpin and Croft (1962) led to the development of a set of scales, the Organizational Climate Description Questionnaire (OCDQ), to measure the openness of the climate of schools. The original OCDQ was designed for use only in elementary schools, but revised versions have been formulated and tested for elementary, middle, and high schools (Hoy & Sabo, 1998; Hoy & Tarter, 1997).

A basic assumption of our analysis of instructional leadership is that a school's organizational climate is closely related to its improvement practices. An open climate, with its authentic interpersonal relations, seems likely to produce a situation where constructive change can succeed. The closed climate, on the other hand, presents an environment of hostility, suspicion, and inauthenticity where the improvement of instruction is doomed to failure. Improving teaching and learning simply will not work in a closed climate; in fact, in such schools it seems futile to attempt to improve the teaching-learning process. If the climate of a school is closed, the first task is to change it. Such change requires a cooperative effort between the teachers and principal; in fact, the principal's leadership is a key to improving the climate. Trust and openness are necessary conditions for effective school improvement.

Research on school climates consistently supports the conclusion that the school's openness and its emotional tone are related in predictable ways. Openness is associated with less student alienation, lower student dropout rates, and more student satisfaction with school (Finkelstein, 1998; Hoy, 1972). Moreover, open schools are generally more effective than closed ones, and teachers are more involved in shared decision making (Hoy & Sabo, 1998; Hoy et al., 1991). Openness, teacher commitment, and teacher loyalty (Hoy et al., 1991; Reiss & Hoy, 1998) are also positively associated. Open school climates increase faculty trust (Hoy, Smith, & Sweetland, 2002) and enhance perceptions of fairness in school (Hoy & Tarter, 2004).

Open organizational relations also have positive consequences in schools because they facilitate the process of improving instruction. No climate can guarantee effective teaching and learning because school climate in and of itself cannot make a poor program good or a weak teacher strong, but an open school climate can provide the necessary atmosphere for reflection, cooperation, change, and improvement. There are three separate OCDQ measures for school climates—one for elementary schools (Hoy & Tarter, 1997), another for middle schools (Hoy & Tarter, 1997), and one for high schools (Hoy & Tarter, 1997; Hoy et al., 1991). There are no copyright restrictions for the use of any of these instruments for research or school improvement; in fact, they are all available at www.coe.ohio-state.edu/whoy. Simply log on, download the instrument, and use it. For some specific examples of changing the openness of the climate of schools see Hoy and Woolfolk Hoy (2006) and Hoy and Tarter (1997).

ORGANIZATIONAL CLIMATE: HEALTHY TO UNHEALTHY

Another framework for defining and measuring the social climate of a school is its organizational health. The idea of positive health in an organization is not new, and it calls attention to factors that facilitate growth and development as well as to conditions that facilitate positive organizational dynamics. The state of health of a school can reveal much about the probable success of change initiatives and improvement. Matthew Miles (1969) defines a healthy organization as one that survives and adequately copes over the long haul as it continuously develops and extends its surviving and coping abilities. Implicit in this definition is that healthy organizations deal successfully with disruptive outside forces while effectively directing their energies toward the major goals and objectives of the organization. Operations on a given day may be effective or ineffective, but the long-term prognosis in healthy organizations is favorable.

Hoy and his colleagues (Hoy & Sabo, 1998; Hoy & Tarter, 1997) used a health metaphor to develop, identify, and measure critical social interaction patterns in schools. They were concerned with the task and social needs of the school. The Organizational Health Inventory (OHI) is a descriptive questionnaire, not unlike the OCDQ, that measures health of the interactions between students and teachers, teachers and administrators, and the school and community. Versions of the OHI are available online for your use at www.coe.ohio-state.edu/whoy. Simply log on, download the appropriate instrument, and use it.

The healthy school is one protected from unreasonable community and parental pressures. The school successfully resists all narrow efforts of vested interest groups to influence policy. The principal of a healthy school provides dynamic leadership, leadership that is both task-oriented and relations-oriented. Such behavior is supportive of teachers and yet provides direction and maintains high standards of performance. Moreover, the principal has influence with his or her superiors as well as the ability to exercise independent thought and action. Teachers in a healthy school are committed to teaching and learning. They set high but achievable goals for students, they maintain high standards of performance, and the learning environment is orderly and serious. Furthermore, students work hard on academic matters, are highly motivated, and respect other students who achieve academically. Classroom supplies and instructional materials are accessible if needed. Finally, in a healthy school, teachers like each other, trust each other, are enthusiastic about their work, and identify positively with the school.

The OHI will provide you with an index of health of your school, and a healthy school climate is essential for effective programs of supervision, evaluation, and professional development. In fact, research shows that school health is positively associated with student achievement, school quality, overall school effectiveness, teacher participation, effective leadership, and a strong culture (Hoy & Sabo, 1998; Hoy et al., 1991).

The Organizational Climate Index

The Organizational Climate Index (OCI) taps both the openness and health of schools. The OCI is composed of 27 Likert-type items that portray the behavior of teachers and principals in the school. Teachers are asked to describe the extent to which each behavior occurs along a scale from rarely to very frequently. The validity and reliability of the scale have been supported in a comprehensive study by Hoy, Smith, and Sweetland (2001). The OCI has four dimensions: Collegial principal behavior and teacher professionalism describe the openness of professional relations, whereas academic press and institutional vulnerability are indicators of the health of the interpersonal dynamics. Each dimension is briefly defined below, and sample items are provided:

- *Collegial Leadership* is principal behavior that is open, egalitarian, and supportive but at the same time sets clear expectations and standards for performance.
  - o The principal treats all faculty members as his or her equal.
  - o The principal maintains definite standards of performance.

- *Professional Teacher Behavior* is teacher behavior that is characterized by respect for colleagues, commitment to students, autonomy, and mutual cooperation and support.
  - o Teachers respect the professional competence of their colleagues.
  - o The interactions between faculty members are cooperative.

- *Achievement Press* describes schools that set high and achievable academic goals, students who persist and strive to achieve and are respected for their academic success, and parents and principals who press for high achievement and school improvement.

o The school sets high standards for academic performance.

o Parents exert pressure to maintain high standards.

- *Institutional Vulnerability* is the extent to which the school is susceptible to vocal parents and citizen groups who cause problems and disrupt the internal dynamics.

o The school is vulnerable to outside pressure.

o A few vocal parents can change school policy.

In sum, climate index is another functional tool for analyzing important aspects of school context. Openness in interpersonal relations and healthy organizational dynamics seem necessary conditions for an effective program of improvement. The principal must first create a positive climate; if it is lacking, it must be developed. The OCI can be found at http://www.waynekhoy.com/. Simply log on, download the appropriate instrument, and use it. Figure 3.4 depicts several school climate profiles as measured by the OCI.

THEORY INTO PRACTICE
ISLLC Standards 1, 2, 3, 5
Select one of the climate measures (e.g. OCI or OHI) and administer the instrument to a dozen or so teachers in your school. Then score the instrument and use the results to write a critical description of your school's climate. What needs to be improved? How would you improve it? Is your school ready for an effective program of supervision, evaluation, and personal development? Make the case for a sound social context in your school in terms of its readiness.

SCHOOL CULTURE

Wang, Haertel, and Walberg (1993, 1997) performed a meta-analysis of more than 10,000 statistical findings on the significant influences on learning. Their results should not be surprising. In general, direct influences have a greater impact on student learning than indirect ones. The key to improving student learning rests with what happens in the classroom. The one exception, however, is that school culture makes an important difference by providing a school context that reinforces important

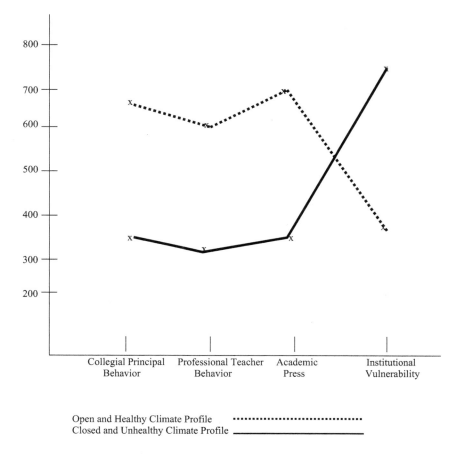

Figure 3.4.   Profiles of Contrasting School Climates.

teaching and learning practices. Instructional leadership takes place when a principal works with teacher colleagues to improve instruction by providing a school culture and climate where change is linked to the best knowledge and practice about student learning.

School climate and culture are complementary ways to examine the atmosphere of a school. Culture is a broader term than climate, and refers to shared *beliefs* rather than patterns of *behavior*. There is not a great difference between beliefs and behavior, so we recommend that you use the framework that seems most useful for improving your school context.

Although there are many definitions of organizational culture (Hoy & Miskel, 2005), we define school culture as the traditions, values, and beliefs that distinguish that school from others and infuse it with a distinctive identity. Culture not only provides the school with a sense of identity, it also binds the organization together, provides appropriate standards for behavior, and cultivates commitment to colleagues. The principal typically embodies the core values of the school and is instrumental in shaping the school culture. We will examine a school culture of academic optimism, which includes collective efficacy, faculty trust, and academic emphasis.

A Culture of Academic Optimism

There are a number of frameworks for examining the culture of a school—for example, a culture of collective efficacy or a culture of trust. Both of these perspectives provide useful views of the school workplace; however, we prefer to examine the workplace of the school as a culture of academic optimism. Academic optimism is a broader and more comprehensive view of school culture that includes both collective efficacy and faculty trust as well as academic emphasis. These three collective properties are not only similar in nature and function, but they complement each other and work together in a unified fashion to create a positive school setting. The academic optimism of a school provides an organizational setting that facilitates high academic achievement for all students regardless of SES, previous achievement, and other demographic characteristics (Hoy & Miskel, 2013; Hoy, Tarter, & Woolfolk Hoy, 2006; McGuigan & Hoy, 2006; Smith & Hoy, 2007). Optimism is often considered a cognitive characteristic (Peterson, 2000; Snyder, Shorey, Cheavens, Pulvers, Adams, & Wiklund, 2002), but the current conception of academic optimism has cognitive, affective, and behavioral elements. Collective efficacy is a cognitive, group belief; faculty trust in parents and students is an affective, group response; and academic emphasis is the behavioral enactment of collective efficacy and trust.

Academic optimism is a collective set of positive beliefs and values about the strengths and capabilities of schools to be successful; optimism unites efficacy, trust, and academic emphasis into a school culture imbued with a sense of the possible. Schools with strong cultures of academic optimism have faculties who believe they can make a positive difference in student learning (collective efficacy), believe students can learn (collective trust), and are committed to high academic performance (academic emphasis). These three collective aspects of academic optimism interact with each other (see Figure 3.4). For example, faculty trust in students and parents promotes a sense of collective efficacy, and in return, collective efficacy reinforces faculty trust. Likewise, if the faculty trusts parents, then teachers believe that they can insist on high academic standards without fear of parents undermining them, and a press for high academic standards in turn reinforces faculty trust in parents and students. Finally, when the faculty as a whole believes it can organize and execute actions needed for academic success, then teachers will emphasize academics, which in turn will reinforce a strong sense of collective teacher efficacy. In short, all the aspects of academic optimism are in transactional relationships with each other and interact to create a strong culture of academic optimism (Forsyth, Adams, & Hoy, 2011; Hoy et al., 2006).

The Dynamics of Academic Optimism

Although academic optimism has been consistently related to achievement regardless of SES (Forsyth et al., 2011; Hoy et al., 2006; Kirby & DiPaola, 2009; McGuigan & Hoy, 2006; Smith & Hoy, 2007; Wagner & DiPaola, 2011), just how academic optimism affects student achievement has received much less attention. Thus we turn to an organizational model that explains the dynamics of the relationship of academic optimism with school achievement.

Two separate, but related, areas of research shed light on the explanation. Bryk and Schneider (2002) conducted a longitudinal study of the Chicago Public Schools designed to examine school effectiveness. In the process of their study, they accidentally discovered the strong importance of trust in schools. They found, "Schools reporting strong levels of trust levels in 1994 were more than three times as likely to be categorized eventually as improving in reading and mathematics than those with very weak reports" (Bryk & Schneider, 2002, p. 111). They theorized that trust facilitated school effectiveness indirectly by promoting the following four organizational conditions that more directly explained achievement: a positive "can do" attitude, outreach and cooperation with parents, professional community, and commitment to school community.

These conditions are remarkably similar to the elements of the construct of academic optimism as developed by Hoy and his colleagues. The "can do" attitude is *collective efficacy*; the outreach and collaboration with parents is embodied in *faculty trust in students and parents*; and finally, professional community in terms of collaboration, commitment to improve teaching and learning, and high expectations and academic standards is captured in *academic emphasis* (Hoy et al., 2006). It seems clear that the key facets that drive student achievement are also the key components of a culture of academic optimism—collective efficacy, faculty trust in students and parents, and academic emphasis (see Figure 3.5).

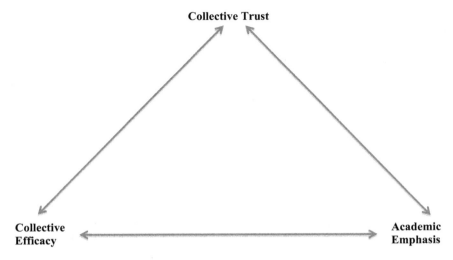

Figure 3.5.   Reciprocal relations of the three components of academic optimism.

The question remains, however, as to how this constellation of organizational properties produces high student achievement. Hoy and his colleagues (Forsyth et al., 2011; Hoy, 2012) provide a theoretical explanation. First, a culture of academic optimism leads teachers and students to set and embrace specific, challenging goals that are achievable, which in turn leads to both high teacher and student motivation. Second, academic optimism and relational trust (working through academic optimism) foster a learning environment in which students and teachers accept responsibility for learning and are motivated to exert strong effort, persist in difficult tasks, and are resilient in the face of difficulties and failures. Third, academic optimism stimulates cooperation among students, teachers, and parents for student learning, which enhances student motivation. Moreover, trust between parents and teachers supports academic optimism as well as furthers cooperation. Both realistic goals and cooperation among students, teachers, and parents lead to strong motivation, which in turn leads to high levels of achievement. High achievement in turn reinforces both relational trust and academic optimism. These interrelationships producing student achievement are summarized and illustrated in Figure 3.6.

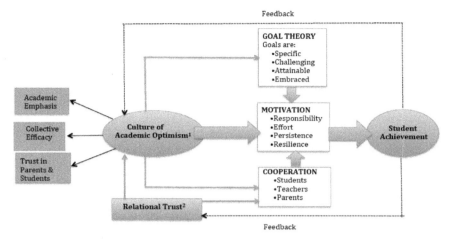

Figure 3.6.   A model of the dynamics of student achievement (Hoy, 2010).

Supervisors and Teachers Working Together to Improve Student Performance

In the latent construct of academic optimism, we have a practical roadmap for supervisors and teachers to improve student learning. The notion of academic optimism provides at least three separate, but related paths to enhance student learning: (1) create collective efficacy, (2) promote collective trust, and (3) support academic emphasis. For example, experiencing achievement, modeling success, and persuading teachers to believe in themselves and their capabilities are paths to collective efficacy (Bandura, 1997; Goddard, Hoy, & Woolfolk Hoy, 2004). Faculty trust in students and parents can be enhanced by useful interchanges and cooperative projects, both formal and informal, between parents and teachers (Forsyth et al., 2011; Hoy et al., 2006). Strong academic emphasis can be developed in schools by recognizing academic achievements and by communicating high, achievable expectations to students and parents. The principal must be the intellectual leader of the school, who has the responsibility to forge a culture in which academic success is a dominant goal. Schools must celebrate intellectual and academic successes of both teachers and students.

A caveat is in order. Any program or intervention to improve one of the elements of academic optimism must be supportive of the other two elements. This guide provides a check and balance for avoiding dysfunctional consequences. For example, some tactics for strengthening academic emphasis, such as more competitive grading and higher standards, could undermine trust among teachers, students, and parents. Avoid such practices. Change in one element at the expense of another is counterproductive. Thus, principals have three criteria (collective efficacy, faculty trust, and academic emphasis) to use as they plan improvement; no change should be made if any of the criteria suffer.

Optimism is a powerful force for improvement. Seligman (1998) was the first to challenge the traditional view of achievement and success as a function of talent and motivation. Seligman offers evidence for a third basic factor in success—optimism. He argues convincingly that optimism matters as much as talent or motivation in success. Learned optimism moves individuals over the wall of learned pessimism. As we have explained elsewhere (Hoy, 2012; Hoy et al., 2006), pessimism is a major inhibitor of success because it leads to a sense of hopelessness and futility.

Pessimism in schools promotes a tired resignation: "These kids can't learn, so why worry?" Unfortunately, such a view is stifling and self-perpetuating. Pessimism also breeds fear—a fear to act, a fear to fail, a fear to experiment—all of which stunt persistence and kill resilience. "Academic optimism, in stark contrast, views teachers as capable, students as willing, parents as supportive, and the task as achievable" (Hoy, Tarter, & Woolfolk Hoy, 2006, p. 40). Thus, the significance of a culture of academic optimism seems essential if principals are going to help teachers improve instruction and student achievement.

Tools for Measuring Culture

Just as there are tools for measuring the climate of schools, measurement tools are available to determine the culture of schools. For example, to measure the culture of trust in a school, use the Omnibus Trust Scale to determine the trust profile for the school (see www.waynekhoy.com). Or to focus on the collective efficacy of a school use the Collective Efficacy Scale and its norms to plot the efficacy of the school (see www.waynekhoy.com). Finally, to map the academic optimism of a high school, go to the same web site for an instrument and scoring direction to determine the relative optimism of the school's culture.

CHANGING CULTURE

Every organization has a unique culture that has been developed and shaped internally by the leaders, followers, and other constituencies as

> **THEORY INTO PRACTICE**
> *ISLLC ISLLC Standards 1, 2, 3, 5*
> What is the academic optimism of your school? Administer the school academic optimism scale to teachers in your school. Use the norms provided (www. waynekhoy.com) to decide the relative academic optimism of your school. Develop short-term and long-term plans to improve the academic optimism. What professional development activities might you use? What informal activities might you use?

well as externally by environmental changes. Schein's (2004) research on leadership and culture remains the seminal work in the field. Rooted in his clinical work with various business organizations, Schein offers a detailed analysis of how leaders can influence culture. For Schein, the guiding principle and assumption underlying his understanding of leadership and organizational culture is that leaders "teach" culture; he wants to emphasize the active role of the leader in transmitting culture as opposed to the passivity of the follower learning culture as it evolves. If leaders are responsible for teaching culture, how should they proceed?

Schein outlines six primary mechanisms for embedding culture:

- what leaders pay attention to, measure, and control on a regular basis
- how leaders react to critical incidents and organizational crises
- observed criteria by which leaders allocate scarce resources
- deliberate role modeling, teaching, and coaching
- observed criteria by which leaders allocate rewards and status
- observed criteria by which leaders recruit, select, promote, retire, and excommunicate organizational members (Schein, 1992).

These six primary, embedding mechanisms outline what is most within a principal's control, and thus highlight domains of influence for the leader and how the leader can interpret and communicate the meaning behind these behaviors. Followers are attentive of the leader's behavior and will interpret the motivation behind it. The leader must deliberately connect his or her leadership behavior (as exhibited in the six primary mechanisms) to the existing culture values and assumptions as embedded in the existing culture. The key for the leader is demonstrating that his or her leadership is consistent and congruent with the core values of the organization.

SUMMARY

The principal of the school is responsible for developing a productive school workplace, one that facilitates teaching and learning. More than any other single individual, the principal creates and cultivates the character of the school workplace. The principal's role is to lead in the development of a collective sense of school identity that transforms the workplace into a distinctive teaching-learning organization.

Effective supervision, evaluation, and professional development cannot occur unless the social context of the school is conducive to such activities. The principal can develop and use both the formal and informal structure of the school to build such a workplace. To that end, the school structure should enable teachers rather than hinder their efforts, and the informal organization must complement rather than compete with the formal. Both the formal and informal structure should support and encourage teachers to experiment and in the process learn from their mistakes.

Just as structure is critical in the development of effective school workplaces, so too are the climate and culture of schools. We have argued that effective school climates are open and healthy in the interpersonal dynamics and that a culture of academic optimism seems necessary for effectiveness and continued growth and development. In brief, we argue that positive social contexts are prerequisites to any effective program of instructional leadership, and, in particular, the school work context should have structures that enable teaching and learning, climates that are open and healthy, and cultures that are optimistic.

A PRINCIPAL'S SUPERVISORY CHALLENGE

Instructions—Read the following account provided by a principal, reflect on her practice, and perform a case analysis.

This is the middle of my second year as principal of Lincoln High School. Lincoln is a small 9–12 school with 68 teachers. A year and a half ago, I was hired to "fix" the school. Morale was low, teachers were discouraged, the principal had been forced to resign, and parents were a constant source of complaint and irritation. I had been an assistant principal in a larger school in a neighboring community for the previous two years, but an opportunity to run my own school and a substantial raise in salary attracted me to the challenge of turning this school around. During my interview, the superintendent had been blunt in describing Lincoln as a school with problems and in need of leadership and change. I believed then as I do now that I can improve Lincoln, and I am, in fact, making progress.

In the faculty meeting the day before classes started, the first thing I did, as a new principal, was to meet my faculty and assess the challenges ahead. My primary agenda for the meeting was clear and simple: to get know the faculty and to let the faculty know what I was all about. The meeting was in the school and I arranged for coffee, donuts, and a fruit platter from a local grocery store. We spent all morning together. After coffee and a little socializing, we went through the formal introductions; then I gave the teachers about 15 minutes of spirited talk—who I was, my core beliefs, my goals, my aspiration, and the challenges we faced. Then we broke into ten groups—nine veteran groups and a group of eleven new teachers. Each group was given the charge of identifying existing problems and providing suggestions for addressing those difficulties. I met with all the new teachers with the explicit goal of getting to know them, developing a support network for them, and to be blunt, to keep them from all the whining that I suspected would take place among the veterans. Actually, the move was a good one because my group of new teachers formed into a cohesive unit of which I was an instrumental part.

The groups of veteran teachers, as expected, came back with a laundry list of problems, including: classes were too large, parents were too critical, the old principal was too harsh, the central administration did not understand their plight, they needed more support, the students did not value schooling, the old principal did not support faculty, the students were unruly, the achievement goals were unrealistic, student absenteeism was high, the school was disorganized, the futility of it all, and on and on. As for suggestions—here too was another laundry list of things *other people* could do to make the job more manageable. It became apparent to me that, in general, the veteran teachers saw virtually all their problems outside their control. My challenge for the first year was to change their perceptions of the school and the administration and to have teachers accept responsibility for some of the problems—for example, lack of collegiality, low achievement, poor classroom discipline, and poor parent–teacher relations. I began by having a regular faculty meeting each month. In addition to routine matters, there were always four items on the agenda: (1) improving classroom management, (2) improving achievement, (3) involving parents, and (4) improving collaboration. In fact, these four items drove virtually all the in-service and professional activity for the year. Focusing on the "big four," we had interactive workshops, formal and informal discussions, and consultations with experts.

How did things go during my first year? Not as well as I had hoped, but I think we did make some progress. Here are the data that I collected after year one. First, let's examine the academic optimism of my school.

Collective Efficacy (SSCE)	458
Trust (SSFT)	498
Academic Emphasis (SSAE)	480
Academic Optimism	477

In addition, the average achievement scores of the students at all levels went up slightly, but we are still a little below average. I lost six teachers the first year: one of my new teachers who decided to have a family, a mid-career teacher who took a position in another district, and four veterans who retired, all of whom I have replaced with young and talented teachers. Parents still complain about some of the teachers, but the complaints are fewer and less intense.

In brief, I have mixed feelings about my school and its progress. We have a long way to go. Although my superintendent seems happy with the progress, I am a little frustrated; my first year was a lot harder than I thought it would be. Change is difficult and slow. This year, I am trying to make more classroom visits—but I remain focused on the big four: academic achievement, classroom management, parental involvement, and teacher collegiality.

REFLECTIVE PRACTICE

Assume you are this principal.

- How do you think the principal did this first year? Defend your judgment.
- What would you do different the next year? Why?
- If you were to focus on only one of the big four, which would it be? Why?
- Sketch a plan to improve one of the big four for the year.

DEVELOP YOUR PORTFOLIO

The principal's role in improving student learning is usually indirect rather than direct. After all, it is the teachers, not the principal, who deliver the teaching and engage most directly with students. An important role for the principal, however, is developing a school context that is open, healthy, enabling, trusting, and efficacious. Select one of the perspectives presented in this chapter and assess the workplace of your school. How conducive is the context to productive programs of supervision, evaluation, and professional development? What can the principal do to improve the work context? In your view, what is the single most important feature of the school context to improve student learning? Why? Make the case. Finally, check out the organizational development strategy for improving the school context used by Hoy and Hoy (2013) at Martin Luther King, Jr. High School to improve the school workplace.

COMMUNICATION EXERCISE

You have been hired as the new principal of an urban school, Samuel DeWitt Proctor Elementary School. The PTA is going to introduce you Friday evening at a meeting they have been publicizing for weeks. You have decided to give a 20-minute presentation on "Schools that Succeed: New Directions for Proctor Elementary School." Develop the outline of your talk using a power point presentation. Be sure to conceptualize the kind of workplace you will be developing, why such a context is important, and how you will lead the school in these new directions. The Power Point presentation should be comprehensive.

READINGS

Forsyth, P. B., Adams, C., & Hoy, W. K. (2011). *Collective trust: Why schools can't improve without it.* New York, NY: Teachers College Press.

Hoy, A. W., & Hoy, W. K. (2013). *Instructional leadership: A research-based guide to learning in schools* (4th ed.). Boston, MA: Allyn and Bacon.

Hoy, W. K. (2012). School characteristics that make a difference for the achievement of all students: A 40-year academic odyssey. *Journal of Educational Administration, 50,* 76–97.

Hoy, W. K., & Miskel, C. G. (2013). *Educational administration: Theory, research, and practice* (9th ed.). New York, NY: McGraw-Hill.

Hoy, W. K., & Sabo, D. (1998). *Quality middle schools: Open and healthy.* Thousand Oaks, CA: Corwin Press.

Hoy, W. K., & Tarter, C. J. (1997). *The road to open and healthy schools: A handbook for change, elementary edition.* Thousand Oaks, CA: Corwin Press.

Schein, E. H. (2004). *Organizational culture and leadership* (3rd ed.). San Francisco, CA: Jossey-Bass.

Senge, P. M., Cambron-McCabe, L. T., Smith, B., Dutton, J., & Kleiner, A. (2000). *Schools that learn.* New York, NY: Doubleday.

WHAT DO SUPERINTENDENTS SAY?

How important are the structure, climate, and culture of a school in developing sound programs for supervision and evaluation? How can principals change the atmosphere of a school to improve student learning?

Superintendent 1: The principal is the singlemost important person in determining the culture and climate of a school building. Structuring a supervision program that is designed to improve teacher performance and convincing teachers of that purpose is the key to improving student learning. A successful principal must display expertise in the teacher/ learning process and establish a means to deliver this expertise to the teachers. Once that is accomplished, the principal can create an atmosphere that fosters teacher improvement and academic success for the students.

Superintendent 2: School culture is one of the most important aspects to developing sound programs for supervision and evaluation. Establishing and modeling a culture of high expectations relative to the teaching and learning process is critical for any school's success. Principals can change the atmosphere in a school by involving staff in the decision-making process and establishing the highest expectations for staff and student performance.

Superintendent 3: Effective supervision and evaluation programs, programs that result in teacher professional development and personal growth, must be developed cooperatively with teachers. Programs imposed upon teachers are likely to yield little more than compliance. Cooperatively developing supervision and evaluation programs requires organizational structure that enables, rather than hinders, productive outcomes; requires an open climate characterized by open, supportive, and nonrestrictive principal leadership; and requires a culture of learning not just among students, but among faculty as well. The principal plays a critical role in defining the structure, climate, and culture of the school, which is precisely how the principal can change the atmosphere of a school to improve student learning.

CHAPTER 4

A MODEL FOR CLASSROOM SUPERVISION

Supervision and evaluation that result in increased learning for all students can be difficult processes to conceptualize because the teaching/learning dynamic is so complex. Some of the factors that impact teaching are the needs, motivation, dispositions, skills, and knowledge of the teacher. Contextual factors such as the overall school climate and culture; federal, state, district and school expectations; available resources; understanding and quality of the standards-based curriculum; and the working relationships of teachers with the principal all impact the teaching process. The expectations of students as well as the relationship of the teacher with the class and individual students also have a significant impact on the teaching/learning process. Norms that develop in the classroom influence the behaviors and attitudes of students and their teacher. The curriculum quality and pedagogy of the individual teacher also affect teaching. Prior to fully developing our model of supervision, we discuss some of the issues that principals should consider.

SOCIAL SYSTEMS

The term "social system" typically refers to large aggregates of human relationships such as neighborhoods, organizations, or society itself. This

Improving Instruction Through Supervision, Evaluation, and Professional Development, pp. 73–102

concept is also a powerful tool for analyzing behavior in small groups. A social system is a set of interacting personalities bound together by social relationships (Homans, 1950; Hoy & Miskel, 2013). This social system is characterized by

- interdependence of elements
- differentiation from its environment
- complex networks of social relationships
- individuals motivated by their personalities and needs
- a distinctive unity that goes beyond its component parts
- interactions with its environment.

Figure 4.1 depicts the major elements of a social system.

Because of the generality of the social systems concept, a wide range of analyses of different social units is possible. It is most useful for supervisory purposes to focus on the classroom as a system, but classrooms exist in the context of a larger social system—the school. Hence, we begin with a conceptual analysis of the social system of the school—the immediate environment that influences classroom activity.

Hoy and Forsyth (1986) argued that behavior in school organizations is primarily a function of the interaction of three basic elements—formal expectations, informal norms, and individual needs. The formal elements

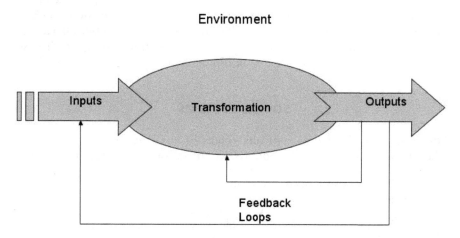

Figure 4.1.   Major elements of a social system.

of an organization refer to the official expectations of positions within the organization. From an array of vague and contradictory expectations, formal organizations select a few formal expectations that are reasonably consistent with the organization's goals. These formal expectations are really role expectations. They include rules and regulations, or policy, and they delineate such things as arrival times, building assignments, job descriptions, and evaluative criteria. Schools employ professionals; hence, there is also an expectation that employees' behavior will be guided by expertise and professional ethics that complement the formal rules and regulations. Thus, teachers and principals are expected to behave in appropriate ways based on both the school's rules and the expertise and behaviors consistent with their professional role.

However, the individuals who occupy formal roles and positions in the school are different and have unique needs. Their different personalities and needs affect their behavior. Teachers' and principals' behaviors in social systems are affected by the underlying need structures that motivate their behaviors.

This complex set of needs and desires produces different behavior in similar situations. Not all students react the same way to group work because they have different needs for structure, order, direction, affiliation, and success, to name just a few. Likewise, not all teachers react the same way to a change of principals, because they have different needs for achievement, recognition, affiliation, and so forth.

Needs affect not only the goals an individual will attempt to achieve but also the way an individual perceives the environment. For example, an individual with a high need for control tends to structure the environment to create opportunities for predictability and order, whereas an individual with a high need for affiliation tries to develop and seek opportunities for sociability. For a teacher of the first type, the school is primarily a vehicle to dominate social interactions; for the second, it is a social setting for the development of friendships and other social relations. In the same way that not all expectations are relevant to the analysis of organizational behavior, not all of the needs of an individual are instrumental in determining his or her role performance.

Work motivation constitutes the single most relevant set of needs for employees in formal organizations like schools. Refer to Hoy and Hoy (2013) for a more elaborate discussion of work motivation. For our present purposes, the individual element is conceptualized in the following manner:

Individual ---> Motivation ---> Needs ---> Behaviors

Because needs affect the way an individual perceives the environment, teachers will have different perceptions of the processes of supervision, evaluation, and professional development. This creates a challenge for principals. Figure 4.2 pictures the major elements at the three basic levels of the school social system.

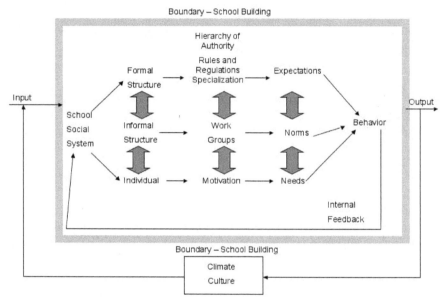

Figure 4.2.   School as a social system.

For example, the formal and informal observations of the teaching staff are affected by district policy as well as the principal's own personality. The rules and regulations may state that the principal is expected to observe each teacher's class at regular intervals. The principal acts to comply with this policy, yet each principal's behavior differs, perhaps because of motivational needs. For example, a principal who has a great personal desire for social acceptance and affiliation with teachers may treat teacher conferences as an opportunity for friendly chatting rather than an opportunity for constructive criticism. Another principal, lacking such a need for social affiliation, focuses on the goal of the process and remains analytical and task oriented during teacher interactions. Both principals are affected by their needs, but the first is more influenced by personality and the second by formal role expectations.

In schools, the work group is the mechanism by which formal expectations and individual needs interact and modify each other. As people are brought together in the workplace, a dynamic relationship emerges between formal role demands and individual needs. The group develops its own informal status structure and culture—its social organization. This informal organization, with its influential group norms, becomes another powerful force that affects behaviors. Thus, behavior in schools is primarily a function of the interaction of the three basic elements we have described: formal expectations, informal norms, and individual needs. Note that congruence of the elements at the three levels is an ideal: formal roles and expectations meeting an individual's needs while conforming to the group's norms.

AUTHORITY RELATIONSHIPS

Student-teacher and teacher-principal relations are integral components of schools and influenced by authority. Yet the concept of authority is

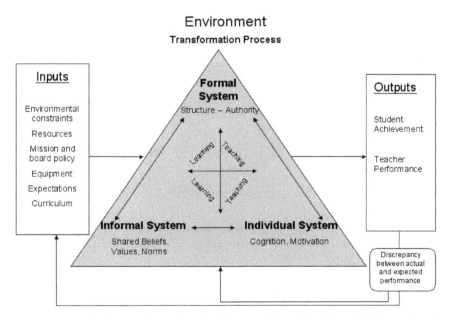

Figure 4.3.   Behavior is a function of the interaction of the formal, informal, and individual systems.

commonly misunderstood and frequently misused. Authoritarian, arbitrary, and dictatorial behavior is not synonymous with authority. Contrary to popular belief, the exercise of authority in schools does not typically involve coercion—that is, forced compliance with directives. Authority in a school exists when teachers believe they have both formal obligations and individual responsibilities.

There are two major sources of authority in school organizations—formal and informal. Formal authority is legitimated by values that have become institutionalized in the positions, rules, and regulations; informal authority is legitimated by shared norms that emerge spontaneously in the work group. Formal authority is vested in the organization and is legally established by contractual agreements. In joining the organization, all employees accept the authority relationship because they agree, within certain limits, to accept the directives of superiors. For example, a principal can direct a teacher to participate in a professional development activity. In contrast, there are a variety of sources of informal authority, such as expertise, personal behavior, or personal attributes. Teachers are often quite willing to comply with directives of principals who have demonstrated technical competence in a specific and relevant area or who have extraordinary qualities or human-relations skills that create a strong interpersonal identification. A common value orientation must emerge within the group to produce normative commitment to school leaders. When such informal norms of support develop, principals have informal authority.

Within the school, individuals can have (1) both informal and formal authority, (2) only formal authority, (3) only informal authority, or (4) no authority. Principals may possess both kinds of authority, but only formal authority is guaranteed by the position. Since we believe that effective instructional supervision is an informal process, principals must first establish informal authority in order to be effective supervisors of instruction.

GROUP BEHAVIOR

In order to engage in supervision as an informal process, the principal must become a "formal leader" by establishing informal authority. This is only possible when a common value orientation emerges within the teachers to produce a normative commitment to the principal. This can be a significant obstacle to principals. For example, some principals are too authoritarian and insecure to generate positive norms among teachers. In other words, some principals don't have the disposition to earn respect and loyalty among teachers.

Table 4.1. Leadership and Authority

		Formal Authority	
		Yes	No
Informal Authority	**Yes**	Formal Leader	Informal Leader
	No	Officer	Follower

Peer pressure among teachers also has a significant impact on principals' behavior. The group, with its informal organization and norms, influences behavior for several reasons. First, communicating feelings is easy and informal among colleagues. Second, informal groups maintain cohesiveness and a feeling of personal integrity, self-respect, and independent choice. Since interactions in the informal organization are neither impersonal nor dominated by formal authority, they provide opportunities for individuals to maintain their unique personalities. Finally, members receive important rewards from the group, and group norms are significant in guiding their behavior. For example, accepted informal procedures, not formal rules, may develop among teachers for disciplining or controlling students; in fact, the informal, custodial norms for controlling students become the criteria for judging "effective" teaching in many schools. Good control is equated with good teaching. Individual teacher behavior, therefore, is influenced both by the formal school structure and the norms and sanctions of the informal group. The principal, using the formal structure, can reinforce appropriate behavior by providing positive rewards or recognition. For example, a lesson well executed can be rewarded in a number of ways ranging from an informal "pat on the back" to a formal written commendation of outstanding teaching for the official record.

Group norms also control behavior. In the school building, norms exist within and among teachers. For example, teachers expect their colleagues to act appropriately in managing students. If a teacher fails to maintain discipline in the classroom, the other teachers apply sanctions such as sarcasm and ostracism in the teachers' lounge.

The culture of the community provides environmental constraints that directly influence formal expectations and group norms and indirectly influence individual needs. As an open system, the school remains open to community, state, and national influences. The reality of high-stakes testing and accountability in a standards-based environment, consequences of the No Child Left Behind Act and the Common Core State Standards, influence expectations, norms, behaviors, and needs of both teachers and principals.

Social behavior in a school is thus affected directly by at least three internal elements: formal expectations, group norms, and individual needs. Appropriate social behavior is reinforced both formally and informally. The principal must see the school as a dynamic entity in which students, teachers, and administrators affect one another's behavior. In that context, the principal functions at both the formal and informal level by providing formal rewards and sanctions in the evaluative process, making appropriate professional development opportunities available to teachers, and informally helping teachers improve the quality of their instruction during the supervisory process.

STRUCTURAL RELATIONS

Schools, like all formal organizations, can be described in terms of levels of the authority structure. The basic work of a school is teaching to facilitate learning. Since the teaching process is the core task, an entire subsystem revolves around the problems associated with effective teaching and learning. Skilled professionals, teachers and principals, are directly responsible for the teaching and learning process in schools.

The principal's role as manager and instructional leader is to integrate organizational activities. Principals must find ways to develop the loyalty of their teachers, motivate their efforts, and coordinate their work. Principals mediate between teachers and parents; they must also procure necessary resources (e.g., financial, personnel, and physical facilities) for teaching and learning. Although principals influence the teaching and learning process, they only have an indirect impact on achievement (Hallinger & Heck, 1996). After all, teachers in schools are the professionals who are interacting with students in the teaching and learning process and, therefore, should be best equipped to know what is necessary for effective student learning. Yet, among school-related factors that influence student outcomes, principal leadership is second only to classroom instruction (Leithwood et al., 2004). Hence, principals must find ways to work with and through their teacher colleagues to help students learn.

Schools are embedded in school districts; hence, both principals and teachers are constrained by district regulations and policies. Chubb and Moe (1990) argue that district control over personnel can be particularly debilitating to a school's effectiveness. This is especially true in light of the research indicating that classroom teachers have the most significant impact on student learning (Hattie, 2009; Sanders & Horn, 1998). When principals have little or no control over who teaches in their schools, they are saddled with teachers whose needs are not congruent with the goals and expectations of the school. The job of effectively supervising teachers is onerous enough without this significant burden. In this age of accountability, expectations for student learning set at the district, state, and national levels direct the goals of both principals and teachers. District policymakers should hold principals accountable, while supporting them with personnel policies that give them a significant role in staff selection.

Thus far, our discussion has focused on the social system of the school. We now turn to the classroom because teaching and learning are classroom functions. The elements of the school social system—formal expectations, informal organization, and individual needs—become key aspects of the classroom environment. Open-systems theory provides a general and useful way of viewing behavior in social organizations of all sizes, yet it is limited as a specific guide to action because it is so abstract. We need a more specific model that principals can use as a practical guide to help teachers improve instruction and student learning. Therefore, a model of classroom performance will now be developed.

THEORY INTO PRACTICE
ISLLC STANDARDS 2, 3, 5

Reflect on your school and answer the following questions. What formal aspects of the school structure help or hinder teachers' professional behavior? What informal aspects of the school structure help or hinder teachers' professional behavior? What motivational needs does your principal have that help or hinder teachers' professional behavior? What motivational needs do you have that help or hinder your professional behavior?

SUPERVISION: AN INFORMAL PROCESS

Instructional supervision is an informal process during which principals and teachers interact in a collegial, professional manner with the expressed goal of improving the quality of classroom instruction and student learning. Identifying teachers' professional development needs, as well as areas for potential professional growth, is an integral component of the supervisory process. Teachers work with their principals to reflect on their classroom practice, identify areas for improvement, and jointly plan strategies to grow professionally.

In our integrated model of supervision, evaluation, and professional development, the three processes are conceptualized as outcome-based and data-driven. They take place within a school context and are influenced by both external (e.g., CCSS, community expectations, state regulations) and internal variables such as culture, climate, resources, authority, and role relationships. The relationship between supervision—an informal formative process—and evaluation—the formal, summative process—is evident. They share the same goal—professional growth of teachers leading to improved classroom instruction and increased student learning. McGreal (1983) argued that all supervisory roads lead to evaluation and cautioned principals not to evaluate teachers until they have spent considerable time working with them in their classrooms. In fact, too often the practice of supervision in K–12 schools shortchanges the original intention of instructional supervision—developing teachers—by supplanting it with evaluation (Sullivan & Glanz, 2000).

Our conceptualization of instructional supervision as a process that helps teachers reflect on their practice and professional development is consistent with earlier progressive models of supervision characterized by teachers who are:

- engaged in reflective practice
- analytical of their own performance
- amenable to assistance from others
- responsible for their own growth and development (Cogan, 1973; Goldhammer, 1969).

Unruh and Turner (1970) describe supervision as "a social process of stimulating, nurturing, and appraising the professional growth of teachers" (p. 17). In their model, the principal's role is to initiate the process of supervision, provide opportunities for teacher learning, and create a professional milieu of continuous learning for teachers that results in greater student learning. Throughout the past three decades, the goals of instructional supervision have been described as

- promoting face-to-face interaction and relationship building between the teacher and supervisor (Acheson & Gall, 1997; Bellon & Bellon, 1982; Goldhammer, 1969; McGreal, 1983),
- ongoing learning (Glickman, 1990; Mosher & Purpel, 1972),
- the improvement of students' learning through improvement of the teacher's instruction (Blumberg, 1980; Cogan, 1973; Harris, 1975),
- data-based decision making (Bellon & Bellon, 1982),
- capacity building of individuals and the organization (Pajak, 1993),
- trust in the processes, each other, and the environment (Costa & Garmston, 1994),

- change that results in a better developmental life for teachers and students and their learning (Sergiovanni & Starratt, 1998),
- principals and teachers working together to achieve a collaboratively developed vision of what teaching and learning should be (Glickman, Gordon, & Ross-Gordon, 2013).

Thus, supervision has been traditionally conceptualized as a formative process that is focused on teacher growth and development. Teachers grow professionally, with the help of principals and other colleagues, through informal interactions that encourage analysis and reflection of their classroom practices (Glatthorn, 1990; Glickman et al., 2010). To reiterate, in this text, supervision is the collaborative and *informal* process among principals and teachers aimed at improving teaching and learning in the classroom.

THEORY INTO PRACTICE
ISLLC STANDARDS 1, 2, 3, 5
Think of your current supervisor. What does your supervisor do to encourage teachers to engage in reflective practice? To take responsibility for their own professional development? To be critically analytic of their classroom performance? To be open to assistance from others?

A SYSTEMS MODEL OF SUPERVISION

To achieve the goals of the supervisory process, increased student learning and teacher performance, a principal must first work to create a school context (see Chapter 3) that is necessary to build collegial, professional relationships with teachers (Figure 4.4).

School Context

Our model identifies contextual elements as the critical inputs for the supervisory process. We discussed the importance of climate, culture, and the nature of school relationships in the previous chapter. These elements are some of the core inputs of our model of supervision.

The context is also affected by overall organizational constraints previously discussed, such as the formal organization, informal organization,

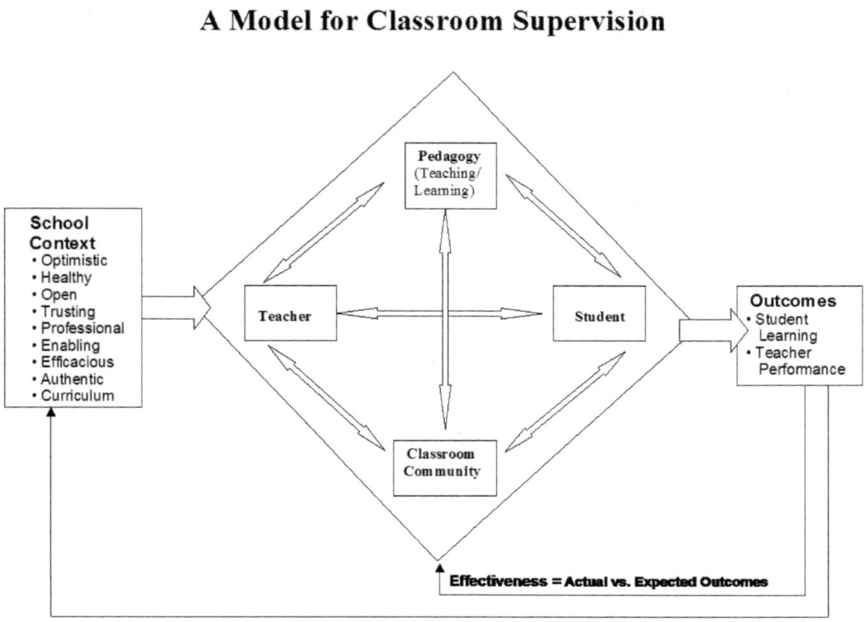

A Model for Classroom Supervision

Figure 4.4.   Classroom Performance Model for Supervision.

and school workplace. The principal's leadership style is critical in creating a context for school improvement. Goleman (1995) argued that "leadership is not domination, but the art of persuading people to work toward a common cause" (p. 149). Nowhere is this truer than in education. Principals must work through teachers to affect student achievement. Given this requirement, it is essential that principals be skilled at building and sustaining relationships. Emotional awareness and regulation are important factors in the daily interactions between principals and teachers (Wong & Law, 2002). A principal's behavior, including interactions with teachers, students, and parents, has a dramatic impact on the kinds of relationships that are forged. When principals interact with teachers in the instructional program, they have the ability to influence student achievement through the teacher. Principals are better able to identify individual and collective strengths and weaknesses within their schools if they maintain continuous dialogue with teachers about standards, curricula, instruction, and assessment. Principals recognize that their sphere of influence on student achievement is mediated through the teacher. As such, principals must align their actions and those of others in the school with the core values and mission of the school.

Improving academic outcomes for all students is impossible if the focus of the activities and dialogue within the building is not centered on instruction. Hawley (1985) found that "teachers who do not subscribe to the goals of the school do not contribute their full efforts" (p. 79). As such, the principal must have the skills, talent, and emotional intelligence to work with and through others to develop a common culture of learning that directs everyone within the school community to work together, persist, and demonstrate learning and resilience in the face of difficulties. Optimism, trust, efficacy, and academic focus, as well as a school climate that is healthy and open, are critical contextual elements of a school culture. Principals can create a context in which informal supervision can be viable and thrive or one in which it is doomed to failure. Another critical element of the school's context in our model is the curriculum.

Curriculum

In this high-stakes, accountability environment, the curriculum is another critical contextual element that impacts achievement. There are three kinds of curricula: the intended curriculum, the implemented curriculum, and the attained curriculum (Schmidt, McKnight, & Raizen, 1996). The intended curriculum is content specified by the CCSS or state standards to be addressed in a particular course or at a particular grade level. The implemented curriculum is content actually delivered by the teacher, and the attained curriculum is content actually learned by students. The discrepancy between the intended curriculum and the implemented curriculum makes opportunities to learn a prominent factor in student achievement—a factor that has continued to show a very strong relationship with student achievement (Brewer & Stacz, 1996; Herman, Klein, & Abedi, 2000; Robitaille, 1993).

In order to impact student learning, the curriculum:

- strives for the best balance of surface and deep understanding
- focuses on developing learning strategies to construct meaning
- includes strategies that are planned, are deliberate, and actively and explicitly teach specific skills and deeper understanding (Hattie, 2009, p. 35).

Therefore, principals should work with district curriculum leaders and classroom teachers to be certain these characteristics are embedded in district curricula. Then, when observing classroom instruction, principals must be vigilant in identifying any discrepancy between the intended curriculum and the implemented curriculum. Today, more than ever, teachers receive explicit guidance on content standards for specific courses and specific grade levels. The existence of CCSS documents, as well as curriculum guides aligned with the standards, does not necessarily guarantee that the implemented curriculum and the intended curriculum are the same.

As supervisors of instruction, principals not only insure that articulated curricula with specified scope and sequence are in place but that teachers have been trained in their implementation. They provide curricular materials aligned with CCSS and state standards as well as adequate teacher resources to help plan lessons that are instructionally sound and content- and grade-level-appropriate. Finally, principals must protect instructional time so that teachers have the opportunity to implement the curricula as intended.

After these curricular resources have been provided, systematic instructional monitoring must take place. Even when highly structured instructional materials are used as the basis for a curriculum, teachers commonly make independent and idiosyncratic decisions regarding what should be taught and to what extent (Doyle, 1992; Stodolsky, 1989; Yoon, Burstein, & Gold, n.d.). This practice of "hobby teaching" frequently creates huge holes in the continuum of content and undermines the students' opportunity to learn.

THEORY INTO PRACTICE
ISLLC STANDARDS 1, 2, 3

In chapter 3 we examined a number of school characteristics that influence the teaching in the classroom. In this chapter, we identify another key element. How can a principal protect instructional time for teachers? How can the supervisor promote diverse learning opportunities? How can principals and teachers align and articulate the curriculum?

CLASSROOM SOCIAL SYSTEM

Four key elements in the classroom social system interact to produce the quality of teacher performance and student learning. These components are (1) the student, (2) the teacher, (3) the classroom community, and (4) pedagogy.

Student

The primary element of the classroom system is the student. The personal characteristics of students in the class are central to any analysis of teaching and learning. What seems intuitively self-evident, that there is a connection between student motivation and achievement, is supported by research (Hattie, 2009). Motivation has an important role in determining the quantity and quality of students' engagement in learning activities, thus impacting their achievement (Anderman, 2013). Motivating students may be more complicated than motivating teachers. Students have needs for safety, a sense of belonging, esteem, and growth. For an in-depth discussion of motivation see Hoy and Hoy (2013, Chapter 5).

The skills, knowledge, values, and abilities that students bring to the classroom are also fundamental factors related to learning. The prior learning students bring to school when they enter has an impact on learning. Many challenges to student learning are directly linked to inadequate preliminary knowledge, skills, and values on the part of students. The correlation between ability and achievement is very high (Hansford & Hattie, 1982). Students who don't have an adequate base to build upon are at a distinct disadvantage, and remediation is necessary. Moreover, limitations in student ability commonly slow progress and produce difficulties within the classroom. The expectations and perceptions that students have of school, teachers, peers, and themselves influence their performance. Research suggests that the relationship between academic self-concept and academic achievement is reciprocal (Marsh & Seaton, 2013). Students who expect to fail frequently do; just as there is a self-fulfilling prophecy when teachers have low expectations for students, the same forces come into play when students have a poor self-image and hold low expectations for themselves. Interests and perseverance of students are other crucial aspects of classroom activities. Other factors such as sex, race, cultural background, and socioeconomic status are also individual characteristics that influence instructional and non-instructional transactions in the classroom.

Teacher

The second component of the classroom system is the teacher. In a study of 60,000 students across grades three through five in Tennessee, Wright, Horn, and Sanders (1997) identified the teacher as the most important factor affecting student learning. Their finding has been supported by subsequent meta-analyses (Hattie, 2009; Marzano, 2003). Of course, the implication for supervisors is evident. The greatest impact they can have on improving student learning is helping teachers become more effective.

Truly effective teachers are successful with students of all achievement levels regardless of the heterogeneity in their classrooms. Perhaps the most striking revelation in the Tennessee study was that on the average, the most effective teachers produced gains of about 53 percentage points in student achievement in one year, whereas the less effective teachers produced achievement gains of about 14 percentage points over the same time. These results are dramatic when we consider that researchers estimate that students typically gain about 34 percentile points in achievement during one academic year (Marzano, 2003).

The knowledge, skills, and dispositions teachers bring to the classroom vary dramatically. Shulman (1987) focused on teacher knowledge and identified different kinds of knowledge of successful teachers. Among them was "pedagogical content knowledge, that special amalgam of content and pedagogy that is uniquely the province of teachers, their own special form of professional understanding" (p. 8). Contemporary definitions of pedagogical content knowledge include not only content knowledge (depth and breadth, fluency with multiple ways of representation), pedagogical knowledge (linking teaching strategies to learning), and contextual knowledge (understanding how student differences impact teaching decisions) (Gess-Newsome, 2013).

Cotton (1995) found more than 150 components of teacher effectiveness. She categorized them into seven major activities: planning, setting goals, classroom management and organization, instruction, teacher-student interactions, equity, and assessment.

Other important attributes of teachers are their perceptions and expectations. The expectation of teachers that all students can achieve and the belief that they can make a difference in that achievement have a positive impact on students' learning (Hattie, 2009). Similarly, low levels of efficacy and negative expectations and perceptions of one's administrator, supervisor, or colleagues often result in a self-fulfilling prophecy (Schmoker, 1999). The adage "you get what you expect" seems to have more than a grain of truth. Teachers' motivational needs also play an important role in their classroom behavior. Strong personal needs for security, dominance, and upward mobility have predictable consequences. Teachers behave in ways that they believe will lead to desired states; hence, both rewards and personal values motivate teacher behavior. The motivational forces of teacher behavior are a complex topic (for further information see Hoy & Hoy, 2013, Chapter 5).

Classroom Community

The next component of the classroom system is classroom community—that is, personal interactions and classroom procedures that facilitate the teaching and learning process. The climate of the classroom has a powerful influence on student learning (Marzano, 2000). Therefore, classroom management is essential—maintaining a positive, productive learning environment, relatively free of disruptive behavior, creates a classroom community in which students achieve (Hattie, 2009). The goal of classroom management is to provide a learning environment where students can make mistakes and learn from them. Teachers are proactive in supporting and facilitating academic and social-emotional learning (Evertson & Emmer, 2013). Good management includes providing students clear expectations, strong guidance, a clarity of purpose, and concern for the needs and opinions of others.

Teacher-student relationships are powerful moderators of classroom management (Cornelius-White, 2007). Positive relationships between teachers and students create classroom communities in which there is more engagement, respect of self and others, group cohesion, fewer resistant behaviors, and higher achievement. Teachers who are student-centered, encouraging, nondirective, empathetic, warm, genuine, and adaptive to student differences create high-achieving classroom communities (Hattie, 2009).

The teacher sets the classroom structure through formal expectations for the students. Marzano (2003) asserts that there are four basic elements of classroom management: "(a) establishing and enforcing rules and procedures, (b) carrying out disciplinary actions, (c) maintaining effective teacher and student relationships, and (d) maintaining an appropriate mental set for management" (pp. 88–89). Few classes are without a body of rules that regulate student behavior; however, there is considerable variation in the degree of structure among classes. Some teachers have rules for almost everything; others have only a few implicit understandings. Teachers develop routine procedures for managing classroom behavior, such as the way in which desks in the room are arranged, what students must do to be called on to speak, whether students must ask permission to leave the room, how the teacher should be addressed, and what format, if any, is to be used on homework assignments. Some teachers involve students deeply, not only in the development of classroom management procedures, but also in planning instructional activities; others do not.

Given the multidimensional, simultaneous, fast-paced, unpredictable, public, and historical nature of classrooms, this is quite a challenge. Gaining student cooperation means much more than dealing effectively with misbehavior. It means planning activities, having materials ready, making appropriate behavioral and academic demands on students, giving clear signals to students, accomplishing transitions smoothly, foreseeing problems and stopping them before they start, selecting and sequencing activities so that flow and interest are maintained—and much more.

Teachers must provide all students access to learning. To achieve this, they ensure that everyone knows how to engage in class activities. The key is awareness. What are the procedures and expectations? Are they understandable, given the students' cultural backgrounds and home experiences? What unspoken rules or values may be operating? Are teachers clearly signaling appropriate ways to participate? For some students, particularly those with behavioral and emotional challenges, direct teaching and practicing of the important behaviors may be necessary (Emmer & Stough, 2001).

The final goal of classroom management is to help students become better able to self-regulate. Self-regulation consists of the processes one employs to activate and sustain thoughts, behaviors, and emotions in order to achieve goals (Zimmerman & Schunk, 2011). Helping students develop self-regulation requires extra time to teach students how to take responsibility for their own emotions, thoughts, and behaviors; this is an investment well worth the effort. When elementary and secondary teachers neglect setting student self-management as a goal, their students often find that they have trouble working independently and taking responsibility for their actions.

Knowledge and expertise in classroom management are marks of expertise in teaching; stress and exhaustion from managerial difficulties are precursors of burn-out in teaching (Emmer & Stough, 2001). Classroom management is mentioned in some form in virtually every major study of factors affecting student achievement.

The teacher determines the structure of the teaching and learning process. For example, a high school mathematics class might consist of the following five activity periods: (1) settling down to work, (2) teacher-directed review of homework, (3) introduction of new skills or concepts, (4) presentation of a new assignment and supervision of student practice, and (5) assignment of independent practice. Thus, the structure of classroom activities can be examined in terms of the formal relations between the teacher and students, the routine management practices in the classroom, student participation in planning, and the organization of learning activities.

Pedagogy

Teaching has been defined in a variety of ways, but for our purposes, it is a system of intentional actions aimed at inducing a permanent change in the learning of skills, knowledge, and values. What factors contribute to quality teaching?

Our definition of teaching implies strategy. Teachers are trying to induce learning in students, but what learning? Teaching and learning are inextricably linked; the purpose of classroom teaching is student learning. Learning is grouped into three categories: (1) skills—learning how to do something (e.g., keyboarding, reading, running); (2) knowledge—learning to know something (e.g., facts and logic systems); and (3) values—learning to make normative judgments (e.g., decisions concerning good or bad, right or wrong). The teaching strategy depends on three factors: the learning task; the teachers' skills, knowledge, and values; and the students' abilities and interests.

Regardless of the pedagogy, good teaching has a number of common phases. Brophy (1997) identified ten keys to successful teaching for understanding:

- The curriculum emphasizes knowledge, skills, and values that will be useful outside as well as inside school.
- Students become more expert by actually using knowledge in practical applications so that conceptual understanding and self-regulation develop simultaneously.
- A few important topics are addressed in depth instead of "covering" the curriculum. Supporters of the constructivist approach believe (with Howard Gardner, 2000) that coverage is the enemy of understanding.
- The content to be learned is organized around a small set of powerful or "big" ideas.
- The teacher presents information but also scaffolds students' efforts to learn.
- The students' role is to actively work to make sense of the information and make it their own.
- Teaching begins with the students' prior knowledge, even if that understanding includes some misunderstanding and conceptual change.
- Class activities include authentic tasks that call for critical thinking and problem solving, not just memorizing.
- Higher-order thinking skills are taught and applied as students learn subject matter, not during separate, stand-alone "thinking" activities.
- The teacher's goal is to create a learning community where dialogue and cooperation promote student understanding of content.

Professional organizations and researchers conclude that teaching expertise is the single most important factor in improving learning for students (Hattie, 2009; Marzano, 2003; National Commission on Teaching and America's Future [NCTAF], 1996). Hattie's (2009) extensive syntheses of over 800 meta-analyses on the influences on achievement in students is to date the largest ever evidence-based research into what actually works in schools to improve learning. He concluded that the quality of teachers and their pedagogy make the most difference in student achievement. Hattie believes the key is making teaching and learning *visible*.

Visible teaching involves teachers deliberately intervening to ensure changes in their students' thinking. This requires teachers to be clear about the learning intentions, know when each student is successful in attaining those learning intentions, and have knowledge of the students' understanding. Teachers must also provide a progressive development of challenging experiences and opportunities for students to develop learning strategies based on surface and deep levels of learning (Hattie, 2009). It also requires teachers to use feedback from students that reveals what they know and understand—to provide direction, but also step back when they see learners are progressing towards success criteria.

Hattie asserts that when learning is visible, students are active; they are involved in determining success criteria, setting higher expectations, and being receptive to different ways of acquiring knowledge and problem-solving. He further argues that in order to make classrooms more effective, teachers should implement those teaching strategies that have the highest impact on student learning. Hattie's meta-analyses examined a range of teaching strategies in relation to how successfully teachers are teaching their students. In the process, he identified those strategies that are most successful for all learners (Hattie, 2009, 2012).

These teaching strategies include, but are not limited to: clarity, reciprocal teaching, providing feedback, meta-cognitive strategies, inquiry-based teaching, cooperative vs. competitive learning, concept mapping, worked examples, and mastery learning (Hattie, 2009).

The pedagogy used by the teacher is a main feature of the teaching-learning process. The litany of research-based, high-yield instructional strategies provides teachers with a variety of vehicles to enhance learning for all students. The curricular guide and its scope and sequence pro-

---

THEORY INTO PRACTICE
ISLLC STANDARDS 2, 3, 4

What do you consider to be the most important motivational needs of teacher? Of students? How would you assist a novice teacher in establishing effective classroom management strategies? In your experience, what are the two most important factors that promote understanding and learning? Why? Are they consistent with the research on teaching for understanding?

vided is central to planning instruction. Books, media, and supplementary materials complement the learning. Moreover, the pacing, sequencing, and coverage of classroom content influence both individual student achievement and class performance. These aspects of the classroom organization are elaborated in Hoy and Hoy (2013, Chapter 6).

OUTCOMES: EFFECTIVENESS OF PERFORMANCE

Two sets of performance outcomes provide the basis for diagnosing classroom performance: teacher performance and student learning. Evidence available in the late 20th century supported a conception of student achievement that placed most of the responsibility on socioeconomic status, family dynamics, and human capital. But the advent of data generated through pre- and post-assessments and the innovation of value-added analysis created a dramatic change in how we view student achievement. The focus today is on teachers and the effectiveness of their teaching.

Teacher performance and student learning are the two basic outcomes of the classroom. The single most important criterion of effectiveness in our model of classroom performance at the student level is achievement and at the teacher level is quality performance. However, at each level for teacher and student, there are multiple criteria of effectiveness that should be employed, and overall performance evaluated by comparing expected outcomes with actual outcomes.

Teacher Performance

The behavior of the teacher is critical in assessing classroom outcomes. The first step in effective teaching is planning. Planning impacts what students will learn because it guides how the available time and intended curriculum will be transformed into learning activities, assignments, and tasks for students (Hoy & Hoy, 2013). Teachers engage in several levels of planning—by the year, term, unit, week, and day. All the levels must be coordinated. Accomplishing the year's plan requires breaking the work into terms, the terms into units, and the units into weeks and days. The plan determines how time and materials will be turned into activities for students. The plan should reduce uncertainty in teaching. There is no single model of planning, but all plans should allow for flexibility. Most plans include instructional objectives, clear and unambiguous descriptions of educational intentions for students. Gronlund's (2000) approach suggests that an objective should be stated first in general terms, then the teacher should clarify by listing sample behaviors that would provide evidence that the student has attained the objective.

In order to plan effectively, teachers should have knowledge about their students' interests and abilities, the content being taught, alternate ways to teach and assess understanding, and the overall expectations. Collaborative planning can be helpful. The process taps the knowledge and expertise of all the individual participants. Collaborative planning can be taken to the next level, in which group members follow the plans with students and videotape the experience. Other group members view the teaching tapes with the goal of perfecting the plans. Some have termed this process *lesson study* and encourage it as a form of professional development for the participating teachers.

Teacher knowledge of the subject is necessary, but not sufficient, for effective teaching. Organization and clarity are important characteristics of good teaching. Teachers who provide clear presentations and explanations tend to have students who learn more and who rate their teachers more positively. Clarity begins with planning. High-performing teachers tell students what they will be learning and how they could approach it. During the lesson, they avoid vague language, make clear connections between facts or concepts by using explanatory links, and check often for understanding. In direct instruction, high-performing teachers provide well-organized presentations, clear explanations, carefully delivered prompts, and feedback. These are all potential resources for students as they construct understanding. In student-centered approaches, these teachers design authentic tasks, monitor student thinking, ask questions, and prod inquiry. Quality performers employ both kinds of teaching as appropriate at different times.

Finally, teacher warmth, friendliness, and empathy seem to be the traits most strongly related to positive student–teacher relationships (Cotton, 2000; Good & Brophy, 1997; Hattie, 2009). To what extent is the teacher actually behaving as he or she desires? There are a number of important dimensions by which to examine teacher behavior. For example, the degree to which instruction is direct or indirect and can be changed as the task or situation changes is significant. In particular, teacher flexibility, the ability to make one's behavior fit the situation, has been found to be predictive of teaching success. It is not easy to become more or less direct in interactions with students as desired, but it is a skill that can be developed. The degree to which teacher behavior is supportive, planned, and stimulating is significant; therefore, each of these classroom behaviors is also a basis for studying teacher performance.

Finally, teachers have affective responses to the classroom environment that influence their behavior. How satisfied are teachers with their jobs, their teaching, and their interactions with students, colleagues, and superiors? Their disposition and classroom demeanor make a difference (Collingson, Killeavy, & Stephenson, 1999; Cotton, 2000).

Student Performance

Student performance refers to the individual rather than the group or the class. How is student performance determined? Today the term *assessment* is used to describe the process of gathering information about students' learning. Assessment is broader than testing and measurement. Assessment is "any of a variety of procedures used to obtain information about student performance" (Linn & Gronlund, 2000, p. 32). Assessments can be formal, such as unit tests, or informal, such as observing who emerges as a leader in a group of students. Assessments can be designed by classroom teachers or by local, state, or national agencies such as school districts or the Educational Testing Service. Also, assessments can go well beyond paper-and-pencil exercises to observations of performances and the development of portfolios and artifacts.

However, the enactment of the federal No Child Left Behind Act (2001) and the subsequent adoption of Core Content State Standards requires each state to categorize its public schools based on results from standardized testing. Consequently, principals and teachers are expected to use results of standardized test scores to make judgments about student performance. However, the cognitive growth for each student needs to be examined with respect to individual ability using multiple assessments. Pre- and post-assessments enable gain scores to be determined for each student. Other factors, such as the socioemotional development of each student, should be carefully monitored as the year progresses. Social and emotional problems should be identified and appropriately addressed. The student's ability to interact successfully in a variety of diverse situations is yet another significant factor in student behavior. So how are expectations for overall individual student learning being established and monitored? Are teacher and school expectations for individual students being met? Finally, individual student satisfaction with school, friends, teachers, and performance in school should be considered outputs. Thus cognitive growth and affective development are the crucial outputs of the classroom teaching/learning system.

SYSTEM EFFECTIVENESS

Since the classroom as a social system is a primary concern, the question of how well the system as a whole is functioning is critical. Four imperative functions of all social systems are goal achievement, adaptation, integration, and culturation (Parsons, 1967). These functions are key criteria for evaluating the operating effectiveness of the system. In our model, goal achievement is the individual student achievement of academic and social performance goals that have been set by the school and teacher. The performance of teachers as they assist students in achieving those goals is the other indicator of goal achievement.

Adaptation denotes the extent to which the operation of the class has accommodated to the basic demands of the school environment. How well has the classroom community met the diverse needs of the individual students? How well does the system meet new demands in the school environment? Integration refers to social solidarity of the class. To what extent has the class been unified into a community of learners? Student esprit, interpersonal conflict, and absenteeism are prime indicators of the degree of integration. Finally, culturation is the maintenance of the integrity of the value system within the classroom community. Effective systems typically require a high commitment to the group and to its norms and values. The degree of student commitment to his/her class work and assignments, to the teacher, to the class as a whole, and to learning is an indicator of how well the class is functioning.

Finally, to what extent are student achievement gains consistent with expected gains? Information or feedback loops transmit outcome results back to the teacher and school. Actual student performance can then be used to make modifications in the system. In brief, we are proposing a model based on open-systems theory to explain teacher performance. The model should be particularly useful to principals as they attempt to understand and help teachers improve the teaching and learning process.

A CONGRUENCE PERSPECTIVE

The idea of fit, or congruence, between system components is not original. Homans' (1950) classic work on the nature of human groups emphasized mutual interaction, consistency, and balance of key elements within a social system. Getzels and Guba (1957) also stressed the importance of congruence among system elements to promote effectiveness and efficiency. Hoy and Miskel's (2013) congruence postulate posits that the greater the degree of congruence among the system elements, the greater the system effectiveness will be. The basic elements of a system can fit together well and function effectively resulting in quality teacher performance and high student achievement, or they can conflict and produce performance problems. Hence, the basic assumption of the diagnostic

Table 4.2. Matches and Mismatches in the Classroom Performance Model

Key Elements/Matches	*Critical Questions/Issues*
Teacher ↔ Classroom Community	To what degree are the needs of the teacher being met by the classroom community? To what extent do the teacher's skills and knowledge create support for a classroom conducive to student engagement and learning?
Teacher ↔ Pedagogy	To what degree are the needs of the teacher being met by the pedagogy? To what extent are teacher's skills and knowledge consistent with their teaching strategies and behaviors (pedagogy)?
Pedagogy ↔ Student	To what degree is the pedagogy consistent with the needs of the students? To what extent do the teacher's strategies and behaviors support students motivation and learning?
Student ↔ Classroom Community	To what degree are the needs of the students being met by the classroom community? To what extent are students' motivations to learn consistent with a classroom climate of student engagement?
Teacher ↔ Student	To what degree are the needs of the teacher consistent with the needs of the students? To what extent do the teacher's skills and knowledge enable the teacher to motivate students to learn?
Pedagogy ↔ Classroom Community	To what degree is the pedagogy consistent with the needs of the classroom community? To what extent do the teacher's strategies and behaviors support a classroom conducive to student engagement and learning?

model presented here is that effectiveness is a function of the congruence among key elements of the system.

The components of the classroom system produce six possible congruence relationships. For example, to what degree are the needs of the teacher consistent with the needs of the students? Is the pedagogy being employed consistent with the needs of students? Table 4.2 above provides examples of some of the critical questions concerning the congruence of each pair of key elements.

SUMMARY

We have developed a systems model of supervision using an open-systems framework (see Figure 4.4). Elements of the school's context influence the ability of the teacher to achieve desired outcomes. They also influence the ability of a supervisor to indirectly influence classroom performance by helping the teacher improve. These contextual elements are essential for the transformation of the classroom into a teaching and learning system. The teacher, the student, the classroom community, and pedagogy are the four basic components that interact to define the system. The model is based on the assumption that teacher and student performance are functions of the congruence among these key components: the greater the fit between pairs of components, the greater the effectiveness of the system. Effectiveness, therefore, is a function of the degree to which expected performance is congruent with actual performance of the teacher and individual students. Feedback loops communicate effectiveness problems when expected behaviors and actual behaviors are not consistent.

THEORY INTO PRACTICE
ISLLC STANDARDS 2, 3
Develop a collaborative plan for assessing the effectiveness of student performance. That is, how would you work with one of your teachers to develop an assessment plan to determine individual student achievement? Be sure that your plan is specific, realistic, and includes both cognitive and socioemotional outcome performances.

A PRINCIPAL'S SUPERVISORY CHALLENGE

Instructions—Read the following account provided by a principal, reflect on her practice, and perform a case analysis.

I am the principal of a relatively small (287 students) K–5 elementary school, with 14 teachers. The vast majority of the students we serve are from middle- to upper-middle-class families. Approximately 1% of our students receive special education services. About 14% receive free and reduced-priced lunch and can be defined as economically disadvantaged. The year I came to the school, our state standardized tests score percentages ranged among the lowest in the school district—in a district in which students in four other schools, with larger special education and disadvantaged populations, were achieving at higher levels. Based on our demographics, we should have been achieving at much higher levels.

My challenge was twofold: first, discover why our students were achieving at such low rates; and second, lead change in instructional practices so that students would learn at higher levels of achievement. During my first year, I engaged staff members in informal conversations, walked through classrooms frequently, examined lesson plans, and made formal observations. I found that teachers enjoyed a tremendous amount of autonomy and had not been held accountable to school district expectations. Through a series of grade-level meetings and full faculty meetings, I reeducated the staff to school district goals, expectations, and initiatives. I outlined the nonnegotiables with regard to instruction—adhere to the curriculum, use the state standardized tests' frameworks—no exceptions. I set this as the standard and began to carefully monitor and reinforce adherence, through the same vehicles: conversation, walk-throughs, lesson plans, and observations.

Naturally, there were pockets of resistance to the changes. By the end of February, one veteran teacher announced her immediate retirement and another requested a transfer to a different school. The superintendent granted their requests upon my recommendation. At the final staff meeting of the year, I reiterated the goals, introduced the new school board goals, and reinforced my allegiance to our district's plan for high achievement for all students. I encouraged each staff member to plan for the next school year using the district expectations, as I would do the same.

That summer, I performed one last directive task. I discovered that many teachers stashed away outdated textbooks, continuing to teach from them long after new ones were adopted. I found that teachers used outdated test preparation materials and were unaware of updated state standardized tests, frameworks, and curricula. I removed and discarded all outdated books and materials so that our teachers could and would focus on the required curriculum rather than their outdated longstanding practices.

At the beginning of my second year, the teachers and I created a list of beliefs and values we all agreed upon and promised to embrace at school. We also wrote a mission, reflective of our beliefs and values, as well as the standards of the state and our district. We asked that each action, each lesson, each component of our school day, be filtered through those values, so that everything we do contributes to our mission. We accomplished this task with the help of an outside facilitator.

Next, our district test coordinator shared our students' results with the staff. Confronting the facts of our reality—extremely low scores relative to our population—was difficult for teachers, but it opened the door to school improvement. Teachers were given the task of mapping their curriculum to cover the essential knowledge, skills, and processes from the state framework. Prior to the start of the year, we met with every grade level to insure that their plan aligned with the county curriculum and state framework.

In addition, this year I have asked that teachers begin each unit fully planned, start to finish, including assessments. Teachers turn in a draft assessment to an administrator prior to teaching the unit. My assistant principal and I evaluate each assessment, using our curriculum guides and the state framework to insure that tests and instruction are aligned and measure adequately the material being taught. This has been a valuable tool for us, in monitoring instruction, and for the teachers, in making sure that what they are teaching is being assessed, as well as insuring that instruction focuses on essential knowledge, skills, and processes. Together with teachers, we now have conversations around the curriculum and we are moving our school toward being more of a professional learning community.

REFLECTIVE PRACTICE

Assess the effectiveness of this principal by reflecting on her practice. What strategies were effective? Why? Which would you change? Why?

If you became the principal of this school when she did, what would you have done? Be sure to consider the following:

- What can and should you do in grade-level meetings and full faculty meetings?
- How can you determine the causes of the poor performance?
- How can you be sure the curriculum is aligned with state standards?
- What kind of professional development is needed?
- How can you get your faculty fully committed to improving instruction and raising student achievement?
- How forceful should you be in your efforts to make teachers accountable for student performance?

Sketch your plan of action. Be sure to address the questions raised above and any other critical issues that you identify. You do have a bright and eager assistant to help you, and you likely have the remainder of this year and two more years to get student achievement to acceptable levels, at least that is what your superintendent says—but there is no doubt that she is holding you accountable for raising the student performance in your school.

DEVELOP YOUR PORTFOLIO

The principal's role in supervision is to help teachers be more effective. Develop a list of "look fors" that you would use as you observe teachers in their classrooms. Be sure to include elements that deal with the following: the classroom teacher, the students, pedagogy, and the classroom community. Also be concerned with indicators of the cognitive and socioemotional features of both teacher performance and student outcomes. Limit your list of "look fors" to 12 items that you believe are most critical in assessing effectiveness.

COMMUNICATION EXERCISE

You have been appointed as the new assistant principal of instruction in a large suburban high school. You have been asked by your principal to address the faculty and make a 10-minute presentation of your vision of a supervisory model that you will implement. Communicate what you expect from teachers and what they can expect from you as you begin observing their classrooms.

READINGS

Acheson, K. A., & Gall, M. D. (2011). *Clinical supervision and teacher development*. White Plains, NY: Longman.

Cotton, K. (2000). *The schooling practices that matter most*. Portland, OR: Northwest Regional Education Laboratory / Alexandria, VA: Association for Supervision and Curriculum Development.

Glickman, C. D., Gordon, S. P., & Ross-Gordon, J. M. (2010). *SuperVision and instructional leadership: A developmental approach* (8th ed.). Boston, MA: Allyn & Bacon.

Hoy, A. W., & Hoy, W. K. (2013). *Instructional leadership: A research-based guide to learning in schools* (4th ed.). Boston, MA: Pearson.

Sergiovanni, T. J., & Starratt, R. J. (2010). *Supervision: A re-definition* (8th ed.). Boston, MA: McGraw-Hill.

Zepeda, S. J. (2009). *Informal classroom supervision*. New York, NY: Eye on Education.

WHAT DO SUPERINTENDENTS SAY?

How do your principals demonstrate that their program of supervision is effective? How do you hold your principals accountable for effective supervision?

Superintendent 1: I think I'll take a pass on this one since all eleven of my principals and vice-principals are nontenured and recently hired by me. I guess the evaluation process was threatening to their predecessors.

Superintendent 2: Principals demonstrate that their program of supervision is effective by spending a majority of their time in the classroom working with teachers to improve their teaching and learning skills. Principals can be held accountable by monitoring the quantity and quality of their teacher observations.

Superintendent 3: Unfortunately, principals are held less accountable for "effective" supervision and more accountable for supervision that is compliant. Attempts to create and maintain effective supervision programs are often constrained by prohibitive, prescriptive, or protective language in the collective bargaining agreement. Knowing that such constraints are beyond the control of the principals reduces my expectation of supervision from one of "effectiveness" to simply one of "compliance."

CHAPTER 5

SUPERVISION OF INSTRUCTION

Before the process of supervision is described in detail, it seems useful to review our basic assumptions about the nature of supervision. The purpose of supervision is to work cooperatively with teachers to improve instruction. The goal of the supervisor is not simply to help teachers solve immediate problems, but also to engage with teachers in the study of the processes of teaching and learning. Clearly, improvement of instruction is a long-term, continuous process that requires collaboration and cooperation.

In the final analysis, only teachers can improve classroom instruction, and teachers need the freedom to develop their own unique teaching styles. Any attempt to change teaching behaviors, however, requires social support as well as professional and intellectual stimulation. Therefore, improvement of instruction is most likely to be accomplished in a nonthreatening atmosphere, by working in a collegial manner, and by creating in teachers a sense of inquiry and experimentation.

WHAT IS EFFECTIVE SUPERVISION OF INSTRUCTION?

Although supervision can be broadly conceived as any set of activities planned to improve the teaching–learning process, it fundamentally involves a cycle of systematic planning, observation, diagnosis, change, and renewed planning. An effective supervisory process must also confront the

Improving Instruction Through Supervision, Evaluation, and Professional Development, pp. 103–131
Copyright © 2014 by Information Age Publishing

organizational constraints and opportunities in each school. The classroom is not an isolated social unit; it is an integral part of the larger school context. The improvement of instruction must be more than a rallying cry for superintendents, parents, principals, and teachers. Clear outcomes of supervision need to be specified and measured to assess the success of supervisory strategies and actions.

In order for supervision to become meaningful and effective, principals must

- define improvement of instruction and guide action toward that end
- provide constructive feedback to teachers
- confront the organizational constraints and opportunities in each school
- foster collaboration and cooperation in the supervisory process
- encourage teacher professionalism by reinforcing norms of autonomy and self-direction
- concentrate on the intrinsic motivation of teachers through teaching itself.

Learning to become an effective supervisor of instruction is a complex, multidimensional task. Effective supervision means growth in student learning. To become a supervisor is to become a leader of leaders, learning and working with teachers and students to improve instructional quality. Goal setting and problem solving become site-based, collective, and collaborative activities. The leadership of the principal is pivotal in ensuring that the process is focused on helping teachers become more effective at helping students learn. In effective schools, individual teacher needs are congruent with organizational goals.

There are three major areas of mastery in order for principals to become effective supervisors: knowledge, skills, and understanding. The knowledge base includes research on teaching, motivation, and change. Principals must also be familiar with subject matter, grade-level, and Core Content State Standards as well as best practices across subject and content areas. Supervisors work with teachers to identify areas for improvement and provide developmentally appropriate professional growth opportunities.

Of course, principals have a key role in creating and maintaining a context that is conducive to teacher growth and development. Those varied tasks require a knowledge base that includes development, alignment, and articulation of curriculum; processes of group development; action research; development of a positive school culture and climate; and school and community relations.

To perform these tasks, the principal must exhibit critical dispositions as well as have interpersonal and technical skills. Interpersonal skills include communication, motivation, decision making, problem solving, and negotiating. Technical skills include ways to approach goal setting, assessment, and planning to implement goals; instructional observation; data collection; and constructive feedback to teachers. The principal must assess the effectiveness of instructional progress. There is an implicit partnership in which teachers ultimately assume responsibility for their own learning with the support of their supervisors. In this partnership, principals promote the exercise of teacher leadership in the learning process.

Principals must acquire the knowledge and skills necessary to become an effective leader of leaders—sharing, facilitating, and guiding decisions about instructional improvement. Instructional improvement is an important goal because effective teaching leads to better student learning (Hattie, 2009, 2012; Wright, Horn, & Sanders, 1997).

Hence, the goal of the supervisory process is to build capacity in teachers by fostering teachers' lifelong learning skills with the overarching goal of improving instruction and student learning. In this ongoing process, the principal supports teachers' growth and development through focused interactions and productive problem solving. If teachers are to model lifelong learning, then their own professional growth and learning must be based on their own unique needs. Supervisors must be able to identify and reflect on these and match supervision to them. With this approach, supervisors work with teachers in the same way teachers are expected to work with students. Principals then become teachers of teachers who initiate, mentor, and coach teachers throughout their careers.

THEORY INTO PRACTICE
ISLLC STANDARDS 1, 2, 3, 5

Reflect on the role of principal as supervisor. What is the minimum skill set a principal needs for effective supervision? What basic knowledge must the principal have to engage in meaningful change efforts with teachers? What fundamental understandings are necessary for a principal who wants to build a collaborative supervisory team with teachers? Provide specific examples in answering the three queries above.

CLINICAL SUPERVISION

Supervision is the set of activities designed to improve the teaching/learning process. It is a collaborative process among professional colleagues. Supervisors do not make judgments about the competence of teachers nor attempt to control them, but rather they work cooperatively with them as colleagues. This clinical approach has been described as the *clinical supervision movement* (Reavis, 1978). The movement has its roots in the work of Robert Anderson, Morris Cogan, and Robert Goldhammer a half century ago as they tried to develop a more effective way of supervising interns at Harvard.

Clinical supervision consists of a cycle of pre-observation conference, observation, analysis and strategy, post-observation conference, and postconference analysis (Goldhammer, 1969). Cogan (1973) elaborated on the approach, which was popularized by Madeline Hunter in the 1980s. Figure 5.1 is a graphic representation of the cycle of clinical supervision. Cogan identified eight specific steps in the process, grouped into three phases: pre-observation, observation, and post-observation.

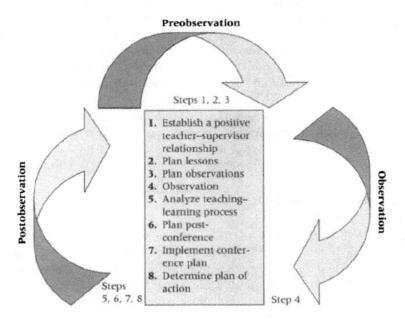

Figure 5.1.   Cycle of clinical supervision.

STEPS IN THE CLINICAL PROCESS

Clinical supervision includes three phases—pre-observation, observation, and post-observation. We begin with the three steps that make up the *pre-observation phase* of the clinical cycle.

Step 1. Establish a positive teacher-supervisor relationship, which involves induction of the teacher into the clinical relationship, clarifying roles and functions, and helping the teacher to understand the purpose and meaning of clinical supervision.

Step 2. Plan lessons cooperatively and emphasize objectives for both students and the teacher, which may include the definition of outcomes, strategies of teaching, reinforcement of learning, and evaluation.

Step 3. Plan observations cooperatively and include the objectives of the visit, data to be collected, and the arrangements for the observation.

Next comes the *observation phase* of the supervision cycle, which follows the initial preparation and planning.

Step 4. Observe the teaching and use mutually determined instruments and data-gathering devices to record classroom events.

Finally, the *post-observation phase* adds four more steps to the cycle and completes the clinical process with planning for a new cycle.

Step 5. Analyze the teaching/learning process by using the data gathered from the observation. The supervisor and teacher perform separate analyses that can be used for constructive discussion of the teaching/learning process.

Step 6. Plan for a post-conference and select a strategy for collegial discussion of the data.

Step 7. Implement the conference plan by engaging in constructive analysis of the teaching/learning process.

Step 8. Determine collaboratively the kinds of actions to be taken and assessed in as the cycle begins anew.

A NEW BEGINNING

The new cycle, however, may be altered. For instance, once an atmosphere of trust has developed between the supervisor and teacher and the teacher understands the objectives and procedures of clinical supervision, the first step of the cycle may be omitted; in fact, occasionally the entire planning phase may be bypassed because the plans are well known. The central objective of the clinical process is the development of a self-directed, analytic teacher who is open to help from other colleagues (Cogan, 1973).

A CRITIQUE OF CLINICAL SUPERVISION

It is difficult to disagree with the goals or even the procedures of clinical supervision as outlined because of its emphasis on analysis rather than inspection. However, we believe that no general supervisory system, clinical or traditional, has been effectively implemented in schools. Most supervisory programs are piecemeal and eventually degenerate into meaningless rituals required by law or by boards of education. But why have supervisory approaches, especially clinical supervision, failed?

The developers of clinical supervision saw supervision as separate from administration. Yet, in practice, the supervisor has most often also been the school principal or assistant principal. The roles of principal and supervisor, however, have potential role conflicts. Traditionally, a principal's focus is on the well-being of the school as a whole, whereas the supervisor's primary concern must be the instructional progress of individual teachers. However, if the principal's primary concern truly is student learning, then the good of the school is consistent with the developmental needs of a particular teacher.

The reality is that teachers know that most principals use observations of their teaching as opportunities to evaluate their performance; consequently, either they resist participating in a collegial manner in appraisals of their teaching or they engage in a hollow ritual of conformity. The principal-supervisor most often accommodates this role conflict by abdicating one of the roles—usually the less clearly prescribed role of supervisor as teacher-helper. We argue that principals can be both effective supervisors and administrators if they recognize the potential conflict, perform the different roles purposefully, and establish an atmosphere of trust and mutual respect.

A second problem for clinical supervision emerges from the conflicting coordinating strategies used by schools. As organizations, schools are designed to accomplish goals; hence, there is a need to coordinate resources and activities. Two coordinating mechanisms, formal authority and professionalism, also have the potential to produce conflict in schools.

The formal authority structure, with accompanying rules and regulations, exercises some control over teachers through the hierarchical chain of command and is embedded in school policy. It involves board policies, record keeping, and the like. It is functional and beneficial for some activities within schools. However, the precise prescription of behavior through a system of rules and regulations conflicts with professionals who value autonomy and presumably have the extensive training, skills, values, and knowledge necessary to accomplish goals without such direction. Unfortunately, the formal structure is more likely to prevail in today's schools because public control and pressures for accountability diminish the authority individual teachers have over their own work. Although the educational task is clearly nonroutine, attempts to standardize their work are a reflection of the uniform standards set for all learners. Coordination of the teaching function appears more likely to be a function of formal structure rather than professional judgments. This reality contradicts the basic philosophy of supervision as a collegial process focused an individual teacher needs and growth.

The clinical supervision approach remains rooted in the formal authority structure of the school. Responsibility and initiative for instructional improvement are understood by both teacher and supervisor to reside with the supervisor. The formal rules require that the supervisor initiate and the teacher respond. Similarly, as practiced, clinical supervision does little to encourage the development of a strong professional orientation among teachers. It clearly places the responsibility for instructional improvement with the officers of the school, creating no need for teachers to develop norms of professional responsibility. In fact, the model encourages teachers to exhibit dependence and seek approval.

Another problem is accountability, which stresses external control and close supervision that undermine teacher professionalism. Although clinical supervision represents a major advance in supervisory philosophy and technology, the problems related to teacher motivation remain. Focusing exclusively on the classroom behavior of teachers, clinical supervision ignores the effects of the school organization itself and the relationship between the school and the teacher. In addition, the impetus for change and improvement of teaching remains external to the teacher.

Although the purpose of supervision is instructional improvement, the clinical model is also flawed by the lack of a specific definition of improvement of instruction. Typically, the teacher and supervisor supply such definitions without benefit of data or conceptual guidelines. Moreover, teacher behaviors that are appropriate and effective in one setting are not necessarily desirable in another.

In summary, clinical supervision appears to offer a plan for improving instruction that is attractive. However, no supervisory system that ignores organizational context is likely to succeed. An effective supervisory model must confront the organizational constraints and opportunities in each school. The classroom is not an isolated social unit; it is an integral part of the larger school context. Finally, improvement of instruction must be more than a rallying cry. Clear outcomes of supervision need to be specified and measured in order to assess the success of supervisory strategies and teacher actions.

THEORY INTO PRACTICE
ISLLC STANDARDS 1, 2, 3, 5
Is it really possible for a principal to be a colleague in the supervisory process? What does a principal have to do to demonstrate to teachers that he or she is interested in helping teachers improve instruction rather than rating teaching performance? Give examples from your own experiences that bolster your position on the principal as a supervisory colleague.

BEYOND CLINICAL SUPERVISION: A DATA-DRIVEN MODEL

If supervision of instruction is to become more meaningful and effective, then a process of supervision must be developed that will:

- define improvement of instruction and guide action toward that end
- confront organizational constraints and opportunities in each school
- foster supervisor-teacher collaboration
- encourage teacher professionalism by reinforcing norms of autonomy and self-direction
- concentrate on the intrinsic motivation of teachers through teaching itself.

The clinical approach is a step in the right direction, but the process needs a stronger theoretical focus. Teachers must be in the forefront of successful instruction—supervision in the background, providing the support, knowledge, and skills that enable teachers to succeed.

COLLEGIAL SUPERVISION

The process of supervision we propose is collegial and consistent with contemporary thinking (Gall & Acheson, 2011; Glickman, Gordon, & Ross-Gordon, 2013; Sergiovanni & Starratt, 2010). The basic features of collegial supervision include:

- a horizontal rather than a hierarchical relationship between teachers and formally designated supervisors
- supervision as the province of teachers as well as principals
- a focus on teacher growth rather than teacher compliance
- teachers collaborating with each other in instructional improvement
- principals supporting and facilitating collaboration
- an emphasis on reflective practice.

Collegial supervision is a vision of what teaching and learning can and should be—one that is developed collaboratively by supervisors and teachers. Colleagues work together to make their vision a reality: all students learning in a manner that enables them to lead fulfilling lives and to contribute to society (Glickman, Gordon, & Ross-Gordon, 2010). Principals share leadership with teachers and engage in coaching, reflection, joint investigation, study teams, and problem solving. Collegial supervision is a peer-driven process with a focus on viable alternatives, instead of criticism or explicit directives.

DIAGNOSTIC CYCLE

The supervisory model outlined in Chapter 4 uses an open-systems approach to consider the major school forces that influence classroom behavior. Effectiveness—improvement of instruction—is defined as the degree to which expected performance is congruent with actual performance at the student and teacher levels. The diagnostic cycle is the basis for linking our supervisory model with collegial supervision. The resulting framework and process of supervision promote harmony, professionalism, and a sense of inquiry and experimentation.

This diagnostic cycle of problem-solving was originally proposed by Hoy and Forsyth (1987). The steps in the cycle are first described as a general systematic approach to problem solving. Then the cycle is illustrated as part of the supervisory process to improve the school context and to improve classroom performance.

The diagnostic cycle is organized into five related steps:

1. *Identify problems.* Identify area(s) where there is a significant discrepancy between the actual and desired state of affairs.
2. *Diagnose causes.* Search for possible causes of the problems by examining key constraints and opportunities.
3. *Develop action plans.* Develop a strategy for action by carefully specifying alternatives, anticipating consequences, deliberating, and selecting a set of alternatives for action.
4. *Implement action plans.* Translate action plans into specific procedures.
5. *Evaluate action plans.* Monitor action plans by collecting data to determine if the plans are producing the intended consequences.

Invariably, the data collection and assessment will trigger the cycle again; hence the process is continuous (see Figure 5.2).

THEORY INTO PRACTICE
ISLLC STANDARDS 2, 3, 5

Compare and contrast the clinical model with the model advocated in this text. What are the advantages of the collegial, diagnostic model proposed above? How can principals make the time required to collect the data that are necessary to implement the model advocated in this text? Is it possible for supervision to be an authentic process of interaction between the teacher and principal?

IMPROVING SCHOOL CONTEXT: APPLYING THE DIAGNOSTIC CYCLE

Although supervision of instruction is centered on classroom activities, the success of the process is directly linked to the school environment. Therefore, the first step in the supervisory process is the development of a context for the systematic study of teaching and learning. Building an atmosphere for effective supervision has two phases. First, the supervisor must be actively involved in developing a healthy, open school climate, one that is conducive to inquiry, analysis, critical examination, improvement, and a culture of academic optimism that enhances student achievement. Second, the supervisor must be intimately involved with teachers in establishing teacher–supervisor colleague relationships. In both cases the goal is the same—to build an atmosphere of optimism and professionalism in which critical analysis leads to improvement.

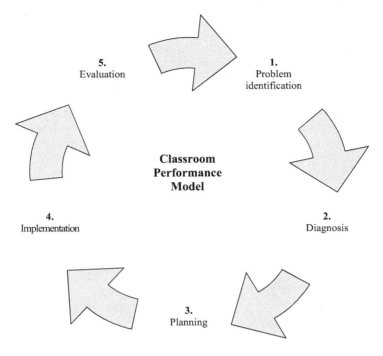

Figure 5.2.   Diagnostic cycle.

School Culture and Climate

A major task facing the supervisor is building a school climate and culture conducive to instructional improvement. What kind of school climate and culture are necessary? Effective supervision is most likely to occur in a nonthreatening atmosphere in which (1) professionals can be open and authentic with each other, (2) the principal and teachers work together to enhance the teaching learning process, (3) satisfaction comes from both task accomplishment (student achievement) and social need fulfillment, and (4) a culture of academic optimism imbues the school; that is, there are collective beliefs of trust, efficacy, and academic focus.

Effective schools are typically characterized by expectations and values that emphasize student achievement and growth. Thus, the basic objectives in climate development are an open and healthy school climate characterized by a culture of trust, efficacy, and academic emphasis—that is, a culture of academic optimism. An open, healthy school climate and a culture of academic optimism are necessary conditions for an effective program of supervision.

The principal is the single most important person in building the climate and culture of the school. Both are major organizational inputs for the classroom social system. A healthy organizational climate and an optimistic culture are critical for supervision and instructional improvement; hence, the principal and teachers should join forces in development of both.

The diagnostic cycle is used to improve school climate and culture. The principal and teachers form a diagnostic team. Teachers bring their expertise and knowledge of classroom dynamics and informal organization; principals bring their knowledge of the formal organization and instruction. Both principals and teachers have a personal stake in the atmosphere of the school as well as the expertise to contribute to its improvement. And if each understands the importance of the other's role, then respect, trust, and teamwork are not only possible, but likely. The principal as formal leader of the school must endorse and support the teacher's role in using our supervisory model. Without such support, supervision is a meaningless ritual.

Identify the Problems

In Figure 5.2, the use of the diagnostic cycle for improving context is outlined. The diagnostic cycle is an example of data-driven decision making. The first step in principal-teachers cycle is to identify problems within the context. Problems in this case are discrepancies between the desired and actual climate and cultural characteristics. In particular, the conceptual capital presented in Chapter 3 provides the tools for analysis and diagnosis.

Openness, health, trust, efficacy, and academic emphasis are desired organizational features. For the principal, such characteristics are expected outcomes, and for teachers, they are needed inputs for effective supervision; therefore, discrepancies in climate and culture are problems to be diagnosed and solved by both the principal and teachers.

Diagnosing the Causes of the Problems

For example, what are the causes of a poor climate? What are the impediments to openness in professional relationships and to an academic press? The Organizational Climate Index (OCI) is a useful measure in diagnosing the roots of climate problems (see www.waynekhoy.com). The following kinds of questions need to be answered in the search for causes of poor school climate and culture:

- Are the informal norms, values, and leadership efforts consistent with the formal rules, policies, and management practices?
- Are the formal rules and regulations consistent with the outcome goals of our supervisory model?
- Are the informal norms and values consistent with the outcome goals of our supervisory model?
- Is the formal authority structure consistent with a model of supervision that stresses collegial behavior and joint problem solving?
- Are both the social and task needs of teachers being met by effective leadership practices?
- Are resources available and compatible with outcome goals of our supervisory model?
- Does the formal organizational enable and foster a culture of academic optimism?
- Does the informal organization promote a culture of teacher responsibility?
- Do leadership practices nurture openness, professional independence, and experimentation?
- Does the curriculum align with supervisory standards and expected outcomes?

Consistency among these key organizational aspects has consequences for improving instruction. The successful use of our supervisory model depends on the appropriate organizational climate and culture. Both have a major effect on the behavior of teachers and should be assessed using the Organizational Climate Index (OCI) or the School Academic Optimism Scale (SAOS) (www.waynekhoy.com). Then the principal and teachers use the data to generate hypotheses about the causes of school problems. The cycle forces them to make some hard choices: (1) they must decide on the critical aspects of climate and culture that are producing the difficulties; (2) they must link the inconsistencies in climate and culture elements to behavioral consequences; and (3) they must decide which school problems to address first. A successful diagnosis is likely if the principal and teachers work together as colleagues engaged in mutual problem solving.

Action Plans

After the school problems have been identified and their possible causes diagnosed, the next step is to develop *action plans*. The formulation of a plan of action involves three steps: (1) generating alternative solutions, (2) comparing possible solutions, and (3) selecting a strategy to be implemented. The process is the same for the teacher–principal group working on solutions to school problems as it is for a teacher-supervisor team solving classroom problems. Each of the proposed alternatives should be directed at overcoming the inconsistencies linked to the negative aspects of climate or culture. Since there are typically many alternative solutions to any set of school problems, each alternative must be evaluated in terms of its probable consequences and likelihood of success. The principal works with a team of teachers to make predictions about the effects of different strategies—an exercise that should help them evaluate the strengths and weaknesses of competing alternative solutions.

Finally, the advantages and disadvantages of each alternative are weighed, and the principal-teacher team agrees on the most favorable way to proceed. The selection of a strategy is the *initial* plan of action, which may be modified as progress is monitored.

Implement Action Plans

After the strategy for action has been designed, the next phase is to *implement the action plans*. Again, cooperation between the principal and teachers is crucial. Fullan (2001) observed that change becomes a learning experience for all the adults involved. During the past decade, teachers have been bombarded with change initiatives about which they have not been consulted. In order to successfully lead the implementation of the selected action plan, teachers must be motivated by understanding how the change will be meaningful for them and their students. Realistic timelines provide time and opportunity to disengage from current behaviors and to prepare for the consequences of the change. Monitoring the progress of planned changes and using feedback mechanisms to make necessary adjustments facilitates smooth transitions.

Evaluation

The last step in the diagnostic cycle is to *evaluate* the consequences of change. Once again, the uses of climate and culture measures, such as the OCI and the SAOS, as tools can determine if the school has changed in a positive direction. This last step often serves as the first in a renewed effort to improve other aspects of school climate. The principal-teacher team can make a difference. The diagnostic cycle can have a major, positive impact on the school atmosphere by (1) measuring the existing climate or culture, (2) comparing the actual climate or culture with the desired climate or culture, (3) identifying priorities for organizational development, and (4) planning and initiating actions to achieve the desired organizational state. A climate of openness and a culture of academic optimism are prerequisites to an effective program of supervision and improvement.

SETTING THE STAGE

The second major task of developing the school context for effective supervision is preparing teachers for collegial supervision and joint problem solving using our supervisory model (review Figure 4.4 in Chapter 4). The process of establishing collegial and trusting relationships with teachers is in large part one of education and socialization. Since in most schools supervision still means the rating of teachers' competence by administrators, teachers remain wary of the rhetoric of supervision. Collegial supervision, partnership, teamwork, professionalism, shared decision making, and joint problem solving are still greeted with skepticism. Thus, the supervisor's initial goal is to reduce the inevitable cynicism and anxiety when another new program of supervision begins.

The first phase of establishing a healthy relationship with teachers should be devoted to the development of a spirit of professionalism and colleagueship. The practices and expectations of any new supervisory process need explanation. The integrated model of supervision, evaluation, and professional development described in chapter two is a good beginning. The role of the principal as a supervisor who supplies advice, shares knowledge, and is professionally committed to improving instruction and learning by direct and cooperative work with teachers should be developed and discussed. Explaining the distinction between the evaluative and supervisory roles of the principal is critical.

As supervisors, principals are teachers of teachers; they are colleagues, not administrators. Indeed, the professional confidentiality of the supervisor-teacher relationship must be nurtured if teachers and supervisors are to be open and candid with each other. The process of developing a sense of self-direction, experimentation, inquiry, and self-study in teachers is a slow and continuous one. Teachers will not be convinced by words alone. Principal supervisors will have to demonstrate by their actions that their first responsibility is helping teachers to improve instruction; in that role they will not make evaluative judgments. Principals can and must understand and protect the integrity of the supervisory role.

After the philosophy and structure of the new model of supervision are understood, the centrality and details of the model (review Figure 4.4) must be introduced. The model is the foundation of a systematic study of instruction. Teachers must not only understand the technical details of the framework, but they must also have or develop the professional orientation necessary to implement it. The model identifies four key areas in which both the teacher and supervisor must have expertise: student needs, teacher needs, appropriate pedagogy, and the classroom community. Moreover, the use of the model requires that the basic performance outcomes of teaching be identified. The teacher and supervisor jointly determine the desired teacher behavior in the classroom and achievement goals for the students. The supervisory team must also agree on appropriate measures for each performance output. Thus, improvement of instruction is jointly defined as the attainment of specific, measurable objectives in teacher behavior and student growth and achievement.

Building the appropriate context rests on the assumption that teachers are professionals. Thus, the school structure should be enabling and encouraging (see Chapter 3), not restricting professional initiative. Much of a teacher's work motivation is linked directly to the actual instruction of students. The heart of the supervisory process is the study and improvement of instruction in the classroom. Hence, success in the process should in itself provide strong motivation and gratification for most teachers. In brief, an open, healthy, and optimistic school environment with professional relationships that stress cooperation, experimentation, and self-study are requisite conditions for effective supervision.

Preparation for the actual study of specific classroom behavior may take a year or more of hard work by the principal and teachers. The school climate and culture may have to be dramatically altered; the principal-teacher relationship may require major restructuring; and the teacher-supervisor relationship will need to undergo a transformation from evaluative to collegial. Furthermore, the technical details and process of the supervisory model must be understood and mastered.

THEORY INTO PRACTICE
ISLLC STANDARDS 1, 2, 3, 5

Picture the school in which you currently work and describe the readiness of the school to engage in collegial and diagnostic supervision. More specifically, briefly discuss the structure of the school, the climate of the school, and the culture of the school. If you were the principal and had one year to make ready your school for the supervisory process that has been developed above, where would you start and what would you do during the next 12 months?

IMPROVING CLASSROOM PERFORMANCE: APPLYING THE DIAGNOSTIC CYCLE AGAIN

In the preceding section, the diagnostic cycle was applied to the organizational context of the school to develop a healthy, open, and optimistic environment. The same diagnostic cycle is used to improve classroom performance, but instead of focusing on contextual problems, attention is now shifted to the individual classroom.

Both classroom and school are in a constant state of change; hence, supervisors and teachers must continually engage in problem-identification and problem-solving activities in order to improve the teaching-learning process. If performance is to be improved, teachers and supervisors need to systematically collect data on performance, compare these results to desired performance, jointly identify problems (discrepancies between actual and desired performance), use the supervisory model to identify possible causes of problems, develop and select action plans, implement them, and evaluate the outcomes. The process is cyclic, with the evaluation of outcomes as the beginning of a new diagnostic cycle (see Figure 5.3). Our model of supervision provides the analytic tools to identify the problems, to diagnose causes, to develop action plans, to implement them, and to guide evaluation and data collection.

The model can be easily made an integral feature of a supervisory process that stresses joint planning and shared decision making between teacher and supervisor. Moreover, the more familiar the supervisor is with the research and theory relevant to the different matches in the model, the more likely the model is to be an effective supervisory tool.

The scope of supervision we advocate is substantially broader than the model of clinical supervision, discussed earlier in this chapter. It includes a series of diagnostic cycles aimed first at the organizational context of the school and subsequently at the classroom. In both cases, the diagnostic cycles constitute a process for identifying and diagnosing problems, using data to develop action plans, and implementing and evaluating those action plans. Each diagnostic cycle is data driven and often incorporates several rounds of data-collection episodes and post-data-collection conferences. We now examine each step of the supervisory process.

DIAGNOSTIC CYCLE FOR IMPROVING CLASSROOM PERFORMANCE

We demonstrated how to use the diagnostic cycle to improve the school context. Now we turn to the use of the cycle to improve classroom performance.

Diagnostic Cycle for Improving Classroom Performance
The Supervisory Process

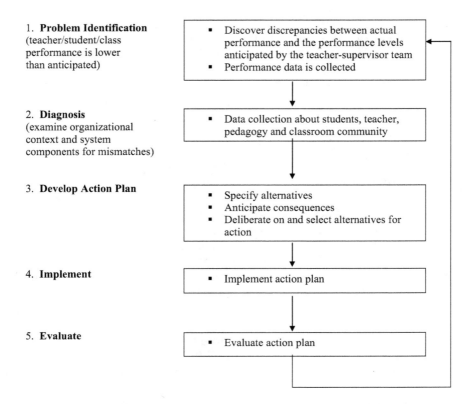

1. **Problem Identification** (teacher/student/class performance is lower than anticipated)	• Discover discrepancies between actual performance and the performance levels anticipated by the teacher-supervisor team • Performance data is collected
2. **Diagnosis** (examine organizational context and system components for mismatches)	• Data collection about students, teacher, pedagogy and classroom community
3. **Develop Action Plan**	• Specify alternatives • Anticipate consequences • Deliberate on and select alternatives for action
4. **Implement**	• Implement action plan
5. **Evaluate**	• Evaluate action plan

Figure 5.3.   Using the diagnostic cycle to improve classroom performance.

Identify Problems

The first diagnostic step is the identification of classroom problems. Problems are frequently suggested by symptoms that things are not working well. A teacher may be having difficulty with classroom management; parents may be complaining frequently about a certain class; teacher or student absenteeism may be inordinately high; teacher morale may be low; student achievement may be low. These are all symptoms of a potential problem; they are valuable pieces of information that may indicate the existence of a problem.

Although symptoms are important guides in problem identification, if one is not guided by the supervisory model, it is easy to confuse symptoms with both problems and causes of problems. A problem is defined in the model as a discrepancy between expected and actual performance. Two classroom outputs have been defined: teacher performance and student performance. When actual behavior in any of these areas is not consistent with expected performance, a classroom problem exists. The specification of a problem, therefore, is a matter of performance outcomes, not inputs or interactions within the classroom system. The latter provide the causes or symptoms of the problem, but they are not the problem itself.

In practice then, problem identification involves discovering discrepancies between actual performance (of the teacher or students) and the performance levels anticipated by the teacher-supervisor team. Typically, the teacher and supervisor would meet, use existing data, and make performance expectations explicit. Then, they agree on the methods to be used in acquiring performance data to test their expectations.

Specific performance data are then collected. These data are then organized in such a way that the teacher and supervisor can judge whether or not their expectations have been met. These post-data-collection conferences produce an answer to the question: Does a problem exist? Remember—a problem is a discrepancy between expected and actual performance.

Diagnosing the Causes of the Problems

After the problem has been identified, the search for possible causes begins. Our supervisory model provides the guiding framework. The starting point in the diagnosis is to identify the nature of the organizational inputs and the four basic elements in the classroom social system. The key constraints and opportunities of the school's contextual elements and resources need to be described and analyzed. Data about the students, teacher, pedagogy, and classroom community are also collected. For each component, the investigation should explore the underlying aspects considered most significant in the particular classroom setting. The point here, of course, is to focus on key dimensions of each variable rather than attempting to analyze everything; such an approach makes the analysis manageable rather than overwhelming. As in problem identification, the collection of data about contextual constraints and components of the supervisory model usually requires a series of planning conferences, one or more data-collection episodes, and post-data-collection analyses.

The crucial step of assessing the matches between each pair of components is performed in post-data-collection conferences. The possible matches defined by the model must be analyzed. Table 5.1 provides a review of some of the crucial issues that should be examined to diagnose the extent to which key components are congruent with each other.

A lack of congruence (mismatches) between major components has negative consequences for classroom behavioral outcomes. The diagnosis of these mismatches in the system needs to be linked to the problems identified in the first step of the process. That is, after describing the components and assessing their congruence, the next step is to relate mismatches to problems. Which mismatches explain the performance problems that have been identified? It is at this point that the supervisor and teacher generate hypotheses about the problem causes, a critical aspect of diagnosis.

The diagnostic phase of the cycle forces the supervisory team (supervisor and teacher) to make some hard decisions. The team must decide on the most crucial aspects of each component, determine the mismatches in the system, link the mismatches to behavioral consequences related to the problem, and decide which problem to attack first. None of these decisions is either obvious or easy. There are many diagnoses for any set of classroom problems. A "best diagnosis" is not possible; the supervisor and teacher will have to settle simply for one that leads to the eventual satisfactory solution to the problem.

Action Plans

After identifying the critical problems and the relationships between system mismatches and classroom performance, the next phase of the process is to develop a strategy for action. This phase involves at least three steps: specifying alternatives, anticipating consequences, and deliberating on and selecting the alternatives for action.

Specify Alternatives

The search for alternatives to solve particular classroom problems is typically straightforward. The process reflects simplified notions of causality and rests on two simple rules: (1) search in the problem areas and (2) search in the area of component mismatches. Although these searches are basically reactive, they will probably be the dominant pattern. A preliminary step in formulating an action plan is to generate as many alternatives as possible. Each of these possible interventions should be directed at overcoming system mismatches linked to the negative

Table 5.1.   Matches and Mismatches in
the Classroom Performance Model

Key Elements/Matches	*Critical Questions/Issues*
Teacher ↔ Classroom Community	To what degree are the needs of the teacher being met by the classroom community? To what extent do the teacher's skills and knowledge create support for a classroom conducive to student engagement and learning?
Teacher ↔ Pedagogy	To what degree are the needs of the teacher being met by the pedagogy? To what extent are teacher's skills and knowledge consistent with their teaching strategies and behaviors (pedagogy)?
Pedagogy ↔ Student	To what degree is the pedagogy consistent with the needs of the students? To what extent do the teacher's strategies and behaviors support students motivation and learning?
Student ↔ Classroom Community	To what degree are the needs of the students being met by the classroom community? To what extent are students' motivations to learn consistent with a classroom climate of student engagement?
Teacher ↔ Student	To what degree are the needs of the teacher consistent with the needs of the students? To what extent do the teacher's skills and knowledge enable the teacher to motivate students to learn?
Pedagogy ↔ Classroom Community	To what degree is the pedagogy consistent with the needs of the classroom community? To what extent do the teacher's strategies and behaviors support a classroom conducive to student engagement and learning?

behaviors associated with the problem. As we have noted, there may be many diagnoses for any set of classroom problems, and more than one action plan may lead to the solution of the problem. Thus, the development of a set of effective alternatives typically requires (1) a willingness of supervisors and teachers to work cooperatively as colleagues, (2) the use of divergent and creative thinking patterns, and (3) time to develop a set of competing alternatives. In general, the greater the number of alternative solutions generated, the greater the likelihood will be of finding a satisfactory solution.

Anticipate Consequences

Since there are usually many alternate solutions to a particular set of classroom problems, each alternative that is developed must be evaluated in terms of its probable consequences and relative merits. By and large, predicting the consequences of proposed alternative solutions is hazardous. On some matters, accurate predictions of consequences may be made; however, when trying to anticipate the reactions of individuals or groups (especially students), the results are typically much more problematic. A number of questions about the proposed solutions must be considered. Do the alternatives come from system mismatches? Does one alternative provide a more adequate solution to the mismatches than do others? To what extent are dysfunctional behavioral consequences likely? It is quite possible to solve one problem, and at the same time, create several others in the process. For example, the classroom arrangement may be adjusted to better meet the teacher's pedagogy, but such a change might produce inconsistencies in the matches between classroom community and the climate.

Since the classroom system is a highly interdependent, open system, careful evaluation of both anticipated and unanticipated consequences of alternative actions must be considered on the basis of theory, research, and experience. The teacher and supervisor must reflectively anticipate the consequences of each alternative action. It is imperative that the supervisory team consider the extent to which the proposed intervention addresses the problem as well as the unanticipated, dysfunctional consequences of the proposed solutions.

Deliberate and Select Alternatives

The final step in developing an action plan is the deliberate analysis of the alternative solutions and consequences. The advantages and disadvantages of the various interventions should be weighed carefully by the supervisory team. The teacher and supervisor must reach agreement about the most favorable way to solve the classroom problems. Occasionally a series of alternate steps are linked in sequential order to provide an action strategy: the more complex the problem situation, the more likely the need for a complex solution. The selection of a plan of action in no way implies an ultimate solution; on the contrary, the choice is a first approximation that will probably be changed and refined as progress toward the problem solution is monitored.

Implement Action Plans

Once a plan of action has been formulated, the decision needs to be implemented. For the most part, the teacher is the key because classroom changes will typically be initiated by the teacher. Thus, the teacher must be both committed to and confident in the plan; it must be the teacher's plan. Intervention plans imposed by the supervisor are doomed to failure. Consensus on plans is imperative.

Action plans should be translated into specific procedures. For example, a plan to change the formal organizational classroom arrangements should contain the mechanics and specific details of action. What steps have to be taken? When? How? By whom? The actions to be implemented must be realistic and consistent with the capabilities of those involved. It is quite possible to diagnose accurately the basic causes of a problem and still have great difficulty solving it. Teachers may recognize the viability of a plan but not have the requisite skills to implement it. We emphasize once again that there is no single way to solve most problems, and a number of action plans can have the same outcomes; hence, it may be necessary to rethink action plans if it becomes apparent that the specific steps to implement a given intervention are impossible or unlikely.

This phase of the process deals directly with the problems of initiating change in an ongoing system. Fullan (2001) identifies three basic problems associated with implementing change. First, individuals are likely to resist change because it produces uncertainty and anxiety. Second, they do not understand the need for the change. Finally, they are not confident that they have the ability to be as successful after the change.

Evaluation

After the action plans have been implemented, they must be monitored and evaluated. Are the plans working in the manner in which they were intended? Specifically, are the expected outcomes being attained? What are the unanticipated consequences, if any? In order to answer these kinds of questions, data from the classroom must be systematically collected and then carefully analyzed.

The monitoring and collecting of data are guided by the expected classroom outcomes that have been jointly agreed upon by the teacher and supervisor. Certainly, reliable and valid data-collection instruments and procedures are imperative and should be determined by the supervisory team. The evaluative phase of the diagnostic cycle is critical; it provides the information both for assessing past practices and guiding renewed effort and planning. Thus, evaluation is both an end and a beginning. Information about the classroom's and organization's responses to the implemented action plans can be used to refine the intervention to more fully fit the system's needs and to deal with any negative, unanticipated consequences and change. The evaluation step closes the loop and starts the cycle again (see Figure 5.2).

> **THEORY INTO PRACTICE**
> *ISLLC Leadership Standards 1, 2, 3*
> Use Table 5.1 that examines the six pairs of elements in The Model for Classroom Supervision (Figure 4.4, Chapter 4) to analyze the harmony and conflict in one of the classes that you are teaching. Use your perceptions of yourself, your students, pedagogy, and the classroom community to evaluate how well these elements fit together. What additional information would make this task more reliable? After all, as this question is posed, we are simply asking for your perceptions. Are they accurate? How do you know?

SUMMARY

We have argued that the supervisory process described here addresses the inherent weaknesses present in conventional and clinical supervision. The scheme has two basic, interrelated phases. The first phase, *improving school context,* consists of developing an open school climate, cultivating a school culture of academic optimism, and establishing collegial teacher-supervisor relationships. A diagnostic cycle is used to identify context problems, diagnose them, and develop a planned intervention to implement and evaluate. The supervisory team uses the process until the school community is prepared for the second phase.

In the second phase, *improving classroom performance,* the diagnostic cycle is again employed, first to uncover performance problems (teacher or student), and then to find their likely causes. As before, the process results in a planned intervention, implementation, and evaluation. In conclusion, the model and process of supervision that we have developed guide action toward the improvement of instruction. Improvement is defined by the teacher and supervisor as the elimination of discrepancies between the desired and actual performance outcomes at two levels—teacher and student. In order for the process to be successful, the climate must be open and a culture of academic optimism must exist. To that end, the principal and teachers work as a team to confront organizational constraints and opportunities and to forge a school context that nurtures systematic diagnosis and change. Moreover, teacher–supervisor relationships are based on professionalism, colleagueship, optimism, openness, and trust. This model of supervision provides the theoretical focus for a diagnostic that encourages improvement of instruction through reflective practice and change. We next elaborate on the nuances of the process.

A PRINCIPAL'S SUPERVISORY CHALLENGE

Instructions—Read the following account provided by a principal, reflect on her practice, and perform a case analysis.

I am the principal of an elementary school with grades four through six. The fifth and sixth grades are departmentalized. Gifted and students with disabilities are included in classes throughout the building. The student body is racially and socioeconomically diverse and consists of approximately 600 students. When I began my first year as principal, I was specifically given the task of raising the achievement level of the students. The students had not done well on the state tests that determined the school's accreditation; hence, my charge was to ensure that the school became fully accredited.

I began my year by meeting with and observing teachers to assess their instructional strengths and weaknesses. I visited every classroom at least two to three times a week and identified a fifth grade teacher, Chris DeSantis, who was weak in a number of areas. He had been teaching social studies or English for the school district for 19 years. His classroom management and instructional skills were so poor that students rarely paid attention to him. When Mr. DeSantis did try to handle disruptive students, it usually led to arguments between the teacher and students and chaos in the classroom. Mr. DeSantis did not use varied instructional strategies, and his lessons were unfocused. Throughout the fall and winter I worked with Chris in pre- and post-observation conferences as well as in one-on-one meetings to try to help him improve his performance.

During this time period, Mr. DeSantis sent me a variety of written correspondences disputing my assessments of his teaching. He also began to misrepresent statements made in our meetings. It was clear to me that I needed to save all of his letters, notes, and e-mails and respond carefully and in writing to his comments and complaints. I also decided to include my assistant principal in any meeting that I had with him in order to ensure that all of our conversations were witnessed by a third party.

By the spring, I concluded that I needed to put this teacher on an informal plan of improvement before engaging in the more formal evaluation system. We met and jointly developed an improvement plan, which included the following elements: observations of other teachers, weekly submission of lesson plans, and professional reading. I also asked a central office supervisor to work with him as a coach. She would observe his teaching and then offer suggestions for change. I wanted to provide assistance from someone who was not part of the evaluation process. Finally, I suggested that Chris videotape some of his lessons so we could examine his teaching. We agreed to meet weekly to discuss the lesson plans and videotapes.

In spite of all our efforts, there was no substantive change in his teaching; parental complaints continued. I assured parents that I was working with Mr. DeSantis closely and that I was addressing their concerns. There simply was little improvement in his teaching even after a year of help. Thus, I notified the Human Resources (HR) office that I was working closely with the teacher and also asked for guidance to ensure that I was appropriately documenting all of my actions and assistance.

Early in the spring, I completed a formal evaluation that assessed his classroom performance as unsatisfactory. At around the same time, I was beginning to make decisions about teacher assignments for the next school year and I asked for teacher preferences. Mr. DeSantis indicated that he was interested in teaching English the following year rather than social studies. I did not want to place him in an English classroom because we had been working with him in social studies instruction for almost two years.

Near the end of the school year, I informed all teachers of their teaching assignments for the following year. The next morning, Mr. DeSantis came into the office agitated and demanded to speak with me. As we entered my office, he began a tirade about my decision. He threatened to have me arrested when I suggested that perhaps he needed to take a sick day. Overall, his behavior was hostile and incoherent. It was obvious that he was too emotional to contend with a classroom of students that morning, so I informed him that I would arrange to have his classes covered for the day. I stepped out of the office to make the arrangement, and when I returned he refused to leave my office as he continued to rant and rave.

I left again to call the central office for assistance from the human resources director, who agreed to speak with Mr. DeSantis. I returned and found the teacher's wife in my office with him. She also started to scream at me and asked why I was out to get her husband. There was no reasoning with either of them. Fortunately, the HR director appeared before I needed to call the police. He spoke with the teacher and assured him that if he went home, a meeting would be arranged the following day to address his concerns.

At the meeting the next morning, Mr. DeSantis again discussed his frustration with his assignment for upcoming year and the belief that he had improved his teaching. He denied the fact that he still was not performing at an acceptable level. Following the meeting, the director contacted the superintendent to discuss the case and we all agreed it was time to move for dismissal of this tenured teacher. I was well prepared by the district's attorney and was able to include all of my memos, observation notes, documentation of conversations, e-mail, and copies of the teacher's notes in a notebook that was presented to the School Board at the hearing. The board and attorney agreed we had a good case for dismissal, one that was carefully and systematically documented.

REFLECTIVE PRACTICE

Assess the actions of the principal. In particular, consider the following questions:

- Was the level of supervisory help adequate, or should the principal have done more? If so, what would you recommend?
- Did the principal provide time for improvement?
- What should be the connection between supervision and formal evaluation?
- How would you evaluate that connection in this case?
- Was the decision to dismiss premature given the 19 years of satisfactory evaluations?
- Do you think the principal made the correct decision in rejecting the teacher's request for a change in subject assignment? Why?
- What would you have done differently and why?
- Can tenured teachers really be removed? Is it worth the effort and expense?
- Do you have a more creative strategy for this problem?

DEVELOP YOUR PORTFOLIO

Use the Diagnostic Cycle in conjunction with the Model for Classroom Supervision to analyze either your class or the class of a colleague. Identify a problem in the classroom and develop a strategy to deal with that problem by going through the steps of the diagnostic cycle. Develop an action plan to address the identified problem. Based on the proposed actions of your plan, anticipate at least one complication that is likely to result in another mismatch of elements. Remember that the classroom is a social system; as you change one element in the system, the change ripples through and influences other elements of the system.

COMMUNICATION EXERCISE

You have just been appointed principal of Evans Junior High, an urban school that is under pressure to make Adequate Yearly Progress (AYP) for No Child Left Behind. The school has a veteran staff who are accustomed to having the principal observe them to evaluate their teaching. You have just completed a course in instructional supervision using this text. At tomorrow's faculty meeting you are planning to make a 10-minute presentation to introduce your views on classroom observation and improving student achievement. Prepare a Powerpoint presentation with the major points you want to make to the teachers.

READINGS

Burke, P. J., & Krey, R. D. (2005). *Supervision: A guide to instructional leadership.* Springfield, IL: Charles Thomas.

Downey, C., Steffy, B., English, R, Erase, L., & Poston, W. (2004). *The three-minute classroom walk-through.* Thousand Oaks, CA: Corwin Press.

DuFour, R. (2002). Beyond instructional leadership: The learning-centered principal. *Educational Leadership, 59*(8), 12–15.

Forsyth, P. B., Adams, C. M., & Hoy, W. K. (2011). *Collective trust: Why schools can't improve without it.* New York, NY: Teachers College Press.

Hoy, W. K. (2012). School characteristics that make a difference for the achievement of all students: A forty year academic odyssey. *Journal of Educational Administration, 50,* 76–97.

Hoy, A. W. & Hoy, W. K. (2013). *Instructioal leadership: A research-based guide to learning in schools.* Boston, MA: Pearson.

Popham, W. J. (2005). *Classroom assessment.* Boston, MA: Pearson.

WHAT DO SUPERINTENDENTS SAY?

A classic problem in supervision of instruction is the role conflict of principals. The principal has to evaluate and rate performance of teachers and also serve as a colleague to help teachers improve their teaching. How do your principals do both?

Superintendent 1: The development of a listing of identifiable and discernable excellent teaching behaviors is essential. Individual dialogue between a principal and a teacher can provide further definition allowing for these behaviors to be mutually agreed upon. The principal has to then create a climate that allows the teacher to work toward these teaching behaviors, with both a coaching component to help the teacher become successful and a rating component to describe the level of success. A non-threatening environment is necessary for everyone making progress toward these identifiable goals. For those who cannot attain these behaviors to an acceptable degree, the evaluation speaks for itself...

Superintendent 2: By establishing an understanding and agreement with staff that the most important job an administrator has is to work with teachers to improve their teaching and learning skills. Principals must establish a culture that teachers want and desire administrators in their classrooms working with them to *improve* their classroom skills and improve student performance.

Superintendent 3: Role conflict is real. No question about it. So in order to balance the competing elements of rater/coach, principals must develop structures and processes that support teacher development that may not require the principal to always be the one-on-one coach. Principals can use teacher leaders, mentors, department meetings, and even staff meetings to promote discussion about effective instruction and assessment to help teachers improve their teaching.

CHAPTER 6

SUPERVISORY SKILLS

The goal of supervision is the improvement of instruction leading to increased student learning. During the supervisory process, principals provide feedback to teachers on what is happening in their classrooms. Hattie (2009) argues that this kind of formative feedback helps teachers assess what they need to do to be more effective and how they are meeting expectations to help all students learn.

EFFECTIVE TEACHERS

Recognizing the positive relationship between effective teaching and student achievement, researchers have described characteristics and skills of effective teachers (Hattie & Timperley, 2007; Hill, Rowan, & Ball, 2005; Pressley, Raphael, Gallagher, & DiBella, 2004; Seidel & Shavelson, 2007). Effectiveness of teachers depends on the nature of educational outcomes and goals; requires certain knowledge, skills, and behaviors; is dependent on providing strong instructional support for academic achievement; and is linked to reflective practice, inquiry, and ongoing professional learning.

When effectiveness is related to student achievement and other important, but hard to measure educational outcomes, research has identified common behaviors of effective teachers. Teacher behaviors that have the highest impact on student learning include, but are not limited to:

Improving Instruction Through Supervision, Evaluation, and Professional Development, pp. 133–158
Copyright © 2014 by Information Age Publishing

- having high expectations for all learners
- communicating the intentions of their lessons and what success looks like if those intentions are realized
- establishing positive relationships with all students
- challenging students by encouraging them to think through and solve problems
- scaffolding instruction to help students construct deep understanding
- monitoring and evaluating student progress (Hattie, 2009).

In the area of professional preparation, formal experiences in content-related pedagogy and high levels of pedagogical content knowledge are linked to student achievement. Effective teachers care about their students, have a good sense of humor, are enthusiastic, recognize students as individuals, and treat them fairly and respectfully. Effective teachers use routines to manage the classroom environment, are organized, and maximize the use of instructional time. Teachers stay clearly focused on instructional activities and student learning while communicating high expectations for their students. Effective teachers also clearly identify and link learning objectives to instructional activities, use a range of instructional strategies as they appropriately relate to the learning objectives and students, incorporate a variety of cognitive levels of questions, and engage students in instruction and the learning process (Walls, Nardi, von Minden, & Hoffman, 2002).

Effective teachers are also able to help students of all ability levels learn. Darling-Hammond and Baratz-Snowden (2005) identified three distinct characteristics of effective teachers: knowledge of learners, understanding of subject matter and skills, and understanding teaching within the context of one's learners. Knowledge of learners includes coming to consensus with the learner about "his or her strengths, interests, and preconceptions" (Darling-Hammond & Baratz-Snowden, 2005, p. 7). Understanding subject matter and skills requires the ability to organize information in such a manner that demonstration of learning can occur. Understanding teaching includes focusing on "what happens next" through feedback and monitoring. This approach informs teachers about the success or failure of their teaching, making learning for both teacher and student visible (Hattie, 2009).

Others describe the affective characteristics of effective teachers, or the social and emotional behaviors that they demonstrate (Hattie, 2009; National Board for Professional Teaching Standards [NBPTS], 2005). They really do care about their students and truly want success for all of their students. These teachers support their students by encouraging an open line of communication and listening and responding to what their students are saying in a positive and trustful way. This is extremely important, as students need to feel that their teachers truly value any questions and concerns that they may have. In addition, effective teachers treat all students with respect, foster self-esteem, motivate them, and have respect for their individual, cultural, religious, and racial differences (NBPTS, 2005).

Effective teachers also demonstrate a real enthusiasm for the learning process and the subject matter they teach. They are able to reach students through varying instructional methods, which, in turn, leads to greater feelings of success and motivation for the students (NBPTS, 2005). When students view their teachers as motivational leaders, there is evidence of a greater willingness to work and higher levels of student achievement (Hattie, 2009).

THEORY INTO PRACTICE
ISLLC STANDARDS 1, 2, 3, 5
How important are teacher dispositions to achieving desired student outcomes? Describe some student outcomes of teacher effectiveness. How can a principal work with teachers to help them attain these outcomes? Be sure to identify some affective outcomes as well cognitive ones. Discuss the relative importance of affective outcomes compared to cognitive ones.

INSTRUCTIONAL STRATEGIES

In addition to the affective characteristics and traits of teachers, there are specific instructional strategies that effective teachers consistently implement with their students.

Questioning Techniques

The process of asking students questions and encouraging students to ask questions allows teachers to actively monitor student learning (Stronge, 2002). Research strongly supports asking questions at varying cognitive levels. While it is important to ask surface questions to establish a knowledge base, it is critical that higher-order questions are frequently asked, as these types of questions generate a deeper understanding of the content being studied (Marzano, 2001; Stronge, 2002). Consider the following two questions:

- "In what year did Columbus discover America?"
- "How did the political, economic, and religious factors influence the exploration of the New World?"

High-level questions can be used to challenge students as it gives them the opportunity to make the connection between subject matter and real world applications. The strategy of questioning at a variety of levels is highly effective with students of all ability levels. Effective teachers also pay attention to the questions students ask. Designing lessons to "entice, teach, and listen to students questioning of students is powerful" (Hattie, 2009, p. 183).

Graphic Organizers

The use of graphic organizers, (e.g., visual representations of information, concepts maps, flow charts, and brainstorming diagrams) promotes student understanding in a nonlinguistic way (Marzano, 2001). Such graphic organizers allow students to organize information and ideas on a given topic, which helps teachers assess student understanding.

THEORY INTO PRACTICE
ISLLC STANDARDS 2 & 3

What are your favorite graphic organizers? Select two graphic organizers and demonstrate how you would use them to help students learn a specific concept or learning objective. How useful are such devices to teachers? What are their limitations? How can principals help teachers become more proficient in the development and use of graphic organizers?

Student Engagement

Keeping students engaged is a challenge for every teacher. Effective teachers are persistent in "challenging and engaging students in all aspects of instruction" (Stronge, 2002, p. 49). This can be accomplished through student questioning, real-world problem solving, and positive reinforcement of desired behaviors. Critical and creative problem solving also encourages student engagement as it solicits multiple ideas and solutions to given situations. Teachers keep students engaged by making the basic work requirements clear, communicating the specifics of assignments, monitoring work in progress, and giving frequent academic feedback (Woolfolk, 2014).

Continuous Assessment

Assessments give teachers the opportunity to sample and observe students' skills, knowledge, and progress in achieving learning goals (Linn & Miller, 2005). Formative assessments prior to or during instruction enable teachers to gather data to plan, to improve instruction, and to help students learn. The data are "nonevaluative, supportive, timely and specific" (Shute, 2008, p. 153) and help teachers make instructional decisions. Using pre-assessment strategies helps teachers to plan more effectively for individual students, leading to greater achievement (Reis & Renzulli, 2003; Stronge, 2002). Such assessment is done at the beginning of a unit or study or at the beginning of the school year for diagnostic purposes, but continuous assessment becomes part of a process to evaluate progress and to change strategies accordingly.

Differentiation

Tomlinson and Allan (2000) define differentiation as "a teacher's reacting responsively to a learner's needs" and state that the "goal of differentiated classrooms is maximum student growth and individual success" (p. 4). Differentiation includes learners of all abilities and a process that is suited to meet the needs of all students. According to Tomlinson (2001), principles of differentiation include a flexible classroom, ongoing assessment of learner needs, and flexible grouping. Teachers can also differentiate for student characteristics in terms of their readiness (i.e., level of difficulty), interest, and learning profile (which includes learning styles, talent, or intelligence).

Differentiation also includes modification of curriculum and instruction to meet the needs of all students; however, the concept highlights key elements of the teaching and learning process:

- modification of content
- focus on student interest
- grouping of students
- instructional strategies
- processing skills.

The various definitions of differentiation described above have lead to discussion about what differentiation should be, look like, and achieve.

Effective teachers maximize the capacity of each student by providing challenging learning opportunities in a supportive way. They recognize that students who are the same age are different in their readiness to learn, interests, learning styles, experiences, and out of school circumstance, and they modify their instruction to meet the needs of individual learners. In differentiated classrooms, students work at different paces, exercise a variety of learning options, and are assessed using measures that accommodate their needs (George, 2005).

Learning Opportunities

Marzano (2000) contends that the opportunity to learn (OTL) content has the strongest relationship to student achievement of all the school level factors he identified. This seems like common sense. OTL highlights the importance of the implemented curriculum. Yet discrepancies do exist all too often between what is taught and what is assessed. Teaching strategies selected to implement the curriculum are as important as the curriculum itself in helping students achieve on standardized tests (Hattie, 2009). The curriculum implemented by teachers and learned by students must be congruent with the curriculum content specified by the Common Core State Standards, or district for that grade level or course, since that is the content that will be assessed in outcome measures (Marzano, 2003).

In sum, effective principals not only focus on the key strategies outlined above but also on Common Core State Standards and school district performance standards that provide benchmark expectations for classroom performance. These standards are most often used to assess teacher performance. Principals need to be familiar with both Common Core State Standards and local standards—a daunting task, especially for those new to the supervisory process. However, it is difficult to supervise and then provide appropriate staff development without the knowledge of standards. Standards are a resource for principals because they help focus on best practices across subject and content areas. Figure 6.1 summarizes the general characteristics of effective teachers.

BUILDING TEACHER SENSE OF EFFICACY

We make the assumption that teachers want to be effective and meet or exceed performance expectations. During the supervisory process, principals can determine whether teachers have the capacity to do so and use the process to help them build their sense of efficacy. As we explained in Chapter 3, *teachers' beliefs in their capabilities to meet or exceed performance expectations in a particular situation* reflect their self-efficacy. Why should teacher sense of efficacy be so important to supervisors? Because self-

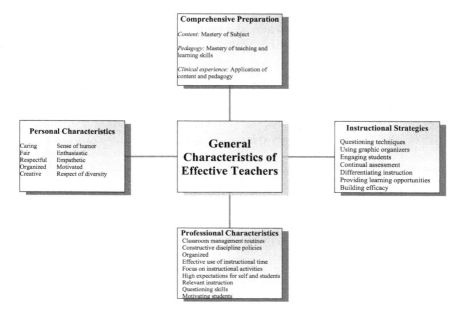

Figure 6.1. Effective teachers.

efficacy, a teacher's belief that he or she can reach even difficult students to help them learn, appears to be one of the few personal characteristics of teachers correlated with student achievement (Hoy & Hoy, 2013; Tschannen-Moran, Woolfolk Hoy, & Hoy, 1998; Woolfolk & Hoy, 1990; Woolfolk, Rosoff, & Hoy, 1990).

Teachers with a high sense of efficacy work harder and persist longer even when students are difficult to teach, in part because these teachers believe in themselves and in their students. Teachers' sense of personal efficacy is higher in schools where the other teachers and administrators have high expectations for students and where teachers receive help from their principals in solving instructional and management problems (Hoy & Woolfolk, 1993). Efficacy grows from real success with students. Any experience or training a supervisor provides that helps teachers succeed in the day-to-day tasks of teaching will give the teachers a foundation for developing an increased sense of efficacy.

Principals should include one or more of the four sources of efficacy expectations (mastery experiences, physiological and emotional arousal, vicarious experiences, and social persuasion) in action plans developed during the diagnostic cycle to help teachers increase their individual sense of efficacy. For example, rather than telling a teacher how to implement a specific teaching strategy, self-efficacy theory suggests that a principal provide the teacher with a model of the strategy, perhaps a colleague next door who is quite effective with that particular strategy. Principals should be cognizant of the fact that efficacy is context-specific; teachers do not feel equally efficacious for all teaching situations. They can feel efficacious in one situation but not in others. Even from one class to another, teachers' level of efficacy can change (Raudenbush, Rowen, & Cheong, 1992; Ross, Cousins, & Gadalla, 1996; Schunk, Pintrich, & Meece, 2008). The key efficacy questions are:

- How difficult is the task at hand and what resources are available?
- Given the situation, do I have the skills and knowledge to be successful?

The interaction of these two components leads to judgments of self-efficacy for the task at hand.

The consequences of these self-efficacy judgments are typically stronger effort, increased persistence, and active teaching when efficacy is high but minimal effort, helplessness, and passive teaching when efficacy is low. Helping teachers establish a strong sense of efficacy supports higher motivation, greater effort, persistence, and resilience.

SUPERVISORY BEHAVIOR

As principals execute their supervisory roles, they display a broad range of supervisory behaviors that have been categorized and placed on a continuum from nondirective to directive behaviors: listening, clarifying, encouraging, reflecting, presenting, problem solving, negotiating, directing, standardizing, and reinforcing (Glickman, 2002; Glickman, Gordon, & Ross-Gordon, 2013). The continuum of supervisory behaviors is depicted in Figure 6.2.

The supervisory behaviors contribute to the decisions made as action plans are devised during post observation conferences. Examples of each behavior follow.

- During *listening*, the principal sits, makes direct eye contact with the teacher and uses affirming head nods and other gestures to indicate comprehension.
- In *clarifying*, the principal asks questions and makes statements to elaborate on the teacher's comments: "I'm hearing you say that...." "Help me understand that."

Supervisory Behaviors

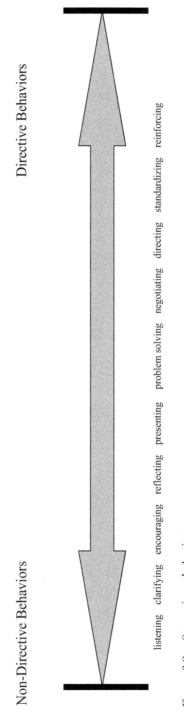

Non-Directive Behaviors

listening   clarifying   encouraging   reflecting   presenting   problem solving   negotiating   directing   standardizing   reinforcing

Directive Behaviors

Figure 6.2.   Supervisory behaviors.

141

- While *encouraging*, the principal verbally acknowledges understanding and urges the teacher to elaborate. "Yes, tell me more about that."
- In *reflecting*, the principal rephrases and synthesizes the teacher's points of view to check for understanding. "I heard you say that.... Why do you think that is the case?"
- During *presenting*, principals provide their own perspectives and ideas about the issue being discussed. "We should consider...." "A solution is...."
- In *problem solving*, the principal leads a discussion with the goal of generating a list of possible actions to solve the problem. "At this point, let's brainstorm alternative solutions."
- While *negotiating*, the principal directs the conversation to examine the anticipated consequences of each proposed alternative, eliminating some and seeking common agreement for action. "Which of the viable alternatives has the most promise?"
- In *directing*, the principal makes the decision and communicates it. "After considering the options, I want you to...."
- In *standardizing*, the principal clarifies the expected outcomes of the action and specifies time-lines for implementation and completion. "In two weeks we want to see..." "Let's meet in ten days so you can provide a progress report...."
- In *reinforcing*, principals communicate the expectation of results by explaining possible consequences, both positive and negative. "After you have been successful, I'd like you to model this...." "It won't be easy maintaining resource support if this doesn't work" (Glickman, Gordon, & Ross-Gordon, 2010, 2013).

At one end of the continuum (listening, clarifying, encouraging), the behaviors allow the teacher to take responsibility; but at the other end (directing, standardizing, reinforcing), that responsibility belongs solely to the principal. In between, there are opportunities for shared decision making and responsibility. There is no best supervisory behavior; each is appropriate depending on the situation.

SUPERVISORY STYLE

Glickman, Gordon, and Ross-Gordon (2010, 2013) identified four approaches to supervisory style: directive, directive informational, collaborative, and nondirective. Hoy and Tarter (2008) conceive of leadership styles along a continuum from director to integrator. Both perspectives

> **THEORY INTO PRACTICE**
> *ISLLC STANDARDS 2, 3, & 5*
> Study Figure 6.2 and the nine types of specific supervisory behaviors
> that can occur in a post-observation conference with a novice teacher.
> Take each of the nine skills and provide an example of how you would
> use each behavior in the context of working with that teacher. Be sure to
> give concrete examples. For instance, how would you demonstrate
> reflective behavior, encouraging behavior, problem-solving behavior,
> and so on?

portray the supervisory approaches along a continuum from directive to
autonomous. We synthesize these two approaches by defining four supervisory styles:

- Director—the principal gives unilateral direction.
- Educator—the principal teaches and then directs action.
- Collaborator—the principal and teachers make joint decisions.
- Professional—the principal empowers teachers to make autono-
  mous decisions.

In the supervisory process, principals' use of any of these approaches is
contingent on the situation, especially the knowledge, interest, and commitment of the teacher. For example, the directive approach may be
appropriate for beginning teachers, while the professional approach is
appropriate for master teachers (see Table 6.1).

During the process of supervision, principals observe teaching while
initiating a wide range of activities that focus on developing the instructional capacity of teachers. Supervising instruction is truly a multifaceted
task that challenges even the most competent principals.

Regardless of the supervisory style, the type of leadership provided by
principals has a dramatic impact on their relationships with teachers during supervision. Teachers need change and evolve during their careers,
not just with their longevity, but also with changing expectations. During
supervision, principals support teachers in a variety of ways depending on
individual strengths and needs. Novice or struggling teachers typically
welcome directive behavior from their principals. Other experienced,
competent teachers prefer to work on their own to foster their professional
development (Glatthorn, 1997). They will take the initiative to select an
area of interest or need, locate available resources for meeting goals, and
develop and carry out a plan of action for continuing development.

Table 6.1.   Matching Supervisory Styles With Teacher Needs

Supervisory Style →	*Teacher Level* →	*Supervisor Behaviors*
Directive Control: Supervisor directs *all* aspects of the process.	Beginners, those on formal plans for improvement, and those struggling with new essential instructional strategies.	Inform, direct, demonstrate, mandate … assign action plan
Directive Informational: Supervisor shares information, emphasizing what must be achieved through action plan.	Beginners and those struggling with new essential instructional strategies	Inform, generate alternatives. Suggest action plan
Collaborative: Open, two-way problem solving; teacher and supervisor are equals. Collaborative decision making; teacher takes the lead in framing questions, posing solutions, and making the final decision shaping the action plan.	Experienced; those with expertise and refined skills	Guide, maintain focus during discussions, connect teachers with similar needs. Collaborate to devise action plan
Nondirective: Self-directing; the teacher develops solutions and ongoing activities to assist with examining practice.	Master	Listen nonjudgmentally; ask open-ended questions; provide clarifications extend inquiry through reflection, role playing, and dialogue. Allow teacher to devise action plan.

Adapted from Glickman (1981)

When principals listen, clarify, encourage, and reflect during the process and allow the teacher to devise a plan of action, they empower teachers to make autonomous decisions based upon their expertise and experience. Principals need to understand what teachers are communicating before they can engage in collaborative problem solving. In this collaborative process, both the teacher and principal have responsibility.

There are times when a principal takes a more directive approach by providing several options from which the teacher makes a selection. The teacher has a choice from among the options the principal offers, but the principal establishes timelines and desired outcomes in this informational directive approach. In this case, the principal is teaching teachers by providing a scaffold for their success. The objective, of course, is to delegate more and more responsibility to the teachers as they develop professionally.

The ultimate directive behavior occurs when the principal makes the decision and directs the teacher to implement a plan of action while specifying the timeline and expected outcomes. When principals use the directive approach, they should be confident that their own knowledge and experience are superior to and different from those of the teachers, placing them in the better position to make the decision. Directive approaches are most appropriate for teachers who are inexperienced as well as those who can't determine an effective plan of action to achieve desired outcomes.

When a teacher implements one or more of the action plans devised solely by the principal, they hold the principal ultimately responsible for the success or failure of the plan(s). Monitoring implementation and principal credibility become issues when the directive approach is employed.

DIFFERENTIATED SUPERVISION

We have already discussed the problems with "one size fits all" clinical model of supervision. Differential supervision is a process through which teachers refine and expand their "instructional repertoire." In order to meet individual teacher learning and development needs, both supports and challenges are provided during differential supervision (Hattie, 2009; Reiman & Thies-Sprinthall, 1998).

For example, there is general agreement that novice teachers need to be supervised differently than experienced teachers (Sternberg, 2000). Beginning teachers have not had the time or experience to develop an extensive repertoire of pedagogy. They generally have more difficulty assessing and responding to unanticipated situations and problems in their classrooms than their experienced colleagues, and thus are in need of more directive assistance.

There are compelling arguments for differentiated supervision that have been described as processes that provide "teachers with options about the kinds of supervisory and evaluative services they receive" (Glatthorn, 1997, p. 3). As adult professionals, teachers should take responsibility for and have some control over their own professional development. They are often best equipped to determine the kind and level of support needed to grow and become more effective.

Outstanding schools are communities built on a foundation of cooperation, mutual assistance, and trust among faculty and staff. Effective principals nurture collegial relationships by sharing power and collegial leadership. Without collegiality, it is unlikely that the supervisory process can be effective in directing ongoing growth and development.

The goal of the supervisory process is to help teachers learn how to build on their own capacity in order to help their students achieve at higher levels (Glickman et al., 2010, 2013). A principal's behavior during supervision can either enhance or diminish teachers' abilities to engage in learning that is appropriate to their professional state of development. A principal must know the faculty well enough to determine which supervisory approach to implement with each individual and then, using the supervisory process, assist each individual to develop professionally. The ultimate goal of the process is to empower teachers by increasing their choices and decision-making responsibility.

DEVELOPMENTAL SUPERVISION

Knowing teachers and correctly assessing their conceptual levels are critical for effective developmental supervision to occur. Effective principals not only correctly assess the conceptual level of teachers but also implement appropriate strategies to meet specific teacher needs (Glickman et al., 2013). Given the diversity and the varied experience levels of any given faculty, this is a real challenge for principals. So how does a principal know what approach is best for each teacher?

The Hoy and Tarter (2008) decision-making model employs three primary criteria for individuals to participate in making decisions: expertise, interest, and commitment to student learning. These same criteria provide basic guidelines to assess a teacher's developmental level and to choose the supervisory approach to employ. Principals assess individual teacher's level of expertise, commitment, and the stake they have in student success by:

- collecting data through observing individual teachers' teaching and working with other professionals
- having conversations with individual teachers and with small groups on their views about students, teaching, awareness of current research on best practices, and their aspirations to develop into master teachers
- assessing teachers' awareness of improvements that can be made in their own classrooms
- articulating how identified improvements can be made
- determining if teachers use multiple data sources to identify needs
- posing instructional problems and assessing how capable teachers are at generating possible solutions
- confronting teachers with a challenging goal

- asking teachers to identify things that would make their classroom or school more effective
- assessing teachers' commitment to students and the school through their behaviors
- identifying teachers who "walk the talk" and do what they say they will do.

After successfully determining the appropriate supervisory approach for each teacher, principals can begin to use our model of the process to help teachers help students more effectively. Remember, the model is based on a collegial rather than hierarchical relationship between supervisor and teacher. Its focus is instructional improvement through teacher development.

When teachers have expertise and interest and are committed to student learning, they are *master teachers*, and the appropriate supervisory approach is a *professional style* in which principals empower teachers to be autonomous actors. In other words, in supervising master teachers, the direction of the supervision is from the teacher to the principal, with the principal serving and supporting the expertise of the teacher. In contrast, when teachers have little expertise and limited interest and are more focused on their own needs rather than those of students, they are *nonprofessional teachers*, and the appropriate supervisory approach is *directive style*. The principal as director decides what teachers should do, instructs them, and monitors them closely. Direct supervision should only be temporary; the principal has the added obligation of helping these teachers develop expertise, interest, and commitment, and as they do, shift more and more autonomy and responsibility to the teachers. As teachers move in this direction, the supervisory style moves incrementally from director to educator to collaborator and ultimately to professional. The model for matching the situation with the appropriate role is summarized in Table 6.2.

PRINCIPALS SUPERVISING TEACHERS: THE DIAGNOSTIC CYCLE IN ACTION

Becoming an effective teacher is an ongoing learning process. Principals work with teachers in the supervisory process in ways that promote such lifelong learning skills as inquiry, reflection, collaboration, and a dedication to professional growth and development. Principals also maintain an academic emphasis in the school with high expectations for students to perform well on standardized tests. These expectations, in turn, focus attention on how teachers must improve their pedagogy so that students can achieve. Essentially, supervisors are teachers of teachers—of profes-

Table 6.2.   A Contingency Model Matching Supervisory Styles With Teacher Characteristics

	Teacher Characteristic			
Supervisory Style	Master	Novice	Marginal	Nonprofessional
	Expertise +	Expertise +	Expertise +	Expertise +
	Interest +	Interest +	Interest +	Interest +
	Commitment +	Commitment +	Commitment +	Commitment +
Director				✓
Educator			✓	
Collaborator		✓		
Professional	✓			

Adapted from DiPaola and Hoy (2008)

sionals with learning needs as varied as those of the students in their classrooms. The challenge for principals is to provide appropriate learning opportunities for each teacher and link them to a unified approach to professional development and growth.

Individual teachers have different personalities, learning styles, and interaction patterns, and they work in different environments. Principals must recognize teacher individuality if teachers are to grow professionally and to improve the quality of their instruction. By employing the diagnostic cycle, the principal and teacher engage in the following six activities:

1. *Identify problems.* Identify area or areas where there is a significant discrepancy between the actual and desired outcomes of student or teacher performance.

2. *Diagnose causes.* Search for possible causes of the problems by examining the mismatches in the classroom performance model.

3. *Develop action plans.* Develop a strategy for action by carefully specifying alternatives, anticipating consequences, deliberating, and selecting a set of alternatives for action to solve the identified problem in order to achieve the desired performance outcomes.

4. *Implement action plans.* Translate action plans into specific and concrete steps to be taken to remedy the problem.

5. *Evaluate action plans.* Monitor action plans by collecting data to determine if the plans are producing the intended consequences.

Invariably, the data collection and assessment will trigger the cycle again; hence, the process is continuous (see Figure 5.2).

OBSERVING TEACHING

In order to use the diagnostic cycle, principals must observe teaching and learning in the teacher's classroom. Supervisory interactions most often manifest as dialogues after principals describe what they observed happening in classrooms in terms of the elements of the classroom social system: students, the teacher, teaching and learning, and the classroom community. In this formative process, there is no need or place for judging or interpreting by the observer. As an observer, the principal collects data that describe what she saw in the classroom, the teacher and principal analyze those data, and through dialogue that follows, move to identify problems, diagnose their causes, and develop and implement a plan to overcome the problems. Both the identification and success of the solution to the problems are driven by data collected either by the teacher or principal. Such observations must be distinguished from formal observations that are a part of the summative evaluative process.

Informal classroom observations should occur frequently and begin at the start of the school year. Teachers who are new to the building feel support and take comfort in the fact that the principal is there for them. Frequent informal observations help principals assess which teachers need support to meet expectations. Principals often cite the lack of time as the reason they do not visit classrooms frequently. Yet the purpose of the school is to help students learn—and most of that learning takes place in classrooms. There are schools that are administratively understaffed or have a large number of novice teachers. In these places, principals may need assistance from master teachers within the faculty to make frequent classroom observations. The alternative, infrequent observations, is unacceptable. Without frequent observation and feedback, teachers become isolated in classrooms and receive professional development opportunities that neither meet their individual needs nor help them deal effectively with problems that confront them in their classrooms. Without helpful feedback, they have limited opportunities for reflection or to improve the quality of their teaching.

Despite the perceptions of some principals, teachers like and want to see them frequently in their classrooms. In addition to collecting data to share with teachers, a review of the literature on frequent classroom observations revealed some very positive outcomes. Frequent principal classroom visits:

- predict increased frequency of teacher satisfaction
- improve teacher self-efficacy
- improve teacher attitudes toward professional development
- improve teacher attitudes toward teacher appraisal

- increase perceived teacher efficacy of other teachers and of the school
- improve classroom instruction
- improve teacher perception of principal effectiveness and support
- improve student discipline
- improve teacher perceived effectiveness of the school (Downey, Steffy, English, Frase, & Poston, 2004).

Thus, research supports the practice of frequent classroom visits. But the data collected and duration of visits can vary greatly. While formal, evaluative observations are often prescribed in number and duration, the informal, formative supervisory observations vary with the focus of the observation. The goal is to provide valid descriptions of classroom events to a teacher. For example, if questioning skills are the focus, then a principal may provide quantitative data on the number of questions asked at each level of Bloom's taxonomy. If searching for classroom patterns, qualitative data like scripting may be provided. Be mindful that the ultimate goal is to improve instruction by helping teachers "see" what has happened in the classroom. Feedback can have a high impact on improving teacher learning when it helps them reduce the discrepancies between current practice, expected performance, and goals. In reality, principals are often required by policy to perform numerous and lengthy summative observations in the process of evaluation that detract from their ability to observe informally and supervise instruction effectively.

WALK-THROUGH OBSERVATIONS

In recognition of this fact, shorter formative supervisory observations have been advocated. These short "drop-in" visits can occur more frequently and give principals snapshots of what is occurring in classrooms. In some models, these observational "visits" are a few minutes in duration.

One example is the Downey walk-through process of observation (Poston, Downey, Steffy, & English, 2009). It advocates thoughtful dialogue focused on developmental supervision. This technique has roots in the practice of management by walking around (MBWA). Adapted from the private sector, MBWA was embraced by those who believe that principals, as instructional leaders, should spend the lion's share of the school day in classrooms (Eisner, 2002). MBWA has a positive impact on student learning across socioeconomic and cultural lines, but especially for those students who come from low-socioeconomic status (SES) homes (Andrews & Soder, 1987; Andrews, Soder, & Jacoby, 1986; Hallinger & Heck, 2010).

With so much time spent in classrooms, principals constantly focus on curriculum and instruction. The Downey observation technique consists of very frequent, short, informal exchanges between principals and teachers that can be used to identify problems, which are discrepancies between what the teacher and principal desire and what actually is happening in the classroom. These short exchanges are also an ongoing and integral part of a reflective teaching practice that is a continuing conversation over time. Short, frequent observations keep the focus on teaching and learning, increase the visibility of the principal as a colleague, and provide a continuous scan for shortcomings in desired outcomes.

We advocate making frequent classroom visits to observe instruction. However, the duration of observations must be sufficient to allow observers to collect data for analysis and reflection. Novice principals often lack complete confidence in their ability to assist veteran or master teachers. Most have been successful classroom teachers but fear that their own practice did not provide an adequate array of strategies to address the variety of problems encountered by teachers in classrooms. By making frequent classroom observations of all teachers, principals' own repertoire of strategies increases dramatically, enabling them to be an effective resource for teachers at all levels of effectiveness.

Frequent informal observations of a teacher's behaviors and interactions give the principal a better chance of collecting valid data. With frequent classroom visits, observations tend to reduce teacher apprehension over time and make formal observations more effective. The more classroom data principals collect, the more they know about the actual functioning of their schools. They more easily identify common areas of mismatched elements that might prove valuable for group professional development at the faculty, grade, or departmental levels. Frequent observations also allow principals to monitor the impact of professional development opportunities that have been provided to individuals and groups of teachers.

In making frequent classroom visits, principals scan, uncover patterns, and can assess which teachers are struggling and in most need of assistance. They can provide help directly or have a master teacher assist before things get out of hand. But remember, we advocate differentiated supervision— that which meets individual teacher needs. However, for all teachers, the duration of the observation should be congruent with the goal of collecting enough data to identify problems and develop an action plan. It is imperative that teachers understand the diagnostic cycle, principal behaviors, and their underlying assumptions. Effective principals engage in discussions with teachers as professional colleagues and explain their supervisory model and observational strategies.

> **THEORY INTO PRACTICE**
> *ISLLC STANDARDS 2 & 3*
> How often does your principal visit your classroom? Typically, how long were the visits? Were the visits sufficient to collect enough data to help you improve your instruction? What kind of feedback did you get after each visit? What was the nature of the feedback? Was it useful? Given your experiences as a teacher, and after reading this chapter, describe what your practices will be as a principal engaged in supervision. That is, how often would you visit classrooms, and how long would you visit each time? What kind of feedback would you provide and how would you provide it? Would you treat all teachers alike when it came to data analysis and action plans? If so, why? If not, why not?

USING THE DIAGNOSTIC CYCLE

In Chapters 4 and 5, we developed a model of supervision and described the essential elements interacting within classrooms: students, the teacher, the teacher's pedagogy, and the classroom community. Problems are discrepancies between the behavior expected by the teacher–principal team and actual outcomes. Thus, "problem" is used here as a discrepancy, which provides an opportunity for improvement. The problem provides the focus, the goal, and the starting point for the supervisory process.

The specific purpose of collecting performance data is to enable the teacher and supervisor to identify "problems." We have discussed the need for teachers to get direct, differentiated, sustained assistance from their principals. Teachers' learning and development are linked to appropriate interactions with their principals during the supervisory process in solving problems (Dinham, 2007; Hattie, 2009; Reiman & Thies-Sprinthall, 1998). Because students, their teachers, and classrooms are so different, the mechanics for identifying discrepancies must be flexible. Ideally, the teacher and supervisor can identify their expectations rather precisely prior to collecting performance data.

In using the diagnostic cycle, problems are identified in a variety of ways—through results of standardized assessments, results of teacher assessments, discipline data, teacher-reported problems, and data collected during direct observation by the principal. In any case, once the problem is identified, action is called for—causes must be diagnosed, and a plan formulated, implemented, and its success evaluated. For example, if a teacher and class appear to be average in every way, students' performance would be expected to be on par with state or national averages on standardized assessments. Lower-than-average performance by the class would result in a discrepancy between expected and actual performance. This problem is likely a function of one or more of six possible mismatches. Table 6.3 summarizes the six possible mismatches in the model.

Table 6.3. Matches and Mismatches in the Classroom Performance Model

Key Elements/Matches	Critical Questions/Issues
Teacher ↔ Classroom Community	To what degree are the needs of the teacher being met by the classroom community? To what extent do the teacher's skills and knowledge create support for a classroom conducive to student engagement and learning?
Teacher ↔ Pedagogy	To what degree are the needs of the teacher being met by the pedagogy? To what extent are teacher's skills and knowledge consistent with their teaching strategies and behaviors (pedagogy)?
Pedagogy ↔ Student	To what degree is the pedagogy consistent with the needs of the students? To what extent do the teacher's strategies and behaviors support students motivation and learning?
Student ↔ Classroom Community	To what degree are the needs of the students being met by the classroom community? To what extent are students' motivations to learn consistent with a classroom climate of student engagement?
Teacher ↔ Student	To what degree are the needs of the teacher consistent with the needs of the students? To what extent do the teacher's skills and knowledge enable the teacher to motivate students to learn?
Pedagogy ↔ Classroom Community	To what degree is the pedagogy consistent with the needs of the classroom community? To what extent do the teacher's strategies and behaviors support a classroom conducive to student engagement and learning?

The challenge for the principal and teacher is to identify which elements are not congruent with each other. That is, which pairs of elements are mismatched? In this instance, the cause of the lower scores might be a mismatch between the teacher and the classroom community. The climate of the classroom may be such that students are antagonistic toward the teacher and the teacher is reacting defensively by asserting formal authority. The consequence of this mismatch is a lot of game playing and posturing between the teacher and students at the expense of time on task. It may also be the case that the teacher's skills and knowledge are not adequate to implement the research-based instructional strategies needed for student success. At any rate, a careful analysis of the congruence of all the elements in the classroom supervisory model must be considered before an action plan is developed and initiated.

In another case, the teacher collects data and initiates a discussion with the principal. For example, the teacher reports that despite efforts to remediate the problem, two students routinely cause uproar in the classroom. In other words, the students in question are not meeting the expectations of appropriate student engagement. Hence, the issue is how to bring student engagement in line with teacher expectations. Teachers need to feel free to ask for help without fear of recrimination, but ultimately the problem cannot be solved until its causes are determined. Treating the symptoms is no substitute for solving the problem. In this case, the crux of the problem may be the teacher's inability to motivate these two individual students. In other words, for these two students there is a mismatch between the teacher's skill and the motivational needs of these students. It may be that the students have such profound personal problems that outside interventions are necessary. Or it may be that the teacher needs the principal's assistance in developing a different strategy to work with the students. In the final analysis, solving classroom problems is a joint endeavor in which both the principal and teacher share responsibility.

SUMMARY

A primary role of the principal is to help teachers become more effective in the classroom. What do effective teachers look like? To answer this question, we reviewed the literature and described the general characteristics of effective teachers in terms of their preparation as well as personal and professional characteristics. We also summarized some instructional strategies, correlated to high student achievement, that effective teachers are most apt to use.

Building a sense of efficacy among individual teachers is a general strategy that principals can use to improve teacher effectiveness. To be successful, it helps if teachers believe that they have the capacity and skill to achieve their objectives in a given situation. The principal's role in helping to build such capacity is critical to success.

As supervisors, principals engage teachers in a collegial fashion to help them succeed. Because the task of supervision is so complex and teachers are so diverse, principals must have a broad repertoire of supervisory behaviors and skills. The challenges of meeting the needs of a diverse teacher population require differentiated and developmental supervision; that is, no one supervisory style is best. We argue that principals must match the situation with the appropriate supervisory style and we provide such a model.

We use the diagnostic cycle introduced in Chapter 5 as a supervisory tool to help teachers understand their problems and take appropriate action to improve. The cycle is a pivotal aspect of supervision; it is a data-driven process to get information, diagnose problem causes, create plans for action, implement those plans, and evaluate their success with hard evidence. To use the diagnostic cycle, principals must get into the classroom, make observations, collect data, provide feedback to the teacher, and then develop an action plan to improve. This process of supervision is more informal than formal; that is, the data are not used to make judgments about the job performance of teachers. Supervision is a formative process rather than a summative one. As such, the informal observations vary in terms of number and duration depending on the needs of teachers.

A PRINCIPAL'S SUPERVISORY CHALLENGE

Instructions—Read the following account provided by a principal, reflect on her practice, and perform a case analysis.

At the beginning of a new school year, I make it a point to observe all teachers new to my building within the first two weeks of school. I conduct brief, informal drop-in observations of all new teachers, usually during the second week of school. This allows me to quickly pinpoint any problem areas and identify teachers who may need some immediate support and help.

I'm in my second year as principal at South Woods, a middle school of 600 students. I observed Melissa Jones, a first-year teacher in the second week of school, who was struggling in two major areas. Melissa was having difficulty in creating coherent lesson plans, and her repertoire of instructional strategies was thin. On the bright side, she had good instincts and had already established rapport with her students.

I dropped into Melissa's classroom on two separate occasions for about 10–15 minutes. Each time I sat down and outlined a plan of action that I thought would best benefit her teaching. Then I arranged to meet with Melissa, and, using my brief outline as a starting point, *together* we crafted a plan that we both felt would help her reach her potential as a teacher. My policy for new teachers is to assign a mentor to help them through their transition year. I quickly decided that Melissa needed a different mentor than the one that I had originally assigned to her, and she seemed relieved at my suggestion that we identify someone else as her mentor. After discussing the possibilities and who might be a better fit for her while still offering the expertise from which she would benefit, we settled on Amanda DeLisi, a young but experienced teacher. Later, when I approached Amanda to ask her to work with the new teacher, she was delighted because she had noticed that the two of them had similar back-grounds and they had "hit it off."

I met weekly with Melissa for three weeks to help her create and write lesson plans. I began by providing her with several different lesson plan formats from which she could choose or mold one that worked best for her, yet contained all of the district-required components. I then sat with her, and through prompting and role modeling, I was able to walk her through the process of crafting a lesson. I supplied the framework, and she supplied the content material. By starting with objectives and outcomes, I was able demonstrate plans that included what she wanted her students to learn and how she could best get them there. These ses-sions also allowed Melissa a venue for reflecting upon her own teaching and heightened her desire to learn about more and varied teaching strategies.

REFLECTIVE PRACTICE

Assume you are this principal.

- Assess the principal's actions during this initial period of supervi-sion. Defend your assessment.
- What would you do differently? Why?
- How would you proceed with your supervision of this teacher? At what point would you observe Melissa teaching? What is your role with respect to the mentor teacher? Do you need to talk to the mentor?
- How structured a plan would you have? Your role here is formative, not summative, so how can you help this teacher in a collegial man-ner? What are the dangers?

Plan a program of supervision for Melissa for the remainder of the year. Be specific and show your timeline for each activity.

DEVELOP YOUR PORTFOLIO

You have observed a teacher about a half a dozen times and you always notice that he asks lower-level questions (recall and factual) and virtually never asks questions that require analysis or synthesis. When you provide this feedback to the teacher, he is defensive and seems unaware of the fact there are different cognitive levels of questioning (e.g., remembering facts, understanding relations, applying facts, analyzing information, evaluating data, creating new knowledge). Develop an action plan to help this teacher improve his questioning skills. Be specific. First, how would you make this teacher aware of the different levels of questioning and their purpose? Second, how would you help him improve his questioning in the context of his classroom? Consider modeling, demonstration, vicarious examples, and teaching him how to question. (For more information on Bloom's revised taxonomy in the cognitive domain and a framework for levels of questioning, see Hoy & Hoy, 2013.) Finally, be sure to include a timeline in your plan. How soon can you expect to see improvement?

COMMUNICATION EXERCISE

Prepare a 20-minute PowerPoint presentation for your faculty on supervision of instruction in which you explain the purposes of supervision, distinguish supervision from evaluation, and describe the principal and teacher's role in supervision. Also explain the model of classroom supervision as well as the diagnostic cycle, and describe how you as the principal will use these tools to help them improve instruction.

READINGS

Fullan, M. (2001). *Leading in a culture of change.* San Francisco, CA: Jossey-Bass.

Gupton, S. (2010). *The instructional leadership toolbox: A handbook for improving practice* (2nd ed.). Thousand Oaks, CA: Corwin.

Hattie, J. (2012). *Visible learning for teachers: Maximizing impact on learning.* New York, NY: Routledge.

Marzano, R. J. (2007). *The art and science of teaching: A comprehensive framework for effective instruction.* Alexandria, VA: Association for Supervision and Curriculum Development.

McEwan, E. K. (2003). *Seven steps to effective instructional leadership* (2nd ed.). Thousand Oaks, CA: Corwin Press.

Wright, S. P., Horn, S. P., & Sanders, W. L. (1997). Teacher and classroom context effects on student achievement. Implications for teacher evaluation. *Journal of Personnel Evaluation in Education, 11,* 57–67.

WHAT DO SUPERINTENDENTS SAY?

What are the purposes of summative evaluation and formative supervision? Can principals supervise and help improve instruction without letting summative evaluation get in the way?

Superintendent 1: The summative evaluation should be the statement of attainment of some agreed-upon goal. With that being said, it is largely bureaucratic and legal in nature. The true training and assistance from a principal comes from formative supervision. A good principal establishes a culture in a building wherein all supervisory activities are focused on improving instruction. If everyone being supervised believes that the principal is focused on making them better, the process of writing a summative evaluation is just the last step of their yearly journey.

Superintendent 2: Any summative and/or formative evaluations should be used to help and assist teachers improve their instructional skills. Any effective principal will use the time spent in the classroom to improve teachers' skill sets.

Superintendent 3: Summative evaluation is a process for gathering information that a principal uses to make decisions about the reemployment of teachers. Formative supervision is an ongoing process by which a principal identifies needs of individuals or groups of teachers in an effort to help improve instruction in a classroom, grade level, department, or staff as a whole. It is seemingly implausible to think formative supervision does not somehow influence or inform a teacher's summative evaluation. However, formative evaluation only gets in the way when a marginal teacher is not exhibiting the skills that merit reemployment.

CHAPTER 7

PROFESSIONAL DEVELOPMENT

Contemporary models of effective professional development vary dramatically from the one-day, one-shot, one-size-fits-all workshops that have traditionally been provided as professional development. Hattie (2009) found that professional development has a significant impact in improving student achievement when opportunities for teachers to learn:

- occur over an extended period of time
- focus on increasing teachers' knowledge and skills in ways to improve student learning
- challenge the prevailing practices and beliefs about how students learn
- provide opportunities for teachers' discourse about teaching that results in learning for all students
- are supported by principals who provide relevant expertise and new knowledge about best practices (pp. 120–121).

Dinham (2007) found that schools with outstanding educational outcomes are led by principals who place a high value on teachers' professional learning—learning that is focused on the quality of teaching and student learning. Increasing teacher knowledge and pedagogy are the goals of professional development. If professional development does not enhance teachers' professional knowledge and classroom practices, little improvement in student learning will result. Transforming the professional

Improving Instruction Through Supervision, Evaluation, and
Professional Development, pp. 159–183
Copyright © 2014 by Information Age Publishing

development learning into classroom practice requires the kind of support principals and teacher colleagues can provide in our model.

A primary responsibility of principals is to ensure that all teachers have the opportunity to grow professionally. In using our model of supervision, once a mismatch has been identified, an individual plan of action is developed with the teacher. These plans of action and the activities required to execute them are individualized professional development opportunities. Since our model of classroom supervision is a continuous process, it creates a school in which teachers can learn and develop as part of regular routines (DuFour, 2004). Executing the action plan within the diagnostic cycle individualizes teacher learning and recognizes that teachers are in various stages of adult growth.

Perhaps the most important work a principal does as a supervisor is working with teachers to facilitate their professional growth and development. Through this informal process, principals encourage and model inquiry, reflection, and collaboration. In this role, principals are teachers of teachers. They recognize that the needs of teacher professionals can be as diverse as those of students in any classroom. Thus, it is through the informal supervisory process that principals first identify the professional needs of the teachers and plan to deliver support for their growth and development. As principals provide learning opportunities for teachers based on individual needs, the entire notion of what is traditionally thought of as "professional development" is transformed. The goal is systemic improvement of teaching that leads to improvement in student learning.

Principals should be mindful in working with teachers to develop action plans that link learning about instructional changes or innovations to teachers' past experiences, and to allow them ample time to integrate innovations gradually into their pedagogy. Since the beginning of the current accountability movement, efforts to meet increasing public expectations have bombarded and overwhelmed principals and teachers. Mandated district or state tasks and strategies ostensibly designed to increase student performance on standardized achievement measures have reduced teacher autonomy and added to the complexity of teacher tasks. Many "educational innovations" introduced in school districts are quick fixes, ill-conceived, and unconnected to the stated purposes of education (Fullan, 1991). Not surprisingly, many of these innovations have failed. One reason for these failures is that principals have not helped teachers integrate the innovations with their past experiences or adapt the innovations to their current teaching practice. Action plans must include realistic timelines, expectations for implementation, and evidence of changes in classroom practice. Teachers often simply are not provided sufficient time to learn about and integrate an innovation before the next innovation is mandated by school districts.

> **THEORY INTO PRACTICE**
> *ISLLC STANDARDS 1 & 2*
> Reflect on your own practice and identify two professional development programs that you believe were good. Who supported you as you attempted to implement the knowledge or skills learned? Did the experience change your classroom practice? If so, how? If not, why not? What impact did the professional development have on the achievement of your students? How did you reach this conclusion?

DEFINING PROFESSIONAL DEVELOPMENT

Improving a teacher's ability to teach is obviously crucial to student learning and school success, and that is the purpose of professional development. *Professional development* is defined broadly as all of the formal and informal learning experiences teachers have throughout their careers, from pre-service training to retirement (Fullan, 2007). A more precise description of professional development is that it is "intensive, ongoing, and connected to practice; focuses on the teaching and learning of specific academic content; is connected to other school initiatives; and builds strong working relationships among teachers" (Darling-Hammond, Wei, Andree, Richardson, & Orphanos, 2009, p. 5). In reality, professional development takes many forms, including short conferences at the end of the school day, half-day work sessions, book studies, joint planning time, week-long seminars, and long-term institutes.

We believe that professional development is inexorably linked to both supervision and evaluation. The goal of both processes is to build the capacity of teachers to help students learn. In the supervisory process, ongoing, one-on-one, focused feedback is used to identify and solve problems linked to the effectiveness of teaching. This is the most powerful staff development approach available to impact and change teacher classroom behavior (Hall & Hord, 2010). It is certainly more powerful than the typical one-day workshops many teachers attend.

The Association for Supervision and Curriculum Development (ASCD) defines effective professional development as activities directly focused on teachers helping students achieve learning goals and supporting student learning needs. Developing and implementing these activities is a collaborative endeavor between teachers and administrators who plan and implement school-based as well as job-embedded, differentiated strategies to improve student learning. The process is a longterm commitment in which principals and teachers work collaboratively to achieve school and district goals (ASCD, 2002). Having a collective responsibility for student learning is an essential element in school improvement and increased student learning (Whalan, 2012). The improvement activities that are embedded in our supervisory model and diagnostic cycle represent individualized professional development for teachers.

Although definitions of professional development provide some guidance on what professional development activities should accomplish, designing an effective program is not easy. Often, school principals' planning for professional development involves plugging an activity into an empty space on the calendar without much thought to the needs of participants. For example, a district may establish a set time for teachers to participate in a professional development activity, and the principal is responsible for filling the allotted time. Rather than planning a comprehensive program with established goals and a process for determining the effectiveness of the program, principals often begin searching for speakers who can fill the space. They may provide little information on the needs of their staff, making it difficult for the trainer to design an effective activity. Instead, the principal should use classroom observations to identify the current status of teachers' knowledge of strategies and content as well as analyze available data in order to determine the training that will have the best chance of positive change in classroom practice. Principals use data to craft professional development experiences in which teachers are able to reflect on their practice, construct professional knowledge with their peers, and develop more collaborative relationships with their fellow teachers (Gregson & Sturko, 2007). Principals collect these data through frequent classroom observations.

Professional development should be provided in a manner that helps the teacher understand the context in which the strategies or content will be presented. There is no better way to accomplish this than through the process of supervision. Through classroom observations and subsequent dialogues, principals provide a mirror so that teachers can reflect on their own teaching, identify problems, devise plans for action, and then implement them. This is truly individualized professional development in the context of teachers' classrooms, meeting their individual needs.

Through frequent classroom observations, a principal can also assess whether small groups of teachers or the faculty as a whole have common development needs. In those instances, principals may provide small group, school–, or district–wide targeted professional development that includes follow up in the context of individual classrooms. Unfortunately, this type of professional development is often ineffective because teachers leave the training without a real understanding of how to implement a strategy or see the relevance to improving their own pedagogy. Rarely are opportunities provided for teachers to plan and organize their lessons to properly implement the "new" strategy or content. Simply presenting the strategy or content and then sending teachers back to their classroom to implement without any follow-up or planning guidance dooms improvement to failure (Yamagata-Lynch, 2003).

CHARACTERISTICS OF EFFECTIVE PROFESSIONAL DEVELOPMENT

The era of educational reform has been underway for over three decades. During this time, professional development has been cited as an essential component of most educational improvement plans. The No Child Left Behind (NCLB) Act (2002) requires all professional development funded by the federal government to be designed around scientifically based research that includes a rigorous, systematic process for identifying the knowledge necessary to measure the impact of training on student achievement. The federal government's definition of professional development includes activities that:

- are sustained, intensive, and content-focused—to have a positive and lasting impact on classroom instruction and teacher performance
- are aligned with and directly related to state academic content standards, student achievement standards, and assessments
- improve and increase teachers' knowledge of the subjects they teach
- advance teachers' understanding of effective instructional strategies founded on scientifically based research
- are regularly evaluated for effects on teacher effectiveness and student achievement (Yoon, Duncan, Lee, Scarloss, & Shapley, 2007).

Learning Forward's (formerly the National Staff Development Council) Standards for Professional Learning (2012) define professional learning as opportunities for teachers to develop their knowledge, skills, and pedagogy to help students perform at higher levels. Their seven standards define professional development as that which increases teacher effectiveness and positive results for all students. Professional development:

- occurs within learning communities committed to continuous improvement, collective responsibility, and goal alignment

- requires prioritizing, monitoring, and coordinating resources for educator learning
- integrates theories, research, and models of human learning to achieve its intended outcomes
- aligns its outcomes with educator performance and student curriculum standards
- requires skillful leaders who develop capacity, advocate, and create support systems for professional learning
- uses a variety of sources and types of student, educator, and system data to plan, assess, and evaluate professional learning
- applies research on change and sustains support for implementation of professional learning for long-term change (Learning Forward, 2012).

An analysis of suggested professional development models revealed consensus that professional development activities should enhance teachers' content and pedagogical knowledge (Guskey & Sparks, 2004). It is obvious that all "teachers should know the subjects they teach and how to teach those subjects to students" (National Board for Professional Teaching Standards [NBPTS], 2004, p. 13). Most models recognized the need for adequate time and resources for educators for professional development to be effective. Extra time for teacher education is often largely viewed as "something done after or apart from regular teaching responsibilities" (Little, 1999, p. 243) rather than as an integral part of teaching practice. It is unlikely that professional development will be effective unless sufficient time is given for observation, reflection, and dialogue with colleagues (Novick, 1996). A review of evidence on how teacher professional development affects student achievement found that sustained professional learning of more than 14 hours showed a positive and significant effect on student achievement from professional development (Yoon et al., 2007). Effective professional development is continuous and supported in both time and resources (Fullan, 1993; Guskey, 1995). Sound professional development results from the continuous collaboration of principals and teachers in our collegial supervisory process.

Another characteristic common of effective professional development is the presence of specific evaluation procedures (Guskey, 2002). Assessing the impact of professional development is critical, since professional development is essential to reforms in teaching and learning (Desimone, 2009). Sykes (1999) argues that good accountability systems are created by using both formative and summative evaluation of teacher professional development.

Keeping professional development activities within the school is another characteristic (Guskey, 2003). The term *job-embedded professional development* is used to describe a direct connection between teachers' work in the classroom and the professional development teachers are provided. Hawley and Valli (1999) agree that professional development should be both "school-based and integral to school operations" (p. 140). Professional development that is job-embedded and aligned with school priorities is more likely to lead to permanent changes in teachers' classroom practices (Teacher Training Center for International Education [TTCIE], 2007). Unfortunately, school-based activity is often overlooked as one of the most powerful forms of professional development. A transformation of school from a workplace to a place from which adult learning arises is indeed a powerful metaphor. Job-embedded professional development is primarily school- or classroom-based and is integrated into the workday, consisting of teachers assessing and finding solutions for authentic and immediate problems of practice as part of a cycle of continuous improvement (Hawley & Valli, 1999; National Staff Development Council, 2010). An integral component of our model of supervision of instruction is job-embedded professional learning.

Joyce and Showers (2003) argue that the only goal of staff development should be student learning. They demonstrate strong relationships between effective, research-based professional development and the development of learning communities of teachers and principals, knowledge of standards and expectations, modifications in instruction, and improved school climate, all resulting in improved student learning. In order to significantly affect student learning, professional development must:

- consist of a community of professional educators who meets regularly to study together, implement what they are learning, share their results and learn from one another
- be connected to curricular and instructional high-yield, research-based strategies that have a high probability of affecting students' learning and students' ability to learn
- produce tangible results in student learning
- enable the educators to increase their pedagogical skills to successfully implement what they learn (Joyce & Showers, 2003, p. 4).

One-shot professional development or a series of workshops that imitate the one-shot professional development experience do not significantly result in either a change in teacher behavior or an increase in student performance (Guskey, 2003). The ten characteristics of effective professional development are summarized in Table 7.1.

Table 7.1. Effective Professional Development

Characteristics of Effective Professional Development

Improves teacher content knowledge and increases pedagogical skills

Clarifies understanding of meanings and relationships

Provides adequate time and resources

Is ongoing and continuous

Is an integral part of collegial supervision and collaboration

Includes evaluation procedures to determine its effectiveness

Is school-based and an integral part of school programs

Has a variety of formats

Accommodates diversity and promotes equity

Uses learning data to drive professional development

THEORY INTO PRACTICE
ISLLC STANDARDS 1, 2, 3, 5
List the last two professional development opportunities that were provided by your principal, and two more provided by your district. Evaluate each of the four experiences in terms of the characteristics of effective professional development. If you were principal of your school, design one professional development program that would meet at least four of the characteristics of effective development programs. What are the four characteristics, and why does your program hold more promise or potential to lead to increased student achievement?

BARRIERS TO EFFECTIVE PROFESSIONAL DEVELOPMENT

Although professional development should be focused on improving the achievement of students, teachers often select activities they find interesting with little connection to student achievement. Unfortunately, teachers can participate and earn recertification points for activities that are unrelated to improving student performance. An example of this is having teachers select conferences and workshops based on location rather than selecting activities with relevant content at the school site. Often, these off-site activities do not focus on the primary purpose of professional development—improving the academic achievement of students. Teacher learning should focus on developing increased pedagogical content knowledge; the cognitive and emotional development of students; and research-based, high-yield instructional strategies to target student achievement (Harvard Family Research Project [HFRP], 2004; Hattie, 2009).

Teachers at all career levels express dissatisfaction with professional development activities, particularly those entering the profession through alternative routes. Often the terminology used presupposes knowledge that is not always understood by individuals new to the profession. An additional struggle exists when schools assign mentors or provide induction programs that assume prior knowledge of strategies and skills that new teachers and alternatively certified teachers have not mastered (Szuminski, 2003). One-shot, one-size-fits-all programs frustrate teachers.

Obstacles to high quality professional development often derail good intentions (see Table 7.2). Trying to fit the programs into an already packed schedule for teachers can be a challenge. In addition, professional development programs can be expensive—sustained, high-quality development requires time, a resource in short supply. When faced with the budget choice of professional development, increased payrolls, technology upgrades, or learning materials, professional development often gets short shrift.

Table 7.2.   Barriers for Effective Professional Development

Barriers to Effective Professional Development
Teachers selecting interesting but irrelevant topics
Teachers selecting activities based on location rather than content
Teachers being placed in programs for which they do not have sufficient background
One-shot programs for everyone
Lack of adequate time and funding for comprehensive development
Lack of follow-up and reinforcement of knowledge or skills

Teachers may be denied the opportunity to participate in professional development during the school day due to reduced funding for substitutes. Coupled with the fact that funding is often not available to pay teachers to attend training during or after school hours or on non-school days, little incentives remain for teachers to volunteer for professional development opportunities (Kerka, 2003). Teachers may also be hesitant to participate in professional development if their involvement will require additional work to implement new strategies or provide training for colleagues with little collaborative planning time provided (Yamagata-Lynch, 2003).

Due to the barriers to designing a comprehensive professional development program, principals often resort to a shotgun attempt to fix identified problems. In other words, during the diagnostic cycle, principals and teachers may identify a specific area of weakness through the analysis of data. The principal may be aware of a program or strategy that is designed to target that specific weakness and arrange for a one-hour training on the strategy. However, the strategy may not be appropriate for some of the staff, although all teachers may be required to attend. Little or no follow-up may be provided to assist teachers in implementing the strategy, but the principal may report that training has been provided to address identified problems. This approach to professional development is rarely successful in accomplishing the ultimate goal of improving student achievement (Desimone, 2009).

THEORY INTO PRACTICE
ISLLC STANDARDS 1, 2, 3, 4, 5

As principal of your school, how would you avoid impediments to effective professional development? Be specific. Be sure to comment on time, other resources, and conventional practices that encourage teachers to select or be assigned to professional development activities. How much freedom can you give to teachers in the selection? How would you determine whether a program of development was a good fit for a teacher or your school? What are your criteria for such a decision?

EVALUATING PROFESSIONAL DEVELOPMENT

As we indicated earlier in this chapter, using specific evaluation procedures is a characteristic common to effective professional development. The evaluation of a professional development program should occur at four levels: reaction, learning, transfer, and results (Kirkpatrick, 1998). A good evaluation first determines the reactions of the participants to the development activity. Next, the evaluation assesses whether participants have learned the intended material. Then, the evaluation turns to whether participants transfer their learning into their classroom practices. Finally, the evaluation assesses the impact on student learning.

Traditional evaluations, however, target only the first level. First level evaluations often consist of a survey distributed to all participants at the end of a program that measures participant satisfaction with the event. Such data will not provide information on whether or not the training was successful in changing classroom behavior of teachers or the level of student achievement. The goals of a strong evaluation program are to measure not only the immediate reaction to the event, but the transfer of knowledge into actual classroom behavior and resulting increase in student learning (HFRP, 2004).

Evaluating the long-term impact of professional development on the accomplishment of established goals is a rare occurrence indeed (HFRP, 2004). Thorough evaluation of professional development rarely occurs for several reasons. One is the lack of resources, including time. Designing an evaluation takes time and must be part of the planning process. When professional development activities are planned without a focused goal, an effective tool to measure desired outcomes cannot be designed. In addition, because complete evaluations in the area of professional development are rare, there is a lack of qualified experts to design such evaluations (HRFP, 2004).

Three phases for the evaluation of professional development have been identified. They are *planning, conducting,* and *reporting* (Killion, 2002). When designing the evaluation tool, it is necessary to first determine the purpose of the development activity to be evaluated. Once the purpose has been established, the method of evaluation must be identified. A variety of evaluation tools can be used, including quantitative surveys, interviews, or open-ended responses (HFRP, 2004). In an effective process to evaluate professional development activities, the *goals* of the development guide the process. Once the goals are determined, designing an effective evaluation includes: *formulating evaluation questions, constructing a framework, developing a timeline, collecting data, organizing and analyzing data, interpreting data, disseminating results,* and *evaluating the evaluation*. The steps in designing an effective evaluation of professional development are summarized in Figure 7.1.

Evaluations should focus on the long-term goals of professional development. Because it is easier to focus on the short-term goals of participant satisfaction, acquisition of strategies, or increased content knowledge, frequently the impact on student achievement is ignored. It is important to realize that the type of professional development should guide the identification of desired outcomes. Consideration should be given to the type of delivery of information as well as the strategies presented and the research behind the strategies (Kerka, 2003). Evaluation of professional development should be a systematic program that measures effectiveness (Killion, 2002). Desimone (2009) argues that recent research knowledge should be applied to improve the conceptualization, measures, and methodology for studying the effects of professional development on teachers and students. The application of a research-based conceptual framework would elevate the quality of professional development studies and subsequently the general understanding of how to shape and implement teacher learning opportunities for the maximum benefit of both teachers and students.

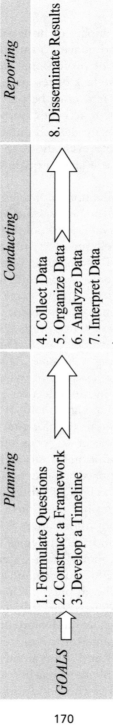

Planning	Conducting	Reporting
GOALS		
1. Formulate Questions 2. Construct a Framework 3. Develop a Timeline	4. Collect Data 5. Organize Data 6. Analyze Data 7. Interpret Data	8. Disseminate Results

Figure 7.1. Evaluating professional development.

PROFESSIONAL DEVELOPMENT THROUGH SUPERVISION

Principals engage teachers in the supervisory process to help them build capacity that leads to improved student learning. In doing so, they make frequent classroom visits, collect data, and share those data in the first step of the diagnostic cycle. The information gleaned from classroom observations and other forms of assessment is used to identify problems, diagnose their causes, devise plans of action, implement the action plans with support, and reassess classroom behaviors. This is truly classroom-imbedded professional development.

Plans of action include both individuals and groups of teachers with common needs to grow and develop their pedagogy. The collective expertise of teacher professionals in every school is an untapped resource. Ongoing support and collaborative learning for teachers can result in improved learning for their students. But teachers must have meaningful opportunities to talk, not only to their principal, but to their teacher colleagues about their teaching, their learning, and meeting common goals (Roberts & Pruitt, 2009). Our model generates reflective dialogue, a focus on student learning, and constant interactions among and between teachers and principals—a community of professional learners.

The processes of supervision, professional development, and teacher growth become systemic and cyclical. Feedback throughout the process is ongoing and creates a spiral of knowledge that leads to improvement of the system, which in turn leads to continued improvement of teaching practices and the implementation of proven instructional strategies, and teachers become immersed in their own learning (Clement & Vandenberghe, 2001; Dudney, 2002; Klinger, Ahwee, Pilonieta, & Menendez, 2003; Roberts & Pruitt, 2009; Sawyer, 2001).

During the supervisory process, principals use their knowledge of classroom curricula and research-based, high-yield practices to help teachers build capacity and increase their effectiveness with students. Principals also involve the entire faculty in this process, encouraging teachers to learn from one another. Throughout the supervisory process, these principals monitor implementation of action plans, evaluate their success, and provide adequate time to determine their long-term impact. Effective principals use research-based strategies, such as modeling, in working with teachers to develop action plans within the diagnostic cycle and provide appropriate resources for collaboration and planning.

Research reveals that the transfer of new initiatives to classroom practice occurs when teachers are shown how specific strategies are implemented through modeling within the context of their classroom. When concepts and demonstrations are given in contrived settings, less than 15% transfers to classroom practice as opposed to over 80% transfer when it occurs in the classroom context (Joyce & Showers, 2003). Administrative follow-up and ongoing discussions on the use of the strategies are also imperative for transfer to practice. If teachers do not use a newly introduced strategy or initiative within several weeks, the likelihood of use significantly decreases. Therefore, an emphasis on modeling and follow-through of strategies is critical to the staff development process. When principals facilitate the learning of teachers, they impact the learning of students and increase the overall success of their schools. In the final analysis, professional development that is embedded in the supervisory process has the greatest potential to make a difference in student learning (DuFour, 2004).

SCHOOL AND DISTRICT INITIATIVES

School– or district–based staff development is a common strategy used to help teachers improve their practice. Such development may be effective when school or district reform initiatives are being implemented. Most often mandatory professional development training is provided for all teachers so they "learn" the standards, curriculum, and instructional strategies and are equipped to implement them with their students. One of the greatest challenges in providing professional development at a school or district level is to keep the development embedded in the classrooms. That is, whatever knowledge or skills are to be mastered should be learned in the context of the job. Principals and staff development personnel are charged to assess the needs for professional development among teachers, define what professional development is and determine effective models for groups of teachers that will have a positive impact on student achievement. However, professional development that occurs as individual teachers work with their principals during supervision to solve problems in their own classrooms has the most promise for sustained change in teacher behavior and improvement in student learning (DuFour, 2004). In designing professional development, Fullan (2001) underscores the importance of developing not only the explicit knowledge of teachers and leaders, but developing applied knowledge as well. Applied knowledge means the learner understands not only know what to do, but also what to do at the right time and for the right reason.

School and district professional development should also be clearly linked to district-defined expectations for teacher performance, research-based best practices, content area standards, and the needs of the student learners (Dudney, 2002; Guskey, 2000; Klinger et al., 2003). However, providing these links at the front end of professional development is not enough. The implementation and impact on student learning of the instructional strategies presented during professional development must also be evaluated (Guskey, 2000).

Literature related to school reform and "reformed" schools also provides insight into school-based staff development practices. Capacity in classrooms was strengthened by the improved performance of the teachers. The content of staff development activities was centered on planning lessons, evaluating student work, and developing curriculum. Pedagogy was a central focus in reformed schools and was the center of the school's staff development plan. All efforts in reformed schools demonstrated an emphasis on improving instruction (Darling-Hammond, 2006; Goodlad, 1994; Johnson & Asera, 1999; Penuel, Fishman, Yamaguchi, & Gallagher, 2007; Sindelar, Shearer, Yendol-Hoppey, & Liebert, 2006).

Professional Learning Communities

Professional development at the school or district level should foster professional interactions among colleagues. In doing so, professional relations are enhanced at the collective level as teachers interact and form groups of professional learners. These groups become learning communities as they continually seek to find answers to enhance student learning and as they develop a culture that reinforces professional development and collective inquiry and supports innovation to improve student learning (Louis, Kruse, & Marks, 1996; Roberts & Pruitt, 2009; Senge, 1990).

School improvement is linked to the school's capacity to deliver job-embedded staff development (TTCIE, 2007). If the capacity of the school to provide quality staff development were limited, then positive change in school improvement did not result. In order to improve the capacity for change in schools, teachers were first trained to reflect on teaching practices, collaborate with other teachers, and work in groups to identify and solve problems.

In high-performing schools, staff development has also been clearly linked to the school improvement plan. Educators in high-performing, high-poverty schools emphasized collective responsibility in helping students become successful. The goal of professional development is to build teacher capacity. Capacity is the ability to help all students learn and meet expectations. Increased teacher capacity linked to the mission of improving student learning can provide the desired outcome—higher student achievement (Comer, 1997; Johnson & Asera, 1999; McDiarmid & Clevenger-Bright, 2008).

Principals in high-performing schools play an important role within the context of how staff development is implemented. These schools have principals who

- engage in instructional support efforts on a daily basis
- persist through difficulties and setbacks
- create opportunities for teachers to work, plan, and learn together
- provide teachers with resources and training perceived necessary to increase student learning (Johnson & Asera, 1999).

These principals give teachers discretion over decisions that enable them to organize in ways that increase their ability to serve students. The goal is to create professional learning communities in which the staff learns together to engage in collective efforts to improve student learning (Roberts & Pruitt, 2009). When a school becomes a professional learning community, its members become interdependent, sharing values and beliefs; they work in a collegial manner to achieve increased learning for all students. In professional learning communities, principals share the supervisory role with teacher colleagues, especially master teachers. Teachers observe one another, engage in a collegial supervisory process such as our model of classroom supervision and the diagnostic cycle to develop plans of action, implement them, and evaluate their success. Professionals support one another and build a culture that enhances collective inquiry, encourages risk-taking, and promotes professional growth for all members of the school's learning community (McLaughlin & Talbert, 2006).

Professional development in successful districts builds well-trained cadres of instructional experts among the teacher and principal corps. Principals are not expected to lead by themselves, and teachers do not work in isolation. The cadre of instructional experts assists teachers and principals in improving practice. In successful districts, mentors are provided to assist new teachers; districts also provide teachers and principals with better data and with more assistance to analyze and use data to guide instructional practice.

With district reform, not only must collaboration take place in each school, each school must build a support framework for other schools in the district. Feedback for low-performing schools needs to include not only the kind of service delivery needed, but input on how to deliver staff development effectively (Carter, 2000; Comer, 1997; Johnson & Asera, 1999). Time must be provided for teachers to plan and work collaboratively. Reflective practice is encouraged, and teachers support each other in these practices. Master teachers lead peer supervision, encourage team teaching, devise internal assessment measures, and keep the mission of the school focused on academic achievement. Teachers evaluate how productive their teaching is in reaching desired outcomes (Carter, 2000; McLaughlin & Talbert, 2006).

In this era of standards and accountability, some districts have focused on systemic district-level reform in which the instructional efforts of the district are more centralized and more support is provided to schools. That is, the central office directs instruction through the implementation of a uniform curriculum framework and assessment program. The roles of central office personnel change in the staff development process. In order for districts to support professional learning communities, they must provide ongoing assessment data to teachers and principals and train them to use the data to diagnose problems. Successful districts establish coherent district-organized strategies to improve instruction (Togneri & Anderson, 2003).

THEORY INTO PRACTICE

ISLLC STANDARDS 1, 2, 3, 5

As principal, how would you encourage the development of professional learning communities in your school? Would you have only one learning community or several? Why? Be specific and describe the nature and character of the communities. Where would you begin? Whom would you enlist for help? Why? How important are learning communities? Why?

NATIONAL AND STATE TRENDS

In response to wide disparities in student proficiency as measured under the No Child Left Behind Act (NCLB, 2002), the Common Core State Standards (CCSS) were developed to provide meaningful and comprehensive comparisons of student performance and achievement among states (ASCD, 2012). The CCSS initiative was conceived to identify and develop college- and career-readiness standards that address what students are expected to know and be able to do when they graduate from high school. The adoption of the CCSS by the vast majority of the states creates an urgency for the professional development of principals and teachers to acquire a deep understanding of the standards and strategies to implement them. Implementing the standards with fidelity has the potential to change the learning and teaching paradigm—and consequently the learning experience of students in most classrooms (ASCD, 2012). Quality professional development that addresses the learning required by the CCSS is:

- scaffolded—begins with basic concepts like "instructional shifts," and then progresses to ongoing engagement delving into the deeper content demands and pedagogy strategies associated with the standards
- grounded in needs of diverse learners—focused on developing teacher skill in differentiating CCSS-aligned instruction for students at a range of levels, with a variety of learning styles and among special populations of students (e.g., English language learners, special education students, gifted and talented students)
- engaging and supportive for teachers—builds working relationships and maintains instructional time while meaningfully engaging educators in using CCSS-aligned professional development.

The current demand that schools graduate *all* students with the complex intellectual skills required to compete successfully in the global society seem daunting. We know a great deal about how students learn, yet classroom practices generally fail to reflect the pedagogy for those principles of learning (Donovan & Bransford, 2005). The challenges for professional development require substantial learning resources. To meet contemporary expectations, professional development must help teachers:

- plan instruction to highlight and reinforce the cognitive skills that are expected outcomes for all students
- work successfully with students from diverse cultural, ethnic, and economic backgrounds
- refocus their roles as facilitators of problem solving and developers of students' knowledge (McLaughlin & Talbert, 2006).

The move toward a more uniform and centralized instructional program like the CCSS can only be successful by building the capacity of all principals and teachers as they work to deliver quality, research-based instructional programs. This capacity building is greatly enhanced through intensive professional staff development efforts. Unless principals and teachers can work together to come to a common understanding of the new standards, develop research-based instructional strategies to implement them, reflect on the successes and failures of their practice, and learn from one another, professional development efforts will fail (McLaughlin & Talbert, 2006). State reform strategies that have not included substantial efforts to improve the nature and quality of classroom practices have shown little success in raising student achievement (Darling-Hammond, 2000).

IMPACT ON STUDENT ACHIEVEMENT

Does professional development make a difference? If so, what is its impact? The answer is complicated and depends on the purpose of the activity as well as the method of delivery (Kerka, 2003). Belzer (2003) defines impact as a change in classroom practice and the attitudes of participants. Both of these are easily assessed using our supervisory model. Most often, however, assessing the impact on actual classroom practice and teacher attitudes takes months, possibly years. Additionally, determining a causal link between a particular training event and student achievement may be difficult, if not impossible (Kerka, 2003). Hattie (2009) performed a meta-analysis of 537 studies on the effects of professional development on student achievement and concluded that professional development can have a high positive impact.

The impact of professional development on student achievement, however, is difficult to measure because of the various factors contributing to student learning. For example, socioeconomic status, family dynamics, attendance rates, teacher turnover, overall school culture and climate, and other contextual variables are some of the other factors impacting student achievement. To credit one event or one program with significant impact is difficult when so many variables are involved. Also, the impact on student achievement may not be evident for some time after a particular event. Isolating that one event as a causal factor is not realistic (Kerka, 2003). The bottom line is that it is difficult to link specific development programs to increased student achievement.

SUMMARY

Principals use professional development to help teachers become more effective. Professional development takes many forms, but regardless of the form, the goal is clear: to build capacity of teachers to help students learn. There are three foci for professional development: improving classroom content, that is, deepening understanding of the subject and how that content can be applied to classroom practice; improving process, that is, activities that increase pedagogy through which content is provided; and enriching context, that is, the classroom environment in which the activities occur.

The process of supervision provides job-embedded professional development at the individual level. This chapter develops professional development at the group level. Whereas supervision is a one-on-one interaction, professional development typically connotes learning in a group process. The traditional notion of professional development is in-service training in the form of workshops and conferences. The grim reality is that this kind of professional development has been a dismal failure.

Effective professional development, whether at the individual or group level, has a number of distinctive attributes. First, it is a continuous and integral part of a systematic program to improve teaching and learning. Inherent in that process is the use of data to evaluate success. Professional development comes in a variety of forms, but successful development requires time and resources, accommodates diversity, and promotes equity. Ultimately, professional development improves teacher content knowledge, increases their pedagogical skills, and produces high levels of student learning.

There are, however, a number of impediments to professional development of teachers, which the principal needs to guard against. Too often teachers select interesting but irrelevant topics for their development or select activities based on the location of a conference rather than the substance of the workshop. One-shot programs for everyone are rarely successful, and the truth of the matter is that effective professional development programs require careful planning, time, and money. Follow-up and reinforcement of new activities is usually as important as initial experience.

Any program of professional development should be continuously evaluated in terms of the goals of the program. Such evaluation includes three phases. First, a coherent plan for evaluation should be developed in which evaluation questions are formulated, a framework constructed, and a timeline set. Next, the evaluation is conducted; data are collected, organized, analyzed, and interpreted. Finally, the results of the evaluation are reported and disseminated.

Professional development takes two forms: individual and group. The individual form is supervision of instruction as we have developed it in the previous chapters. The group form typically involves a grade level, department, school, or district. Group professional development fosters professional interaction among colleagues. As teachers interact in groups, they form professional learning communities, which seek to find ways to enhance student learning, and they develop a culture that reinforces collective inquiry and risk taking to improve student learning.

Principals have an important role in high quality professional development programs. Research shows that such principals engage in instructional support on a daily basis, persist when things get difficult, create opportunities for teachers to work together, and provide teachers with the necessary resources and training to be successful (Drago-Severson, 2004).

There are a number of school improvement models for staff development. First, instructional enhancement models sharpen the focus on teaching. Second, professional leadership models create new roles for teachers such as mentors, coaches, and curriculum developers. Finally, program development models limit outside staff development and promote the expertise of staff within. Staff training is embedded in the job and becomes an integral part of the school improvement plan.

Without question, adoption of the CCSS has a profound influence on professional development. In order to meet implementation deadlines, both principals and teachers need intensive professional development to acquire a deep understanding of the standards as well as strategies to implement them successfully. In order to have a chance of being successful, professional development programs must be classroom focused, aligned with the new learning standards, and research-based.

If professional development programs are to make a difference in student learning, then they should be embedded in the practice of teaching, encourage professional learning communities, and make supervision an authentic and collegial activity rather than a hollow ritual.

A PRINCIPAL'S PROFESSIONAL DEVELOPMENT CHALLENGE

Instructions—Read the following account provided by a principal, reflect on her practice, and perform a case analysis.

I was appointed the principal of a "failing" elementary school with 400 students in a suburban school district. Teachers and staff were all working hard, yet students' standardized test scores were abysmal. The school had a bimodal distribution of students (over 50% free and reduced lunch generally living in low-rent housing and at the other end of the spectrum, children from the most exclusive neighborhood in town). Some of the more educated and affluent parents were sending their children to private schools. We were losing enrollment. The demographics indicated that approximately 60% of the students who entered school in kindergarten did not complete their fifth grade year at this school. Student mobility, poverty, and mix of majority to minority students posed a huge problem. The divide was evident the minute you entered the school. It was evident when you spoke with parents, majority and minority alike, and when you spoke or listened to the students. The community perception was very negative as well because there had been many unflattering stories in the local newspaper about the school's struggles with academics and behavioral issues. Something had to be done.

I initiated discussions with teachers individually and at team meetings. It became evident that the instructional focus varied among teachers, even the same grade level. They were teaching, but their focus was random at best. I also reviewed the curriculum. With the assistance of the school's reading specialist, an outside facilitator from central office, and a great taped series from ASCD, we began a systematic review of our school's curriculum. Some teachers were resistant at first because they were losing their planning periods; there were many morning meetings before school and additional team meetings.

The pay off came with the first "Aha" moment. Several grade levels were working together to analyze what they were teaching by month and by subject. We had a longitudinal chart up in the room, and it was visible that in September and October, several grade levels and teachers had a two-week unit on apples. When this unit was compared to or aligned with the district's curriculum and state's learning standards, the apple was no where to be found! This was a wonderfully enjoyable unit for teachers and students but had no relevance across the kindergarten to second-grade span. Teachers began to find more and more areas that did not align. When this endeavor first began, the staff questioned why central office mandated what they wanted taught. In the end, it was the staff actually plowing through the curricula, making wall charts and timelines, and really reading and discussing each objective that provided the biggest growth for teachers and a huge payoff for students and the school. By spring, the hallways were filled with curriculum maps! Each grade level had developed a curriculum map that was disseminated to parents. New parents and visitors were handed curriculum maps so they knew immediately what unit was being studied. The main hallway had a huge chart for each grade level and it was clear to everyone what was to be taught in each grade and each subject and how the units of study related to the objectives of the state learning standards.

These displays were a visible sign to assure parents and visitors that the school was indeed teaching what was required. Teachers could speak with authority about the curriculum because they had in fact "unpacked" it. When the state test results arrived at the end of the year, there was a collective sigh of relief that the school passed every standard at every grade level! We were on our way to changing the image of a school from a "Can't do" to a "Can do" place for students.

REFLECTIVE PRACTICE

- What are the professional development activities that occurred in this case?
- How were the professional development activities related to student outcomes? Teacher performance?
- Assess the professional development using the criteria in Table 7.1.

- Reflect on your own recent professional development and compare it with the professional development activities in this case.
- This case depicts a problem-centered and integrated approach to professional development. Compare and contrast this case with a typical professional development program in which you have recently participated.
- As a principal, how would you connect the process of supervision with the professional development that was demonstrated in the case?

DEVELOP YOUR PORTFOLIO

You have been charged by your superintendent to increase the student achievement in your school. Although you have worked with the teachers to align the curricula with state learning standards, when you visit classrooms you don't see evidence of changes in teacher practices. Your district has state funds to help you provide an effective professional development program. In order to use these funds, however, your program design must align with best practices for professional development (see Table 7.1). Outline the content of your proposed program, strategy for delivery, the timeline, and your evaluation procedures to demonstrate that you have been successful. Be sure to illustrate how your plan aligns with best practices.

COMMUNICATION EXERCISE

Teachers in your district have traditionally determined what activities they will participate in during district-wide in-service days; that is, they have been given choices. Unfortunately, there is no evidence to suggest that the current practices are effective; in fact, most teachers admit they have no impact on their teaching. Develop a presentation that you will make to your faculty at the next regular meeting in which you will do the following:

- Describe what the literature and research suggests as an effective model for effective professional development.
- Present a rationale for change.
- Present a plan to change the professional development in your school.

READINGS

American Educational Research Association. (2005). Teaching teachers: Professional development to improve student achievement. *Research Points, 3*(1), 1–4.

DuFour, R. (2004). The best staff development is in the workplace, not in a workshop. *Journal of Staff Development, 25*(2), 63–64.

Guskey, T. R. (1995). Professional development in education: In search of the optimal mix. In T. R. Guskey & M. Huberman (Eds.), *Professional development in education* (pp. 114–131). New York, NY: Teachers College Press.

Guskey, T. R. (2003). What makes professional development effective? *Phi Delta Kappan, 84*(10), 748–750.

Harvard Family Research Project. (2004). *Promoting quality through professional development: A framework for evaluation.* Cambridge, MA: Author.

Croft, A., Coggshall, J. G., Dolan, M., Powers, E., & Killion, J. (2010). *Job-embedded professional development: What it is, who is responsible, and how to get it done well.* Washington, DC: National Comprehensive Center for Teacher Quality.

Danielson, C. (2007). *Enhancing professional practice: A framework for teaching.* Alexandria, VA: Association for Supervision & Curriculum Development.

Stiles, K. E., Mundry, S., Hewson, P. W., Loucks-Horsley, S., & Love, N. (2009). *Designing professional development for teachers of science and mathematics.* Thousand Oaks, CA: Corwin Press.

WHAT DO SUPERINTENDENTS SAY?

Do the professional development activities in your school district increase student achievement? How do you know?

Superintendent 1: The short answer is No! Most of our professional development activities are workshops, conferences, and speakers focusing on cutting edge technologies and changes in state testing requirements. We should do more systematic evaluation of these activities as they affect student achievement, but up until this point we have not. I don't think our activities are having an impact on student achievement in spite of the fact that teachers generally rate the professional activities as useful and well done. On the other hand, our test results on the state tests have been consistent for the past three years. The results are good, but they have not improved. The improvement of student achievement on these tests will become a system-wide goal for next year.

Superintendent 2: I'd like to think so. We initiated a systemic development program around professional readings that highlight research-based best practices related to increased student achievement. Principals are conducting professional meetings in each school, facilitating discussions and encouraging dialogue around the readings. They then ask teachers to demonstrate or model an "effective" practice in their classroom.

Superintendent 3: We bring in nationally recognized speakers for our district-wide in-service workshops that begin each school year. The intention is that during the remainder of the year, teachers continue to focus on that theme or strategy. We still have many individuals requesting permission and resources to attend conferences and workshops. Although we assess each request individually, we tend not to approve or encourage this type of professional development. When we do, we require that participants return to the district and conduct a workshop or information session for their colleagues to share what they have learned.

CHAPTER 8

EVALUATION

Although the functions and responsibilities of principals as supervisors and evaluators are qualitatively different (formative versus summative) and have different authority relations (informal versus formal), both processes work toward the same goals of improving teacher performance and student learning. The responsibility for identifying, planning, and providing professional growth and development is a critical element linking supervision and evaluation; the common goal is increased teacher effectiveness and student achievement.

Our model supports formative supervision as the primary means of helping teachers grow and improve professionally. We believe classroom observations should be used to collect classroom performance data to help teachers reflect on their practice and identify, with their principals, areas for improvement. Certainly summative evaluation does have a function in our model, but it is not the primary vehicle for instructional improvement. The process of evaluation, like the supervisory process, is cyclic. The length of the cycle can vary, but more typically is an annual cycle. Figure 8.1 represents a model evaluation cycle.

Improving Instruction Through Supervision, Evaluation, and Professional Development, pp. 185–206

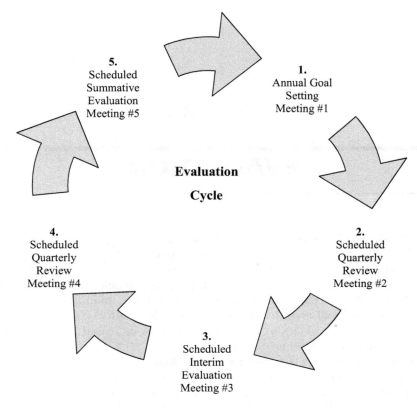

Figure 8.1.   Evaluation cycle

WHY EVALUATE?

We believe that the process of supervision holds the most promise to assist the vast majority of teachers to improve their effectiveness; however, supervision, as an informal, collegial process, cannot achieve other formal goals that summative evaluation achieves, especially:

- satisfying federal and state requirements to evaluate for quality assurance
- formally documenting the overall performance of professional staff (both in and out of the classroom)
- getting the attention of professional staff who are not interested in professional growth, are not cooperating in the supervisory process, or otherwise not behaving professionally

- obtaining the data necessary to make sound judgments concerning recommendations for contract renewal or termination of employment.

The Personnel Evaluation Standards of the Joint Committee on Standards for Educational Evaluation (2013) identifies ten distinct purposes for teacher evaluation (see Table 8.1). Others echo and modify these purposes. For example, Peterson and Peterson (2006) argue that evaluations provide positive feedback to the majority of teachers, as well as assure parents and other interested stakeholders of teacher quality. Evaluations also inform personnel decisions such as retention, assignment, advancement, and dismissal, and they provide rationales for extra duty and leadership assignments.

Despite a few discrepancies among lists, there is common agreement that the overall purposes of personnel evaluation are accountability and professional growth leading to student learning. We agree with Danielson and McGreal (2005), however, that the process of evaluation is "oversold" to educators and the public alike as a panacea to achieve both accountability and teacher growth. Decades of research lead to two general conclusions concerning teacher evaluations: First, the importance and necessity of evaluations have long been recognized by educators—they have, however, been disappointed about the process and lack of impact on teacher growth and student learning; second, when the focus of evaluation is teacher growth in a formative process of reflection and development, classroom practices have a greater chance of improving. Thus, classroom observations should be used as both formative data to drive professional development and evidence to make summative judgments about teaching quality. Constructive teacher feedback, improved teaching, and recognition can be achieved for most classroom teachers through the formative process of supervision and the summative process of evaluation.

Summative performance evaluations of professional employees in schools are required in all states. The focus on high-quality, effective teachers has never been greater. Findings that the effects of teacher quality on student learning are long-lasting with profound effects on student achievement (Chetty, Friedman, & Rockoff, 2011; Sanders, 1998) have placed a real focus on teacher quality. In this era of accountability, teacher evaluation has been emphasized and has evolved into an increasingly high-stakes activity. The public wants guarantees that their students are being instructed by quality teachers. Given increased public demand for accountability and the responsibility of protecting the rights of employees, fair, data-driven personnel evaluations are necessary.

Table 8.1.   Standards for Educational Evaluation

Propriety Standards	Utility Standards	Feasibility Standards	Accuracy Standards
Service Orientation *Is a service mission present in the standards?*	Constructive Orientation *Does evaluation help schools develop teachers and propel them to excellence?*	Practical Procedures *Is information gathered with minimal disruption and cost?*	Defined Responsibilities *Is the role of the evaluatee clear?*
Formal Guidelines *Are guidelines agreed upon and written in a formal document?*	Agreed Upon Uses *Have the uses been identified so that appropriate questions can be addressed?*	Political Viability *Is the evaluation system set up and monitored collaboratively in order for the system to work?*	Work Environment *Is the context identified, described, and recorded so that it may be considered in the evaluation?*
Process for Conflicts of Interest *Are conflicts of interest avoided?*	Evaluator Credibility *Is the evaluator qualified and professional?*	Fiscal Viability *Are time and resources provided for effective and efficient evaluation and implementation?*	Documentation of Procedures *Are procedures documented so that other users can assess the procedures?*
Accessibility of Reports *Are reports available?*	Functional Reporting *Is the report clear, timely, accurate and germane?*		Valid and Reliable Measurements *Is the information obtained accurate and consistent?*
Professional Perspectives *Is everyone protected from unfair practices that may damage?*	Follow-Up Evaluation *Do users and evaluatees understand the results and take appropriate actions?*		Systematic Data Control *Is the information used kept secure, carefully processed and maintained?*
			Fairness and Monitoring *Does the process guard against bias and is the evaluation system reviewed? Is it revised when appropriate?*

QUALITY PERSONNEL EVALUATION

Inherent in the vast majority of efforts to improve teacher evaluation are some common key components. First, quality teaching must be defined and specific teaching behaviors linked to quality. In this process, expectations for teacher performance must be clearly defined and a variety of opportunities provided that enable teachers to demonstrate teaching ability. Such opportunities should enhance teaching ability in a way most appropriate to individual teacher needs and abilities as trained evaluators provide assessment and feedback to teachers (Danielson, 2001; Danielson & McGreal, 2005; Dudney, 2002; Goldrick, 2002; Howard & McColskey, 2001; Sawyer, 2001).

Although there may be unique aspects to different professional roles (teacher, counselor, media specialist, etc.), all educational personnel have a common need—the need for fair, job-relevant, and meaningful evaluations. Unfortunately, meeting this need has not been common (Danielson & McGreal, 2005; Peterson & Peterson, 2006; Stronge, 2006). The Joint Committee on Standards for Educational Evaluation (2013) concluded that personnel evaluation has been ineffectively conducted in educational organizations despite the centrality of the process. Dominant criticisms of personnel evaluation include issues such as lack of constructive feedback, failure to recognize and reinforce outstanding service, and dividing rather than unifying collective efforts to educate students.

Evaluation needs are basic: the need for a thoughtful, thorough, and fair evaluation based on performance and designed to encourage improvement in both the person being evaluated and the school. The evaluation process should conform to the standards developed by the Joint Committee on Standards for Educational Evaluation (2013): *propriety, utility, feasibility,* and *accuracy.*

Propriety Standards

In order to conform to propriety standards, evaluations must be conducted legally, ethically, and with consideration for the welfare of those being evaluated (evaluatees) and clients of the evaluations (Joint Committee, 2013). Ultimately, the evaluative process should establish a process that directly supports the primary principle that *schools exist to serve students.* To that end, evaluation should promote and support sound educational practice that achieves the school system's mission so that educational needs of students, community, and society are met. Guidelines for the evaluations should be agreed upon and communicated in appropriate written form (e.g., negotiated contract, employee's handbook) to avoid unnecessary conflict. In addition, any conflicts of interest should be identified early and dealt with to avoid compromising the process and results of the evaluations. Finally, the results of the evaluation should be provided in a timely fashion to all personnel, and the process should always be conducted in a professional manner, one that enhances, and does not damage, reputations and performance. In sum, propriety standards should be characterized by a service orientation, formal guidelines, processes to deal with conflicts of interest, accessibility to evaluation reports, and a professional perspective.

Utility Standards

Utility standards are guides for evaluations so that they will be informative, timely, and influential (Joint Committee, 2013). The evaluation of all educators should inform decision makers regarding goal accomplishment. The collective evaluations of all employees should relate individual performance to the overarching organizational goals, including student learning (Danielson & McGreal, 2005; Stronge, 2006). This concept of utility is illuminated in five specific standards. First, the intent and practice of evaluations should be constructive in order to assist the professional educators in providing excellent service. Second, the intended uses of the evaluation process should be agreed upon in advance in order to facilitate the most appropriate design. Third, the evaluations should be conducted credibly and professionally so that the results of the evaluation are respected and used. Next, the evaluation reports should be clear, timely, accurate, and germane in order to enhance practical value. Finally, there should be appropriate follow-up to ensure that the results of the evaluation are understood and that appropriate actions are taken as needed.

Feasibility Standards

In order to meet the feasibility standards, evaluation processes must be as easy to implement as possible, efficiently utilizing time and resources, and be adequately funded (Joint Committee, 2013). An evaluation process that satisfies the feasibility standards will specifically address the various jobs within a school, while at the same time being sensitive to the practical issues (e.g., time) that relate to proper evaluation within the school system. To this end, evaluation should be planned and implemented so that the process yields needed information while minimizing disruption and costs. The evaluation should also have political viability; that is, it should be a collaborative process in both its design and implementation and have adequate resources to guarantee effective and efficient implementation. In brief, the evaluation process should be politically and fiscally viable as well as practical.

Accuracy Standards

Accuracy standards require that information be technically accurate and that conclusions be linked logically to the data (Joint Committee, 2013). Thus, evaluation should be based on well-defined job responsibilities and integrated into a system in which contextual issues are considered as part of the assessment. The use of multiple data sources, valid and reliable measures, and systematic data analysis procedures should also be included in the design of evaluations. Fairness is critical in both the evaluation process and proper training of principals who conduct the evaluations. Finally, periodic monitoring to refine and improve the process over time is essential. Table 8.1 synthesizes the Standards for Educational Evaluation.

THEORY INTO PRACTICE
ISLLC STANDARDS 2, 3, 5
Assess your own district's evaluation process in terms of the propriety, utility, feasibility, and accuracy standards (use Table 8.1). Are the evaluation guidelines clear and assessable? Are individuals protected from unfair practices? Does the evaluation focus on developing teachers? Are evaluators qualified, professional, and credible? Is your principal a skillful evaluator? Is the principal's feedback useful to you and your colleagues?

PERFORMANCE CRITERIA: THE FOUNDATION OF EVALUATION

Danielson (2001) argues that evaluation procedures should assess performance using data collected for each of the evaluative criteria while simultaneously producing teacher reflection and development. But what criteria should be used to evaluate the various school professional personnel? The foundation of an effective performance evaluation process is clear, comprehensive, and well-documented performance criteria with sufficient detail and accuracy so that everyone understands the expectations of the job. In essence, performance criteria must guarantee that the teacher (or other professional) is evaluated based on what she or he is expected to do; thus, these criteria describe the specific job expectations and serve as the cornerstone of the performance evaluation process.

Impact on Students

Evaluation systems should focus on student learning. Performance evaluations need to measure the effectiveness of school professionals, but the problem with that charge is that the definition of an effective teacher or counselor varies. Working as professional colleagues, teachers and principals must come to a common understanding of what good teaching looks like. In the past several years, research-based, high-yield instructional strategies (Hattie, 2009; Marzano, 2007) have been identified and should be reflected in the expectations of a contemporary evaluation system. Standards of exemplary practice have been established and should be used in evaluation systems.

Tucker and Stronge (2005) argue that measures of student achievement should be used to assess the quality of instruction. They believe that links between teacher classroom performance and student achievement can be assessed by the:

- quality of student work and how it reflects the outcomes specified and taught by the teacher
- level of student content knowledge during pre- and post-instruction assessments
- student progress toward annual, quantifiable academic goals
- learning gains achieved by students in relation to their growth-rates in previous years.

Another method is to evaluate teachers based on their impacts on students' test scores, commonly termed the "value-added" approach. Most contemporary models of teacher evaluation include increased student learning as a criterion of effective teaching. How exactly to assess learning contributed by individual teachers is a controversial issue. But sound evaluation requires the assessment of all aspects of teaching. Evaluation systems should focus attention on the importance of teaching and learning for students and teachers alike, but evaluation systems must meet the propriety, utility, feasibility, and accuracy standards.

DEFINING EXPECTATIONS

Job descriptions should clearly specify job expectations. Unfortunately, most often they are general, are vague, and exclude important expectations of the position. Expectations are better defined by asking the question: *What criteria are used to determine if the job responsibilities are met?*

Organizations, especially those who serve clients, like schools, depend on the professional behaviors of their employees to do what is in the best interest of their clients. Many expectations are not usually included in job descriptions. For example, expectations for the performance of some professional staff, including teachers and counselors, extend well beyond the four walls of the classroom. Consequently, it is imperative to clarify performance expectations for individuals who occupy all of the professional roles in a school.

As we see, a credible evaluation is based on the premise that both evaluators and those they evaluate know and understand all the elements of the job, the performance expectations, and how their performance will be assessed. To that end, the first step is describing and categorizing expectations into the major aspects of each job. Clearly defined professional responsibilities constitute the foundation of the teacher *performance standards*. *Performance standards* define categories of expected behaviors as teachers perform their duties. A fair and comprehensive evaluation system provides sufficient detail and accuracy so that both teachers and principals understand the job expectations for those being evaluated. *Performance indicators* under each standard describe some actual evaluatee behaviors that indicate if specific expectations were met. This two-tiered framework is a useful way to operationalize an evaluation process for both evaluators and evaluatees. For example, in Marzano's (2011) evaluation model, a classroom teacher has four major responsibilities: planning and preparing, classroom strategies and behaviors, reflecting on teaching, and collegiality and professionalism, all leading to student learning.

Other models, such as the Uniform Performance Standards of Virginia (Virginia Department of Education, 2011), are more specific in describing expectations and therefore have more performance standards. The Virginia performance standard categories include professional knowledge, instructional planning, instructional delivery, assessment of and for student learning, learning environment, professionalism, and student academic progress. Within each of the performance standards exist specific indicators of performance for teachers. Thus, performance indicators are examples of observable behaviors that indicate the degree to which teachers are meeting each performance standard.

Performance indicators specify expected teacher behaviors. Performance indicators are provided as examples of the types of performance that will occur if a standard is being fulfilled. For example, under the Instructional Delivery standard, performance indicators provide greater specification of role expectations. An example of a teacher performance indicator within the Instructional Delivery standard is: *The teacher differentiates instruction to meet the students' needs* (Virginia Department of Education,

2011, p. 10). Observable behaviors (performance indicators) constitute the most specific description of how performance will be assessed in the two-tiered hierarchy, and they can be documented and directly assessed. Several observable behaviors should be used to define each performance expectation (standard). Examples of observable behaviors for a classroom teacher in the Instructional Delivery standard are specified in Table 8.2.

Table 8.2.   Sample Performance Indicators

Examples of teacher work conducted in the performance of the standard Instructional Delivery may include, but are not limited to:

- Engages and maintains students in active learning.
- Builds upon students' existing knowledge and skills.
- Differentiates instruction to meet the students' needs.
- Reinforces learning goals consistently throughout lessons.
- Uses a variety of effective instructional strategies and resources.
- Uses instructional technology to enhance student learning.
- Communicates clearly and checks for understanding.

These performance indicators are not intended to be all-inclusive lists but rather examples of typical behaviors that indicate satisfactory performance of the specific expectation (standard). Performance is assessed using the observable behaviors that relate to the performance expectation of the job responsibilities. In sum, they need to be representative of a particular job responsibility, objectively documented and measured, and providing a representative sample of expected behaviors. A comprehensive sample of teacher performance standards and performance indicators is located in Appendix A. Although every school district has an evaluation procedure that should include expectations for performance, this comprehensive sample provides a model of one state's teacher evaluation system.

THEORY INTO PRACTICE

ISLLC STANDARDS 2, 3, 5

Assess your school district's evaluation instrument. Are the performance expectations clear? Do teachers in the district find the instrument fair and reliable? Does the instrument contain behavioral exemplars to define expectations? How objective and subjective are the expectations? How can you improve the expectations? The instrument?

DATA SOURCES IN EVALUATION

Although the foundation of an effective performance evaluation process is a comprehensive set of clearly defined performance expectations, they alone are not adequate to ensure a quality evaluation process. Performance expectations describe what the professionals are expected to do, but performance expectations do not address how professionals fulfill responsibilities or how well they do them. In other words, a good performance evaluation process provides the ways and means for documenting the performance and includes a rubric for judging that performance.

In order to execute a fair, comprehensive evaluation process, at least two issues must be resolved:

- What are appropriate information sources for documenting the professional's performance?
- How can the various information sources be integrated?

Primary reliance on formal observations in teacher evaluation presents significant problems (e.g., contrived situation, very limited sample, only occurs in classroom). Additionally, direct observation provides data on only one aspect of the performance of evaluatees—that of their own behaviors in the classroom on a given day and time—and not on their impact on student learning.

Appropriate use of multiple data sources can provide a more accurate measure of teachers' performance; this measure should be made using data that reflect the broad array of duties teachers perform as they help students learn and contribute to the overall effectiveness of the school. Therefore, a variety of data sources such as classroom observations, student achievement data, client surveys, artifacts of performance, portfolios, professional goals, and other relevant sources of information are useful.

Systematically documenting performance in a variety of settings using a variety of means enhances the breadth and depth of both the evaluatee's and the evaluator's understanding of performance strengths and weaknesses. However, for data sources to be acceptable, they must meet the tests of logic, reliability, fairness, and legality (Peterson, 1995). For example, consider the following important questions:

- Are the data the responsibility of the individual being evaluated?
- Do the data reflect the person's responsibilities described in the job description?
- Are the data linked to student learning and other key classroom tasks?

- Are the data of primary importance in judging quality?
- Are there better data available?

A sound evaluation process is based on actual performance data collected through multiple means that are representative of the professional's total performance, thus using a comprehensive data set. Multiple data sources provide for a comprehensive and authentic "performance portrait" of the professional's work. A three-year study supports combining three types of measures: classroom observations, student surveys, and student achievement gains in evaluating teachers (Bill & Melinda Gates Foundation, 2013). The sources of information described in Table 8.3 provide a comprehensive and accurate feedback on professional performance.

Table 8.3.   Data Sources for Documenting Teacher Performance

Direct Observation
Goal Setting
Student Achievement
Client Surveys
Review Artifacts of Performance

PERFORMANCE GOALS

One method to employ in measuring progress for student learning or other expected outcomes is establishing annual performance goals. These performance goals should be aimed at desirable, yet realistic, improvement targets that are congruent with the student needs. Once established, the goals can be reviewed and adjusted as necessary.

With the use of performance goals, the professional typically reports progress on achieving the goals at regular intervals throughout the evaluation process. Indicators of goal attainment include documentation via oral and written reports, as well as other relevant evidence; objective data are better than subjective judgments. When actual measures of student achievement data are used, contextual factors, often beyond the teacher's control, should be considered.

DOCUMENT REVIEW

Analyses of artifacts (i.e., the collection of written records and documents produced under the professional's auspices as a part of his or her job responsibilities) are also important in evaluation. Artifacts for a counselor, for example, might include correspondence to parents; group counseling agendas; reports of sessions; logs of individuals counseling session; and records of communication with parents, community members, and social service agencies. Artifacts for classroom teachers include planning documents, assessments, examples of student products, and logs of contacts with parents.

A portfolio is a formal collection of documents—or artifacts—that are useful for demonstrating the performance of the professional. Portfolio evaluation involves the systematic collection of data concerning the fulfill-ment of the duties or responsibilities of the professional. Sample items include journal notes, newspaper clippings, programs from various activi-ties organized, results of action research, events and functions attended, and accounts of professional activities and publications. The portfolio provides a forum for dialogue on the full scope of responsibilities for the professional's job and provides additional information that may not be available in any other form.

CLIENT SURVEYS

In virtually every school district in America, principals receive feedback, often unsolicited, regarding particular programs, events, and personnel. The feedback can come in e-mails, telephone calls, casual conversations in the grocery store, or a variety of other informal venues. In the absence of a more systematic method for collecting perceptions of stu-dents, parents, staff or community members, these anecdotal comments can form the basis of the principal's impression of the perceptions of the performance of an individual. In recent years, there has been a growing movement for educators to adopt *360-degree* assessment principles. The 360-degree evaluation is often used in private-sector human resource management. It is a process for evaluating individuals' performance based on feedback from everyone with whom they come in contact—supervisors, coworkers, partners, subordinates, and the general public. For use with teachers, it would require collecting input data from admin-istrators, colleagues, students, and parents (Manatt, 2000; Peterson & Peterson, 2006; Stronge, 2006). Client-centered feedback provides an avenue for the principal to receive systematic and representative feed-back regarding overall performance.

Both students and parents have the ability to provide other perspec-tives that principals cannot obtain. In fact, research reveals that principals and parents emphasize different components of a teacher's job. Parents focus on how teachers communicate and work with their children, whereas principals focus on classroom behavior and performance of administrative tasks. Peterson (1988) cautioned, however, that although data provided by parents of elementary students are on target, less contact and communication between teachers and the parents of secondary students result "in more global or halo ratings for the teachers of older students" (p. 247). Samples of student surveys can be found in Appendix A2. Although costs and procedures must be considered, the challenge is to collect survey data that are reliable, valid, and fair.

Reliability

Does the client survey provide consistent results? Surveys used for students or parents to provide data on the performance of professionals must meet the challenges of consistent, stable feedback. Research has demonstrated that "student ratings of teachers are consistent among students and reliable from one year to the next" (Peterson, 2000, p. 106). Large samples, careful selection of participants, and representativeness of the sample are important considerations.

Validity

Does the survey measure what it purports to measure? Professionals often question the ability of students or parents to provide valid data about professional performance. Three factors of their concern are:

- how well the rating scales capture the nature of effective teaching
- the students' ability to accurately perceive what is going on in the classroom
- biases that might affect the accuracy of the students' judgment (Alkin, 1992).

A review of the research on student survey data, however, found that students in fact do a credible job in providing valid data. It is obvious, but important, that only job-related questions should be asked that the respondents are in a position to answer (Stronge & Ostrander, 2006).

Fairness

The goal of using client surveys is to gather factual descriptions of the individual behavior and performance (Stronge & Helm, 1991, p. 193).

Therefore, only individuals who can provide valid information should be surveyed. Students and parents have different kinds of experiences with educational professionals; thus, questions must be specifically designed to address those behaviors and performances on which they have reliable information. Haphazard sampling should be avoided; systematic sampling is important for both the validity and reliability of the information.

STUDENT ACHIEVEMENT DATA

The use of student achievement data in the evaluation process is controversial (Berk, 1988; Sacks, 1999), but such data are invaluable (Tucker & Stronge, 2001). How can the assessment of teacher effectiveness be valid without assessing student learning? Student data address expected learning outcomes and, if used wisely and carefully, can provide valuable feedback to teachers. Not surprisingly, there is compelling evidence that effective teaching is the most significant factor in student learning (Mendro, 1998; Nye, Konstantopoulos, & Hedges, 2004; Rivkin, Hanushek, & Kain, 2001; Wright et al., 1997). The use of student achievement data ensures that evaluations hold teachers accountable while providing feedback that can be used to help teachers improve their effectiveness. The current trend toward value-added or growth models attempt to measure the impact of each teacher on students' test scores (Chetty et al., 2011). Proponents support the use of value-added factors as the basis for teacher evaluations (Bill & Melinda Gates Foundation, 2010, 2013). Opponents question the value of student achievement data as a significant component of teacher evaluations. They argue that research "casts substantial doubt on the utility of student test score gains as a measure of teacher effectiveness" (Rothstein, 2011, p. 3).

Significant obstacles to the fair and effective use of achievement data in the evaluation process exist. Consider, for example, the absence or lack of availability of good tests, multiple-year data, multiple-year scores, and the inability to match student data with teachers over time. In addition, many achievement tests are not accurate at high and low ends. Also, experts disagree on the concept of degree high-stakes achievement testing (Peterson & Peterson, 2006). Currently it is difficult to collect technically defensible pupil achievement data for those pre-K–3 students in schools with high turnover student populations, and for extremely high- or low-performance students.

In an attempt to address concerns of inappropriate uses of achievement data in the evaluation process, Tucker and Stronge (2006) propose a series of recommended practices to increase the fairness, accuracy, and usefulness of data, which are summarized in Table 8.4.

Table 8.4.   Recommended Practices to Increase the Fairness, Accuracy, and Usefulness of Data

Use student learning as only one component of a teacher assessment system that is based on multiple data sources.

Use fair and valid measures of student learning.

Recognize that gain scores have inherent liabilities (e. g. regression to the mean, ceiling effect).

Use measures of student gain or growth versus a fixed achievement standard or achievement status, but recognize that value-added models of teacher need further research and have limitations.

Consider the context in which teaching and learning occur when judging teacher effectiveness.

Compare learning gains from one point in time to another for the same students, not different groups of students.

Use a time frame for teacher assessment that allows for patterns of student learning to be documented.

Use measures of student learning to focus on improvement in teaching, learning, and schooling as a whole.

Measures of student learning have the potential to provide valuable feedback on the achievement of individual students, the instructional effectiveness of specific teachers, and the soundness of instructional strategies and programs. The standard catalogues of teacher performance descriptions are no substitute for using good student achievement data (Peterson & Peterson, 2006). When good student achievement data are available, use those data. When such data are not available, develop the means to get it, and involve teachers in the process.

THEORY INTO PRACTICE

ISLLC STANDARDS 2, 3, 5

What sources of data are used in your school district to evaluate the performance of teachers? Are they adequate? Are they useful, reliable, and valid? What other sources of data might be used to improve the quality of the judgments? How would your colleagues react to the suggestion that students and parents provide data on teacher performance? What is your candid opinion on the matter? Are standardized achievement scores reliable and useful standards to judge teacher performance?

SUMMARY

During the summative process of evaluation, principals make overall assessments of the effectiveness of educational professionals in their schools. In doing so, principals identify strengths and areas for improvement and assist teachers and other professionals in developing a plan of action for improvement. The process of evaluation, like the supervisory process, is cyclic. The length of the cycle varies, but teachers are generally on annual cycles.

The process of evaluation is necessary to achieve goals that cannot be achieved through supervision. Remember supervision is informal, formative, and supportive, and the goal is to help teachers improve. Evaluation, however, is formal, summative, and judgmental, and the goal is to rate and assess the competence of teachers. Consider the following evaluation demands:

- satisfying federal and state requirements to evaluate for quality assurance
- formally documenting the overall performance of professional staff (both in and out of the classroom)
- getting the attention of professional staff who are not interested in professional growth, are not cooperating in the supervisory process, or otherwise not behaving professionally
- obtaining the data necessary to make sound judgments concerning recommendations for contract renewal or termination of employment.

Although evaluations are performed in virtually every school in the nation, the quality and results of evaluation vary greatly and most often do not meet the two minimum goals of accountability and improving effectiveness. In order to meet these goals of evaluation, evaluations must conform to the standards of *propriety, utility, feasibility,* and *accuracy.* Useful evaluations are grounded in the actual performance duties of each individual. Fair and accurate judgments of the overall effectiveness of a professional require reliable, valid data from multiple sources. Conforming to these minimal standards and goals ensures viable, constructive, and defensible evaluation process.

A PRINCIPAL'S SUPERVISORY CHALLENGE

Instructions—Read the following account provided by a principal, reflect on her practice, and perform a case analysis.

I was hired as the new principal of Xavier Middle School at the beginning of the school year. I was familiar with the culture, climate, and makeup of Xavier Middle because I had worked at the school as an assistant principal just two years prior. While the student demographics had not changed since my departure (population of 1,100 students—55% Caucasian, 45% minority, 45% on free/reduced lunch), there were several faculty members new to the school.

One new teacher was Tracey Cooper, a seventh-grade mathematics teacher. Ms. Cooper was beginning her third year of teaching at Xavier Middle. In the summer, I reviewed evaluations from her previous administrators, and found that on paper Ms. Cooper was a teacher who was rated *slightly above average* when compared to her peers. For example, while her previous principal rated her *satisfactory* in the majority of the job responsibilities on the teacher evaluation instrument, there were several ratings of *exemplary* in such areas as *professionalism* and *rapport with students*.

When I recall my first conversation with Ms. Cooper, which occurred during an impromptu meeting a week before all teachers were scheduled to arrive, I found it strange that her first statement to me was, "Hi. I'm Tracey Cooper, and I teach math on Team 7-2. Just a heads-up, my room is always pretty noisy, but I want you to know that my kids get results." I smiled, introduced myself, and informed Ms. Cooper that I looked forward to working with her and visiting her classroom.

By the end of the second week of school, I had made several visits to Ms. Cooper's classroom. The visits were informal ones, stopping for 5 to 10 minutes during each visit. In my opinion, it appeared that Ms. Cooper was off to a relatively reasonable start, but true to her warning her classroom was always chaotic—noisy, disorganized, and confusing.

During the third week of school, I conducted an unscheduled formal observation in Ms. Cooper's classroom. It was during this observation when my concerns regarding Ms. Cooper's ability to teach crystallized. Specifically, Ms. Cooper was weak in her classroom management skills and instructional strategies. For example, student conversations were being held while she was providing direct instruction, and Ms. Cooper seemed completely oblivious to the problem. In addition, the pacing of the lesson was inappropriate and at no time did Ms. Cooper check for student understanding prior to assigning the homework for the evening.

Of the 18 job responsibilities listed in our teacher evaluation system, I was able to observe 12 of them during my first formal observation of Ms. Cooper's class. While I assessed performance on eight of the responsibilities documented to be *satisfactory*, three ratings of responsibilities were *needs improvement* and one rating was *unsatisfactory*. Ms. Cooper and I met the following afternoon to discuss the observed lesson.

During the post-observation conference, I provided specific feedback to Ms. Cooper in reference to the concerns I had regarding her lesson. According to Ms. Cooper, she was unaware of any deficiencies she had in the areas of classroom management or instructional skills. While she admitted the lesson I observed was not her best lesson, she became defensive when I shared the ratings of *needs improvement* and *unsatisfactory*. Ms. Cooper stated that, based on previous administrators' observations, she had always received good ratings regarding her performance in the classroom. Ms. Cooper also informed me that I would be impressed by her students' performance on the benchmark tests that would be administered at the end of the quarter. I then shared with Ms. Cooper that, based on district policy, the one rating of *unsatisfactory* she received necessitated that a performance improvement plan (PIP) be initiated.

Ms. Cooper and I met at the beginning of the following week to discuss the PIP. I wanted this to be a collaborative process. Although I knew there were several strategies that I would certainly include in the plan, I wanted Ms. Cooper to be able to provide some input as well. For example, one component that Ms. Cooper wanted to include in the plan was the opportunity for her to observe some teachers outside of the building. This strategy was incorporated into the plan, along with components such as submitting lesson plans for approval ahead of time, using a rubric to scan the classroom for inappropriate student behaviors during lessons (to be submitted daily for each core), videotaping her lessons periodically in an effort to self-reflect on targeted areas of concern, and conducting walk-through observations with building administrators in an effort to learn from some of the veteran teachers in the building.

A target date in about a month and a half was set to review the PIP and Ms. Cooper's performance, particularly in the identified areas of concern. When this date arrived I found it necessary, based on a lack of progress of specific objectives outlined in the PIP, to continue with the plan. For example, after several additional formal classroom observations, Ms. Cooper's students' results on benchmarks were low. Moreover, she exhibited an overall lack of concern regarding specific requirements listed in the PIP. Clearly, adequate progress had not yet been made.

I recall feeling disappointed that Ms. Cooper was not only not willing to follow the plan as agreed upon, but that she simply was not taking the matter seriously. It was at this point when I began to think about moving forward with a decision of nonrenewal of her contract, particularly because this is the year she would gain tenure if her contract were renewed. Following several additional weeks of unsatisfactory improvement of Ms. Cooper's classroom performance, I began to compile the documentation I would need to present to my supervisor in the near future.

I was fully aware of the district's policy regarding the dismissal of non-tenured and tenured teachers. I was also confident in the case I was preparing. First, I knew that I had approached Ms. Cooper's PIP from the standpoint that I, as her evaluator, wanted to support her in hopes of enabling her to become a better teacher by improving in areas of deficiency. Second, I knew it would be obvious from the documentation that Ms. Cooper neither took the PIP seriously nor did she put forth much effort to remedy the situation. Third, all steps outlined in the district's policy regarding PIPs were followed and all timelines were adhered to throughout the process.

I presented my case to the superintendent's designated panel during the last week of February. Because I knew what the state code required regarding the dismissal of nontenured teachers, I was confident that the case I presented was a solid one and that my recommendation to move forward with the nonrenewal of Ms. Cooper's contract would be supported.

A great deal of the discussion from the panel focused on the observations from previous administrators. Questions such as, "I wonder why she seems to be having a hard time this year?" and, "Why do you think it was that she never had a rating below *satisfactory* before this year?" Suddenly the discussion shifted to my evaluation. Based primarily on previous administrators' observations, the panel then began to question whether or not the teacher needed more time to rectify the noted deficiencies.

Following a lengthy discussion, the panel eventually agreed to move forward with a recommendation to the superintendent of nonrenewal. In reflecting upon the situation, I could not help but imagine how difficult this process would have been had Ms. Cooper been a tenured teacher. As a principal, we need to take an honest approach toward the process of teacher evaluation. Inflating ratings and providing meaningless feedback to teachers do nothing to improve the performance of poor teachers. In addition, such practices make it nearly impossible to successfully remove incompetent teachers from the profession.

REFLECTIVE PRACTICE

Assess the effectiveness of this principal by reflecting on her practice. What happened to this teacher? Was it fair? If a school gives a new teacher two years of good evaluations, and then a new principal views her work as unsatisfactory, what should be done?

If you were confronted by the challenge of working with this teacher, what would you have done? Be sure to consider the following:

- Was this teacher provided enough time to improve?
- Did the teacher get a fair shake?
- How much credibility do you give to your predecessor's evaluations?
- Should you talk to your predecessor about this teacher? Why?
- Is this teacher beyond help? Can you get an experienced master teacher to help her? Should you?
- Was this principal too tough? Did the principal take the easy way out?
- What would you do differently in evaluating this teacher?

DEVELOP YOUR PORTFOLIO

Observe a colleague teaching and use your district's evaluation instrument to assess the effectiveness of the teaching. Then use the sample instrument found in Appendix A to assess the effectiveness. Contrast the two instruments and their ability to provide specific feedback about strengths and weaknesses. As a principal, which would you prefer? Why? Include copies of the results of both assessments along with your analyses of both tools.

COMMUNICATION EXERCISE

Select either the instrument used by your district *or* one in the appendix. Prepare a presentation for new teachers in which you provide a clear explanation of the instrument. Be sure that you articulate expectations. For example, don't simply tell teachers that "they should plan well." Explain what good planning is and provide examples. Your goal is for the teachers to leave confident that they know what the expectations are and how they will be used to assess their teaching performance.

READINGS

Danielson, C., & McGreal, T. L. (2000). *Teacher evaluation: To enhance teacher professional practice.* Alexandria, VA: Association for Supervision and Curriculum Development.

Goldrick, L. (2002). *Improving teacher evaluation to improve teaching quality.* Issue Brief. Washington, DC: National Governors Association Center for Best Practices.

Peterson, K. D. (2000). *Teacher evaluation: A comprehensive guide to new directions and practices* (2nd ed.). Thousand Oaks, CA: Corwin Press.

Stronge, J. H., & Tucker, P. D. (2003). *Handbook on teacher evaluation: Assessing and improving performance*. Larchmont, NY: Eye on Education.

Tucker, P. D., & DeSander, M. (2006). Legal considerations in designing teacher evaluation systems. In J. H. Stronge (Ed.), *Evaluating teaching: A guide to current thinking and best practice* (2nd ed., pp. 69–97). Thousand Oaks, CA: Corwin Press.

WHAT DO SUPERINTENDENTS SAY?

Is the process of evaluation used in your school district effective in identifying incompetent teachers?

Superintendent 1: Yes, our evaluation procedures are clear and we identify weak teachers early. Our goal is to make sure that incompetent teachers don't get tenure. I admit that we have a few incompetent teachers who have tenure, but we have done a good job recently to award tenure only those teachers who show promise to be outstanding teachers. Our major focus is the early identification and development of talented teachers. Success early prevents long, acrimonious, and litigious battles later. Our beginning teachers know specifically what they must do to succeed.

Superintendent 2: Our evaluation process and instrument are sound. However, the effectiveness of the process to identify individuals who are not performing up to expectations depends on the evaluator—the principal who makes the final judgments about performance. I review all summative evaluations and rarely see certain principals identify any individual as performing unsatisfactorily, while others do a great job in identifying those who are not performing up to our standards.

CHAPTER 9

IMPLEMENTING EVALUATION

Designing performance standards, selecting sources of data, and creating documents and materials for a performance-based assessment of professional educators are critical initial steps for appropriate evaluation. Equally important, however, is the actual implementation of the performance evaluation process.

In Chapter 8, we described the standards that the evaluation process should meet as well as the categories, job expectations, and behavioral indicators that provide a description of well-defined expectations for professional educators. The multiple data sources (e.g., direct observation, student achievement measures, client surveys, artifacts or portfolio review, and goal setting) are vehicles the principal uses to get information concerning overall performance. After collection, these data must be synthesized and used in a meaningful judgment to assess individual overall performance.

IMPLEMENTATION TO MEET FEDERAL AND STATE MANDATES

Determining exactly how and how often teachers should be evaluated emerged front and center in the American Recovery and Reinvestment Act of 2009. That federal stimulus plan set aside more than $4 billion for states that invested in new ways to overhaul their education systems, including how best to evaluate teachers. A resulting federal initiative,

*Improving Instruction Through Supervision, Evaluation, and
Professional Development,* pp. 207–227
Copyright © 2014 by Information Age Publishing
All rights of reproduction in any form reserved.

Race to the Top (2011) and resulting grant competitions, such as School Improvement Grants, require more thorough evaluations of teachers based on frequent classroom observations and their students' performance on standardized tests. Requirements to evaluate all teachers annually and include value-added growth measures as a significant component of teachers' evaluations present real practical challenges. In fact, a body of research suggests that value-added teacher ratings are not sufficiently reliable or valid to support high-stakes, individual-level decisions about teacher quality or performance (Darling-Hammond, Amrein-Beardsley, Haertel, & Rothstein, 2012).

States that adopted Common Core State Standards are revamping teacher evaluation processes so that all educators will be evaluated annually on multiple measures of effectiveness, including student learning growth in meeting the standards as well as observations of teachers' instructional practices. Teacher evaluation systems are aligned to the CCSS if:

- statewide assessments, student learning objectives, and other classroom assessment tools focus on the instructional shifts (e.g., for ELA/literacy teachers: "Does the teacher consistently employ text-dependent questioning?")
- teacher observation rubrics and model teaching standards clearly articulate the knowledge and skills with which teachers must become proficient to deliver instruction aligned to the CCSS
- teacher evaluation reports and results (e.g., the formative information received throughout the year before and after observations and the summative rating a teacher receives annually) are framed in the language of CCSS
- both formative and summative teacher evaluation results are used to direct targeted, individualized support to educators and to inform large-scale teacher professional development around the CCSS, with a focus on the instructional shifts (Peltzman, Porter, Towne, & Vranek, 2012).

Under the new evaluation systems, teachers who are rated poorly face losing tenure or their jobs. Federal authorities argue that the requirements for the new teacher and principal evaluation systems are critical to the success of the entire school reform movement. Proponents of the new evaluation policies argue that teachers have a significant impact on students' academic progress, either preparing them for future success or setting them back so they can't be successful. Critics say that observations are subjective, and test scores aren't a reliable measure of a teacher's performance.

They argue that evaluation should be designed for professional development and the improvement of teaching.

Not suprisingly, the movement to redefine how teacher performance is assessed has been controversial. Rating and rewarding teachers based on student test score data became the flashpoint that sparked public battles between school officials and teacher unions across the country. Most states do not have data systems in place to collect and analyze student achievement data in terms of tying it to individual teacher performance. Those few states with advanced data systems must figure out how to measure student academic progress for the vast majority of teachers whose students don't regularly take standardized tests. Certainly, the best way to use value-added factors in evaluations has yet to be discovered (Chetty et al., 2011). For example, counterproductive responses such as teaching to the test could result, which make value-added factors a poorer measure of teacher quality. The challenges of implementing mandated valued-added or growth models are many.

Value-added measurement and other criteria may help to identify strong or weak teachers; however, identification does not create more good teachers—interventions required to improve performance must be identified and implemented. Our model supports formative supervision as the primary means of helping teachers grow and improve professionally. The formative process can and should co-exist with the summative process in a sound evaluative system. We applaud the renewed focus on classroom observations, but not the inspection model. We believe classroom observations should be used to collect classroom performance data to help teachers reflect on their practice and identify, with their principals, areas for improvement. Certainly summative evaluation does have a function in our model, but it is not the primary vehicle for instructional improvement.

PRINCIPALS AND EVALUATION

Principals' primary orientation is to the entire school. They are responsible for student learning, an orderly environment, coordination of all the school activities, the solution of immediate problems, holding people accountable, and in general, the smooth functioning of the school. Efficient school performance relies primarily on professional behavior of classroom teachers. The principal is the individual directly responsible for and involved in virtually all the day-to-day school operations; hence, it should come as no surprise that the principal's perspective is often more pragmatic and systemic than teachers' views.

Principals articulate the official organization's goals, objectives, and values. They occupy a formal position of authority and power. Although principals may be supportive and helpful to teachers, they also have the burden of making organizational decisions about competence. Federal and state policy mandates formal evaluations of personnel. The principal is the individual who is given the responsibility of providing formal feedback to teachers, holding them accountable, disciplining faculty, imposing formal sanctions when such action is appropriate, and recommending nonrenewal or termination when warranted.

Although the task is time consuming and at times confrontational, principals can neither ignore nor neglect their formal responsibility of evaluating the performance of individuals. Recall that in our integrated model, supervision is the informal process of assisting teachers to become more effective in helping students. Evaluation, on the other hand, is a formal process in which judgments about the quality of overall performance are made. In supervision, the primary focus is on classroom performance that results in student learning; in evaluation, principals make judgments of the overall performance of school professionals in performing all of their duties, in the classroom as well as other assigned duties and responsibilities. Evaluation is the overall assessment of the competence of teachers.

Principals are commonly responsible for both supervising and evaluating teachers, and both teachers and principals believe the processes have considerable value (Blase & Blase, 2001; Holifield & Cline, 1997). Both processes provide visible principal leadership in the school (Peterson & Peterson, 2006). Both processes require that all involved parties understand expectations. In working with teachers to clarify expectations, set goals, or develop plans for improvement, principals promote both school and district priorities. Supervision and evaluation are processes that emphasize high student achievement and sound professional practice.

The principal is responsible for documenting cause and recommending the removal of incompetent, ineffective teachers from the profession. Systematic evaluation is the tool principals use to judge teacher performance and the front line of quality control and accountability. Constituents expect principals to provide an effective teacher in each classroom. Evaluation, not supervision, is the high-profile process that at one extreme is a vehicle for teacher affirmation and growth and at the other extreme a means to document the reasons for dismissal.

DIFFERENTIATED DEVELOPMENTAL EVALUATION

We advocate for differentiated and developmental evaluation, just as we advocated for differentiated, developmental supervision. Principals use walk-throughs, observations, conversations, and other informal interactions with teachers in the process of supervision. Although the informal data of supervision are not used in evaluation, they give the principals a good indication of which professional staff members may require more time and attention in the process of evaluation. Obviously, more principal time should be invested where it is needed and will do the most good. Prime candidates for special attention include beginning teachers, teachers who are struggling, and those whose students are performing unsatisfactorily. Professional experience and past performance should be considered as the frequency, nature, and extent of evaluations are planned (Peterson & Peterson, 2006).

We emphasize that differentiated supervision does not mean different expectations for professionals performing the same job. Fair, legal evaluation requires equal application of performance expectations. However, differentiated, developmental evaluation does require modification in elements of the process. For example, data collected through direct observation and post-observation conferences should occur more frequently for beginning teachers, nontenured teachers, and those whose performance has been identified as less than satisfactory, than for veteran teachers who have a history of satisfactory performance; the evaluation cycle should be shorter for those in need while veteran teachers with histories of satisfactory performance may have an annual evaluation cycle. Of course, formative, informal supervision is ongoing and continuous throughout the cycles. Quality evaluation requires a major investment of principals' time, so it should be focused where it will reap the greatest benefit. Schools that have high teacher turnover rates pose an extraordinary challenge because more teachers require more time for direct observation and individual conferences. Making time for quality evaluation is critical, and differentiating the process enables the principal to focus attention where it is most needed.

ROLE CONFLICT

There is inherent tension between the supervisory and evaluative roles of the principal (Holland, 2004; McLaughlin, 1990); our model, however, views these two processes as complementary, yet our framework recognizes the tension. In the real world of practice, principals are expected to help teachers improve their effectiveness through supervision as well as making judgments about their performance in evaluation. Principals must be aware of the potential conflict between the roles of supervision and evaluation. This role conflict requires a very deliberate effort on the part of principals to fulfill their obligation of improving instruction. But the administrative role of the principal is an evaluative one, and that reality prevents some teachers from being completely candid with principals about classroom problems (Popham, 1988).

Recognition of this potential conflict has lead to experiments in restructuring school administration, such as creating roles of "instructional principal" and "operations principal" or associate principals with very specific distinct roles in the school—one for instruction and the other for management. In large school organizations, it may be possible to separate the administrative and supervisory roles. In such cases, master teachers and other specialists with instructional expertise are welcome additions to the supervisory team. In most schools, however, the principal is required both to help teachers improve (supervision) and to assess their competence (evaluation)—a major challenge.

THEORY INTO PRACTICE
ISLLC STANDARDS 1, 2, 3, 5

In your school, who evaluates and who supervises instruction? Is it the same person? If so, is that a problem? Are the processes differentiated? If so, how? If not, why not? Are all teachers treated the same—that is, are veteran teachers observed as often as beginning teachers? Should they be? Why? Is your principal more skillful at supervision or evaluation? Does the principal know the difference?

PRINCIPALS' RESPONSIBILITIES

Professional educators want and need feedback, both formative and summative communications, to help them grow professionally. Both principals and teachers recognize that there are sound reasons to evaluate performance, and if evaluation is done well, it increases effectiveness and communication. Unfortunately, however, most often evaluation is merely a paper shuffle that doesn't help teachers and sends the wrong message. Studies of large samples of principals' summative ratings of teachers reveal that virtually every individual is rated above average; teachers do not believe that teacher evaluation, as generally practiced, works well (Bernstein, 2004). When the process of evaluation does not discriminate between those who perform at high levels of competence and those who do not, no one benefits, and teachers become cynical about the entire process (Scriven, 1981).

Principals recognize the importance of securing performance data directly from primary sources such as direct observations, client surveys, student achievement scores, and artifacts of performance. In securing and using such multiple data sources, principals recognize the complexity of the duties of professional educators, the variety with which they can be successfully executed, and the variety of settings of their practice (Peterson & Peterson, 2006). As evaluators, principals do not try to assess the performance of an educator in each one of the many expectations at a point in time, but assess holistically using multiple data sources.

Selecting the appropriate data sources for each individual and documenting performance can be a challenge. The variety of settings and the capacity in which educators serve students requires that all teachers have an equal opportunity to document their quality in the ways most appropriate to them. Certain data are not relevant or may not be available for every professional educator. For example, student value-added data may be available and used in teacher evaluation for some but not all teachers.

Thus, a completely uniform evaluation process is inappropriate and not good practice. Evaluation is subjective—it requires principals to make judgments. Quality judgments require that principals:

- are well versed in the process
- are experts in teaching/learning
- use the best objective data available
- recognize and compensate for their own biases
- involve stakeholders in the process.

A principal's feedback and evaluation can influence student learning, classroom instruction, and the satisfaction of teachers (Downey et al., 2004). Sometimes evaluation results in planning and providing appropriate professional development, while other times evaluation leads to a decision not to renew a contract. Both kinds of decision require quality judgments.

It is the principal's job to make hard management decisions about the effectiveness of all teachers as well as the recommendation to retain teachers. Confronting ineffective teachers is often the most negative experience for principals. The resultant interpersonal conflicts can undermine the morale, effectiveness, and future practice of principals. Such acrimonious and time-consuming experiences can prove detrimental and difficult, but a principal's first responsibility is to the students. Incompetent teachers must be dismissed. Constituents and stakeholders rely on the principals to support effective teaching and root out ineffectiveness. Principals can and must eliminate the small percentage of incompetent professionals (Annunziata, 1998, 1999; Peterson, 2000).

THE TENURE MYTH

We would be remiss not to address a general deficiency in the practice of teacher evaluation across the nation—the failure to hold teachers accountable for effective performance because they have earned tenure status. All too often, when principals, superintendents, and school boards are queried about the continued employment of ineffective teachers the responses cite tenure as the culprit—the reason the poor performers cannot be dismissed. This is a misrepresentation of reality. Zirkel (1996) refers to this tenure myth as "professional lore" that most often substitutes for "pertinent law" (p. 18) regarding minimal legal requirements.

Although administrators perceive that the courts favor the rights of teachers over school boards, the record reveals just the opposite. Analyses of cases brought by school boards to dismiss teachers reveal that school districts prevail the vast majority of the time (Cain, 1987; DeSander, 2005; Rossow & Tate, 2003). The courts are generally reluctant to substitute decisions of the school board as long as teachers were afforded proper due process—that is, if job performance was unsatisfactory, adequate notice of concerns, clear directions for improvement, and assistance in that improvement were all provided (Tucker & DeSander, 2006).

Tenure status originated to protect teachers from arbitrary or politically motivated dismissal. Tenure provides teachers with due process rights—in other words, a vested property interest in the position (Tucker & DeSander, 2006). The specific requirements of due process vary from state to state, but place the burden of proof for dismissal of an employee with tenure status squarely on the shoulders of the school board (Alexander & Alexander, 2004; Cambron-McCabe, McCarthy, & Thomas, 2004; La Morte, 1996; Rebore, 1997; Valente, 1998).

A LEGAL EVALUATION SYSTEM

Since requirements of due process vary by state and other mandates by school district, devising one universal evaluation process is not possible (Gessford, 1997). Some general elements, however, are recommended. Evaluation procedures must

- meet the judicial standard of "reasonableness" and "fairness" through clear explanation and uniform application (Beckham, 1985)
- satisfy the general substantive, as well as procedural, aspects of the law
- make the conditions of employment known by distributing a clear explanation of these conditions to every teacher.

In order to conform to these three requirements, an evaluation process should include a statement of purpose, clear performance criteria, standards of performance defined by a rating scale, specific procedures used to collect performance data, and a method to summarize the data on performance such as an evaluation summary (Frels & Horton, 2003; Gessford, 1997; Stronge & Tucker, 2003). In addition, a manual describing the entire evaluation process, including the elements listed above, should be distributed to all teachers prior to the implementation of the evaluation process (Frels, Cooper, & Reagan, 1984). The manual should detail both the expectations for performance and possible rewards or disciplinary action that may be a consequence of the evaluation. Each element is described in Table 9.1.

Table 9.1.   Evaluation Training Program Components

Collection of data
Use of data for evaluation
Application/implementation guidelines
Measures of student achievement, value-added and other goals
Orientation/overview of district policies and procedures
Legal requirements for evaluation
Conferencing skills

The evaluation process and the policies that guide it must conform to legal requirements, state and local school board regulations, and contractual agreements. Principals and other administrators must be careful to comply with the policies of the board that govern the evaluation process in the district. Principals and others school administrators must also provide due process in all phases of teacher evaluation. In meeting the standards of due process, principals not only must meet legal requirements, but also model fair and ethical behavior, which supports professional growth and effective teaching.

The stated expectations that will be used to assess teachers' performance are the heart of the evaluation process (Frels et al., 1984). These expectations must be specific enough so that those being evaluated clearly understand the expectations and how performance will be assessed (Beckham, 1985). Direct observation is generally how evaluators gather data to determine performance—these data are essential to justify and defend an evaluation (Frels et al., 1984). The use of other data sources "increases both the validity and the legal credibility of a teacher evaluation, and it is especially important in cases of unsatisfactory evaluation" (Tucker & DeSander, 2006, p. x). The evaluation process should assess a broad sampling of each employee's job responsibilities over a sufficient period of time to identify a pattern of behavior. It is imperative to have written records of teacher performance in which growth and development as well as lack of improvement are noted. Summaries should include specific examples of teacher behavior to illustrate and justify summative assessments, especially those that indicate exemplary or less than satisfactory performance (Frels & Horton, 2003). In essence, the summary of an educator's performance should document the personnel recommendations made by the evaluator (Frels & Horton, 2003).

Principals are often intimidated by the legal requirements inherent in the evaluation process. Nevertheless, evaluation is one of their primary responsibilities and should be no cause for alarm. There are specific legal requirements that define a fair and rational evaluation process. When evaluations and personnel decisions result from such a process, the courts have supported school districts' decisions if teachers have been accorded fundamental due process rights. There is no question that guaranteeing due process takes time and resources, but there is no alternative if principals are to act responsibly and professionally. Students, parents, and the community deserve effective teachers in every classroom, which is only possible when principals maintain high expectations and engage professional educators in a fair, rigorous, and legally sound evaluation process.

MAKING SOUND EVALUATION DECISIONS

Thus far we have provided the distinction between supervision and evaluation, described the goals of evaluation, discussed the principal's role, and outlined the elements of a sound, legal evaluation process. What district specific information do principals need for evaluation?

Implementation Prerequisites

Principals must understand the district policies governing personnel evaluations and the procedures that specify the "nuts and bolts" of the process in order to fairly and legally implement the evaluation process. Our experience is that the best-designed evaluation process will fail to achieve its goals without the adequate training. Although often overlooked, training is a critical component of the evaluation process. Training must be provided for principals and other administrators new to a district and for all administrators when a new evaluation process is adopted. The absence of adequate training places administrators in a frustrating, uncomfortable position—they must initiate and participate in the evaluation process, yet they do not have a clear understanding of their role and existing constraints, a condition that undermines the process.

The basic components of sound evaluation training are summarized in Table 9.1.

Once principals become familiar with the district policies, procedures, and implementation guidelines, they need to develop a working knowledge of the district's expectations of employee performance as identified in the clusters of job responsibilities for each position. Sample behavioral indicators of expected performance for each expectation help both the principal and teachers clearly understand the expectation. Next, principals need to develop familiarity with the rating scale employed to describe acceptable/unacceptable behavior for each job responsibility.

Finally, principals need to verify that data sources used to document and assess the overall job performance are appropriate for each individual being evaluated. District expectations and responsibilities, such as the number and duration of formal observations for each individual being evaluated, should be clear. Unfortunately, all too often, principals are expected to "hit the ground running" and are not provided any basic training or review of the district's evaluation procedures. Such procedures vary from district to district. Even though deadlines are dictated by legal requirements, there is variability among districts, and new principals must be brought up to speed quickly in implementing the elements of the process.

Rating Scales

One tool that is useful in making evaluation decisions is a rating scale—or rubric—against which performance can be assessed. Rating scales can be designed as a simple dichotomous scale (e.g., satisfactory versus unsatisfactory, meets expectations versus does not meet expectations). A more descriptive approach, however, is a three- or four-point scale that offers opportunities to explain and justify performance ratings. These behaviorally anchored scales are helpful as principals focus on relative growth and continuous improvement with professionals during the evaluative process. One such example would be the four-point rating scale as illustrated in Table 9.2.

In this example of a rating scale, four distinct ratings are available for use in assessing a professional's performance. The four-point scale enables the principal to acknowledge exemplary work quality and to provide useful feedback for work that is judged in need of improvement. Ratings typically are assigned to individual performance expectations, but not to behavioral indicators. Additionally, ratings can be applied to the overall clusters of responsibilities to provide a more global assessment of performance. Table 9.3 illustrates how the ratings would be applied in a final evaluation, and Appendix B offers a sample summative evaluation format done in the four-level rating scale.

Table 9.2. Rating Scale Definitions

Rating	Definition
Level 4: Exemplary Performance	Exemplary performance by the teacher that continually impacts students, and programs in the school in a positive manner. For performance to be rated in this category, the performance must consistently exceed the expectations set forth in the performance standards and the principal should cite specific examples in a narrative format.
Level 3: Performance Meets Criteria	Performance that consistently meets expectations resulting in quality work in the accomplishment of the job performance standards identified for the teacher. This is the acceptable performance level that is expected.
Level 2: Performance Requires Improvement	Performance that does not meet standards and requires an improvement to produce desired results (i.e., to meet criteria). The principal should cite specific evidence in a narrative format (i.e., describe examples of specific behaviors on the part of the teacher that illustrate the deficiency).
Level 1: Performance Is Unsatisfactory	Unacceptable performance that requires significant improvement to justify continued employment. The principal should cite specific evidence in a narrative format (i.e., describe examples of specific behaviors on the part of the teacher that illustrate the deficiency).
Level 0: Cannot Judge	The principal does not have enough information to rate performance on an identified standard *(see note below)*.

Adapted from Stronge, DiPaola, and Tucker (2001).

Note: The rating *"Cannot Judge"* would be used only when the principal lacks sufficient information to make a fair or accurate assessment of the teacher's performance on a specific job standard. However, in the final evaluation, the principal would determine a rating drawn from an overall review of evidence.

**Table 9.3. Sample Teacher
Performance Evaluation Format**

Teacher's Name_____

Principal_____

Academic Year_____

DIRECTIONS

Domain: Instructional Delivery

The teacher: Differentiates instruction to meet the students' needs.

Exemplary Performance	Performance Meets Criteria	Performance Requires Improvement	Performance Is Unsatisfactory	Cannot Judge

Comments:_____

_____

_____

Source: Virginia Department of Education (2011)

In the previous chapter, we provided criteria to select appropriate information sources for documenting a teacher's performance. In order to develop a complete picture of a professional's contribution to the over all success of the school, we advocated that the principal use broad-based, multiple sources of information (Peterson, 2000; Stronge & Tucker, 2003). The advantages of each of the recommended data sources were discussed and methods for integrating them were suggested. Here, we proposed using a rating scale as a tool to make evaluation decisions. We now turn to basic guidelines and suggestions for principals as they implement a performance evaluation process.

COMMUNICATING EVALUATION DECISIONS

Throughout the data collection phases of the evaluative process, communication occurs between the principal and those being evaluated. Most often, dialogue is a result of a formal observation, but discussion can also occur during analysis of student achievement data or another data-gathering event. The formal summative conference is the capstone communication event of the process. It confirms that which has been communicated throughout the evaluation process. When regular feedback is a component of the process of evaluation, there are no surprises in the summary evaluation conference (Derven, 1990; Mancision, 1991; Pennock, 1992).

During the summative conference, the overall assessment of performance is discussed, which often leads to problem-solving, strategizing, and goal-setting (Anderson & Barnett, 1987; Krayer, 1987; Losyk, 1990/1991; Meyer, 1991). Successful evaluation conferences not only inform teachers about their job performance, but also formally document the assessments and motivate higher levels of performance (McGregor, 1961).

Helm and St. Maurice (2006) argue that the success of a conference is contingent on the careful planning of the principal. They recommend eight steps for principals to prepare for an evaluation conference. While their suggestions involve principal action, corresponding teacher involvement in the planning contributes to the success of the conference. Whether principals make requests or not, teachers can make significant contributions to the success of the evaluation conference through their own actions. The actions advocated are summarized in Table 9.4.

A summative conference is an ideal forum for the principal to collect additional data from teachers by listening and helping them reflect on their performance, as well as their perceptions of the culture, climate, and other contextual factors of the school. Although evaluation is a formal process, the conference should occur in a setting conducive to relaxed, open communication. Research suggests that the principal should initiate the dialogue by asking the individual to share a self-assessment (Alexander Hamilton Institute, 1995; Buzzotta, 1988; Pennock, 1992). Evaluation conferences based on self-assessments tend to be more positive and helpful to all concerned. Focusing on self-assessment also motivates employees to improve performance (Meyer, 1991); in fact, the greater the participation of the teacher in the evaluation conference, the greater the satisfaction with both the conference and the principal will be (Anderson & Barnett, 1987; Krein, 1990; Webb, 1989).

One of the most difficult things for principals to do during a conference is to listen. Pertinent information about teachers' performance and professional development can be determined by listening rather than talking during the conference. Successful summative conferences have the following characteristics:

- two-way dialogue in which the principal spends most of the time listening
- a balanced review of past performance and plan for the next evaluation
- agreement on the teacher's strengths and successes
- agreement on problems affecting the teacher's performance
- teacher-initiated goals for improving performance (Helm & St. Maurice, 2006).

Table 9.4. Preparing for an Evaluation Conference

Principal Action	*Teacher Action*
Set and confirm with teacher the date, time, and place of evaluation conference.	Collect, organize, and analyze documentation generated during the evaluation period (sample assignments, tests, student work, pictures of displays, etc.).
Give teacher a copy of the evaluation form, if applicable, request teacher to use for self-appraisal.	Review job description, previously set goals or objectives, and mission statement.
Ask teacher to organize, review, and submit any performance documentation collected.	Complete copy of the evaluation form provided by the principal.
Ask teacher to be prepared to discuss successes, unmet challenges, and factors interfering with best performance; how can the principal help the teacher achieve his/her goals.	Identify major strengths and successes of the year.
Review job description and previous evaluation with performance goals.	Identify any unmet expectations/goals and analyze possible reasons for failure, paying careful attention to factors both within and outside your control.
Complete a tentative evaluation and create notes which summarize teacher's successes and concerns.	Identify areas for growth (improvement or new directions) and possible goals or objectives for the next year.
Plan a "script" for addressing concerns tactfully.	Identify how the principal or school system can help you become a more effective teacher.
Prepare questions which enable the teacher to provide a meaningful self-analysis.	

Adapted from Helm and St. Maurice (2006)

COMMUNICATING DISSATISFACTION

Sometimes it is necessary for principals to communicate that performance has been unsatisfactory. Earlier in this chapter, we provided the basic guidelines for providing due process. Unsatisfactory performance cannot be substantiated by a single event; rather, a pattern of performance over time is required. Data collected over time and based on classroom observations, reviews of artifacts, student outcomes, parent testimonies, and other related evidence is important.

In order to substantiate a judgment of unsatisfactory performance, it is critical that a principal demonstrate that the teacher has received notice of the specific performance expectation, was provided a remediation plan by the principal, and was given the assistance and time needed to correct the inadequate classroom performance (McGrath, 1993). When principals make hard personnel decisions to take corrective action, such as denying tenure or firing a teacher, their credibility and competence are on the line.

Other important sources of information in cases of unsatisfactory performance are parent and student complaints. Principals should request that parents put complaints in writing. Parent and/or student complaints can help document an ongoing pattern of unsatisfactory performance, but complaints should be documented and demonstrate a pattern of behavior. Transfer requests, nurse's referrals, and disciplinary referrals are also used to show a pattern of conduct (McGrath, 2006).

REMEDIATION PLANS

Before taking punitive action against an employee, principals must make a good faith effort to help remediate the deficient performance, unless the deficiency is so egregious that it provides grounds for immediate dismissal (Frels et al., 1984). Good remediation plans address the specific performance to be improved, resources needed for improvement, follow-up assessments of improvement, benchmarks of progress, consequences for not improving, and criteria for satisfactory performance.

When a principal recommends termination of a tenured employee, the burden of proof falls on the principal. To substantiate the action, principals must document that due process has been provided and that a remediation plan was implemented with unsatisfactory outcomes. Summative evaluations typically are part of the permanent employment record of employees. The record and thoroughness of the documentation also provides an account of the principal's behaviors, and may serve as an artifact of principal performance.

Principals who have been called to testify during dismissal hearings feel as if they are on trial because their competence and integrity are questioned. They often leave proceedings wondering whether their actions were worth the angst and insults. There is little question that recommendations to terminate the employment of an individual are difficult, but the task is a critical part of being a principal. Protecting students from incompetent teachers is an instrumental principal task.

THEORY INTO PRACTICE
ISLLC STANDARDS 1, 2, 3, 5

Does your principal clearly make the distinction between satisfactory and exemplary performance? Between satisfactory and unsatisfactory performance? Is the evaluation process in your school fair; that is, does it produce sound decisions based on reliable and valid data? If not, how can the process be improved? If the process is fair, what can be done to fine-tune the process? Does feedback to teachers help them improve their teaching? What is the evidence for your claim? How subjective and objective are the evaluations?

SUMMARY

In this chapter, we discussed the challenges that confront principals as they perform one of their most important duties—the evaluation of professional staff. Juggling the informal process of supervision with the formal process of evaluation is difficult for even seasoned principals. The role conflict is real, but it can be minimized if all individuals involved have a clear understanding of the mechanics of the processes of supervision and evaluation.

Because principals have professional staff members in their schools at different stages of their careers and with different levels of competence, evaluation should be differentiated and developmental. The length of the evaluation process, time spent with individuals, and amount of data collected should vary according to the needs of the individual and the school. In most cases, feedback is focused on setting goals to improve teacher effectiveness. The principal is responsible for a holistic written assessment of the overall performance of professional staff. Although these judgments are subjective to some degree, principals should use objective data, recognize their own biases, and involve teachers in the process.

Legal requirements of the evaluation process need not be intimidating. Recommendations concerning the retention of nontenure staff are not as complex as those to reprimand or dismiss a professional who has tenure, a property right. Although all evaluations should be fair and legal, it is critical that those with tenure be afforded due process throughout the evaluation and include notice of any unsatisfactory performance, as well as a plan to improve. Principals are the front line of accountability and quality control in schools. All stakeholders expect them to help teachers improve as well as eliminate those who cannot be effective.

A PRINCIPAL'S INSTRUCTIONAL LEADERSHIP CHALLENGE

Instructions—Read the following account provided by a principal, reflect on her practice, and perform a case analysis.

I became principal of Fairmount Elementary during this past summer. Fairmount serves a very heterogeneous group of students in grades K–5. As a new principal, I wanted to get to know the staff and share my instructional expectations with them prior to making any classroom visits. I explained my belief that one of my responsibilities was to help them grow and become more effective classroom teachers. I intended to use the informal process of supervision in working with them. In that process I would help them reflect on their practice by providing both outcome data and data collected during classroom visits. I also explained that another one of my responsibilities was to annually evaluate their overall performance in a more formal process. To that end, we reviewed the school district's evaluation process. I was not sure how the previous principal handled the evaluation cycle, but I shared my plans with the faculty.

I wanted to be absolutely sure that we all had a clear understanding of the difference between my supervision and evaluation procedures. I also made clear my expectations. I explained that in addition to the unannounced informal classroom visits and announced formal classroom observations that I would be doing daily walk-throughs. I wanted the data that I was gathering to be reflective of what a typical day was like in the classroom, at lunch, at recess, and in assemblies. In other words, over time, I would have a pretty good idea of the teaching and management style of any teacher within the building.

I varied the times of my visits and kept a log of my walk-throughs so that no one could say that I was "picking" on them. There were 62 teachers in my school with most teachers having about five years of teaching experience. In other words, this was a young faculty.

It didn't take many weeks into the school year for me to take note of Ms. Yancy, a tenured teacher with seven years of "successful" third grade teaching experience. I noticed that the students in Ms. Yancy's room were doing a lot of worksheets (busy work). Ms. Yancy was generally at her desk but would pop up when I came into the classroom. Lesson plans were not well developed, if done at all. There was no evidence of differentiating instruction, despite the fact that the class was heterogeneously grouped. There were other signals that things were not going well, such as parent phone calls indicating that their children were "unhappy," "bored," or "not challenged." Teachers were also complaining that Ms. Yancy wasn't pulling her fair share of the team's responsibility. Her own teammates felt that she was dragging their team down because when students changed classes and rotated for math or science or social studies her students were not on the same page as the rest of the third grade classes.

During several meetings with Ms. Yancy over the course of 10 weeks I provided data collected during classroom visits concerning the number of minutes that no active teaching occurred. She explained that on all the occasions I happen to come in after the teaching had taken place and students were engaged in independent practice. I shared concerns expressed by parents and students that her class was not enjoyable and did not provide appropriate challenges. Ms. Yancy took issue with these assessments and explained that learning was hard work and wouldn't be enjoyable for many students. When I asked how she worked with her team to ensure that all third graders were working on the same units, she explained that it was impossible to keep pace with the other team members and meet the individual needs of her students. During all of our informal discussions, Ms. Yancy either dismissed my suggestions or promised to make minor alterations in her practice, but subsequent observations revealed no differences. Obviously, my informal supervision wasn't working; it was time to be more formal and forceful.

I wanted to be sure that I followed district procedures for evaluation and referred to the procedures manual for documentation. I began by making more frequent visits to her classroom at various times of day and also requested that my assistant principal assist in monitoring her teaching. I completed multiple unannounced and announced visits and held pre-observation and post-observation meetings. We discussed various strategies that she could use and each of these observation discussions was written up and filed. She received a copy of all paperwork and signed off on the summaries of conferences.

I worked to find a mentor for her within our school to provide support. I requested written weekly lesson plans along with a scope and sequence for covering all of the third grade objectives. Ms. Yancy clearly needed a roadmap to cover all of the material by the end of the year; however, plans were not submitted on time and then not executed in the classroom. Multiple supports were provided for Ms. Yancy, and she had input into what she felt was needed for improvement, but some things were non-negotiable, such as written lesson plans.

A performance plan was developed and discussed with Ms. Yancy. Included in the plan was the opportunity for Ms. Yancy to visit other classroom teachers within our building and visit other schools. Conferences with Ms. Yancy were frequent and intense. As the expectations and pressure increased, her performance actually got worse. Keep in mind that her previous seven years of evaluations were good, but it became evident that this year's summative evaluation was going to be poor, and Ms. Yancy was going to be placed on a formal improvement plan. I was surprised when Ms. Yancy came to see me in the spring and informed me that she would be taking Family Medical Leave (FMLA); she claimed she was having difficulty coping with all the stress in her life.

REFLECTIVE PRACTICE

If you were the principal in this school, what are your next steps?

- Would you support Yancy's request for Family Medical Leave? Would it matter?
- After all this work, how would you insure that it was not wasted when Yancy returned from leave?
- How does the evaluation process continue?
- Should you try to counsel Yancy to find a school in which she will be more successful?
- Do you think this application for leave is a tactic for dealing with the negative evaluation? If so, what would you do?
- What would be your recommendation to the superintendent about this case?
- How will you deal with the teacher's claim that she was successful for seven years before you arrived, and that the evaluation is a personal vendetta?

DEVELOP YOUR PORTFOLIO

Select an evaluation instrument that you will use to evaluate teachers as a principal. Discuss the rationale for making the selection and how you would use the tool to get reliable and defensible results. Be sure to specify data sources and how you would insure an objective evaluation that will help the teacher improve, that is constructive, and at the same time could stand the scrutiny of an attorney if the case arose to that level.

COMMUNICATION EXERCISE

In the case above, assume the role of the principal. Craft a letter to the superintendent that responds to the claim that you are on a personal vendetta with this teacher that is causing deterioration in her mental health. Also make a clear recommendation concerning her request for a Family Medical Leave.

READINGS

Annunziata, J. (1997). Linking teacher evaluation and professional development. In J. Stronge (Ed.), *Evaluating teaching: A guide to current thinking and best practice* (pp. 288–301). Thousand Oaks, CA: Corwin Press.

Nevo, D. (1994). How can teachers benefit from teacher evaluation? *Journal of Personnel Evaluation in Education, 8*(2), 109–117.

Peterson, K. D., & Peterson, C. A. (2006). *Effective teacher evaluation: A guide for principals.* Thousand Oaks, CA: Corwin Press.

Rossow, L. F., & Tate, J. O. (2003). *The law of teacher evaluation.* Dayton, OH: Education Law Association.

Zirkel, P. A. (1996). *The law of teacher evaluation: A self-assessment handbook.* Bloomington, IN: Phi Delta Kappa Educational Foundation.

WHAT DO SUPERINTENDENTS SAY?

How do you help your principals be effective evaluators, that is, support them in retaining only effective teachers?

Superintendent 1: I reinforce the message that it is easier to screen out poor teachers before tenure; therefore, the focus in our district is on ensuring that only successful teachers are given tenure. My principals know they are accountable for an incompetent teacher. On those rare occasions when a tenured teacher is not performing adequately, it is the principal's job to gather the evidence for termination. In my state, the weight of the evidence to terminate a tenured teacher is on the district. That means the principal is responsible for building the case for termination, which is a long and arduous job. All my principals are aware of the difficulty, and we make a strong effort to retain only effective teachers before granting tenure. I believe granting teachers tenure is one of the most important decisions a school district makes.

Superintendent 2: We do several things to assist them. First, we invest a lot of time in training them in implementing our evaluation process. We establish consensus around the expectations we have in every area of performance. Principals new to our district are required to participate in a simulation in which we provide a data set that they use to make judgments and complete a summative evaluation. We communicate our belief that the best chance they have as principals to improve schools is to hire and retain effective teachers and not employ ineffective individuals. We encourage nonrenewal of nontenured teachers whenever there is a question about their potential to be stellar performers. We also provide legal assistance to principals who decide to begin documentation for the dismissal of a tenured teacher.

CHAPTER 10

HIGH-QUALITY INSTRUCTION

We have described all the elements of our integrated model of supervision, evaluation, and professional development (Figure 2.1, Chapter 2). The relationship between effective teaching and student achievement has been firmly established (Hattie, 2009, 2012; Marzano et al., 2001; Sanders & Horn, 1998). Therefore, principals work with teachers in the processes of supervision of instruction, evaluation of performance, and professional development to help teachers improve instruction and contribute to the increased student learning that results.

Principals use data in both supervision and evaluation. The specific performance outputs of teaching should help determine appropriate data collection devices and methods. For example, research has provided compelling evidence about effective teacher behaviors associated with increased student learning (see Chapter 6). Research related to all elements of teaching (teacher performance) and student learning provides a focus for observing, analyzing, planning for, and improving teacher performance.

THE TEACHING TASK

Hattie (2009) completed one of the largest ever evidence-based research studies of its kind. He analyzed over 50,000 studies that investigated what

Improving Instruction Through Supervision, Evaluation, and Professional Development, pp. 229–255

actually works in schools to improve learning. His conclusion is not surprising—the quality of teachers and their pedagogy make the most difference in student achievement. Hattie's notion of teacher quality is a metric that reflects what teachers do and the effects they have on all students. In essence, teachers need to know (1) the learning intentions and success criteria of their lessons, (2) how well all students are attaining these criteria, and (3) where to go next when there is a gap between students' current knowledge and understanding and the success criteria. Active teaching involves backward design—that is, starting backwards from the desired results—success criteria related to learning intentions.

In describing the four interacting elements of our model (students, the teacher, pedagogy, and classroom climate) that produce the outcomes (teacher performance and student learning), we discussed the characteristics of effective teachers and classroom practices. The core teaching task can be conceptualized as having three basic elements: planning, implementing, and assessing. These elements can be further subdivided into the various decisions and activities that comprise each of the elements (Figure 10.1). The elements of teaching will be discussed along with the implications for principal actions as supervisor of instruction and evaluator of effectiveness.

PLANNING

Teaching is a complex task designed to result in learning among students with varying abilities, interests, and previous learning; not surprisingly, it often requires complex and lengthy planning efforts. Planning influences what students will learn; in fact, it transforms the available time and curriculum materials into activities, assignments, and tasks for students (van Gog, Ericsson, Rikers, & Paas, 2005; Wiggins & McTighe, 2005). Principals expect teachers to plan, and principals often require plans be submitted to them for review. During supervision and evaluation, principals should differentiate expectations for teacher planning based on the competence of individual teachers. For many experienced teachers, planning is a creative problem-solving process (Shavelson, 1987). Experienced teachers know how to successfully execute many lessons and know what to expect and how to proceed; thus, they often don't follow the detailed lesson-planning models they learned during their teacher-preparation programs. Planning is more informal—focused on success criteria, but less scripted. Beginning teachers and those who are having difficulty in planning require more scrutiny and assistance.

Planning requires long-term thinking guided by objectives (success criteria). Teachers should coordinate plans for a year, semesters, units, weeks, and days. Studies reveal that planning done at the beginning of the

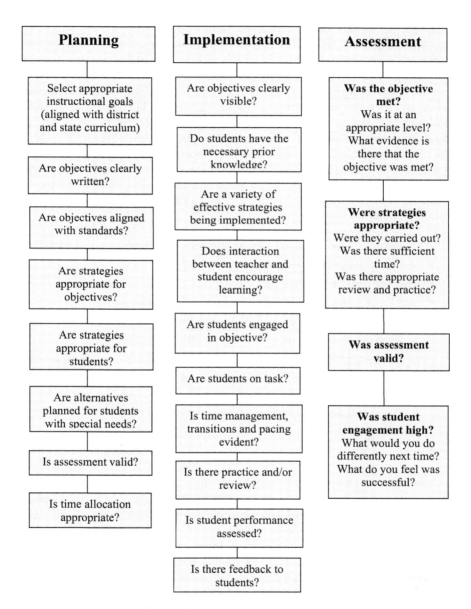

Figure 10.1.   Core teaching task.

year is particularly important because it establishes important routines and patterns early. For experienced teachers, unit planning is most important, followed by weekly and then daily planning. For beginning teachers, however, isolated day-to-day lesson planning seems more important. Inexperienced teachers often have difficulty integrating discrete lessons into comprehensive units (Koeppen, 1998; McCutcheon & Milner, 2002).

Sound planning reduces uncertainty in teaching, but planning should guide instruction, not control it; planning should be flexible, not rigid (Calderhead, 1996). In fact, when teachers rigidly adhere to plans, teaching and learning often suffer. Teachers must be flexible in reacting to how students interpret, accommodate, reject, and/or reinvent the content and skills; how the students relate and apply the content to other tasks; and how the students react in light of success and failure (Hattie, 2009). In order to plan creatively and flexibly, teachers need to have wide-ranging knowledge about

- Common Core State Standards (CCSS) and district expectations
- subjects (content) being taught
- the learning intentions and success criteria of their lessons
- students' prior knowledge, interests and abilities
- effective teaching, e.g.,
  o moving from the single idea to multiple ideas
  o relating and extending these multiple ideas so that learners construct and then reconstruct knowledge and ideas
  o working with groups
  o applying and adapting materials
  o using all their knowledge to create meaningful activities
- expectations of the community

Principals can assist teachers with planning in many ways. For example, principals can help insure that appropriate instructional goals are aligned with district and state standards. Figure 10.2 summarizes essential planning elements.

Appropriate instructional planning means that the teacher (1) targets some specific content related to the instructional goals of the district curriculum/school/state, (2) translates the targeted content into instructional objectives, (3) selects instructional strategies to take the learners from where they are to mastery of the objectives, and (4) assesses the extent to which the objectives are achieved.

The initial step in the planning process usually involves examining the lesson's objective(s) and success criteria. It is, of course, not an arbitrary

Process for Identifying Problems

✓ Teacher and principal select performance outputs to be studied.
✓ Teacher and principal identify performance expectations.
✓ Teacher and principal agree on data collection measures and procedures.
✓ Data are collected.
✓ Teacher and principal review and analyze data.
✓ Teacher and principal determine whether a problem/opportunity exists.
✓ If a problem/opportunity exists, the diagnostic cycle continues.

Figure 10.2. Identifying supervisory problems.

decision, but it requires the teacher to select an objective(s) aligned with the state/district learning standards or curriculum guides. CCSS and district standards provide the context in which the teacher makes content decisions about instructional units and lessons. All too often, decisions about the content of units and lessons have been made by textbook sequences or the particular interest of a teacher. No single textbook or resource is likely to provide adequate content to meet the explicit learning outcomes and needs of all learners. Therefore, it is important that teachers know how to access curriculum guides, maps, and other resources that specify expectations.

INSTRUCTIONAL OBJECTIVES—LEARNING INTENTIONS

An instructional objective is a clear, unambiguous description of educational intentions for students. Instructional objectives are "intended learning outcomes ... the types of performance students are expected to demonstrate at the end of instruction to show that they have learned what was expected of them" (Gronlund, 2000, p. 4). Although there are many different approaches to writing objectives, each assumes that the first step in teaching is to decide what changes should take place in the learner—the goals of the teaching. Learning intentions of lessons should explicitly describe what it is that the teacher wants students to learn. The clarity of learning intentions "is at the heart of formative assessment" (Hattie, 2012, p. 47). Good instructional objectives describe the behavior, the conditions (how and when) under which learners will demonstrate learning, and the criteria (degree) that learners must meet or exceed—criteria of success. Instruction guided by learning intentions and success criteria frames the lesson (Clarke, 2001) and results in higher achievement levels for learners. Instructional objectives help teachers to develop learning strategies, individualize instruction, and construct quality assessments.

Hattie (2012) argues that there are five essential components of learning intentions and success criteria. Planned lessons:

1. are challenging and engage the students' commitment to invest in learning
2. take advantage of and build students' confidence to achieve the learning intentions
3. have high, appropriate expectations of students' outcomes
4. lead to students setting goals to master and reinvest in their own learning
5. have learning intentions and success criteria that are explicitly known by the students (p. 51).

COGNITION

The cognitive view conceptualizes "learning as an active mental process of acquiring, remembering, and using knowledge" (Woolfolk, 2014, p. 312). Bloom and his colleagues developed a taxonomy of educational objectives and provided a description of the objectives in each area: cognitive, affective, and psychomotor (Bloom, Engelhart, Frost, Hill, & Krathwohl, 1956). Therefore, instructional objectives may focus on cognitive, affective (behavioral), or psychomotor changes in the learners. In reality, of course, behaviors from these three domains occur simultaneously. For example, while students are entering data in a spreadsheet (psychomotor), they are also remembering or reasoning (cognitive), and they are likely to have some emotional response to the task as well (affective). The original taxonomy has been updated. Six basic levels were retained in the revision, but the names of three were changed to indicate the cognitive processes involved and the order slightly altered (Anderson & Krathwohl, 2001). The six cognitive processes of the revised taxonomy are remembering (knowledge), understanding (comprehension), applying, analyzing, evaluating, and creating (synthesizing). In addition, the revisers added a new dimension to the taxonomy to recognize that cognitive processes must process something—one has to remember or understand or apply some form of knowledge. Figure 10.3 summarizes the revised taxonomy. There are six processes or verbs—the cognitive acts of remembering, understanding, applying, analyzing, evaluating, and creating. These processes act on four kinds of knowledge—factual, conceptual, procedural, and metacognitive.

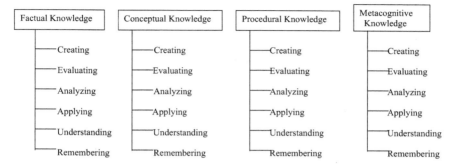

Figure 10.3. Levels of knowledge and cognitive levels.

Conceptual Understanding

Curriculum guides/maps that reflect CCSS and district expectations should drive the decision about what is taught—the knowledge and understanding that is important. Then planning should reflect actions that lead to the highest cognitive understandings and gains for students. Hattie (2012) posits three levels of understanding: surface, deep, and conceptual. Surface learning is focused on understanding ideas; deep understanding is demonstrated by relating ideas; and conceptual understanding involves abstract processing to extend ideas (Hattie, 2012). In gaining both surface and deep understandings, students develop conceptual understanding. In planning lessons, teachers should consider these levels of understanding and explicitly state learning intentions at the different levels. Such specificity helps students better understand the learning intentions and is of great value in constructing both pre and post assessments. Figure 10.4 provides an example of an application at the different levels of understanding.

Affective Domain

The affective domain, the domain of emotional responses, runs from least committed to most committed (Krathwohl, Bloom, & Masia, 1964). At the least committed level, a student would simply pay attention to a certain idea. At the most committed level, the student would adopt an

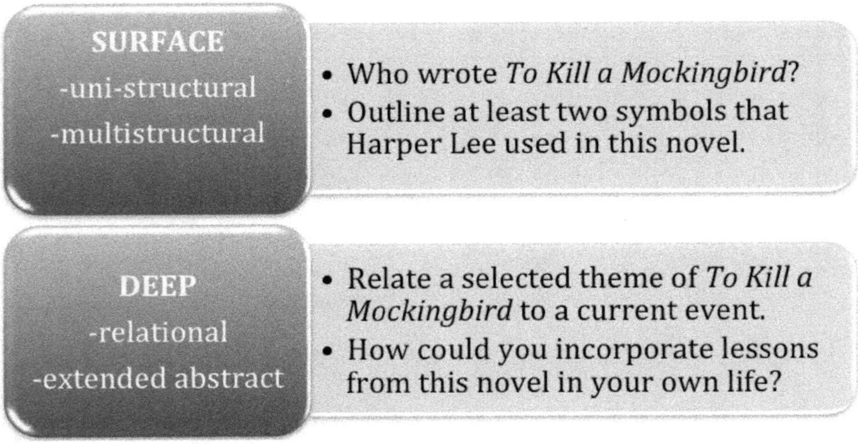

Figure 10.4.   Example of different levels of understanding.

idea or a value and act consistently with that idea. There are five basic objectives in the affective domain:

- receiving—being aware of or attending to something in the environment
- responding—demonstrating some new behavior as a result of experience
- valuing—showing some definite involvement or commitment
- organizing—incorporating a new value into one's general set of values, giving it some ranking among one's general priorities
- characterizing by value—acting consistently with the new value.

Like the basic objectives in the cognitive domain, these five objectives are very general. To write specific learning objectives, teachers must state what students will actually be doing when they are receiving, responding, valuing, and so on.

Psychomotor Domain

Objectives in the psychomotor domain can be characterized as either voluntary muscle capabilities that require endurance, strength, flexibility, agility, or speed; or the ability to perform a specific skill (Cangelosi, 1990).

Objectives in the psychomotor domain should be of interest to a wide range of educators, including those in fine arts, physical education, vocational-technical education, special education, and other subjects. The use of technological devices also requires specialized movements and well-developed hand–eye coordination. Hence, using lab equipment, the mouse of a computer, or art materials means learning new physical skills.

Constructivist Perspective

Unlike traditional planning in which the teacher has sole responsibility, in constructivist approaches, planning is shared and negotiated. In the constructivist model of planning, the teacher and students together make decisions about content, activities, and approaches. Rather than having specific student behaviors and skills as objectives, the teacher has overarching goals—big ideas that guide planning. These goals are understandings or abilities that the teacher returns to repeatedly.

KNOWING THE STUDENTS

Instructional objectives are created in response to the task analysis and diagnosis of learners. In order to make decisions that will result in viable instructional plans, teachers must have knowledge about the students. Without proper diagnoses, teachers are likely to make false assumptions about what learners know and can do.

Principals can help teachers determine what learners know and can do relative to instructional goals by providing and interpreting longitudinal student achievement data. Initially, teachers use existing school data to determine knowledge, skill, and attitudes of learners. Then teachers employ formative assessments before and during instruction to guide them in planning and modifying instruction to help improve student learning. Therefore, formative assessment is "non-evaluative supportive, timely, and specific" (Shute, 2008, p. 153). The formative assessment data and anecdotal records about individuals' and groups' readiness for future learning experiences help determine who does and does not possess the prerequisite knowledge, skills, and attitudes for proposed instructional goals. Formative teacher assessments also help teachers consider attention spans and learning styles when designing lessons (Stronge, 2002).

Learning Activities

In order to plan effectively, teachers must identify the knowledge and skills learners must be able to access in order to achieve the learning intentions. A comprehensive list of knowledge and skills necessary for learners to achieve instructional goals is important; in fact, the more comprehensive the list, the less likely the teacher will be to make incorrect assumptions about the learners' preparedness for instruction. In other words, sound instructional objectives include all the prerequisite skills, knowledge, and attitude levels not yet acquired by the learners.

In planning, teachers need to think of ways to engage students that will elevate their thinking levels during the lesson. Good thinking can and should be developed during lessons. A culture of thinking can be created in classrooms by selecting learning activities that require inquiry, creativity, and challenge to students to make and counter arguments based on evidence (Perkins, Jay, & Tishman, 1993).

Effective teachers recognize that learning is collaborative and requires dialogue. Plans should include activities that create peer-to-peer interactions and constructions while encouraging and creating opportunities for all viewpoints, comments, and criticisms (Shayer, 2003). Such planning helps teachers assess both the processing levels during different parts of activities as well as the levels of individual students' responses.

Principals can help teachers create appropriate plans by asking the right questions throughout the planning process. Figure 10.5 summarizes the steps and decisions to be made as a plan is developed once the content goal has been selected.

Effective principals also provide an instructional framework containing research-based strategies that positively affect student achievement to guide the planning process (Hattie, 2009; Marzano, 2003). High-yield, research-based teaching strategies are summarized in Table 10.1. See Hattie (2009) for a comprehensive explanation of each of these high-yield instructional strategies. Each strategy is supported by multiple research studies and describes specific teacher behaviors or actions. For example, in *reciprocal teaching*, the teacher enables students to learn and use cognitive strategies such as summarizing, questioning, clarifying, and predicting through dialogues between the teacher and students and students and students as they attempt to gain meaning (Rosenshine & Meister, 1994).

Principals, working with instructional personnel, can use these teaching strategies to create the *school's instructional framework*. Each strategy can be learned and perfected. As teachers design lessons, they can incorporate a variety of these strategies as they plan to achieve their learning intentions with all students.

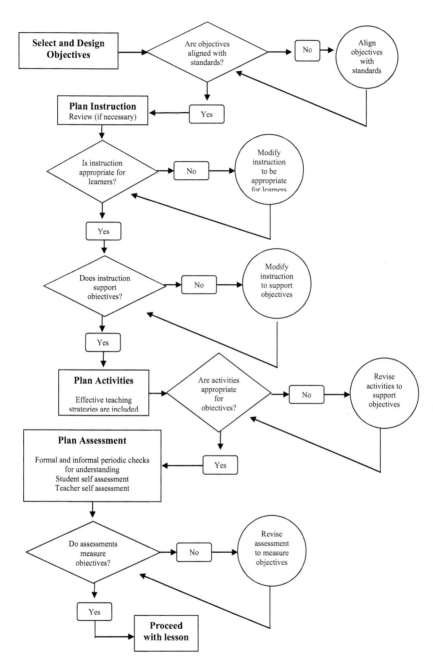

Figure 10.5. Translating instructional goals into classroom practice.

THEORY INTO PRACTICE

ISLLC Leadership Standards 3 & 4

What is your reaction to the implementation of Common Core State Standards? Has your classroom instructional practice changed? How? Have your principal's supervisory and/or evaluation procedures changed? How? Assess the merit of these changes. How has the community reacted to the legislation and subsequent changes? Have the changes produced a more efficient and effective learning environment? If so, how? If not, why?

IMPLEMENTING

In this phase, teachers implement the lessons they have designed—putting the plans into actions. Implementation describes the time the teacher spends with learners in an effort to meet the instructional objectives. One way to describe the teaching task in the classroom is to discuss the behaviors of effective teachers (Darling-Hammond & Baratz-Snowden, 2005; Hattie, 2009; Marzano, 2003). Table 10.2 summarizes effective teacher behaviors. See Chapter 6 for our discussion of effective teaching practices.

Another way to view the teaching task is to focus on research-based instructional methods that have a positive impact on student learning. There are many high-yield instructional strategies. Unfortunately, many teachers may be familiar with only a few of them. Teachers tend to employ strategies with which they feel most comfortable, despite the most current research on the strategies' effectiveness. It is difficult to convince teachers to change their instructional methods. The best motivator to change is data that demonstrate the methods they employ have not been successful for all their students. When students are not achieving, they don't need more of the same unsuccessful teaching methods—they need different teaching strategies.

Although recent meta-analyses have identified the most successful methods, it is important not to rush to implement the strategies that research identified as having the highest impact on achievement. It is more important to understand the "underlying reasons for the success of the strategies and use this as the basis for making decisions about teaching methods" (Hattie, 2012, p. 84). Having a sound understanding of how and why research-based strategies are effective holds the promise of enabling teachers to develop a rich repertoire of instructional strategies for their practice.

Table 10.1.   Instructional Strategies With High Impact on Student Achievement

Reciprocal teaching—help students actively bring meaning to the written word; they learn to monitor their learning & thinking.

Teacher clarity—clearly communicate the intentions of the lessons and success criteria.

Strategies that emphasize feedback—at four levels: task, process, self-regulation, and self-levels.

Spaced vs. mass practice—frequency of different learning opportunities.

Metacognitive—plan how to approach a given learning task, evaluating progress, and monitoring comprehension.

Interventions for learning disabled students—combination of direct instruction and strategy instruction.

Problem-based learning—place more emphasis on meaning and understanding than on surface level knowledge.

Interventions for learning disabled students—such as sequencing, drill repetition, and strategy cues.

Cooperative learning—best effects when designed with high levels of peer involvement.

Study skills—interventions outside what the teacher would normally undertake in the course of teaching; combining study skills with subject content creates deeper understanding.

Source: Adapted from Hattie (2009, Appendix B)

Table 10.2.   Effective Teacher Behaviors

Instructional Behaviors	*Affective Behaviors/Characteristics*
Effective use of instructional time	Constructive discipline policies
Focus on instructional activities	High expectations for self and students
Relevant instruction	Cares about students
Establishes classroom management routines	Has a sense of humor
Questioning skills/techniques	Fair in decisions
Motivates students	Enthusiastic
High expectations for self and students	Respectful
Uses graphic organizers	Empathetic
Engages students	Motivated and motivating
Continually assesses students	Creative
Differentiates instruction	Respects diversity
Provides learning opportunities	Mastery of subject
Builds efficacy	Mastery of teaching/learning skills
Application of content and pedagogy	

Another way to view the teaching task is consider the elements of successful instruction for student understanding at all levels—surface, deep, and conceptual (constructed). Brophy (1997) identified 10 keys to successful teaching for understanding:

1. The curriculum emphasizes knowledge, skills, and values that will be useful outside as well as inside school.

2. Students become more expert by using knowledge in practical applications so that conceptual understanding and self-regulation develop simultaneously.

3. A few important topics are addressed in-depth instead of "covering" the curriculum. Supporters of the constructivist approach assert that coverage is the enemy of understanding.

4. The content to be learned is organized around a small set of powerful or "big" ideas.

5. The teacher presents information but also scaffolds students' efforts to learn.

6. The students' role is to actively work to make sense of the information and make it their own.

7. Teaching begins with the students' prior knowledge, even if that understanding includes some misunderstanding, and conceptual change must be the goal.

8. Class activities include authentic tasks that call for critical thinking and problem solving, not just memorizing.

9. Higher-order thinking skills are taught and applied as students learn subject matter, not during separate, stand-alone "thinking" activities.

10. The teacher's goal is to create a learning community where dialogue and cooperation promote student understanding of content.

In brief, effective teachers organize content to be learned around a small set of big ideas. Then teachers present information and scaffold students' efforts to learn. Teaching begins with the students' prior knowledge and includes authentic class activities that call for critical thinking and problem solving, not just memorizing. Higher-order thinking skills are taught and applied as students learn subject matter, not during separate, stand-alone "thinking" activities. This kind of teaching creates a learning community where dialogue and cooperation promote student understanding of content (Brophy, 1997).

Another way to describe the teaching task in the classroom is to discuss the skills a teacher uses in instruction: structuring, soliciting, and reacting (Martin, 1983). Although it is not a comprehensive description of classroom teaching, it does provide another framework to think about and discuss teaching.

Structuring Skills

Structuring skills are the ways teachers organize instructional activities and make them meaningful for learners; an example of this is when a teacher provides the instructional objective and outlines how it is connected to prior learning. Teachers focus the learners' attention on the tasks at hand, create smooth transitions from previously learned material to new material, and explain how (through instructional activities) students will achieve the new objective. Part of structuring skill, then, entails keeping students informed about what they will know after the learning and helping students recognize what they have learned and how it fits in with what they previously knew.

Soliciting Skills

Teachers provide opportunities for students to be engaged and involved in the learning process. These skills most often refer to questioning, which is the most common and therefore the most critical form of interaction between teachers and students (Jacobsen, Eggen, Kauchak, & Dulaney, 1981). Learning to question skillfully is an important part of learning to teach. Questioning is complicated by the fact that the wording of questions influences the kind of response elicited. That is, the teacher's construction and posing of the question essentially determines the level of response—whether a mere factual one or some more cognitively complex response such as synthesis. In constructing and asking questions, teachers should strive to develop higher-level thinking skills by asking questions at the various levels of Bloom's taxonomy. Questions eliciting not only knowledge responses, but also the higher cognitive levels of understanding and synthesis should be standard practice. Examples of conceptual questions include those that require cognitive manipulation of several facts to produce an answer. Manipulation may include noting similarities and differences, breaking a whole into component parts, forming a whole from parts, or describing the application of a general principle to a specific situation.

Such questions require higher-order cognitive activity and help develop those higher-order thinking skills in students. Although questioning is one of the most important skills a teacher can master, teachers can also solicit engagement by employing constructivist approaches—for example, modeling, scaffolding, inquiry-based teaching, and the Socratic method.

Reacting Skills

Teacher feedback or instructional responses to learner activities are sometimes called reacting skills. Compelling research on feedback indicates that academic achievement in classes where effective feedback is provided to students is considerably higher than the achievement in classes where it is not. In fact, a review of almost 8,000 studies identified feedback as the most powerful single modification enhancing achievement (Hattie & Timperley, 2007). Optimal feedback provides "cues or reinforcement to the learner in the forms of video, audio or computer-assisted instruction ... or relate[s] feedback to learning goals" (Hattie, 2009, p. 174).

In order to influence student achievement, feedback must be timely and specific. Teachers should provide feedback to students at regular intervals throughout their learning (Bangert-Drowns, Kulik, Kulik, & Morgan, 1991). Many teachers claim that they provide feedback, but the key is whether students receive and act on the feedback. Is it specific enough? Does it make a difference in helping students improve?

Regular feedback can be thought of as formative assessment in that it is provided during the learning and is not a summative assessment at the end of the process (Airasian, 1994; McMillan, 2000). For example, teachers get feedback from assessments they administer, make adjustments in their teaching, and consequently provide feedback to students. Systematic provision of formative assessment data has the potential to improve student achievement. Feedback must also be specific to the content being learned (Bangert-Drowns et al., 1991). Teacher assessments should be specific to the actual curriculum taught. Consequently, it is important for principals to ensure that teachers are using appropriate assessments to monitor teaching success.

All three categories of instructional skills discussed here are vital to effective teaching. All three can be learned and improved by every teacher. Principals can assist teachers in their development by supervision, which is supportive, focuses on these skills, and provides constructive feedback. Figure 10.6 summarizes implementation stages.

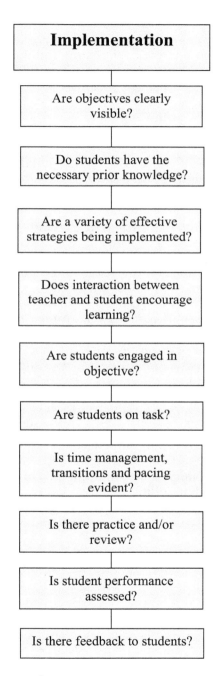

Figure 10.6.   Implementation stage.

ASSESSING

Assessment is an important part of teaching, and the selection of assessment procedures should be done when the other key decisions about instruction are made—during the planning process while the instructional objectives are being identified. In fact, it is a good idea to consider expected outcomes in constructing objectives. There should be congruence between what a teacher intends for the students to learn and how that learning will be assessed. Assessment takes on a specific purposeful function: to let learners and teachers know whether the instructional objectives have been met. If not, assessment points the teacher and students to the area where remediation or review is necessary. Assessment is as much an indicator of the success of teaching as it is of learning.

Student learning is only one of the important expected outcomes of teaching. The other is the performance of teachers. People, especially high achievers like teachers, seek feedback about their performance because it gives them another perspective from which to evaluate their own performance and development. Performance information can challenge, revitalize, and stimulate change. Without performance feedback, individuals, as well as whole organizations, cannot determine true effectiveness, and their perceptions can easily become distorted. In addition to these general needs for performance data, the supervisory and evaluation processes we have proposed use these data to spotlight the problems that activate classroom performance analysis.

Performance output information is vital to increase effectiveness in individual classrooms. Students, and especially teachers, consciously and unconsciously tend to standardize activities and relationships to compensate for the uncertainty and unpredictability inherent in classroom dynamics. While it is necessary to have a few standards to keep order, overemphasis in standardizing activities and relationships results in boredom and disinterest while stifling creativity and enthusiasm for learning. Teachers and principals must be vigilant in guarding against practices that reduce the effectiveness of teachers; classroom observations are helpful in this regard.

In this era of accountability and high-stakes testing, teachers feel great pressure and stress when they are confronted with assessment data. They fear that student achievement data will be the primary criterion used to assess their competence. We have warned about the pitfalls of using student achievement data alone to judge teacher effectiveness. Achievement data can be used as *one* data source to assess teacher effectiveness and should be used only when data provide actual gains as a result of a particular classroom experience (pre- and post-data) or show trends in achievement over time.

THEORY INTO PRACTICE
ISLLC Standards 1, 2, 3, 5

In your school, how do teachers generally assess the progress of their students? Textbook tests? Teacher-made tests? What format is typical—essay, objective, authentic assessment? To what extent do the instructional objectives guide the development and use of tests? When was the last time the school or district had a session on developing assessments? Are teachers generally expert in developing tests and interpreting results? How do teachers use the results of their tests? Grading? Learning? Diagnosing? In general, make the case that testing is either well and healthy or in need of improvement in your school. Be specific and give some examples to substantiate your argument.

In the supervisory process, however, achievement data are of mutual interest to teacher and supervisor. Assessments reveal the students who are not meeting expected learning outcomes. The data enable the teacher and principal, working as a team, to diagnose trends and jointly plan for reteaching using different instructional strategies or remediation as appropriate. Principals can help teachers become more effective in assessment by providing a framework of salient questions to consider. Figure 10.7 summarizes assessment queries.

It would be naïve to neglect a critical element in successful teaching—teacher reactions to how students interpret, accommodate, reject and/or reinvent the content and skills; how students relate and apply the content to other tasks; and how students react in both the cases of success and failure in relation to the content and methods that the teacher taught. Learning requires passion, patience, and attention to detail, from teachers and students alike (Hattie, 2009). The most powerful single influence enhancing student achievement is feedback. What is needed is quality feedback—where that feedback has the greatest effect is when teachers receive more and better feedback about their teaching, and then the ripple effect back to the student is high (Hattie & Timperley, 2007).

IDENTIFYING PROBLEMS

In reviewing our supervisory model and the diagnostic cycle of problem solving (Chapters 4 and 5), the specific purpose of collecting performance output data is to enable the teacher and supervisor to identify problems. By problems we simply mean discrepancies between the behavior expected by the teacher–principal team and what the outcome data reveal. In this context, a "problem" often refers to an opportunity. The

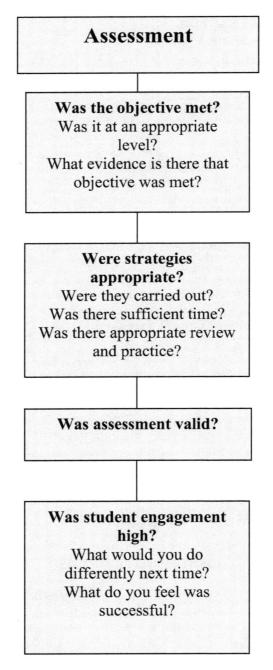

Figure 10.7.   Assessment stage.

problem provides the focus, the goal, and the starting point for the supervisory process. We have defined a problem (opportunity) as a discrepancy between expected and actual performance. The mechanics for identifying discrepancies are necessarily somewhat flexible. Ideally, the teacher and principal can identify their expectations fairly accurately prior to collecting performance output data. For example, in order to make adequate yearly progress (AYP) under No Child Left Behind (NCLB), 90% of students in the third grade must pass the state third-level mathematics test. This would represent the expected outcome for third grade teachers. When assessment data reveal that not all students achieve that expectation, a problem is identified.

To illustrate this example, the data-collection and problem-identification phases of the diagnostic cycle are expanded in Table 10.3.

Table 10.3. Identifying Supervisory Problems

- Teacher and principal select performance outputs to be studied.
- Teacher and principal identify performance expectations.
- Teacher and principal agree on data collection measures and procedures.
- Data are collected.
- Teacher and principal review and analyze data.
- Teacher and principal determine whether a problem/opportunity exists.
- If a problem/opportunity exists, the diagnostic cycle continues.

In Step 1, the teacher and supervisor meet to select some performance outputs for investigation. In our example, the expected output was externally selected. Selection from among the two types of performance output (teacher performance or student learning) is based on mutual discussions about what data might reveal as problems (opportunities) related to teacher effectiveness.

Steps 2, 3, and 4, while logically distinct and ordered, are in fact interdependent and may require simultaneous consideration. In most instances, the identification of the student performance output depends on the school, district, or state goals and data-collection mechanism. Some adjustment of the expectation may be warranted by circumstance. For example, if a particular third grade teacher had an unusually high number of students who had not performed well in mathematics in the previous year, adjustments in expectations might be made for that teacher.

Data collection is next (Step 5). It is also characterized by a great deal of flexibility in terms of whom, how, and when. Individual student performance output data might be collected by the teacher or through standardized assessments. It might be collected during a single class or it might be longitudinal—that is, collected periodically over an extended time. It might be collected with a digital camera, smart phone, tablet, computer, pen and paper, an assessment instrument, and so on. When multiple data sources are used, a more accurate understanding of student learning in its dimensions should result.

Step 6 is very important, partly because of the temptation to speculate wildly about data. In most cases it seems reasonable that teacher and principal take the raw data and independently try to make sense of them. Further analyses, reflection, and time usually yield valuable insights about the data.

Eventually, teacher and supervisor come together to order and evaluate the data. At the same time, they determine whether problems or opportunities exist. If either or both exist, the diagnostic cycle continues. The entire cycle of the supervisory process is described in Chapter 5.

We have discussed a somewhat ideal process in which the expected student output was capable of being measured and stated as a specific quantity. That is not always the case. For example, a teacher and principal might decide to investigate teacher behavior outputs like displays of caring for students such as listening, warmth, and encouragement. Manifestations of such behaviors are decidedly more vague than scores on student mathematics assessments; thus, deciding expected performance output levels is more difficult. Despite the elusiveness of such outputs, a teacher and principal may use observation data provided by the principal, as well as video recordings of the teacher, and mutually conclude whether expectations for teacher caring behaviors have been met or not. Thus, even when expected performance output levels are not easily determined in advance, teacher and supervisor can evaluate whether what is observed is acceptable to them. Although far from the ideal process discussed earlier, this process might very well serve as a springboard to continue the diagnostic cycle.

MEASURING TEACHER OUTPUTS

Each of the two sets of classroom outputs (teacher performance and student performance) will be discussed separately in the next chapter as we articulate actual methods and instruments for collecting performance output data. Some cautions are appropriate at this point. No single measure of performance output should be depended upon to provide ultimately reliable data. It is best to assess performance outputs with several different kinds of measures. Supervision is a process that involves a balance between collecting scientifically accurate data while maintaining the enthusiasm and motivation of the teacher and principal. The measures and methods for collecting performance output data we suggest here represent some useful methods but by no means are all-inclusive.

Teacher effectiveness is synonymous with student achievement. Research has demonstrated that teacher effectiveness is influenced by many factors—some are concerned with instruction and some address affective issues. Examples of factors in each of these two categories are represented in Table 10.2. Principals and teachers concerned with improving teacher effectiveness should focus on these factors because they are directly linked to the critical output, student achievement.

SUMMARY

We related our integrated model of supervision, evaluation, and professional development to the complexities of the teaching task. The three core elements of the teaching task—planning,implementing, and assessing—were examined, discussed in detail, and related to evidence-based research that identified what actually works in schools to improve student learning. The process of using observational data to identify mismatches between desired and actual classroom outputs was outlined. By using such data teachers and their observers can identify needs for professional development and teacher growth.

A PRINCIPAL'S INSTRUCTIONAL LEADERSHIP CHALLENGE

I have been principal of Proctor Middle School for five years, during which time the state test scores in all areas have consistently increased to meet the rising expectations of NCLB. Jamal Washington is a second-year science teacher. I have established a good relationship with Jamal. Last year we worked together on his classroom management techniques and from midterm on, Jamal had no problems with discipline; in fact, students and faculty alike marvel at how willing students are to comply with his directions. During walk-through observations as well as the final formal observation last spring, I noted that Jamal's instructional strategies were highly directive. We met and decided that this year we would work together to help him improve his pedagogy. During the first observation of Jamal's class I used an observation tool as a guide to collect data. In particular I was concerned about student participation. My observation confirmed my suspicions. Jamal had become a skillful lecturer whose students were well behaved and attentive (see classroom observation form in Figure 10.8). It was time to help him enhance his instructional repertoire.

TEACHER BEHAVIORS

A check (√) appears if an item is observed. Note that in a single observation, not all items will be observed. Indicators are not checked without evidence. Observers are to write specific examples or non-examples in the far right column for discussion with the teacher.

THE TEACHER: Jamal Washington, Science 8	Observed √	SPECIFY EXAMPLES/NON-EXAMPLES
1. Clarifies and articulates specific learning objectives/learning intentions.	√	*Objective posted and explained*
2. Identifies and communicates challenging success criteria in checklists and rubrics.		
3. Assesses and builds upon students' existing knowledge and skills.	√	*Made assumption about prior learning*
4. Engages and hooks		
5. Provides input, explains, and models	√	*Lectured the entire time*
6. Guides practice: monitors, coaches and remediates as needed 7.		
8. Provides closure and assesses lesson impact on students, engages students in reflection		
9. Provides time for independent practice		
10. Develops vocabulary and connects concepts and ideas. 11.		
12. Questions for high level thinking and deep learning, responds appropriately to students queries, promotes student questioning.		
13. Uses small group options, specify a, b, c, d, e: a) Pairs, c) Cooperative learning, b) Guided reading, d) Reciprocal teaching, e) other	√	*Whole group instruction entire time*
14. Assigns/uses varied and leveled text, specify: a. Nonfiction b. Fiction c. Textbook d. Real world e. Leveled or differentiated text		
15. Integrates student use of technology to enhance learning.		
16. Assesses individual learning to provide specific descriptive feedback at the task, product and process levels; does not mix/confuse praise with feedback.	√	*Praised oral responses to questions posed*
17. Differentiates instruction through re-teaching, acceleration, and enrichment, etc.		
18. Uses existing products or samples as models for student products.		
19. Provides choices in assessment products.		
20. Uses a variety of assessment strategies and appropriate instruments.		
19. Arranges classroom configurations to maximize learning.		
20. Uses management strategies to reduce disruptions in learning: clear expectations, rules, procedures, safety, etc.	√	*Students were orderly, well-behaved, and knew classroom routines*
21. Maintains and reinforces instructional clarity and alignment across learning goals, lesson organization, explanation, examples, guided practice and assessments.		

2012 SURN Principal Academy: School of Education, at The College of William and Mary, SCHEV, and VDOE.

Figure 10.8.　Teacher behaviors.

I met with Jamal during his planning period and we reviewed my sketchy notes on the class I observed. It was clear that Jamal has mastered classroom management and developed appropriate objectives that were clear, visible, and aligned with the curriculum. He had written the lesson's objective on the board and continuously referred to the objective throughout his lecture. I was impressed with his skills with direct instruction, but we agreed it was time to branch out. The observation revealed that there were few genuine opportunities for student questions. The classroom atmosphere suggested a climate of trust and respect. Students seemed to genuinely like Jamal and cooperate with him. Jamal agreed that he should involve students more in the lesson. As a first step we decided to focus on three cognitive levels of questioning—questions that involve remembering, understanding, and applying (see Figure 10.3).

REFLECTIVE PRACTICE

Assume the role of this principal and proceed to develop a plan for next steps.

- Review the Model for Classroom Supervision (Figure 4.4) and the Diagnostic Cycle in Figure 5.3.
- Use the diagnostic cycle to identify a problem.
- Is there a discrepancy between Jamal's pedagogy and student needs?
- Is Jamal ready to expand his pedagogical repertoire?
- Evaluate their proposed strategy—that is, focusing on three levels of questioning. Is that too much? Not enough?
- Should you have Jamal observe other teachers skillful at questioning?
- Specifically, how would you help Jamal expand his questioning skills?
- How much time should intervene before an observation to assess his progress?
- What observational tool would you use to collect data?

DEVELOP YOUR PORTFOLIO

Use the observation tool, Teacher/Student Behavior Observation Form (Figure 10.12), to observe two different teachers in your school. Analyze the data that you collect by writing a description of the teaching that occurred. Be sure to include a summary of the different teaching behaviors and student reactions to them. Also describe the research-based strategies that each teacher used. Point out the strengths and weaknesses of each teacher. Compare the approaches of the two teachers. Which is more appropriate? Why? How would you use these data to help teachers improve their instruction? End your analysis with the one event in each class with which you would begin your improvement plan.

COMMUNICATION EXERCISE

Use *one* of the two observations above and write a script to communicate what you observed. Try to be positive and constructive in your description. Speak not only to the interaction patterns observed but also the kinds and levels of questions that the teacher posed. Accentuate the positive, but select at least one area in need of improvement and use a constructive approach to tackling the problem.

READINGS

American Federation of Teachers. (2003). *Setting strong standards*. Washington, DC: Author.

Blase, J., & Blase, J. (2001). *Empowering teachers: What successful principals do*. Thousand Oaks, CA: Corwin Press.

Byrk, A. S., & Schneider, B. (2002). *Trust in schools: A core resource for improvement*. New York, NY: Russell Sage Foundation.

Copland, M. A. (2002). *Leadership of inquiry: Building and sustaining capacity for school improvement in the bay area school reform collaborative*. San Francisco, CA: Center for Research on the Context of Teaching.

Darling-Hammond, L., & Baratz-Snowden, J. (2005). *A good teacher in every classroom: Preparing the highly qualified teachers our children deserve*. San Francisco, CA: Jossey-Bass.

Tschannen-Moran, M. (2004). *Trust matters: Leadership for successful schools*. San Francisco, CA: Jossey-Bass.

WHAT DO SUPERINTENDENTS SAY?

How much help do your principals need in observing the teaching and learning process and helping teachers improve?

Superintendent 1: All my principals except one do a reasonably good job observing their teachers and helping them improve. That is no accident. One of the most important criteria we use to hire principals is their capacity to demonstrate instructional leadership. By that, I mean the principals must know curriculum, understand teaching and learning, have great interpersonal skills, and know how to work positively and constructively on instructional improvement. If there is any question about their capacity to work collegially with teachers to improve instruction as well as make the hard tenure decisions when required, I simply will not recommend them to the board. The one principal I have who is not especially skillful in supervision and evaluation is someone who has been around a long time—too long. My attention has turned to trying to move him out of the school into a central office position, which does not require a broad knowledge of curricular and instructional issues. Next year, he will not be a principal.

Superintendent 2: I feel one of the major responsibilities as superintendent is to free principals to get into the classrooms to supervise and evaluate teachers. Thus, I ask my principals frequently how much time they spend in the classroom. To be candid, I am rarely happy with their answers. All my principals spend too little time in the classroom. I expect them to be in the classroom with teachers about half of the time each day or preparing for teacher conferences. If they are not in the classroom, I want to know why. Then it is my responsibility to free them to take care of their supervision, evaluation, and professional development requirements—the trinity of school improvement.

Superintendent 3: The important work in schools occurs in classrooms. That's where principals should spend the lion's share of their time. Monitoring instruction and working with teachers directly to help them become more effective is a major responsibility. Principals can determine when they need additional help, such as specialized assistance from content area specialists or from master teacher coaches. Generally, the help they require is in performing some of the managerial responsibilities of their jobs. We have assigned individuals to relieve them of some of those duties in order to free up time for principals to be in classrooms and spend time with teachers.

CHAPTER 11

IMPROVING INSTRUCTION

Schools are only as effective as the teachers who practice within them. School leaders, however, have a very powerful role in influencing the teachers, curricula, school and home contributions to effectiveness through instructional leadership. Instructional leaders focus on teaching, learning, and student outcomes (Hallinger, 2011). When principals focus their work on the processes of teaching and learning, they can have a positive influence on student learning (Robinson, Lloyd, & Rowe, 2008). Effective school leaders promote challenging goals and develop a school culture in which teachers question, critique, and support their colleagues in collectively achieving those goals. Leaders who pay attention to teaching and are focused on achievement have the highest impact on achievement (Hattie, 2009).

School leaders as teacher colleagues are in a unique position to help teachers improve professionally by providing feedback for reflection, identifying potential areas for growth, and providing appropriate professional development. In this chapter we highlight some of the research-based, high-yield instructional strategies and provide observation tools for data collection during classroom observation that help principals and teachers assess the two sets of classroom outputs—teacher performance and student performance in our supervisory model.

School leaders must not only know what research-based, high-yield instructional strategies are, but know what they look like in classroom

Improving Instruction Through Supervision, Evaluation, and Professional Development, pp. 257–286

practice. They also must be able to collect relevant data for reflection. In essence, observers are another set of eyes collecting data on what actually is occurring in classrooms while teachers are engaged in making constant, rapid instructional decisions in working with students. In this chapter we introduce a variety of data collection tools that focus on research-based, high-yield instructional strategies. Principals and other observers can use these tools in collecting data for reflection and analysis.

MEASURING TEACHER OUTPUTS

Each of the two sets of classroom outputs—teacher performance and student performance—will be discussed separately as we articulate actual methods and instruments for collecting performance output data. Some cautions are appropriate at this point. No single measure of performance output should be depended upon to provide completely reliable data. It is best to assess performance outputs with several different kinds of measures. Supervision is a process that involves a balance between collecting scientifically accurate data while maintaining the enthusiasm and motivation of both the teacher and principal. The measures and methods for collecting performance output data we suggest here represent some useful methods but by no means are all-inclusive.

Teacher effectiveness is synonymous with student achievement. Research has demonstrated that teacher effectiveness is influenced by many factors—some are concerned with instruction and some address affective issues. Examples of factors in each of these two categories are represented in Table 11.1. Principals and teachers concerned with improving teacher effectiveness should focus on these factors because they are directly linked to the critical output: student achievement.

Collecting Classroom Data

You will recall that our supervisory model defines a problem as the discrepancy between what is planned and expected versus what actually happens in classrooms. Observers assist teachers by providing another set of eyes that can focus on the constant, complex interactions that occur in classrooms. A series of research-based, classroom data collection tools have been developed to assist observers in providing teachers with actual objective data about their teaching for reflection and analysis. Observers meet with teachers and review the goals of the different data collection

Table 11.1.   Effective Instructional and Affective Teacher Behaviors

Instructional Behaviors	*Affective Behaviors/Characteristics*
Uses instructional time effectively	Implements constructive discipline policies
Focuses on instructional activities	Has high expectations for self and students
Practices relevant instruction	Cares about students
Establishes classroom management routines	Demonstrates a sense of humor
Implements questioning skills/techniques at different cognitive levels	Makes fair decisions
Motivates students and builds efficacy	Demonstrates enthusiasm
Has high expectations for self and students	Is respectful
Uses graphic organizers	Demonstrates Empathy
Differentiates instruction and engages students	Is motivated and motivating
Assesses students continually	Is creative
Applies content and pedagogy	Respects diversity
Provides learning opportunities	Demonstrates mastery of subject and of teaching/learning skills

tools. Familiarity with the different data collection tools facilitates analysis and reflection. The tools are all designed to focus on research-based, high-yield instructional practices—those strategies with the most promise of helping students learn and find success in the classroom. Some tools collect data more broadly, while other are narrowly focused on a particular high-yield strategy.

Once the observer collects classroom data, the data are shared with the observed teacher. We advocate providing a copy of the data to the teacher immediately—certainly the same day. This immediate feedback reduces anxiety and enables the teacher to reflect on the data while personal perceptions of what occurred in the classroom are fresh in his or her memory. When you begin observing classes and collecting data, we urge you to photocopy the data tools provided. Then copy the completed form to share the data with the teacher. You may then arrange to meet to discuss the data after you both have had the opportunity to analyze and reflect on those data.

Electronic versions of the data collection tools are available at: onlineobservationtools.com/. When you get to the website, register by providing your e-mail address and use "30daytrial" as the invite code. The electronic versions of the tools make it possible to provide immediate feedback by enabling the observer to save the completed data form as a PDF file and e-mailing a copy to the teacher. You can e-mail a copy of the forms from the website to yourself in order to have tools to use as you practice observing classes. The electronic tools enable the observer to collect data on a laptop or tablet device, transfer the data to a searchable database, and access all collected data for analysis at the individual teacher or school level. The web-based, electronic versions of the data tools save time, as well as paper, and allow for easy comparison of observations made over a period of time. Data collection tools can also be found in Appendix D.

RESEARCH-BASED INSTRUCTIONAL STRATEGIES

We would be remiss not to provide some details on several teaching strategies that have been identified by recent meta-analyses as having the most positive impact on student achievement. These examples focus on high-yield mathematics and literacy instruction, although they cut across all subject areas.

The first example, from a meta-analysis of the most effective instructional strategies in algebra (Haas, 2005), reveals the four teaching methods that had the greatest impact on improving student achievement: direct instruction; problem-based learning; manipulatives, models, and multiple representations; and cooperative learning. An elaboration of these four teaching methods follows.

Direct instruction, not to be confused with didactic teaching, can be effectively employed across all subject areas in the curriculum. Direct instruction involves these stages:

- Teachers have a clear idea of the learning intentions—what students will be able to understand, do, and so on as a result of the teaching.
- Success criteria are clearly defined and students are informed about the standards of performance.
- Commitment and engagement in the learning task are established by using a *hook* to grab the students' attention.
- The lesson is sequenced—input (providing information), modeling (provide examples of what is expected as an end product), and checking for understanding (monitoring whether students can demonstrate they got it).
- Students participate in guided practice under the teacher's direct supervision.

- Teacher provides closure—helping students make sense out of what was taught.
- Students engage in independent practice for reinforcement (Adams & Engelmann, 1996).

Problem-based learning cuts across all subjects when students apply knowledge to new situations by induction or deduction. Teachers engage in problem-based learning when they:

- focus on the problem-solving process rather than the solution
- use the interests of individual students to create problems
- challenge students with open-ended and long-term problems
- explore alternative methods of solving a problem with students (Gijbels, 2005).

Manipulatives, models, and multiple representations include a variety of activities, such as creating graphic representations, making physical models, generating mental pictures, drawing pictures and pictographs, and engaging in kinesthetic activities (Haas, 2005). Some examples of this method include:

- providing multiple representations (words, symbols, graphs, tables, etc.)
- using pictures to illustrate concepts
- diagramming to help students learn
- engaging students in games to practice skills

The second example of strategies that have the most impact on student achievement is *reciprocal teaching*, which is an instructional process designed to teach students cognitive strategies that might lead to improved learning outcomes. It is one of the most effective strategies in improving student achievement (Hattie, 2009). Reciprocal teaching was initially used to develop reading comprehension by enabling students to learn and use cognitive strategies such as summarizing, questioning, clarifying, and predicting. As students attempt to gain meaning from the text, dialogue between the teacher and students and students and their peers supports the embedded strategies (Rosenshine & Meister, 1994). Each student takes a turn at being the "teacher," and often the teacher and students take turns leading a dialogue concerning sections of a text. Students check their own understanding of the material by generating questions and summarizing. Expert scaffolding is essential for cognitive development as students move from observer to performer after repeated modeling by adults. The aim, therefore, is to help students actively bring meaning to the written word, and assist them to monitor their own learning and thinking.

Our final example of effective strategies is *cooperative learning*, which also reaches across all subject areas. It is much more effective than individualistic learning, highlighting the positive influence of peers in enhancing student learning (Hattie, 2009). Cooperative learning has a prime effect on enhancing interest and problem solving when it is structured with high levels of peer involvement. Peers play a powerful role, for example, as demonstrated in the strategies involving reciprocal teaching. Under cooperative conditions, interpersonal relations have the strongest influence on achievement (Roseth, Fang, Johnson, & Johnson, 2006). In well-constructed cooperative situations, students are more able to collectively make and learn from errors, and their conversations can assist in having the goals, learning intentions and success criteria clarified (Nuthall, 2007).

Cooperative learning activities include a positive interdependence (sense of sink or swim together), face-to-face promotive interaction (helping each other learn, applauding successes and efforts), individual and group accountability (each individual has to contribute to the group achieving its goals), interpersonal and small-group skills (communication, trust, leadership, decision-making, and conflict resolution), and group processing (reflecting on how well the team is functioning and how to function even better) (Johnson & Johnson, 1999). Some examples of teaching methods in this category are when:

- students are engaged in cooperative problem solving
- students start homework in class with peer assistance
- students brainstorm and discuss solutions to problems with peers
- students serve as peer tutors.

Principals, as supervisors and evaluators, can help teachers become more effective by helping them learn and effectively practice those research-based teaching methods and strategies that have a positive impact on the achievement of students.

TEACHERS' KNOWLEDGE

It is clear that a teacher's knowledge of the subject is critical for teaching (Ball, Lubienski, & Mewborn, 2001; Borko & Putnam, 1996). Part of that knowledge is pedagogical content knowledge, or knowing how to teach a subject to particular students (Shulman, 1987). We know that the quality of teachers—as measured by whether the teachers were fully certified and had a major in their teaching field—is related to student performance (Darling-Hammond, 2000). Content knowledge is necessary, but not sufficient, for effective teaching. Teachers who know more facts about their subject do not necessarily have students who learn more. But teachers who know and understand their subject may make clearer presentations and more easily recognize student difficulties. They answer student questions and do not have to be evasive or vague in their responses; they generate another example or analogy when the students need more help understanding.

EXPECTATIONS

Hattie (2009) argues that the greatest single issue in helping students achieve is the need for teachers to have a common perception of progress. When a student moves from one teacher to another, there is no guarantee that he or she will experience increasingly challenging tasks, have a teacher with similar (high) expectations of progress through the curricula, or work with a teacher who will grow the student from where he or she is, as opposed to where the teacher believes he or she should be at the start of the year. To have high expectations and to share a common conception of progress requires teachers to be concerned about the nature of their relationships with their students—the power of these relationships is critical for learning to occur.

CLARITY AND ORGANIZATION

Research reveals the importance for the teacher to communicate the intentions of the lessons and the notions of what success means for these intentions—criteria of success (Hattie, 2009). Fendick (1990) found a high impact on student achievement when he investigated teacher clarity, which he defined as organization, explanation, examples and guided practice, and assessment of student learning—clarity of speech was a prerequisite of teacher clarity.

Teachers who provide clear presentations and explanations tend to have students who learn more and who rate their teachers more positively (Hines, Cruickshank, & Kennedy, 1982, 1985; Land, 1987). Teachers with more knowledge of the subject tend to be less vague in their explanations to the class. The less vague the teacher, the more the students learn (Land, 1987).

Research offers guidelines for greater clarity in teaching (Berliner, 1987; Evertson, Emmer, Clements, & Worsham, 2000; Hines et al., 1985). When planning a lesson, teachers should try to anticipate the problems students might have with the content. Principals can facilitate this anticipation by encouraging teachers to complete written components of a lesson to identify potential problems. Providing definitions for new terms and several relevant examples for concepts facilitates clarity. Lessons should be delivered in a logical sequence, including checkpoints, that incorporate oral or written questions or problems to make sure the students are following the explanations. Clear introductions to lessons, as well as telling students what they will be learning and how they will learn it, also contributes to clarity.

Being precise about "how" to do the work is even harder. One study found that teachers seldom, if ever, explain the cognitive processes they want their students to practice in a seatwork activity. More capable students often figure out the right process, but other students simply guess or give up. As principals observe instruction, they should determine whether teachers make clear connections between facts or concepts by using explanatory links such as because, if ... then, or therefore. Explanatory links tie ideas together and make them easier to learn (Berliner, 1987). Explanatory links are also helpful in labeling visual material such as graphs, concept maps, or illustrations.

Effective teachers also signal transitions from one major topic to another with phrases such as "The next area...," "Now we will turn to...," or "The second step is..." Teachers might help students follow the lesson by outlining topics, listing key points, or drawing concept maps on the board or on an overhead projector. Teachers monitor the group to see if everyone is following the lesson. Principals should scrutinize the learners as they observe instruction. Look for confident nods or puzzled stares. Is the teacher using words that are familiar to the students? Defining new terms and relating them to what the students already know? Vagueness is the enemy of understanding. Is the teacher being precise and encouraging students to do so also? Is the teacher avoiding vague words and ambiguous phrases? Refraining from using pet phrases such as "you know," "like," and "Okay"? Principals can encourage teachers to make an audio recording of a lesson to self-check for clarity.

LEARNING TIME

Simply making more time for learning will not automatically lead to achievement. The key to enhancing learning is to increase productive time—engaged learning time or time on task. Engagement is higher when students work in groups or laboratories. The greater the academic demands on students and more they feel challenged, the more the students are engaged with instruction and the less prone they are to distractions. The frequency of different learning opportunities is much more important than spending more time on task (Hattie, 2009).

Student success in learning new skills depends not on the amount of practice or experience, but the amount of deliberate, relevant effort to improve performance. This deliberate practice needs to be at an appropriate, challenging level of difficulty and enable successive refinement by allowing for repetition. Time must be provided to make and correct errors, and provide informative feedback to students (van Gog, Ericsson, Rikers, & Paas, 2005). Deliberate practice requires students to stretch themselves to higher levels of performance and requires much concentration and effort over extended periods, usually of fixed times over many days.

Students may be struggling with inappropriate content and/or teaching strategies. When students are working with a high rate of success—really learning and understanding—the time spent is called academic learning time. One important goal of supervision is to help teachers efficiently and effectively use the minutes available for learning. Good classroom management increases academic learning time by keeping students actively engaged in worthwhile, appropriate learning activities. Teaching is active with a great deal of time devoted to teacher–student interaction, explanation, and questioning. Less time is spent in independent seatwork or review worksheets.

Assessing classroom time spent directly related to academic activities and the degree to which students are engaged provides an indication of teachers' emphasis on instructional activities. A number of very simple techniques can be used, with varying degrees of precision, to collect information about the academic behaviors of teachers and the effects of those behaviors on students. From the perspective of the teacher, a simple monitoring of what the teacher and students are doing every minute of a class session would be an indicator of academic focus. It might be stated as a percentage of total time available, for example, a teacher's behavior might be described as academically focused 75% of the time. The rest of the time was used in keeping order, housekeeping, and so on. Audio or video recording might be used to record teacher behavior, or the principal might actually use a watch to determine academically engaged time.

Another technique, and probably a more useful one, would be for the principal to record the behavior of the teacher at short intervals. In reviewing this record of what the teacher was doing throughout the class period, teacher and principal can quite accurately determine how much academically focused time there was and also identify trends of teacher behavior that interfere with or distract from academic focus. Perhaps the most interesting and useful technique is one that focuses on how students spend their class time. Often a description of teacher behavior alone is misleading, particularly when the teacher works with small groups.

DiPaola and DiPaola (2009) designed the *Student Engagement* form that is very simple and useful for recording how students are engaged. Each circle represents a student seated in the classroom. On the first line in each circle the principal indicates the gender and name, or some other identifying characteristic, of each student. The remainder of each circle is divided into six, numbered sections. A coded legend is provided to represent on-task behaviors and off-task behaviors observed. The observer systematically examines the behavior of each student for a few seconds to determine whether the student appears on task, or off task, during an activity or time interval. This is indicated for each student by recording the appropriate behavior code in the circle on the seating chart that represents that student. The principal can repeat these student observations at six time intervals or six activities during a lesson using the same legend codes to indicate observed behavior. Figure 11.1 is a sample student engagement data-collection record.

The detail and simplicity of the system are apparent. Once completed, the principal and teacher can meet or conduct independent analyses of the data on the form. A careful analysis of on-task and off-task behaviors will reveal problems, particularly if the percentage of time-on-task does not meet their expectations. This technique allows the information about student behavior to be displayed in a manner that is sure to provoke thought and discussion.

OPPORTUNITIES TO LEARN

It is the frequency of different opportunities rather than merely spending more time on task that makes the difference in learning (Hattie, 2009). Teachers should increase the rate of correct academic responses to planned, varied opportunities to practice until minimum levels of mastery (defined by success criteria) are met (Walker, Greenwood, Hart, & Carta, 1994). This is a common denominator of many effective practices, such as direct instruction, peer tutoring, mastery learning, and feedback. Planned, varied instructional practice increases opportunities not only to enhance mastery but also to gain fluency. By this we do not mean "drill and practice," which is often dull and repetitive, involves minimal feedback, and does not extend or provide multiple different experiences. Planned, varied instructional practice can involve specific skills and complex performances. The attainment of success criteria can be motivating

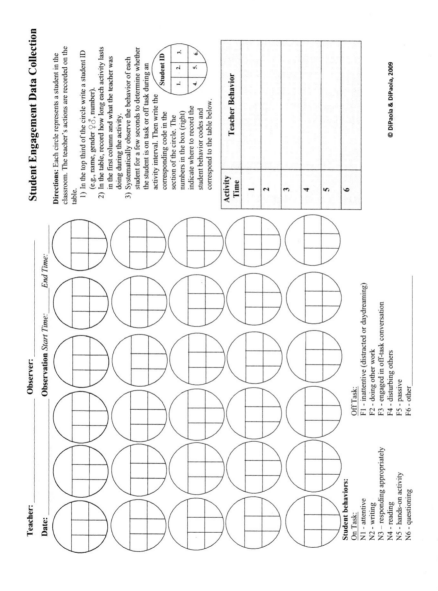

Student Engagement Data Collection

Teacher: _____ Observer: _____

Date: _____ Observation *Start Time:* _____ *End Time:* _____

Directions: Each circle represents a student in the classroom. The teacher's actions are recorded on the table.

1) In the top third of the circle write a student ID (e.g., name, gender ♀♂, number).
2) In the table, record how long each activity lasts in the first column and what the teacher was doing during the activity.
3) Systematically observe the behavior of each student for a few seconds to determine whether the student is on task or off task during an activity interval. Then write the corresponding code in the section of the circle. The numbers in the box (right) indicate where to record the student behavior codes and correspond to the table below.

Student ID

1.	2.	3.
4.	5.	6.

Activity Time	Teacher Behavior
1	
2	
3	
4	
5	
6	

© DiPaola & DiPaola, 2009

Student behaviors:

On Task:
N1 - attentive
N2 - writing
N3 - responding appropriately
N4 - reading
N5 - hands-on activity
N6 - questioning

Off Task:
F1 - inattentive (distracted or daydreaming)
F2 - doing other work
F3 - engaged in off-task conversation
F4 - disturbing others
F5 - passive
F6 - other

Figure 11.1. Student engagement.

267

and lead to longer retention of sometimes over-learned surface and deep knowing (Péladeau, Forget, & Gagné, 2003).

Providing students such opportunities to learn is directly related to student achievement. To provide opportunities, teachers must make sure everyone knows how to participate in class activities. The key is awareness. What are the rules and expectations? Are they understandable, given the students' cultural backgrounds and home experiences? What unspoken rules or values may be operating? Are teachers clearly signaling appropriate ways to participate? For some students, particularly those with behavioral and emotional challenges, direct teaching and practicing of important behaviors may be required (Emmer & Stough, 2001).

CLASSROOM ROUTINES

The overall positive effect of a well-managed classroom is not surprising. Teacher-student relationships are powerful moderators of classroom management. The following aspects of classroom management have significant impact on achievement:

- teacher's ability to identify and act quickly on potential problems
- teacher maintaining emotional objectivity
- effective disciplinary interventions
- group contingency strategies
- tangible recognition of appropriate behavior
- direct and concrete consequences for misbehavior (Hattie, 2009, p. 102).

Effective teachers capture instructional time by using efficient rules and procedures. They have planned procedures and rules for coping with generic situations that can be anticipated easily. For example, how will materials and assignments be distributed and collected? How will grades be determined? What are the special routines for handling equipment and supplies? Procedures describe how activities are accomplished in classrooms, but they are seldom written down; they are simply the ways of getting things done in class. Weinstein (2003) and Weinstein and Mignano (2003) suggest that teachers establish procedures to cover the following areas:

- administrative routines (e.g., taking attendance)
- student movement (e.g., getting out of assigned seat)

- housekeeping (e.g., storing personal items)
- routines for accomplishing lessons (e.g,. how to collect assignments or return homework)
- interactions between teacher and student (e.g., how to get the teacher's attention when help is needed)
- talk among students (e.g., group work or giving help).

Principals can use these six areas as a framework for helping teachers think through their procedures and routines.

ENGAGING STUDENTS

Being seated in the "action zone"—the front row and down the center for most classrooms, tends to increase participation for students who are predisposed to speak in class, whereas a seat in the back will make it more difficult to participate and easier to sit back and daydream (Woolfolk & Brooks, 1983). To better engage all students, Weinstein and Mignano (2003) suggest that teachers move around the room when possible, establish eye contact with students seated far away, and direct comments to students seated at a distance. Effective teachers often vary the seating so the same students are not always assigned to the back of the room and arrange classrooms to be appropriate for particular objectives and activities.

Different classroom arrangements have advantages and disadvantages. For example, horizontal rows and traditional row and column arrangements are useful for independent seatwork and teacher, student, or media presentations; they encourage students to focus on the presenter and simplify housekeeping, so they are good arrangements for the beginning of the school year—especially for new teachers. Horizontal rows also permit students to work more easily in pairs. However, this is a poor arrangement for large-group discussion. Clusters of four or circle arrangements are best for student interaction. Circles are especially useful for discussions but still allow for independent seatwork. Clusters permit students to talk, help one another, share materials, and work on group tasks. Both arrangements, however, are poor for whole-group presentations or tests and may make class management more difficult. On the other hand, the fishbowl can create a feeling of group cohesion and is helpful when the teacher wants students to watch a demonstration, brainstorm a class problem, or see a small visual aid. Principals can help teachers design spaces for learning that match the teacher's learning intentions and activities. If there are problems with an activity, maybe the physical design is hindering rather than supporting learning.

> **THEORY INTO PRACTICE**
> *ISLLC Standards 1, 2, 3, 5*
> How is instructional time protected in your school? Be specific. What
> does the principal do to insure that most time is focused on instruction
> with minimal interference? What are the specific things in your school
> that erode instructional time? If you were principal, list five strategies
> you would employ to protect instructional time. How many of these does
> your principal use? If the principal employs all five, then develop three
> more that you would suggest.

INTERACTING WITH STUDENTS

Interaction refers to verbal behaviors that keep the learning activity
directed, focused, and organized by the teacher. Providing information,
questioning, answering, clarifying, praising, giving directions, scolding,
and redirecting skills and techniques are of particular interest. An indicator of these behaviors and skills could be obtained by simply clocking
the percentage of available time the teacher spends engaged in each
behavior during a lesson. More useful data for analysis and reflection
would reveal the kind and frequency of interactions with each student
in the class. DiPaola and DiPaola (2007) developed the *Student-Teacher
Verbal Interactions* form to collect these data. Observers simply indicate
an interaction from the teacher to a student by placing an arrow pointing down in one of the boxes when teacher directs an interaction to
that student. Likewise, an arrow pointing up is drawn when the student
directs an interaction to the teacher. The observer also places the
appropriate code from the legend for the kind of verbal interaction
observed (Figure 11.2).

Analyses of a full seating chart containing these interaction data can
indicate behavioral patterns relevant to a teacher's direction of activity.
Data may reveal, for example, that the teacher interacts with only a limited number of students in a certain manner while others are virtually
ignored. They may reveal that the teacher has a tendency to interact
differently with girls than boys or not interact with one gender at all. By
using the code provided in the legend, the kind of interactions with
individual students can also be determined and patterns revealed. If
interactions do not meet expectations, a problem is revealed and appropriate planning follows. This technique allows the information about
teacher verbal behavior to be displayed in a way that facilitates analysis
and discussion.

Teacher/Student Interactions

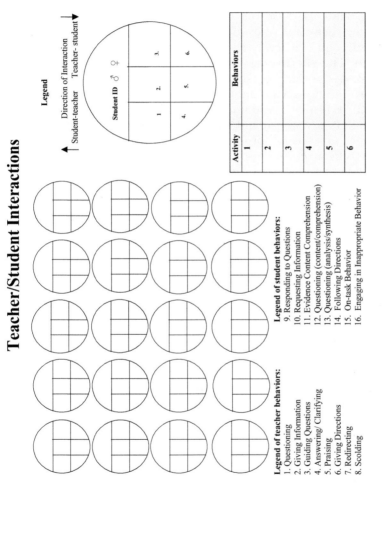

Legend of teacher behaviors:
1. Questioning
2. Giving Information
3. Guiding Questions
4. Answering/ Clarifying
5. Praising
6. Giving Directions
7. Redirecting
8. Scolding

Legend of student behaviors:
9. Responding to Questions
10. Requesting Information
11. Evidence Content Comprehension
12. Questioning (content/comprehension)
13. Questioning (analysis/synthesis)
14. Following Directions
15. On-task Behavior
16. Engaging in Inappropriate Behavior

Legend

Direction of Interaction
Student-teacher   Teacher- student

Student ID ♂ ♀

© DiPaola & DiPaola 2011

Figure 11.2.   Student/teacher verbal interactions.

271

QUESTIONING SKILLS AND TECHNIQUES

Good questioning is a critical component of effective teaching—a powerful strategy for building comprehension (Mantione & Smead, 2003). "Good questions lead to improved comprehension, learning, and memory of the materials" (Craig, Sullins, Witherspoon, & Gholson, 2006, p. 567) among students. Research has established a direct link between student achievement and the effective use of questioning at different difficulty and cognitive levels (Brophy & Good, 1986; Cawelti, 1999; Hattie, 2009). The effectiveness of questioning depends on the types of questions asked—"surface questions can enhance surface knowing and higher-order questions can enhance deeper understanding" (Hattie, 2009, p. 182). Effective questioning also enables teachers to assess student learning. Principals should focus on questioning skills and techniques in the supervisory process as they attempt to help teachers become more effective. An observer can collect questioning data by simply recording verbatim the questions the teacher asks during a lesson or lesson segment. Both the frequency and cognitive level of teacher questions can be examined to see if they are appropriate for the particular class and grade level. Teacher reinforcement statements and praise and criticism of students can also be recorded and examined by teacher and supervisor.

In another method of data collection, the principal records the cognitive level of each question the teacher poses during a lesson or lesson segment using a data collection tool (DiPaola & DiPaola, 2007). Figure 11.3 provides a sample instrument to collect questioning data during an observation. Note that the observer records the wait time in seconds next to the cognitive level of each question during the observation. Of course, the observer must be familiar with the cognitive hierarchy and question stems that cue to specific cognitive levels.

The principal can then summarize the number of questions asked at each cognitive level during the duration of the observation. Joint analysis by the teacher and principal of these data may reveal patterns or the fact that most questions are at one cognitive level—recall, for example. If the questioning skills and techniques of the teacher do not meet the expected outcomes of teacher performance, a problem is identified and an opportunity to become more effective revealed.

Teacher: _____

Date: _____

Class Observed: _____

Follow up Dialogue Date: _____

Administrator: _____

Observation: *Start Time:* _____ *End Time:* _____

Number of Students in the Class: _____

Directions: The purpose of this form is to record the cognitive level of each question the teacher poses during a lesson or lesson segment. For each question, identify the level of the question and count the number of seconds the teacher waits until letting a student respond. Record the number of seconds in the corresponding row in each question's column.

Cognitive Level	\multicolumn{11}{c}{Wait Time in Seconds}											Total Questions Asked
	Q1	Q2	Q3	Q4	Q5	Q6	Q7	Q8	Q9	Q10	Q11	
Remembering												
Understanding												
Applying												
Analyzing												
Evaluating												
Creating												

Sample Stems

Remembering
What is the definition for…
What happened after…
How many…
Who did…
When was…
Define the word…
Which is true or false?

Understanding
Explain what happened after…
Provide a definition of…
What is the purpose of…
Explain why _____ caused _____
What are some examples?
Who was the key character?
How are these ideas different?
What do you think could happen?

Applying
What is another instance of…
Demonstrate the way to…
Which one is most like…
Could this have happened in…
How would you organize these ideas?
Which factors would you change?

Analyzing
What steps are important in the process of…
The solution would be to…
What's the relationship between…
What other conclusions can you reach about…
If ____, then ____
What do you see as other possible outcomes?

Evaluating
How would you have handled…
How would you feel if…
Defend your position about…
What do you think should be the outcome?
What changes would you recommend?

Creating
Devise your own way to…
Develop a proposal for…
How would you deal with…
Can you see a solution to…
What would happen if…
How many ways can you…
Design a ____ to ____

© *DiPaola & DiPaola 2009*

Figure 11.3. Cognitive levels of questions and wait time.

> **THEORY INTO PRACTICE**
> *ISLLC Standards 1, 2, 3, 5*
> Use your own teaching experience and give examples of questions that facilitate remembering. Then turn to questions that enhance understanding and give a few more examples. What is the difference between these two types of questions? Now compare and contrast questions that call for application with those calling for analysis. Be sure and give an example of each. The final two levels of questioning are evaluating and creating. Illustrate each of these levels with specific questions. To what extent do you expect teachers to use all six cognitive levels of questions? Should some teachers be content if they get most of their students understanding, applying, and analyzing the basic concepts of the lesson? How realistic is it to expect teachers to teach students to be creative?

TEACHING ACTIVITIES

The goal of a teacher and principal is finding the balance of classroom activities that is most effective for a particular class at a particular grade level to achieve the instructional objective. Given the array of research-based teacher strategies related to student achievement, principals often collect data on teacher and student behaviors in the classroom. Various data collection tools focusing on research-based teaching strategies have been developed in order to assist principals and peers in collecting data for teacher reflection and joint analysis. One example is an observation form designed at the School University Research Network (SURN) at the College of William and Mary for use in their Principals' Academy. Focusing on both principal performance standards and research-based, high-yield strategies, Rozzelle (2012) and her colleagues developed the *SURN Teacher Observation and Feedback Tool* to give principals the opportunity to assess the variety of research-based teacher behaviors exhibited during an observation, as well as make anecdotal comments (see Figure 11.4). The tool gives the observer the opportunity to record occurrences of both high and low yield practices by the teacher. An analysis of these data with the teacher provides an opportunity to assess the range of behaviors being employed to help students achieve.

Another tool was designed by Rozzelle and her colleagues to collect data on how students are engaging with the content of the lesson. Principals and other observers can use the *SURN Student Engagement Observation and Reflection Tool* (Rozzelle, 2012) to collect data on student participation in both high-yield and low-yield practices (see Figure 11.5). Reflection and

Name_____   School_____   Grade/Content_____

Date_____   Time In _____   Time Out _____Observer _____

The observer uses this form to record occurrences of high and low yield practices by the teacher. A check appears if an item is observed. Note that in a single observation, not all items will be observed. Indicators are not checked without evidence. Observers are to write specific examples or non-examples in the far right column for discussion with the teacher. An observation crosswalk resource aligns items with *Virginia Uniform Teacher Performance Standards.*

Pre-observation review:
Lesson Plan reflects: the use of student learning data, appropriate pacing and rigor, differentiated activities, alignment with curriculum, and alignment of lesson activities and assessments to lesson's objective (Virginia Uniform Teacher Performance Standard 2).

Feedback:

OBSERVATION "LOOK-FORS"	*Observed*	*SPECIFY EXAMPLES/NON-EXAMPLES*
1. Clarifies and articulates specific learning objectives/learning intentions.		
2. Identifies and communicates challenging success criteria in checklists and rubrics.		
3. Assesses and builds upon students' existing knowledge and skills.		
4. Engages and hooks		
5. Provides input, explains, and models		
6. Guides practice: monitors, coaches and remediates as needed		
7. Provides closure and assesses lesson impact on students, engages students in reflection		
8. Provides time for independent practice		
9. Develops vocabulary and connects concepts and ideas.		
10. Questions for high level thinking and deep learning, responds appropriately to students queries, promotes student questioning.		

Figure 11.4.   SURN teacher observation and feedback tool. *(Figure 11.4 continues on next page.)*

joint analysis of such data enable both the teacher and principal in assessing the quality of student interaction with instructional activities and whether a discrepancy exists between the desired and actual outcomes.

A final example is to collect data on teacher and student behaviors simultaneously. DiPaola and DiPaola (2007) designed the *Teacher/Student Behavior Observation Form* (Figure 11.6) focusing on the high-yield strategies identified by Marzano (2003). Observers use this form to collect data

OBSERVATION "LOOK-FORS"	Observed	SPECIFY EXAMPLES/NON-EXAMPLES
11. Uses small group options, **specify a, b, c, d, e:** a) Pairs, c) Cooperative learning, b) Guided reading, d) Reciprocal teaching, e) other		
12. Assigns/uses varied and leveled text, **specify:** a. Nonfiction b. Fiction c. Textbook d. Real world e. Leveled or differentiated text		
13. Integrates student use of technology to enhance learning.		
14. Assesses individual learning to provide specific descriptive feedback at the task, product and process levels; does not mix/confuse praise with feedback.		
15. Differentiates instruction through re-teaching, acceleration, and enrichment, etc.		
16. Uses existing products or samples as models for student products.		
17. Provides choices in assessment products.		
18. Uses a variety of assessment strategies and appropriate instruments.		
19. Arranges classroom configurations to maximize learning.		
20. Uses management strategies to reduce disruptions in learning: clear expectations, rules, procedures, safety, etc.		
21. Maintains and reinforces instructional clarity and alignment across learning goals, lesson organization, explanation, examples, guided practice and assessments.		

Lower-Yield Practices for Teachers		
1. Questions in series-interrogative		
2. Assigns practice without explicit instruction		
3. Tells/lectures		
4. Uses whole class instruction		

Observation Overview Environment Assessment: Establishes a climate of trust and teamwork by being fair, caring, enthusiastic. Respects and promotes cultural sensitivity. Specify Examples or Non-Examples:

Figure 11.4.   SURN teacher observation and feedback tool. *(continued).*

using the three keys—teacher behavior, student behavior, and teaching strategies—at the bottom of the form. A rich data set for reflection and analysis results by focusing on the three key elements simultaneously. These data provide an opportunity to examine student reactions to the teacher's behaviors. Are the students' reactions congruent with the teacher's reactions? Do they conform to student behaviors anticipated based on the teacher's behaviors? Are the behaviors focused on learning? Do the teacher's behaviors reflect research-based instructional strategies that affect student achievement?

THEORY INTO PRACTICE

ISLLC Standards 1, 2, 3, 5

Review the *Teacher Observation and Feedback Tool* in Figure 11.4 to be sure you become familiar with the format and have an understanding of the specific data it enables one to collect and how the data are collected on it. Then use the form to collect data in a teacher's classroom. Remember that all the look-fors listed will not be observed. Just focus on those that you observe but be sure to specify examples or non-examples for those you do observe. After your observation and data collection, analyze the data. Describe the instructional strategies that the teacher used—were they high-yield, research-based? Appropriate for the learning expectations? How many were low-yield strategies? Summarize the strengths and weaknesses of this teacher during the lesson. How would you use these data to help the teacher improve instruction?

TEACHER-STUDENT RELATIONSHIPS

Building positive relationships with students has a dramatic impact on their achievement and success in school. Establishing such relationships with students "implies agency, efficacy, respect by the teacher for what the child brings to the class ... and allowing the experiences of the child to be recognized in the classroom" (Hattie, 2009, p. 118). Teachers who have the most positive relationships with students are person-centered and demonstrate a high degree of emotional intelligence. Research revealed that teachers who are non-directive, empathetic, warm, and encourage learning and higher order thinking have the highest positive impact on student learning (Hattie, 2009).

Hamre and Pianta (2001) followed all the children in a small school district who entered kindergarten one year and continued in the school district through the 8th grade. The researchers concluded that the quality of the teacher–student relationship in kindergarten (defined in terms of level of conflict with the child, the child's dependency on the teacher, and the teacher's affection for the child) predicted a number of academic and behavioral outcomes through the 8th grade, particularly for students with high levels of behavior problems. Even when the gender, ethnicity, cognitive ability, and behavior ratings of the student were accounted for, the relationship with the teacher still predicted aspects of school success. The researchers concluded that "the association between the quality of early teacher-child relationships and later school performance can be both strong and persistent" (Harme & Pianta, 2001, p. 636). Based on the results of this carefully conducted study, it appears that students with significant

Name_____   School_____Grade/Content_____

Date_____ Time In _____ Time Out _____   Observer _____

OBSERVATION "LOOK-FORS"	Observed	SPECIFY EXAMPLES/NON-EXAMPLES
1. Engages in setting learning goals		
2. Engages in making choices.		
3. Engages in reading.		
4. Engages in writing.		
5. Engages in discussing text or other input.		
6. Engages in problem solving.		
7. Creates products.		
8. Engages in peer tutoring, cooperative learning, reciprocal teaching, and other cooperative group structures: **Specify**		
9. Engages in relevant, real-world learning experiences.		
10. Applies meta-cognition strategies, *Specify:* a) Making connections e) Summarizing b) Inferring/Generating Hypotheses/Predicting f) Visualizing c) Asking/generating questions g) Synthesizing d) Determining importance/big ideas h) Monitoring and clarifying		
11. Creates/uses learning tools, *indicate:* a) Concept mapping b) Advance/graphic organizers c) Manipulatives d) Technology e) Other, *Specify*		
12. Engages in self-assessment of their work, what they learn, and how they learn		
13. Engages in asking for and giving specific feedback to peers and to the teacher.		
Lower-Yield Practices for Students		
1. Completes worksheet, homework		
2. Engages in oral turn taking		
3. Responds orally		
4. Engages in listening		
5. Engages in off-task behaviors		

Figure 11.5.   SURN student engagement observation and reflection tool.

behavior problems in the early years are less likely to have problems later in school if their teachers are sensitive to their needs and provide frequent, consistent feedback.

Some teachers are much more enthusiastic than others. Studies have found that ratings of teachers' enthusiasm for their subject are correlated

Teacher / Student Behavior Observation Form

Teacher: _____   Date: _____

Objective:

	Teacher Behavior	Student Behavior	Specific Examples
Activity / Clock time			
Activity 1 Time:			
Activity 2 Time:			
Activity 3 Time:			
Activity 4 Time:			
Activity 5 Time:			
Activity 6 Time:			
Activity 7 Time:			
Activity 8 Time:			

Teacher Behavior Key
T1. Clarifying learning objective/outcomes
T2. Identifying success criteria/rubric
T3. Engaging & Hooking
T4. Explaining and modeling
T5. Guiding practice
T6. Providing closure
T7. Employing small group options
T8. Listening
T9. Assigning varied & leveled text
T10. Providing descriptive feedback

Student Behavior Key
S1. Setting learning goals
S2. Reading
S3. Writing
S4. Discussing text/input
S5. Problem Solving
S6. Creating a product
S7. Peer tutoring/cooperative learning
S8. Asking questions
S9. Using learning tools
S10. Self-assessing

Figure 11.6.   Behavior observation form.

with student achievement gains (Rosenshine & Furst, 1973). Studies revealed that teachers who are warm and friendly tend to have students who like them and the class in general (Murray, 1983; Ryans, 1960; Soar & Soar, 1979). The research also links teacher caring, warmth, and enthusiasm with effective teachers and student achievement (Marzano, 2000; Stronge, 2002). As early as 1970, teacher behaviors rated as animated, enthusiastic, stimulating, energetic, and mobile were related to student achievement (Rosenshine, 1975). The frequency of eye contact, voice fluctuation, movement, and gesture were also related to student achievement. Teacher warmth, caring, and enthusiasm are observable and are reasonable foci for teacher-principal analyses during the supervisory process.

Teacher behaviors identified as characteristic of enthusiastic teaching include requesting interpretation, opinions, and facts; frequently praising students; gesturing; speaking rapidly; moving around the classroom; asking varied questions; making eye contact with students; and raising and lowering vocal inflection (Rosenshine, 1975). These behaviors can simply be counted by the principal during an observation; however, slightly more precise data-collecting procedures are available for some of the behaviors. For example, aspects of enthusiasm can be studied by reviewing audio- or audio-videotapes. Electronic transcription is a very useful way to examine enthusiasm since no data are lost in making the record.

More focused techniques allow the teacher and supervisor to concentrate on one aspect of enthusiasm at a time and consequently design a limited and manageable plan for change. For example, the teacher's physical movement in the classroom can be recorded by a principal recording movement patterns on a seating chart. Such data may demonstrate that a teacher moves infrequently and that when movement does occur, it is always toward the same side of the classroom. The principal may notice that the teacher always moves toward a student speaker, causing the student speaker to lower his or her voice and thus depriving the rest of the class from hearing.

A teacher's raising and lowering vocal inflection can be examined through audio recordings that are later listened to by the teacher and supervisor in order to make judgments about the adequacy and variety of the teacher's vocal inflection. Often the discovery that one's teaching lacks observable enthusiasm can be responded to by a plan involving gesture, voice pitch and volume modulation, and movement. Any of the behaviors constituting enthusiasm can be monitored by a principal or electronic transcription, and improvements can be built into the teacher's planning. For a teacher just to discover that his or her teaching is less enthusiastic than it might be, however, is not sufficient. A plan of action, focusing on specific behaviors and including a system for self-monitoring progress is necessary for enduring instructional improvements.

Although it is more difficult to assess the warmth a teacher exhibits, some of the behaviors constituting warmth can be observed, including:

- accepting and clarifying the emotional tone of the students in a non-threatening manner
- praising student action or behavior

- encouraging student action or behavior
- joking to release tension
- turning minor disciplinary situations into jokes
- believing that students can behave themselves without constant supervision (Gage, 1975).

Of all the teacher behaviors discussed, warmth is perhaps the least tangible and the most difficult on which to collect data. But perhaps the most useful technique would be the selective verbatim approach, in which the observer makes a verbatim transcript of verbal events that are indicative of warmth. As a result of such a transcript, a teacher and principal may decide that warmth is not exhibited often enough or is not shown to certain students. Another method to assess the important teacher traits is to use a simple list of indicators. The *Classroom Observation Form* (DiPaola & DiPaola, 2007) summarizes those behaviors linked to enthusiasm and warmth (see Table 11.2). This form can be used to record the frequency of those behaviors during a classroom observation.

Table 11.1.   Classroom Observation Form: Teacher Behaviors Linked to Student Learning

Teacher ...	*Observed*	*Comments*
exhibits warmth, friendliness, and understanding		
provides student-initiated and student-regulated activities		
uses routines to manage the classroom environment		
fosters an atmosphere of trust and respect		
is constructive in their discipline		
maximizes the use of instructional time		
communicates high expectations for students		
identifies and links learning objectives to instructional activities		
uses a range of instructional strategies that appropriately relate to the learning objective and students		
incorporates a variety of cognitive levels of questions		
engages students in instruction and the learning process		
stays clearly focused on instructional activities and student learning		

Observation notes:

SUMMARY

In this chapter we focused on the teacher performance output of our supervisory model. We first summarized some research-based, high-yield instructional strategies to focus on performance that has the best promise of positively influencing the other output—student achievement. Next we introduced some ways to collect focused information on individual teacher performance with regard to those teaching strategies. The observation tools that we use to collect classroom data may appear to be complicated on initial review; however, hundreds of observers who have used them attest to their effectiveness in data collection—naturally, the more you use them, the more familiar they become and the easier it is to collect and share data. Equally obvious is the fact that other measures can be employed to examine teachers' performance outputs. However, these particular tools are simple and easy to explain to teachers. The forms organize collected data in a manner that is easy to analyze and that facilitates dialogue between teacher and observer. As the teacher and principal become more experienced in classroom analysis, they may well elect more precise and sophisticated measures and procedures. Appendix D provides some guidelines for observing classroom behavior.

DEVELOP YOUR PORTFOLIO

Go to onlineobservationtools.com. When you get to the website log in or register, If you have not done so, by providing your e-mail address and use "30daytrial" as the invite code. Access the digital version of the Teacher/Student Observation Form on a laptop or tablet, to observe two different teachers in your school. Analyze the data that you collect by writing a description of the teaching that occurred. Be sure to include a summary of the different teaching behaviors and student reactions to them. Also describe the instructional strategies that each teacher used—were they high-yield, research-based? Appropriate for the learning expectations? Point out the strengths and weaknesses of each teacher. Compare the approaches of the two teachers. Which is more appropriate? Why? How would you use these data to help teachers improve their instruction? End your analysis with the one event in each class with which you would begin you improvement plan.

COMMUNICATION EXERCISE

Use **one** of the two observations above and write a script to communicate what you observed. Try to be positive and constructive in your description. Speak not only to the interaction patterns observed but also the kinds and levels of questions that the teacher posed. Accentuate the positive, but select at least one area in need of improvement and use a constructive approach to tackling the problem.

A PRINCIPAL'S SUPERVISORY SUCCESS STORY

Jake Johnson is a fifth year math teacher at Fallsville High School. Fallsville has 1,320 students and is located in a working class neighborhood. The student population consists of 62% African American, 25% Caucasian, 5% Asian, and the remaining 8% of students are self-identified as multiracial. Sixty-one percent of students qualify for free or reduced lunch. As an English as a Second Language school district site, 120 students from 41 nations attend Fallsville. About one third of graduating seniors pursue college. Until 2011, Fallsville was accredited by the state board of education. With the introduction of the new math standards and state assessments in 2012, Fallsville is accredited with warning.

For the past five years Jake has taught statistics, pre-calculus, and geometry. When principal Troy Fox arrived in July of 2012, he was eager to meet with teachers, students, parents, and community members. As the third principal in three years, in a school where student performance on standardized tests had declined steadily for the past four years, Troy aimed to learn as much as possible about Fallsville prior to the arrival of teachers and the first day of school. In his first week on the job, Troy sent a letter to teachers to introduce himself and invite them to meet with him at their convenience. More than two-thirds of teachers came during their summer break to meet the new principal and talk about their programs and experiences at Fallsville. As the school year approached, Troy was impressed with the number of teachers and students who came into the building over the summer break to prepare their classroom or get ready for the fall sports season.

Troy met the remaining staff at the first faculty meeting of the school year. After receiving the school meeting schedule, Jake introduced himself and stated that he would not be able to attend any faculty meetings because he is taking courses in advanced statistics at a local university. He also stated that due to traffic, he would not be able to stay for after-school tutoring for his students on most days. Troy asked a few questions about the classes he will be taking as well the program he was pursuing. He informed Jake that he would like him to attend faculty meetings and that whenever possible he would work with him to ensure he would get to his university class on time. Troy also told Jake that for the second semester he would like him to avoid registering for classes that meet on Wednesdays as these days are designated for meetings at Fallsville. Jake was friendly and seemed agreeable to work together with the new principal around the new meeting schedule.

After catching up with all teachers, Troy returned to his office for a scheduled meeting with his assistant principal, Rachel Mueller. Troy shared the conversation he had with Jake, and Rachel was not surprised. Rachel explained that Jake has been taking graduate classes for a few years now and he had not been able to attend many faculty meetings or be available for his students after school. Rachel said that Jake was a good teacher who deeply cared about his students. Though Jake's students performed below the performance of similar students in both the school district and the state, Jake was a team player and was willing to improve his practice. Rachel has been an assistant principal at Fallsville for the past three years. With a mathematics background, Rachel felt camaraderie with the math teachers as well as the lead teachers at Fallsville. Though apprehensive about the change in leadership, Rachel was excited at the opportunity to collaborate with Troy to realize the potential of Fallsville teachers.

During the first few weeks of school, Troy spent most of his time visiting classrooms talking with both students and teachers. Each time Troy visited a classroom, he gave teachers data collected during the observations, and often he met with teachers for post-observation conferences. Because Fallsville was given a warning by the State Department of Education for low mathematics student achievement, Troy spent a disproportionate amount of time observing math classes, observing Jake several times. During one observation of Jake's fifth-period geometry collaborative class, Troy observed numerous students in off-task conversations and a reluctance of students to engage in academic work. Troy and the special education collaborator assigned to this class spent most of their time correcting student behavior, delivering teacher-centered instruction, and providing students with easy solutions to complex mathematical problems. Students in Jake's class were seated in rows, and the off-task students appeared to be seated at the rear of the class.

The following day Troy met with Jake for a post-observation conference. Jake was on time to the meeting and brought a copy of his lesson plan. Troy set Jake at ease by asking a few questions and then provided Jake with copies of data collected during prior observations of his classes in the areas of professional knowledge, planning, delivery of instruction, assessment, and learning environment. Each data set was nonjudgmental and described specific student and teacher behaviors. Troy asked Jake to reflect on the lessons and the data. Jake responded that the lessons did not meet his expectations—although he has a nice group of students this school year, they had very low mathematical prior knowledge. Troy directed specific questions about how the data reflected the engagement of Jake's students during the observed lessons. Jake admitted that some students didn't seem that motivated and really did not seem to be that interested—thus, not engaged as much as he would like. Troy suggested that making classes more student-centered and differentiating instruction would help Jake motivate and engage his students. Troy told Jake that he would like him to attend two sessions of professional development on differentiated teaching strategies for geometry students at a local university. Jake agreed to attend the sessions and to include new strategies into his plans.

Troy provided Jake with a copy of the released practice items for the geometry state tests, the testing blueprint, and the cutoff scores for student passing rates at both the proficient and the advanced level. He further provided Jake with mathematical learning "look-fors" that emphasized student-centered differentiated instruction that targeted the application, analysis, and synthesis of mathematical content knowledge. Jake seemed to appreciate the resources and promised to make a greater effort to help his students be more successful.

Jake attended the sessions of professional development on differentiated teaching strategies provided by the district's instructional specialists. He was enthusiastic and began implementing strategies, inviting both Troy and Rachel to his class to provide additional feedback and help him improve his practice. Troy and Rachel made several observations of Jake's classroom and were very pleased at the transformation. Students were working in groups of three to four and rotated in stations around the room solving mathematical problems. Each time a problem was solved, the students had the pieces of the puzzle needed to solve the next problem. Students collaborated on solving each problem and appeared to take pride in their work. Ms. Fryer, the special education collaborator, provided support to all students. Students were discussing math and appeared to have fun doing so. Jake asked questions of each group and served as a resource for his students. Over the coming months, Troy and Rachel visited Jake's classroom on four other occasions. Each time, students worked in groups to solve problems while Troy provided the support they needed. Troy visited Jake's classroom after school, and each time, desks were arranged to maximize student collaboration in solving math problems. During the last two months of the school year, Jake even volunteered to come in on Saturday mornings to provide academic assistance to all geometry students. Throughout the spring, Jake continued to stay after school for his students and attended all faculty meetings. On the last school benchmark test, his students performed above the school and school division average for similar classes. His students are well prepared for the End of Course test and he is often seen collaborating with his content team during common planning and after school meetings.

REFLECTIVE PRACTICE

Review this principal's supervisory success story. Analyze the principal's strategies and behaviors as they relate to the Model for Classroom Supervision and the Diagnostic Cycle. What specific strategies and actions are congruent with the model and cycle? What gaps can you identify? Imagine you are Jake's principal. How would your strategies and interactions differ from Troy's as you planned to help Jake improve his classroom performance? What observational tool would you use to collect data? Who else would you include in the process? What steps will you take to help Jake make the positive changes in his teaching behavior permanent and prevent backsliding to his old bad habits?

CHAPTER 12

SUPERVISION AND PROFESSIONAL DEVELOPMENT

An Application

Effectiveness of quality schools includes data-driven decision making (Schmoker, 1999); committed instructional leaders (Hoy & Miskel, 2013; Marzano, Waters, & McNulty, 2005); commitment to a comprehensive school reform model (Marzano et al., 2005); shared mission, vision, and values (DuFour & Eaker, 1998); a positive school culture and climate (DuFour & Eaker, 1998; Hoy & Miskel, 2013); and commitment to positive change and incremental monitoring of successes (DuFour & Eaker, 1998; Fullan, 1999; Marzano et al., 2005). All of these elements are embedded in the processes we have examined in this book—the supervision of instruction, the evaluation of professional staff, and their professional development.

Research has established a direct link between the instructional strategies employed by classroom teachers and the degree to which students learn (Hattie, 2009). While research has demonstrated the importance of implementing specific instructional strategies to increase student understanding, it is also true that these behaviors are not frequently encouraged and/or systematically monitored, nor are the implementations of these

Improving Instruction Through Supervision, Evaluation, and
Professional Development, pp. 287–304
287

strategies linked to evaluation in a meaningful way. If students are ever to enjoy the benefits that specific strategies offer, it is imperative that teachers are provided opportunities to learn these strategies through professional development. Teachers can then implement these strategies with their students, receive feedback regarding their implementation through the process of supervision, and tailor future professional development experiences to specific needs. Finally, teachers' success in the implementation of these strategies can be linked to the assessments of their overall performance through the process of evaluation.

The critical work of schools, teaching resulting in learning, most often occurs in classrooms. Throughout this book, we have conceptualized the classroom social system as a four-component system, a subsystem of the school. The case presented in this chapter is designed to demonstrate how that system is used to analyze instructional problems and opportunities. A crucial requirement for the implementation of a collegial approach is an atmosphere of trust, colleagueship, and participation. As we engage in this case, it is assumed that the efforts to prepare the organizational context have been successful. The case provides an example of what might happen in a real supervisory and evaluative situation. Although a simplification of what may occur in a real situation, it demonstrates how the diagnostic cycle, classroom social system, and organizational context come together to improve instruction.

INSTRUCTION AT CREST MIDDLE SCHOOL: AN APPLICATION

Ann Blair teaches sixth grade at Crest Middle School. Crest has 880 students in grades six, seven, and eight. Ms. Blair teaches language arts and social studies to a total of 71 students in her three class blocks each day. The students in Ms. Blair's classes reflect the overall population of Crest—about 50% White, 35% African American, and 15% other group members from very diverse socioeconomic backgrounds. Students at Crest are not grouped by ability, and the students in Ms. Blair's three classes reflect that practice—diversity in both group membership and abilities.

Ms. Blair is in her second year of teaching. Her summative evaluation last year reflected unsatisfactory performance of her teaching. As a result, Ms. Blair participated in a summer workshop on effective instructional strategies that the principal, Rich Hout, hoped would help her become more effective in the classroom. Unfortunately, several observations conducted during the first two weeks of school by both the principal Hout and assistant principal, Mary Jacobs, revealed little change in her pedagogy.

Ms. Blair is bright and fairly articulate. As an undergraduate college student, she double-majored (American literature and history) and graduated in the top third of her class. She is an avid reader and genuinely enjoys being with her students. Despite these attributes, Ms. Blair has some serious classroom problems.

Crest Middle School has just begun to implement the classroom performance model and diagnostic cycle to improve instruction. The principal and assistant principal have worked closely to develop the school context and to foster collegial relationships between the teachers and themselves. Prior to the opening of school this year, they introduced the staff to the classroom performance model. The principals worked hard to create a school context that is rather ideal for introducing this phase of classroom improvement. There is a high level of trust, a culture of optimism, an open climate, and a real collective focus on helping all students become successful.

Teachers were asked if they would be interested in participating in the new instructional improvement program. Ann Blair and seven of her colleagues at Crest Middle volunteered to participate in the experimental round of the process. Ann was eager to participate because she perceived that it would give her more specific feedback about her performance and assistance in improving it. During her first year she had come to know Mary Jacobs, the assistant principal. Mary often talked with Ann about her teaching and students. Ann was confident Mary could be helpful in assisting her improve her classroom performance in the new program.

In late September, Ann and Mary got together briefly to discuss beginning the new program of supervision. Ann already knew about the program in general. She knew that it was a data-based program for working at instructional improvement. She also knew that the program involved a series of collegial decision-making episodes in which she and Mary would carefully study her classroom and what goes on there.

Ann and Mary spent most of the first session talking generally about performance indicators—performance outputs of the teacher and individual students. The model and process are driven by data reflecting the actual performance of the teacher and individual students. Ann and Mary ended their discussion by agreeing to review Chapters 10 and 11, "Working With Teachers" and "Improving Instruction," so that they could prepare to specify desired performance levels when they next met.

A week later, Ann and Mary discussed their perceptions about some dimensions of performance that appear to overlap in many ways. Ann was most interested in beginning with teacher performance rather than individual student performance since her summative evaluation last year was not satisfactory in that area.

Mary said she had created a flow chart representing some of the basic steps of the diagnostic cycle and the classroom performance model. Ann and Mary studied the flow chart together (see Figure 12.1) and talked about what it represented. The chart made it obvious that the first step would require Ann and Mary to specify desired performance.

Since they agreed to focus on teacher performance, they referred to the section in Chapter 11 on Measuring Teacher Outputs. Ann and Mary agreed to focus on the performance standards that were unsatisfactory on Ann's evaluation last year. Specifically, the evaluation was unsatisfactory on performance indicator: *demonstrating an ability to engage and maintain students' attention and to recapture or refocus it as necessary during the lesson.*

Returning to the flow chart (Figure 12.1), Ann and Mary responded to the question: Are there data about actual performance output? Mary suggested that performance data could be collected for these indicators by using two of the observation tools found in Chapter 11 while she observes Ann's classes. Ann and Mary examined Figures 11.2 and 11.3 and agreed the data they captured would serve as a useful and convenient starting place for the diagnostic cycle.

They used the flow chart and agreed on the following:

- to initially focus on teacher performance
- to focus on performance expectations related to engaging students and maintaining their attention during class
- to engage all students and have them remain on task during class
- to collect data through observation using the observation tools 11.2 and 11.3

Ann noted that they had not targeted other specific performance indicators judged unsatisfactory in her evaluation. She wondered whether they could proceed by following several paths of the flow chart simultaneously. There are many different ways to proceed, all of them exciting, somehow interconnected, and having the same purpose—instructional improvement. Since they were both using the process for the first time, they agreed to focus on this one issue: student engagement during her lessons. Ann and Mary set a time to meet again in a week. In the interim, Mary promised that she and principal Hout would visit her classroom and use the observation tools to collect data that focused on their agreed upon performance indicator.

Mary and Rich each visited one of Ann's classes and recorded their observations. Five days later, Ann and Mary met again and Mary brought with her a copy of the principal's and her observations (Figure 12.2 and 12.3). It was immediately clear to both Ann and Mary that Ann did not

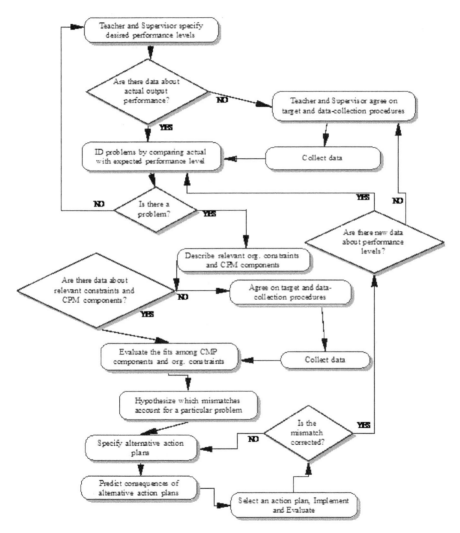

Figure 12.1.   Steps of diagnostic cycle and classroom performance model.

meet the expectations set in their last meeting. Ann revealed that she was terribly surprised by these data and was anxious to go forward with the analysis.

When it has been determined that a problem exists, the principal and teacher should then set about describing any relevant organizational constraints and the components of the classroom performance model. In essence, this means analyzing relevant organizational constructs (inputs) and components of the classroom system (transformational process) to determine how the unsatisfactory performance (outputs) occurred. In this case, too many students in Ann's classes continue to be off task, and Ann spends too much time giving information and scolding students. How can Ann improve her classroom performance? How can Mary assist Ann in the improvement? Figure 12.4, introduced in Chapter 4, is included here to reinforce your memory of dimensions integral to the classroom performance model.

Recall that in this process, the teacher and principal focus their efforts on the classroom system elements (students, the teacher, classroom climate, pedagogy) to improve outcomes. In response to the low student engagement in the classes, Ann and Mary began by examining the process components of the classroom performance model that seemed likely to be related to the low engagement.

Ann and Mary started to talk about the four components of the classroom performance model (teacher, student, classroom climate, pedagogy). They conclude that it would be a good idea for them to review the chapters of this text pertaining to those components so they could refresh their memories and be better prepared to describe the components and eventually evaluate the fits or mismatches between them.

During the review, Mary noted a series of questions based on the descriptions of each component in this text to help guide their discussion and analysis (see Figure 12.5). For the analysis of the "teacher" component, Mary had written:

- What is your knowledge about social studies instruction?
- How developed are your teaching skills (in classroom management, questioning, and interpersonal areas)?
- What are your feelings toward students? Administrators? Self?
- Are you enthusiastic about your job and this school?
- Do you expect high performance from your students? Do you have challenging but realistic expectations for all children?

Using the questions as a guide, Ann and Mary discussed the "knowledge" component. Ann certainly met the criteria and held a state license

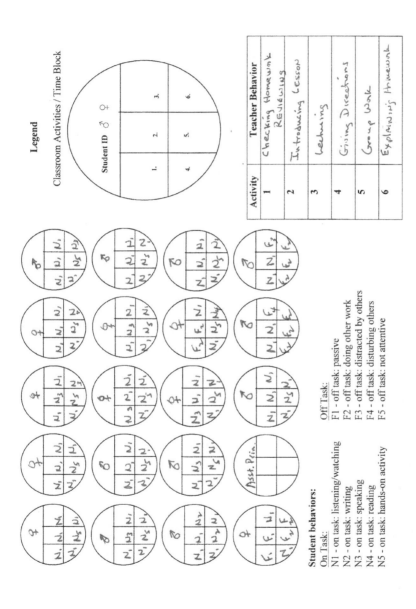

Figure 12.2. Student engagement.

293

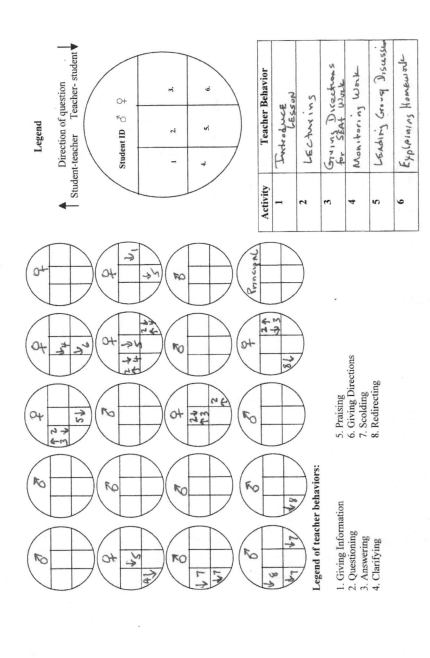

294

Figure 12.3. Student-teacher verbal interactions.

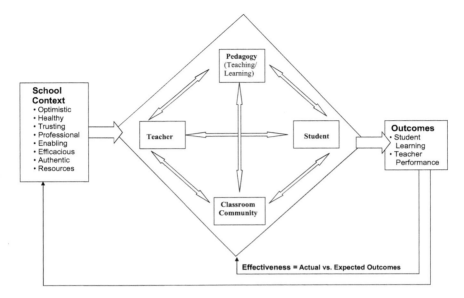

Figure 12.4.   A model for classroom supervision.

to teach social studies. She did admit that she didn't practice many of the strategies she learned in her methods classes during her student teaching in a neighboring school district. The teacher she worked with, Pat Ruffin, was a seasoned veteran who "ran a tight ship." She encouraged Ann not to "experiment" with her students, but to follow the routine that Pat had established. Ann modeled Pat's instructional practices and received high ratings for her performance from Pat.

Next, they discussed the "teaching" component. In responding to the question about teaching skills, Ann indicated that she was most comfortable directing instruction in her classroom. She believed that her students were not mature enough to engage in group work. Yet she believed that she asked many questions to stimulate interest and that she tried to be very encouraging.

Her feelings about the job of teaching and the people she worked with were very positive. She was not having any problems with colleagues or administrators. She thought she was very enthusiastic about her job and really wanted to improve her performance. With regard to teaching, she said that she enjoyed teaching most of the time, but got frustrated by her students' lack of motivation.

Ann raised the question of the Pygmalion effect—that is, could it be that she had been treating the students differently, based on differing

expectations? Mary asked Ann whether she believed she did have different expectations for different students. Ann said she didn't know. Mary
suggested an exercise. She asked Ann to comment on the potential of
each child as Mary called out the names of Ann's students at random.
Mary took notes. When they had finished, it appeared that Ann's expectations were in fact different for different students based on her perception
of their interest and motivation to learn. To analyze the student component, Mary noted the following questions:

- What are the students' attitudes toward language arts and social
  studies?
- Do the norms of the students support academic performance?
- What about the academic self-concept of the students?
- Do the students appear to be motivated?
- Are there relevant background characteristics of the children?

Some of the questions about the student component could not be
answered without specific data. For this first round of the diagnostic cycle,
Ann and Mary were relying primarily on Ann's informal observations in
response to Mary's questions. Each time a diagnostic cycle is completed,
however, there should be contributions to the overall data, which will
make future analyses more precise. If the descriptions of the components
and subsequent match analyses don't lead to productive and specific suggestions for instructional improvement, it is a likely indicator that the
descriptions were based on data that were too general and unsystematic.

Ann and Mary discussed Ann's students as a class, being mindful of the
purpose of description. Ann thought the attitude of the class toward language arts and social studies was less enthusiastic than it would be for
some of their other subjects, particularly those that had hands-on activities like math (manipulatives) or science (lab exercises). She believed her
students were a little more restless and inattentive during social studies.
Ann thought only about a third of her students were motivated, but she
believed they were all capable.

To assess the classroom climate component, Mary posed several questions including:

- What kind of informal structure exists among students?
- Are the norms of the classes supportive of the teacher and the sub-
  ject matter?
- How does the teacher manage the classroom?
- What kind of leadership does the teacher engage in?

In discussing these questions, Mary came to the conclusion that Ann attempted to have very structured classes focused on learning the social studies content specified by the curriculum guide. Ann agreed with this assessment, explaining that students got out of control or take advantage when she attempted to give them some leeway. Ann described the learning in her classroom primarily driven through her lectures and the notes she provided for students to copy. Ann described her classroom as orderly. Although she was aware that tight classroom control was not a style popular among many contemporary teachers, she was also aware of advice from Pat and other experienced teachers that it is easier to loosen up than tighten up when it comes to classroom routines and rules. During her student teaching, Ann found that this style suited her. She didn't feel comfortable with the "chaos" in the classrooms of some of her colleagues. As her second year of teaching was more than half completed, she felt very comfortable with the behavioral arrangements in place. She was proud of the orderliness of her classroom.

The final component of the classroom system for them to discuss was Ann's pedagogy. Ann and Mary agreed that it would make sense to use Ann's current teaching units to describe her pedagogy. The questions Mary posed were:

- What was the long-term planning for units and classes?
- How did you prepare for classes?
- How is each class structured?
- What kinds of questions do you ask?
- What kind of assessment is done and how frequently?

In responding to Mary's questions, Ann talked about her unit and class preparations. She said that she taught to the curriculum guide, which required that students complete eight of the units in the textbooks assigned. Ann had assumed that if the class completed the materials required by the curriculum outline, her students would perform well on the state assessment test. She prepared for her classes finding ways of making sections of the curriculum interesting. Ann thought her classes were structured traditionally. Usually she would begin a class with some relevant fact or story that would interest students in the lesson. Then, Ann would explain the content and provide notes for the students to copy during her explanations. Sometimes a reading segment would be assigned to be read silently in class, and each student would be asked to answer questions based on their reading. This was repeated in subsequent classes until each unit was completed. After each unit, a short written test was given that focused on facts and events introduced in the chapter.

It had been a long but interesting meeting. Both Ann and Mary were satisfied with their tentative descriptions of the four classroom system components. They knew that if their descriptions proved inadequate for the remaining steps of the analysis, they could stop and collect more specific and objective data. They referred to the flow chart (see Figure 12.1).

They were now ready to evaluate the matches among the components. They were hopeful that these analyses would give them some idea of why Ann's students' engagement had not improved to the extent they had hoped.

EVALUATING THE MATCHES

Ann and Mary examined the matches among the components of the classroom social system. Mary brought with her the diagram of the system she often used in talking about the performance-based instructional improvement program. She thought they might use the diagram to visualize the different relationships as they talked (see Table12.1).

Mary also suggested that they use the questions from Table 12.1 to structure their analysis of component matches. They each had before them the notes from yesterday's descriptions of the components of Ann's classroom. A summary of Ann and Mary's discussion and the conclusions they reached as they analyzed each pair of components follows.

1. TEACHER<-> CLASSROOM CLIMATE *To what extent are teacher needs supported by the classroom climate?*

Both Mary and Ann thought the classroom climate did support Ann's needs, particularly her needs for order, predictability, task organization and teacher control. Ann felt comfortable with the structured task-oriented climate (Match).

2. STUDENT <-> CLASSROOM CLIMATE *To what extent are student needs met by the classroom climate?*

The students in Ann's class are generally not motivated to learn. The climate, as described, stifles student engagement. There is little innovation or even opportunity for students to learn and work together (No match).

3. TEACHER <-> PEDAGOGY *To what extent are teacher needs met by the pedagogy employed? Does the teacher have the skills and abilities to achieve the task?*

Table 12.1. Matches and Mismatches in the Classroom Performance Model

Key Elements/Matches	*Critical Questions/Issues*
Teacher ↔ Classroom Community	To what degree are the needs of the teacher being met by the classroom community? To what extent do the teacher's skills and knowledge create support for a classroom conducive to student engagement and learning?
Teacher ↔ Pedagogy	To what degree are the needs of the teacher being met by the pedagogy? To what extent are teacher's skills and knowledge consistent with their teaching strategies and behaviors (pedagogy)?
Pedagogy ↔ Student	To what degree is the pedagogy consistent with the needs of the students? To what extent do the teacher's strategies and behaviors support students motivation and learning?
Student ↔ Classroom Community	To what degree are the needs of the students being met by the classroom community? To what extent are students' motivations to learn consistent with a classroom climate of student engagement?
Teacher ↔ Student	To what degree are the needs of the teacher consistent with the needs of the students? To what extent do the teacher's skills and knowledge enable the teacher to motivate students to learn?
Pedagogy ↔ Classroom Community	To what degree is the pedagogy consistent with the needs of the classroom community? To what extent do the teacher's strategies and behaviors support a classroom conducive to student engagement and learning?

As described, both the teacher and the teaching task are very structured. The teacher has a great need for order, and the way she teaches is very orderly and predictable. Text, notes, and readings follow curriculum guide. (Match).

4. STUDENT <->PEDAGOGY *To what extent are student needs met by classroom instruction?*

Student needs do not appear to be met. Ann's classes are performing below reasonable expectations, and they are bored, restless, or disinterested in the class. The methods being employed by Ann and reading materials assigned do not engage students (No match).

5. STUDENT <-> TEACHER *To what extent are student and teacher needs consistent?*

The teacher has great order needs. These needs prohibit the teacher from gradually releasing control to students. The students are not flourishing. They are capable but vary in ability levels. Learning needs of students are not being met (No match).

6. PEDAGOGY <-> CLASSROOM CLIMATE *Does the classroom climate facilitate the teaching task? Does the classroom climate hinder or promote learning?*

The climate, such as it is, does facilitate the pedagogy as described. Both pedagogy and climate promote order and predictability (Match).

IDENTIFYING WHICH MISMATCHES ACCOUNT FOR THE PERFORMANCE PROBLEMS

After describing the components and assessing their congruence, the next step is to relate mismatches to problems. In this case, the next step for Mary and Ann is to determine the mismatches that account for or explain the teaching performance problem.

It was immediately clear to both Ann and Mary that the needs of the students were at the core of the problem; they were out of step with the rest of the classroom social system, which is controlled by the teacher. However, the reality is that the students are those that the system is designed to serve. Therefore, everything but the student component will have to be changed: the classroom climate, the pedagogy, and Ann. Table 12.1 summarizes the matches and mismatches of elements.

THEORY INTO PRACTICE
ISLLC STANDARDS 1, 2, 3
Help Ann and Mary. Is it possible to change the climate in Ann's classroom, her pedagogy, and Ann's need for control? If not, why not? If so, where would you begin this monumental task? Use Table 12.1 to identify a pair of elements to begin the changes. What happens to the other pairs of elements if they change the classroom climate so that it matches the students' needs?

We believe that by using this process, Ann and Mary can work together and make progress one step at a time. Mary suggested that some of the components would have to be adopted simultaneously, but that they could think and plan change in some kind of sequence. If they plan and implement opening up the classroom climate first, for example, the student <-> climate relationship would become a match, but two new mismatches would be created (pedagogy <-> climate and teacher <-> climate). How should that progress?

If they proceed, however, and change each of the components to make it congruent with the student component (reduce Ann's need for order and provide a variety of teaching strategies to meet the needs of students), then the number of mismatches is reduced to zero!

Ann and Mary agree that their first concern is with the climate component. Their next step is to develop a plan to align the classroom climate to the needs of the students. Mary was encouraged by Ann's willingness to change and identified a master social studies teacher who could be a real asset in helping Ann improve her performance.

DEVELOPING A PLAN OF ACTION

Mary and Ann were anxious to move the supervisory process forward. They have constructed an informal hypothesis about the causes of the problem, namely that every component in the classroom system was incongruent with the student component. They also outlined a three-step plan to bring the components into congruence and produce a classroom social system conducive to the development of this particular group of students. They now turned their attention to the first step of the three-step plan—development and implementation of ways to open up Ann's classroom climate and modify the culture.

At the time, the climate in Ann's classroom was low in involvement and innovation and high on task orientation, order and organization, rule clarity, and teacher control. In order to open up the classroom climate, it is crucial to increase student involvement and innovation, and probably affiliation. Mary suggested that Ann's students need to be much more actively involved in both processes of teaching and learning. She also suggested that Ann begin deemphasizing task orientation, order, and teacher control somewhat in order to begin addressing another of the issues—Ann's need for control.

Ann expressed a willingness to implement Mary's suggestion. She had been thinking about how to increase involvement, innovation, and affiliation and suggested planning a group project for her students. Mary complimented Ann and reinforced the suggestion by noting that student group work, even when supervised by the teacher, reduces teacher control and task orientation. Mary suggested that Ann speak with one of her peers, Jamie, who also taught social studies. Mary asked Jamie if she would be willing to work with Ann. Jamie is a master teacher who can help Ann plan lessons that emphasize small-group work, provide opportunities for students to interact, and become creative and more involved.

After Jamie and Ann had time to work together to plan the next unit, Ann met with Mary to review the plans. They also talked about monitoring the progress of and evaluating their plan. Ann and Mary agreed on two monitoring sessions in which Mary and Rich, the principal, would observe the classes and make further suggestions if necessary. During the last class of the planned unit, Mary would observe and take notes on the frequency levels of student engagement as well as students' contributions to the class discussions in each of Ann's class section. They both hoped those data would verify that Ann's performance had positively changed.

A preliminary problem had been identified (insufficient student engagement and participation), and an action plan was formulated and ready for implementation. Ann and Mary planned two monitoring sessions to assist the implementation phase. They decided that classroom observation would be done at the end of the planned reading unit. During the observation, Mary was to collect data that she and Ann agreed upon that were relevant to the planned changes. The post-observation conference would then be used to evaluate the success of the implementation of the action plan and to determine whether the mismatch had been adequately corrected.

If the action plan were successful, Ann and Mary would presumably go on to Step 2 of their long-range, three-stage plan to bring the classroom social system in congruence with the needs of the students. After the completion of that plan, as suggested in the flow chart (Figure 12.1), they might analyze the newly collected performance data relative to teacher and student and begin a whole new cycle. The supervision process is never-ending. It is a process that engages the teacher and principal in constant renewal and professional development leading to instructional improvement.

SUMMARY

We have proposed a theory and practice of supervision and professional development aimed at improving instruction. Our approach is based on the assumption that the improvement of instruction ultimately rests with teachers themselves. Any attempt to change teaching behavior, however,

> **THEORY INTO PRACTICE**
> *ISLLC STANDARDS 1, 2, 3, 5*
> If you were Mary or Rich, what three changes in Ann's behavior would
> you hope to observe that reflect success in the plan to meet the needs of
> her students by altering the classroom climate? What three changes in
> the students' behavior would you hope to observe? The example of the
> supervisory process described in this chapter involves professional
> development. Ann, Mary, and Jamie participate in professional
> development events during this example of the supervisory process.
> Describe at least two professional development activities for each one of
> them.

is facilitated by social support as well as professional and intellectual stimulation from colleagues. The primary goal of the supervisor is not simply
to help teachers solve immediate problems but to engage with teachers in
the collaborative study of classroom activities that are effective with students. Successful teacher-principal relationships are based on professionalism, colleagueship, and trust. If supervision of instruction and
professional development are to be meaningful and effective, they must
be guided by theory. The theoretical model should define improvement
of instruction, direct action toward that end, and identify the organizational constraints and opportunities in each school. A diagnostic process
must link the model to action, foster teacher and principal collaboration,
encourage teacher professionalism by reinforcing norms of autonomy and
self-direction, and concentrate on the intrinsic motivation of teachers
through teaching itself.

The classroom performance model (see Figure 12.4) provides a strong
theoretical focus for a diagnostic cycle of supervision that encourages
improvement through self-study and change. The model uses an open-
systems framework to examine classroom behavior.

Performance in the classroom is viewed as a consequence of the
interaction of four key classroom elements: teacher, student, pedagogy, and
classroom climate. Effectiveness is a function of the congruence among
these four elements; hence, classroom performance is analyzed in terms of
the congruence patterns of the system elements. Improvement is the
elimination of discrepancies between the desired and actual performance
outcomes of the teacher and individual students. The diagnostic cycle is the
mechanism for linking the classroom performance model with the
improvement of instruction. The cycle is a generic approach to problem
solving organized into five related steps: (1) problem identifying, (2)
diagnosing, (3) planning, (4) implementing, and (5) evaluating. The

process is used both to improve school context and to improve classroom performance. Improving school context consists of developing an open, participative school climate of trust, and establishing colleagueship in teacher-principal relationships. After such a climate has been established, the diagnostic cycle is used to uncover performance problems (teacher or student); to identify the likely causes of the problems; and to plan, implement, and evaluate classroom interventions.

REFLECTIVE PRACTICE

This entire chapter has been a leadership challenge involving the supervision and professional development of Ann Blair at Crest Middle School. Consider the following questions:

- Were the data collection tools adequate?
- What other data might have been collected?
- How difficult was it to identify a problem using the model—a discrepancy between expected and actual behavior?
- What problem (discrepancy) was addressed in this case?
- What were the matches and mismatches in this case?
- Which mismatches were attributed to the problem?
- How realistic was the plan of action?
- Is it probable that a teacher's needs can be modified?
- Did overcoming one mismatch solve all mismatches or create others?
- What are the next steps in this case?

DEVELOP YOUR PORTFOLIO

Use this case and specify an expected performance level for Ann Blair. Then answer the questions in Table 12.1. In other words, use Table 12.1 as a guide to apply the diagnostic cycle and classroom performance model. Answer the questions using the data from the case of Crest Middle School.

COMMUNICATION EXERCISE

Prepare a presentation to explain the classroom performance model and the diagnostic cycle to the teachers in your school.

CHAPTER 13

EVALUATION, SUPERVISION, AND PROFESSIONAL DEVELOPMENT

Applications

In this final chapter we provide an example of the evaluative process and its link to professional development. The cases presented in this chapter were designed to demonstrate how evaluation is used to provide feedback on overall performance and to guide professional development. A crucial requirement for sound implementation of the evaluation process is the collection of multiple sources of data that principals use to make judgments concerning the performance of teachers. As we engage in these cases, it is assumed that the efforts to prepare the organizational contexts have been successful. It is also assumed that the informal process of supervision also occurs in these schools—that is, improvement of instruction is not attempted solely through the formal process of evaluation. Thus, all three processes, evaluation, supervision, and professional development, are embedded in the cases. The cases provide examples of what might happen in real school situations. Although simplifications of what may occur in a real situation, they demonstrate how the evaluative cycle is operationalized with the goal of helping individuals improve their overall performance.

Improving Instruction Through Supervision, Evaluation, and Professional Development, pp. 305–321

WEST PEAK HIGH SCHOOL: AN APPLICATION

A.J. Syler teaches ninth grade at West Peak High School. West Peak has 1,480 students in grades 9–12. Mr. A.J. Syler teaches Earth science to a total of 104 students in his five class sections daily. The students in Mr. Syler's classes reflect the overall population of West Peak—about 45% White, 30% African American, and 25% other group members from diverse socioeconomic backgrounds. Those seeking an academic diploma versus a general high school diploma differentiate the two main groups of students at West Peak. The students in three of Mr. Syler's classes are seeking an academic diploma; those in the other two sections are working for a general diploma. Earth science is a required course in the state high school curriculum; all of A.J.'s students must pass the state proficiency test in Earth science to receive the required credit.

A.J. is in his 11th year of teaching. His summative evaluation last year reflected overall satisfactory performance in the domains of planning and assessment, instruction, communication and community relations, and professionalism. In the domain of safety and learning environment, it was noted that in the performance indicator *"The teacher maximizes instructional time and minimizes disruptions,"* A.J.'s performance required improvement. Pat Horton was completing his second year as principal and believed that A.J.'s students could achieve at higher levels if A.J. didn't waste so much class time. During the past year, A.J. was absent four times and did not leave lesson plans for his substitute teachers. His emergency substitute folder was not updated, and emergency lesson plans were nothing more than games to keep students occupied. During walk-throughs and more formal observations, Pat and her assistant principals noted that A.J. often took more time than necessary to handle administrative routines like taking attendance, getting instruction started, and making transitions, and he terminated class instruction several minutes prior to the actual end of the class periods. They often noted students in his classroom lined up at the door waiting for the bell to ring. Despite attempts to work with A.J. in the supervisory process throughout the past year, his behavior did not change. As a result, Pat created a remediation plan for A.J. and met with him to discuss the plan's components (Figure 13.1).

A.J. disputed the judgment of the principal in an attachment to the summative evaluation document; he argued that his students' pass rates on the state exam were acceptable and students enjoyed his classes because he often told stories and rewarded students with a few minutes to socialize if they all behaved and completed their assignments. When they met to create a professional remediation plan to help A.J. increase his effectiveness in using instructional time, A.J. objected to participating in an afternoon two-week summer workshop on advanced instructional

Name: A. J. Syler		Date: June 3, 2013	
Goal: Increase instructional time during classes			
Objective: Effectively plan and manage routine daily tasks and transitions			
Competency Area: Classroom Management			
Steps/Strategies: • **Submit emergency lesson plans and provide lesson plans when absent.** • **Observe peers who demonstrate effective us of instructional time.** • **Participate in summer workshop and earn certificate.**	**Time Frame:** • **Submit emergency/substitute plans by September 15.** • **Complete observations of designated peers by October 1.** • **Participate in summer workshop on effective classroom management techniques.**	**Support Team:** • Principal • Assistant Principal • Peers	
Evaluation: • **Emergency substitute plans submitted on time and substitute plans are provided when absent.** • **Demonstrate effective use of instructional time during class sessions by efficiently managing routine tasks and transitions.**			
Documentation: • Substitute Plans • Lesson Plans • Informal Observations • Formal Observations			
Signatures: Principal	**Teacher:**	**Date:**	

Figure 13.1. Professional Development Plan.

strategies—he was, after all, a veteran tenured teacher and had a lucrative job during the summer months. However, Pat was determined to "get A.J.'s attention" and substituted participation in an evening graduate level course in classroom time management as a required component of the plan. Pat knew the instructor of that course, and several of the teachers in the high school who participated in the past found it to be very helpful. A.J. also agreed to plan transitions more carefully and submit his plans to Pat every Monday by 7:30 A.M. He invited Pat and any other administrator to visit his classes anytime to monitor his progress.

THEORY INTO PRACTICE
ISLLC STANDARDS 1, 2, 3, 5
What do you think of the Professional Development Plan devised for A. J.? Did it meet criteria of good professional development? Use the template Figure 13.2 to create a Professional Development Plan that addresses A. J.'s in need of improvement performance (a review of chapter 9 may be helpful).

Pat hoped the plan would help A.J. become more effective in the classroom. When he returned for the new school year, A.J. submitted his lesson plans promptly on the first day of classes and the next Monday morning. He noted transitions and seemed to be conscious of how time would be used. His emergency lesson plans and substitute folder were in good order prior to the September 15 due date. During several walk-through observations conducted during the first two weeks of school, both Pat and an assistant principal noted that students were engaged and seemed to be working right up to the bell ending class periods.

Pat scheduled a meeting with A.J. to follow up on his progress. During their meeting she inquired about the course in advanced instructional strategies. A.J. reported that he attended the first two classes but dropped the course because he didn't believe it would help him—he knew all the stuff in the syllabus. Besides, it was summer and he worked hard during the day and wanted some down time with his family. Pat was dismayed. She asked why he hadn't contacted her to inform her about his decision to not participate in the course. A.J. replied that he was addressing the concerns and could perform all of his duties satisfactorily without additional coursework, as he had for 10 years.

Pat wanted to give A. J. the benefit of the doubt but was concerned by his cavalier attitude. She suggested they review all the domains, performance standards, and indicators in the district's evaluation instrument. She wanted to not only emphasize the expectations in the performance standard in which A.J. needed to improve his performance, but also make

Name: **Date:**

Goal:

Objective:

Competency Area:

Steps/Strategies:	Time Frame:	Support Team:

Evaluation:

Documentation:

Signatures: Principal _____   **Teacher:** _____   **Date:** _____

Figure 13.2.   Professional Development Plan Form.

him aware of the expectations in the other domains, especially *Profession-alism* (see Appendix A). Pat specifically noted the performance indicator, *The teacher engages in activities outside the classroom intended for school and student enhancement.*

A. J. became agitated and told Pat that the course she required in this plan was not *meaningful.* Pat calmly told A. J. he was missing the point. She wanted A.J. to understand that both she and the district expected the performance of all teachers to meet all the established evaluative criteria. The plan was designed to help him. A.J. insisted he could meet expectations this year and would comply with all other components of the plan.

By early October, both Pat and an assistant principal each had formally observed two of A.J.'s classes. They specifically recorded data concerning the use of instructional time during the class periods observed. The data revealed that A. J. was making progress but still seemed to be taking too much time taking attendance, collecting papers, and distributing materials. Pat met with A.J. to share the data. A.J. wondered whether Pat's expectation for "housekeeping" time was realistic. After all, the data revealed that it took only seven minutes to take attendance, collect assignments, and get the class started. Pat explained that seven minutes in a 42 minute period was a substantial percentage of class time. There was also time lost during other transitions in class. She suggested that A.J. spend time observing two other science teachers who used class time efficiently. A.J. agreed to do so if Pat arranged to have his "duty" period covered for a couple of days.

A week later, A.J. and Pat talked about his observations of the other two teachers. A.J. quite frankly wasn't impressed with their performance and questioned whether the administrator scrutiny of his use of time was a bit nit picking. Pat knew that both the teachers A.J. observed used "warm up" activities for students as they entered the classroom. They were both very organized and had very little "down" time during their classes. She attempted to engage A.J. in a discussion of what he observed in the other classes, but he simply replied that different teachers had different styles of teaching and insisted that his students were learning and performing well. Pat suggested he attempt to incorporate relevant "warm-up" activities into his planning. A.J. agreed to consider it and ended the meeting abruptly, citing an appointment he had to keep.

Pat was getting frustrated. She decided to continue to walk-through and observe A.J.'s classroom and asked her assistants to do so on a regular basis, collect data, and complete an interim evaluation of A.J.'s performance at the end of the quarter. During the weeks that followed, A.J. was not as diligent in submitting lesson plans. In fact, during the first week of November, Pat requested to see his plans since they had not been submitted in over eight days. Data collected by her administrative team during classroom observations indicated that A.J. was not really making further progress in using instructional time. Both assistant principals and Pat noted that he was curt during their interactions with him. Through the grapevine, there was talk of A.J. claiming harassment in the faculty lounge and suggesting that not every teacher was being held to the same standards.

Pat continued to monitor A.J.'s performance by collecting data. Additionally, she performed an analysis of student performance on last year's Earth science exams. Of the four Earth science teachers, A.J.'s students scored lowest overall, although overall their pass rates were above the state's passing score. Pat wished she could go back several years to analyze data, but the state began reporting student results by teacher just last year. She used the data to complete the interim evaluation form. She liked the form because it included all the performance indicators and enabled him to refer to them specifically as he reviewed the evaluation with teachers. Pat gave A.J. a copy of the interim evaluation to review prior to their evaluation conference. Based on the data, Pat rated A.J.'s performance satisfactory in all performance standards except two (see Figure 13.3). The data revealed that he still was not taking advantage of available instructional time and was not participating in the professional development plan that had been agreed upon.

THEORY INTO PRACTICE
ISLLC STANDARDS 1, 2, 3, 5

Based on the information provided, has Pat been fair in her interim assessment of A. J.'s performance? Why or why not? Are there performance standards in the domains of Planning & Assessment or Instruction in which A. J.'s performance was not satisfactory (see Appendix A)? If so, which standards and performance indicators?

During the conference, A.J. and Pat agreed to focus on the performance standards that were *in need of improvement* on A.J.'s interim evaluation. Pat expressed concern that A.J. was not taking the process seriously. She communicated her belief that A.J.'s performance could in fact become satisfactory if he would cooperatively work with the administrators. Pat asked A.J. to identify any obstacles he perceived in improving his performance. A.J. expressed his feeling that at the beginning of the school year he really tried to meet Pat's expectation, but he couldn't seem to satisfy her. It was a busy time for A.J. because his part-time lawn irrigation business took most of his out-of-school time. He got especially upset when Pat sent him to observe a teacher with only two years of experience. A.J. felt that he was a good teacher. Now that it was late fall, his part-time job was no longer taking time and he could focus again on what he needed to do to satisfy Pat and the other administrators.

THEORY INTO PRACTICE
ISLLC STANDARDS 1, 2, 3, 5
Why didn't Pat use the test data in A. J.'s interim evaluation? Would you have used it? If so, why? If not, why not? Based on this most recent interim evaluation conference, use the template (Figure 12.1) to create a Professional Development Plan that addresses A. J.'s in need of improvement performance in the two standards cited.

Pat was relieved to hear A.J. agree to actively participate in improving. In the end, she didn't cite him for insubordination for failing to complete the summer course that was included in the plan he signed. She wanted A.J. to be successful and believed he could become a more effective teacher if he reflected more and stopped acting like a victim. Pat suggested that A.J. work with the science department chairperson, Roger, in planning and exploring strategies to get his classes off to a quicker start. Roger was a seasoned veteran whom A.J. respected. Additionally, A.J. agreed to submit plans on time and attempt to use instructional time more effectively. Pat promised to follow up by visiting A.J.'s classes regularly and making observations to collect data and give him feedback.

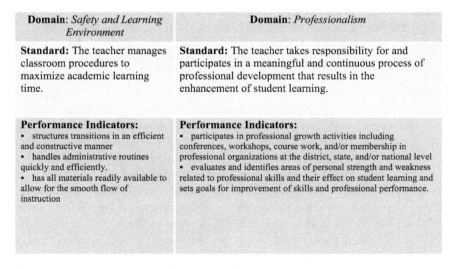

Domain: *Safety and Learning Environment*	**Domain**: *Professionalism*
Standard: The teacher manages classroom procedures to maximize academic learning time.	**Standard:** The teacher takes responsibility for and participates in a meaningful and continuous process of professional development that results in the enhancement of student learning.
Performance Indicators: • structures transitions in an efficient and constructive manner • handles administrative routines quickly and efficiently. • has all materials readily available to allow for the smooth flow of instruction	**Performance Indicators:** • participates in professional growth activities including conferences, workshops, course work, and/or membership in professional organizations at the district, state, and/or national level • evaluates and identifies areas of personal strength and weakness related to professional skills and their effect on student learning and sets goals for improvement of skills and professional performance.

Figure 13.3.   Samples of Performance Indicators for Two Domains.

During the next two quarters Pat and her assistant principals visited A.J.'s classes both formally and informally. They provided both informal and formal feedback specifically directed at the use of instructional time. Roger, the science department chair, gave A.J. some suggestions for warm-up activities that he modeled for him. A.J. adapted them for his classes and improvement became evident in A.J.'s effectiveness in using the available instructional time. A.J.'s attitude improved, and he seemed to enjoy talking shop with Roger.

As May approached, Pat reviewed data collected during formal observations in preparation to complete summative teacher evaluations. In reviewing the data collected on A.J.'s classes, she noticed that the two assistant principals had noted that A.J. seemed to direct most of his questions during class to students who had the answers. Although, as observers, they were spending time focused on A.J.'s use of instructional time, a pattern of calling on a select group of students seemed to emerge from data collected on observation forms and in narrative notes. A discussion with her assistant principals confirmed the trend. However, neither Pat nor her assistants ever mentioned their observations that A.J. interacted only with a limited number of students during their formal or informal conversations with him.

Pat decided to observe A.J.'s class and specifically focus on his interactions with students. She decided to collect data on student–teacher verbal interactions using an observation tool designed for that purpose (Figure 10.9). Pat observed one of A.J.'s classes and recorded interactions. A review of the data confirmed the trend—A.J. was interacting with only about a third of his students. It seemed like the intensive attention A.J. received to confirm improvement in one area of performance uncovered another concern in a different area. The more time administrators spend in classroom, the more opportunities they have to identify potential areas in which to help teachers become more effective.

As Pat completed A.J.'s summative evaluation, she was undecided. On one hand, A.J. had a successful year. He completed a portion of the improvement plan and was using instructional time more efficiently. On the other hand, he did not complete a major component of the improvement plan, and observations revealed concerns in the area of student engagement. She decided to overlook the partial completion of the improvement plan. After all, the plan's objective had been met. Pat then turned to the domain of instructional delivery and the performance indicator concerning student engagement: *The teacher engages and maintains students in active learning*. Based on the data, A.J. was not soliciting comments, questions, examples, and other contributions from all students in his classes and was not using questioning strategies effectively. Should his summative evaluation reflect this deficiency?

Pat met with A.J. to discuss his summative evaluation. A.J. began the dialogue by expressing how pleased he was that his performance in all evaluative criteria met district expectations. He thanked Pat for working with him during the past year and recognized that he probably didn't act very professionally during October and November. Pat explained that although the summative evaluation did indicate improvement in standards previously rated *in need of improvement*, progress was a continuous goal. In fact, there were some data she wanted to share with A.J. as they prepared to develop his professional development plan for the next school year.

First, Pat showed A.J. the performance data of his students on the prior year's state Earth Science exam. Pat pointed out that the overall performance of A.J.'s students was the lowest of the four Earth Science teachers. She cautioned that she drew no conclusions from these data because they represented only one administration of the test. Pat did remind A.J. that now that scores were reported for individual teachers, similar data would be collected each year, and trends over several years could reveal patterns in achievement based on individual teacher performance.

Next, Pat revealed the data on student engagement in A.J.'s classes. She explained that she could have included them in the summative evaluation and rated A.J. *in need of improvement* in that performance expectation. However, she decided to use the informal process of supervision with A.J. to address this problem during the next school year. They would begin now by reviewing the student engagement data collected, identify the problem, and jointly develop a professional development plan.

THEORY INTO PRACTICE
ISLLC STANDARDS 1, 2, 3, 5

Did this principal make the correct decision to use supervision and not evaluation to help A. J. address student engagement in his classroom? Why or why not? What are the next steps? Devise a Plan of Action in the supervisory process (be sure to use the diagnostic cycle to examine the matches and mismatches, identify the problem, etc.). A review of Chapter 11 may be helpful in completing this task. Has this case become too personal? Should the principal turn the case over to one of his assistants for a year and maintain a low profile?

BLUE LAKE HIGH SCHOOL: AN APPLICATION

Roy Hall is a veteran math teacher at Blue Lake High with 24 years of service. Blue Lake has 930 students in grades 10 through 12 in a nice suburban community. The students are predominately White, with Asian and African American students comprising the remainder of the population. The students are from middle- and upper-middle-income families, and 93% attend college after leaving Blue Lake.

For the past decade, Roy has taught all the advanced math classes: AP calculus, trigonometry, advanced algebra, and algebra II. When principal Juanita Diaz arrived in July, she was eager to meet and spend time with as many of the teachers as she could contact prior to the opening of the new school year. She sent an open invitation to faculty members to come in to meet with her at their convenience during the summer; many accepted the invitation to meet the new principal and spend some time talking about their programs and experiences at Blue Lake. As the beginning of the school year approached, Juanita was impressed by the number of teachers who came into the building to prepare their classrooms and get materials ready for their classes.

Juanita finally met Roy on opening day for teachers. She was making rounds visiting teachers as they readied their classrooms and introduced herself to Roy. Juanita expressed regrets that they were unable to meet and discuss his programs during the summer. Roy was polite but explained that he didn't come to the building unless he was required to by contract. Juanita thought this was an unusual response for him to make to the "new" principal, but she expressed interest in getting to know him and work with him, then moved on to the next room.

When Juanita returned to the office she ran into Jack Miner, one of the assistant principals. Jack has been at Blue Lake for over 20 years. He was a teacher and head coach until six years ago when he was selected for his current position. Jack was happy that Juanita was selected to be the principal. She was an outsider, and Jack believed the school needed a principal with a different perspective. There was very little turnover at Blue Lake, and therefore the school had a veteran staff. It was a very good school, but Jack thought it had so much more potential and hoped that someone like Juanita would come to Blue Lake and help folks realize that potential.

Juanita couldn't resist mentioning her encounter with Roy Hall and Roy's comment about not coming to the building unless required to do so. Jack was not surprised. Roy was a good teacher and his students did well by all accounts (e.g., AP scores, state tests, SAT math). But it was well known that Roy was not someone who would participate in any extracurricular or volunteer programs. When Roy was a young teacher with a wife and three small children, he took a course in tax preparation and had a part-time job preparing tax returns in order to "make ends meet." Over several years, his little gig turned into a lucrative tax preparation business. He does year-round accounting for many of his clients and in fact prepares the tax returns of many of the faculty members at Blue Lake, including the former principal. Juanita was dismayed by the information Jack provided. A component of her vision of Blue Lake was to have students and school programs fully supported by all faculty and administrators. It was hard for her to believe that was possible when some of the individual faculty members functioned only in their classrooms.

During the first several weeks of school Juanita spent the majority of each school day visiting classes. She decided to visit each English class because every student at Blue Lake was required to take English. It gave her an opportunity to meet students in small groups and interact with their teachers. By the fourth week, she began visiting other classes. One of first was Roy Hall's Algebra II class. Juanita noted that although Roy was a bit formal and businesslike with his students, his class was well planned and executed. Roy involved each student in meaningful activities during the lesson, often checked for understanding, and used the class time effectively. Juanita also noted that Roy was conscientious as he performed his assigned cafeteria duty. Juanita walked through Roy's different classes several times during the following weeks. Her brief visits confirmed what she had observed during her initial observation of Roy's Algebra II class—no-nonsense classes in which students were engaged in learning with little time for anything but work on mathematics.

THEORY INTO PRACTICE
ISLLC STANDARDS 1, 2, 3, 5
Based on the data that Juanita has obtained on Roy's classroom performance, complete an interim evaluation using the evaluation tool in Appendix C. Is Roy's performance generally satisfactory? If not, where is improvement needed?

The annual back-to-school night in late October was well attended. Juanita was chagrined that it had not been scheduled sooner, but she inherited the event schedule from her predecessor. The number of parents who participated that evening impressed her. Several days later she received a phone call from Mrs. Turner, a parent of a student in Roy Hall's Algebra II class. Evidently her daughter, Alex, was struggling to earn a passing grade. During Mr. Hall's meetings on back-to-school night, he explained to parents that he was available to help students two days a week after school during the 35 minute time he was required to remain in the building. Her daughter was generally able to attend Hall's sessions, but evidently needed more help. When Mrs. Turner contacted

Mr. Hall to request additional assistance for her daughter, Mr. Hall suggested she hire a private tutor. He explained that he would devote two days to tutoring but the other two days he was required to remain after school he devoted to grading papers for his classes. Mr. Hall explained to Mrs. Turner that it wasn't unusual for his students to have private tutors.

THEORY INTO PRACTICE
ISLLC STANDARDS 1, 2, 3, 5

Based on the data that Juanita has obtained on Roy's classroom performance, complete an interim evaluation using the evaluation tool in Appendix C. Is Roy's performance generally satisfactory? If not, where is improvement needed?

Juanita listened to Mrs. Turner's account of the conversation with Mr. Hall. She told Mrs. Turner that she'd speak with Mr. Hall after school that day and that she would call Mrs. Turner the following morning. Juanita immediately asked her secretary to get a message to Roy Hall asking him to meet her in her office after school. She was surprised a few moments later when her secretary reported that Mr. Hall reported that he was providing extra help to his students after school, had an appointment after that but could meet with Juanita tomorrow during his planning period at 11:15 A.M. or after school. She decided to meet with him at 11:15 the next morning. During their meeting Roy was cordial but direct in his responses to Juanita's questions. He reported that his routine is to provide assistance to students two days a week after school, but that is the limit because grading students' papers takes the remaining two days. Historically, students do enroll for his upper level classes who aren't recommended and may be inadequately prepared. He is willing to help them, but prior experience demonstrated that many require more help than he can provide and he therefore recommends private tutors. Juanita inquired about the possibility of using additional after-school sessions for helping students. Roy politely told her that he used his preparation period to plan, and after-school sessions to grade and provide extra help. He couldn't do much for students who weren't adequately prepared for his classes or didn't have the ability to earn high grades; hence, he suggested private tutors for those students. Although most parents expected their children to achieve at high levels, not every student could earn an A in his classes. Juanita was concerned by his attitude and worried about the message Roy was sending to parents. Juanita asked Roy whether it was possible to have some of his more capable honor society students tutor their peers who needed help. Roy thought that was a wonderful idea and suggested that the advisor to the honor society organize such a program—he certainly didn't have the time, nor was it his job. Juanita expressed disappointment that Mr. Hall didn't feel that helping students was his job. Roy Hall adamantly expressed his belief that he in fact was helping students during the time available and shouldn't be expected to do more. Roy then got up and excused himself because his next class was about to begin.

Juanita was furious. How could a teacher who was so capable ignore his responsibility to assist his students? Was she being unreasonable and expecting too much? She decided to call Mrs. Turner as promised and then meet with the superintendent. Mrs. Turner became angry when Juanita suggested that Mr. Hall did not have additional time to tutor her daughter. She paid high taxes to live in this community and expected to get more than lip service from the principal. Juanita explained that she could not compel Mr. Hall to do more than he was already doing. Mrs. Turner let the principal know in no uncertain terms that she was calling a school board member.

After Juanita explained the situation and her frustration to Dr. Aaron Brooks, the district superintendent, he shook his head. Aaron knew there were several teachers in the high school who worked to the letter of the contract and had urged the former principal to use the evaluation process to let them know that they were not meeting the district's overall performance expectation. Of course, the former principal failed to follow up, and to date Dr. Brooks hadn't seen one summative evaluation indicating unsatisfactory performance for any of those "clock watchers." Juanita explained that Hall's classes were well planned and executed. Most of his students were successful. However, she was frustrated that someone with so much to offer students, colleagues, and the school would not become more involved.

Juanita returned to her office and carefully examined the district's evaluation instrument. It was evident that her boss expected her to use it formally to inform Hall of their dissatisfaction. The first thing Juanita noted was the rating scale. The categories gave her the opportunity to indicate that performance was *in need of improvement*. The rating of *unsatisfactory* could be used if the individual did not improve after being given an opportunity to do so.

REFLECTIVE PRACTICE

Situate yourself in the role of the principal. Consider the following issues and questions:

- What is your evaluation goal for this mathematics teacher?
- Does the evaluation instrument used in your school enable you to address the concerns of the superintendent and principal in this case?
- Is the expectation that teachers should first focus on helping students during the school day a realistic top priority?
- If helping students is a top priority, what do you do with teachers who refuse?
- Is the issue of helping students in school worth a confrontation with such a teacher?
- What is your position as principal?
- Regardless of your own feelings, if the superintendent maintains that "helping students comes first," how will you act on that expectation?
- Can you still be collegial in your interactions with teachers? How?

DEVELOP YOUR PORTFOLIO

Prepare an interim evaluation on Roy Hall using either the instrument used in your school or the form provided in Appendix C. In which major areas of teacher responsibilities are Roy's performance satisfactory? In which area(s) does his performance need improvement? Cite the specific performance standard(s) that need attention. Devise an improvement plan to address the standards that need improvement. Be sure that your plan is reasonable and feasible. What help will you provide to ensure Roy's success? What strategies will you use to engage a resisting Roy Hall?

COMMUNICATION EXERCISE

You are a new principal in your current school district. Prepare a faculty presentation to introduce yourself and to communicate your expectations for the faculty, administration, and students. Make sure that your expectations are consistent with the formal expectations in your school district's evaluation process.

SUMMARY

We have provided a rationale and model for the evaluation of personnel that meet the standards for professional personnel evaluations and that can achieve the formal goals of summative evaluation, including:

- satisfying state and district requirements to evaluate
- formally documenting the overall performance of professional staff (both in and out of the classroom)
- getting the attention of professional staff who are not cooperating in the supervisory process or otherwise not behaving professionally
- obtaining the data necessary to make sound judgments concerning recommendations for contract renewal or termination of employment

During the summative process of evaluation, principals make overall assessments on the effectiveness of educational professionals in their schools. In doing so, principals identify strengths and areas for improvement and assist in the professional development of teachers by developing action plans. The process of evaluation, like the supervisory process, is cyclic. The length of the cycle varies depending on the requirements of the state and local district. Beginning and nontenured staff members are generally on annual cycles, while veteran, tenured staff may be on a multi-year cycle.

Although evaluations are performed in virtually every school in the nation, the quality and results of evaluation vary greatly and most often do not meet the two minimum goals of accountability and improving effectiveness. In order to do so, evaluations must conform to the standards of propriety, utility, feasibility, and accuracy. Evaluations must be grounded in the actual duties each individual is expected to perform. In order to be fair and accurate, judgments concerning overall effectiveness of a professional should be made using reliable, valid data from multiple sources. In conforming to these standards and meeting these minimum requirements, evaluation can be a viable and constructive process. On the other hand, a poorly developed teacher evaluation process leaves principals without the necessary tools and procedures to deal with unsatisfactory teachers.

FINAL NOTE

We illustrated the use of the model and process in improving the school context (Chapter 3) and in improving classroom performance (Chapters 12 & 13). These cases represent only a few of a myriad of problems that confront teachers and principals. It should be obvious that supervision, evaluation, and the related professional development are complex, demanding, and continuous processes. The models we proposed provide no panacea; rather, they are useful tools. Improving instruction requires a long-term perspective, one in which goals are dynamic. Success merely becomes a step toward a new goal. There are no ultimate goals. There is only the continuous process of improving teaching and learning.

APPENDIXES

APPENDIX A:
SAMPLE EVALUATION PERFORMANCE
STANDARDS AND PERFORMANCE INDICATORS

Standards of Performance

1. Professional Knowledge
2. Instructional Planning
3. Instructional Delivery
4. Assessment of and for Student Learning
5. Learning Environment
6. Professionalism
7. Student Academic Progress

Professional Knowledge

The teacher demonstrates an understanding of the curriculum, subject content, and the developmental needs of students by providing relevant learning experiences.

Improving Instruction Through Supervision, Evaluation, and Professional Development, pp. 323–352
Copyright © 2014 by Information Age Publishing

Sample Performance Indicators

Examples of teacher work conducted in the performance of the standard may include, but are not limited to:

1.1 Effectively addresses appropriate curriculum standards.

1.2 Integrates key content elements and facilitates students' use of higher level thinking skills in instruction.

1.3 Demonstrates ability to link present content with past and future learning experiences, other subject areas, and real-world experiences and applications.

1.4 Demonstrates an accurate knowledge of the subject matter.

1.5 Demonstrates skills relevant to the subject area(s) taught.

1.6 Bases instruction on goals that reflect high expectations and an understanding of the subject.

1.7 Demonstrates an understanding of the intellectual, social, emotional, and physical development of the age group.

1.8 Communicates clearly and checks for understanding.

Instructional Planning

The teacher plans using the Virginia Standards of Learning, the school's curriculum, effective strategies, resources, and data to meet the needs of all students.

Sample Performance Indicators

Examples of teacher work conducted in the performance of the standard may include, but are not limited to:

2.1 Uses student learning data to guide planning.

2.2 Plans time realistically for pacing, content mastery, and transitions.

2.3 Plans for differentiated instruction.

2.4 Aligns lesson objectives to the school's curriculum and student learning needs.

2.5 Develops appropriate long- and short-range plans and adapts plans when needed.

Instructional Delivery

The teacher effectively engages students in learning by using a variety of instructional strategies in order to meet individual learning needs.

Sample Performance Indicators

Examples of teacher work conducted in the performance of the standard may include, but are not limited to:

3.1 Engages and maintains students in active learning.

3.2 Builds upon students' existing knowledge and skills.

3.3 Differentiates instruction to meet the students' needs.

3.4 Reinforces learning goals consistently throughout lessons.

3.5 Uses a variety of effective instructional strategies and resources.

3.6 Uses instructional technology to enhance student learning.

3.7 Communicates clearly and checks for understanding.

Assessment of and for Student Learning

The teacher systematically gathers, analyzes, and uses all relevant data to measure student academic progress, guide instructional content and delivery methods, and provide timely feedback to both students and parents throughout the school year.

Sample Performance Indicators

Examples of teacher work conducted in the performance of the standard may include, but are not limited to:

4.1 Uses pre-assessment data to develop expectations for students, to differentiate instruction, and to document learning.

4.2 Involves students in setting learning goals and monitoring their own progress.

4.3 Uses a variety of assessment strategies and instruments that are valid and appropriate for the content and for the student population.

4.4   Aligns student assessment with established curriculum standards and benchmarks.

4.5   Uses assessment tools for both formative and summative purposes and uses grading practices that report final mastery in relationship to content goals and objectives.

4.6   Uses assessment tools for both formative and summative purposes to inform, guide, and adjust students' learning.

4.7   Gives constructive and frequent feedback to students on their learning.

Learning Environment

The teacher uses resources, routines, and procedures to provide a respectful, positive, safe, student-centered environment that is conducive to learning.

Sample Performance Indicators

Examples of teacher work conducted in the performance of the standard may include, but are not limited to:

5.1   Arranges the classroom to maximize learning while providing a safe environment.

5.2   Establishes clear expectations, with student input, for classroom rules and procedures early in the school year, and enforces them consistently and fairly.

5.3   Maximizes instructional time and minimizes disruptions.

5.4   Establishes a climate of trust and teamwork by being fair, caring, respectful, and enthusiastic.

5.5   Promotes cultural sensitivity.

5.6   Respects students' diversity, including language, culture, race, gender, and special needs.

5.7   Actively listens and pays attention to students' needs and responses.

5.8   Maximizes instructional learning time by working with students individually as well as in small groups or whole groups.

Professionalism

The teacher maintains a commitment to professional ethics, communicates effectively, and takes responsibility for and participates in professional growth that results in enhanced student learning.

Sample Performance Indicators

Examples of teacher work conducted in the performance of the standard may include, but are not limited to:

6.1 Collaborates and communicates effectively within the school community to promote students' well-being and success.

6.2 Adheres to federal and state laws, school and division policies, and ethical guidelines.

6.3 Incorporates learning from professional growth opportunities into instructional practice.

6.4 Sets goals for improvement of knowledge and skills.

6.5 Engages in activities outside the classroom intended for school and student enhancement.

6.6 Works in a collegial and collaborative manner with administrators, other school personnel, and the community.

6.7 Builds positive and professional relationships with parents/guardians through frequent and effective communication concerning students' progress.

6.8 Serves as a contributing member of the school's professional learning community through collaboration with teaching colleagues.

6.9 Demonstrates consistent mastery of standard oral and written English in all communication.

Student Academic Progress

The work of the teacher results in acceptable, measurable, and appropriate student academic progress.

Sample Performance Indicators

Examples of teacher work conducted in the performance of the standard may include, but are not limited to:

7.1   Sets acceptable, measurable, and appropriate achievement goals for student learning progress based on baseline data.

7.2   Documents the progress of each student throughout the year.

7.3   Provides evidence that achievement goals have been met, including the state-provided growth measure when available as well as other multiple measures of student growth.

7.4   Uses available performance outcome data to continually document and communicate student academic progress and develop interim learning targets.

Note: Performance Standard 7: If a teacher effectively fulfills all previous standards, it is likely that the results of teaching—as documented in Standard 7: Student Academic Progress—would be positive. The Virginia teacher evaluation system includes the documentation of student growth as indicated within Standard 7 and recommends that the evidence of progress be reviewed and considered throughout the year.

Appendix A2: Sample Client Survey
Student Assessment of Learning Environment Grades 3–5

Information About Me

I am a	I am	My grade in school is .....
⬭ Boy	⬭ African-American	⬭ 3rd
⬭ Girl	⬭ Asian/Pacific	⬭ 4th
	⬭ Hispanic	⬭ 5th
	⬭ White	

Choose "**I agree**" or "**I'm not sure**" or "**I don't agree**" for each statement. Color in the ⬭ under your choice.

Give your opinion about the following:	I agree	I'm not sure	I don't agree
My teachers always help me when I need it.	⬭	⬭	⬭
I look forward to coming to school.	⬭	⬭	⬭
My teachers care about how I'm doing in school.	⬭	⬭	⬭
My teachers expect me to work hard and do my best.	⬭	⬭	⬭
The work I do in school is interesting.	⬭	⬭	⬭
I learn new things in my classes.	⬭	⬭	⬭
I feel safe in this school.	⬭	⬭	⬭
My teachers show respect to all students.	⬭	⬭	⬭
My teachers use many ways to teach.	⬭	⬭	⬭
My teachers listen to student ideas.	⬭	⬭	⬭
My teachers give us extra practice to help us learn.	⬭	⬭	⬭
My teachers make sure we learn new material.	⬭	⬭	⬭
My teachers get everyone involved in learning.	⬭	⬭	⬭
My teachers review what we learned earlier in the year.	⬭	⬭	⬭
My teachers give us extra help during lunch and after school if we need it.	⬭	⬭	⬭
Awards are given for coming to school and doing good work.	⬭	⬭	⬭
Teachers talk to my parents about how I'm doing in school.	⬭	⬭	⬭
My teachers make sure students understand what we are learning.	⬭	⬭	⬭
Students in my classes care about learning.	⬭	⬭	⬭
Students behave themselves in my classes most of the time.	⬭	⬭	⬭

This instrument was developed by Pamela D. Tucker and Meliss K. Levy for use with schools involved in the Virginia School Turnaround Specialist Program.

APPENDIX B

Teacher's Name_____**Subject/Grade**_____
Evaluator_____
Academic Year_____

<u>DIRECTIONS</u>

To be completed by the principal as documentation for the teacher's evaluation

Performance Standard 1: Professional Knowledge

The teacher demonstrates an understanding of the curriculum, subject content, and the developmental needs of students by providing relevant learning experiences.

Sample Performance Indicators

Examples of teacher work conducted in the performance of the standard may include, but are not limited to:

1.1   Effectively addresses appropriate curriculum standards.

1.2   Integrates key content elements and facilitates students' use of higher level thinking skills in instruction.

1.3   Demonstrates an ability to link present content with past and future learning experiences, other subject areas, and real-world experiences and applications.

1.4   Demonstrates an accurate knowledge of the subject matter.

1.5   Demonstrates skills relevant to the subject area(s) taught.

1.6   Bases instruction on goals that reflect high expectations and an understanding of the subject.

1.7   Demonstrates an understanding of the intellectual, social, emotional, and physical development of the age group.

1.8   Communicates clearly and checks for understanding.

Exemplary	*Proficient is the expected level of performance.*	*Developing/ NeedsImprovement*	*Unacceptable*
In addition to meeting the standard, the teacher consistently demonstrates extensive knowledge of the subject matter and continually enriches the curriculum.	The teacher demonstrates an understanding of the curriculum, subject content, and the developmental needs of students by providing relevant learning experiences.	The teacher inconsistently demonstrates understanding of the curriculum, content, and student development or lacks fluidity in using the knowledge in practice.	The teacher bases instruction on material that is inaccurate or out-of-date and/or inadequately addresses the developmental needs of students.

Performance Standard 2: Instructional Planning

The teacher plans using the Virginia Standards of Learning, the school's curriculum, effective strategies, resources, and data to meet the needs of all students.

Sample Performance Indicators

Examples of teacher work conducted in the performance of the standard may include, but are not limited to:

2.1   Uses student learning data to guide planning.

2.2   Plans time realistically for pacing, content mastery, and transitions.

2.3   Plans for differentiated instruction.

2.4   Aligns lesson objectives to the school's curriculum and student learning needs.

2.5   Develops appropriate long- and short-range plans, and adapts plans when needed.

Exemplary	Proficient is the expected level of performance	Developing/Needs Improvement	Unacceptable
In addition to meeting the standard, the teacher actively seeks and uses alternative data and resources and consistently differentiates plans to meet the needs of all students.	The teacher plans using the Virginia Standards of Learning, the school's curriculum, effective strategies, resources, and data to meet the needs of all students.	The teacher inconsistently uses the school's curriculum, effective strategies, resources, and data in planning to meet the needs of all students.	The teacher does not plan, or plans without adequately using the school's curriculum, effective strategies, resources, and data.

Performance Standard 3: Instructional Delivery

The teacher effectively engages students in learning by using a variety of instructional strategies in order to meet individual learning needs.

Sample Performance Indicators

Examples of teacher work conducted in the performance of the standard may include, but are not limited to:

3.1   Engages and maintains students in active learning.

3.2   Builds upon students' existing knowledge and skills.

3.3   Differentiates instruction to meet the students' needs.

3.4   Reinforces learning goals consistently throughout the lesson.

3.5   Uses a variety of effective instructional strategies and resources.

3.6   Uses instructional technology to enhance student learning.

3.7   Communicates clearly and checks for understanding.

Exemplary	Proficient is the expected level of performance.	Developing/Needs Improvement	Unacceptable
In addition to meeting the standard, the teacher optimizes students' opportunity to learn by engaging them in higher-order thinking and/or enhanced performance skills.	The teacher effectively engages students in learning by using a variety of instructional strategies in order to meet individual learning needs.	The teacher inconsistently uses instructional strategies that meet individual learning needs.	The teacher is instruction inadequately addresses students' learning needs.

Performance Standard 4: Assessment of and for Student Learning

The teacher systematically gathers, analyzes, and uses all relevant data to measure student academic progress, guide instructional content and delivery methods, and provide timely feedback to both students and parents throughout the school year.

Sample Performance Indicators

Examples of teacher work conducted in the performance of the standard may include, but are not limited to:

4.1 Uses pre-assessment data to develop expectations for students, to differentiate instruction, and to document learning.

4.2 Involves students in setting learning goals and monitoring their own progress.

4.3 Uses a variety of assessment strategies and instruments that are valid and appropriate or the content and for the student population.

4.4 Aligns student assessment with established curriculum standards and benchmarks.

4.5 Uses assessment tools for both formative and summative purposes, and uses grading practices that report final mastery in relationship to content goals and objectives.

4.6 Uses assessment tools for both formative and summative purposes to inform, guide, and adjust students' learning.

4.7 Gives constructive and frequent feedback to students on their learning.

Exemplary	Proficient is the expected level of performance.	Developing/Needs Improvement	Unacceptable
In addition to meeting the standard, the teacher uses a variety of informal and formal assessments based on intended learning outcomes to assess student learning and teaches students how to monitor their own academic progress.	The teacher systematically gathers, analyzes, and uses all relevant data to measure student academic progress, guide instructional content and delivery methods, and provide timely feedback to both students and parents throughout the school year.	The teacher uses a limited selection of assessment strategies, inconsistently links assessment to intended learning outcomes, and/or does not use assessment to plan/modify instruction.	The teacher uses an inadequate variety of assessment sources, assesses infrequently, does not use baseline or feedback data to make instructional decisions and/or does not report on student academic progress in a timely manner.

Performance Standard 5: Learning Environment

The teacher uses resources, routines, and procedures to provide a respectful, positive, safe, student-centered environment that is conducive to learning.

Sample Performance Indicators

Examples of teacher work conducted in the performance of the standard may include, but are not limited to:

5.1 Arranges the classroom to maximize learning while providing a safe environment.

5.2 Establishes clear expectations, with student input, for classroom rules and procedures early in the school year, and enforces them consistently and fairly.

5.3 Maximizes instructional time and minimizes disruptions.

5.4 Establishes a climate of trust and teamwork by being fair, caring, respectful, and enthusiastic.

5.5 Promotes cultural sensitivity.

5.6 Respects students' diversity, including language, culture, race, gender, and special needs.

5.7 Actively listens and pays attention to students' needs and responses.

5.8 Maximizes instructional learning time by working with students individually as well as in small groups or whole groups.

Exemplary	Proficient is the expected level of performance.	Developing/Needs Improvement	Unacceptable
In addition to meeting the standard, the teacher creates a dynamic learning environment that maximizes learning opportunities and minimizes disruptions within an environment in which students self-monitor behavior.	The teacher uses resources, routines, and procedures to provide a respectful, positive, safe, student-centered environment that is conducive to learning.	The teacher is inconsistent in using resources, routines, and procedures and in providing a respectful, positive, safe, student-centered environment.	The teacher inadequately addresses student behavior, displays a harmful attitude with students, and/or ignores safety standards.

Performance Standard 6: Professionalism

The teacher maintains a commitment to professional ethics, communicates effectively, and takes responsibility for and participates in professional growth that results in enhanced student learning.

Sample Performance Indicators

Examples of teacher work conducted in the performance of the standard may include, but are not limited to:

6.1 Collaborates and communicates effectively within the school community to promote students' well-being and success.

6.2 Adheres to federal and state laws, school policies, and ethical guidelines.

6.3 Incorporates learning from professional growth opportunities into instructional practice.

6.4 Sets goals for improvement of knowledge and skills.

6.5 Engages in activities outside the classroom intended for school and student enhancement.

6.6 Works in a collegial and collaborative manner with administrators, other school personnel, and the community.

6.7 Builds positive and professional relationships with parents/ guardians through frequent and effective communication concerning students' progress.

6.8 Serves as a contributing member of the school's professional learning community through collaboration with teaching colleagues.

6.9 Demonstrates consistent mastery of standard oral and written English in all communication.

Exemplary	Proficient is the expected level of performance.	Developing/Needs Improvement	Unacceptable
In addition to meeting the standard, the teacher continually engages in high-level personal and professional growth and application of skills, and contributes to the development of others and the well-being of the school.	The teacher maintains a commitment to professional ethics, communicates effectively, and takes responsibility for and participates in professional growth that results in enhanced student learning.	The teacher inconsistently practices or attends professional growth opportunities with occasional application in the classroom.	The teacher demonstrates inflexibility, a reluctance and/or disregard toward school policy, and rarely takes advantage of professional growth opportunities.

Performance Standard 7: Student Academic Progress

The work of the teacher results in acceptable, measurable, and appropriate student academic progress.

Sample Performance Indicators

Examples of teacher work conducted in the performance of the standard may include, but are not limited to:

7.1 Sets acceptable, measurable, and appropriate achievement goals for student academic progress based on baseline data.

7.2 Documents the progress of each student throughout the year.

7.3 Provides evidence that achievement goals have been met, including the state-provided growth measure when available as well as other multiple measures of student growth.

7.4 Uses available performance outcome data to continually document and communicate student academic progress and develop interim learning targets.

Exemplary	Proficient is the expected level of performance.	Developing/Needs Improvement	Unacceptable
In addition to meeting the standard, the work of the teacher results in a high level of student achievement with all populations of learners.	The work of the teacher results in acceptable, measurable, and appropriate student achievement.	The work of the teacher results in student academic progress that does not meet the established standard and/or is not achieved with all populations taught by the teacher.	The work of the teacher does not achieve acceptable student academic progress.

EVALUATION SUMMARY

Strengths

Areas for Improvement

_____   _____

Teacher   Principal

Date_____   Date_____

TEACHER'S SIGNATURE ACKNOWLEDGES RECEIPT OF THIS FORM.
WRITTEN COMMENTS MAY BE ATTACHED.
COMMENTS ATTACHED:____YES____NO

APPENDIX C: SAMPLE INTERIM REVIEW FORM

Teacher's Name_____**Position/Grade**_____
Principal_____
Academic Year_____

Directions: Evaluators use this form in the fall to maintain a record of evidence documented for each teacher performance standard. Evidence can be drawn from formal observations, informal observations, portfolio review, and other appropriate sources. This form should be maintained by the evaluator during the course of the evaluation cycle. This report is shared at a meeting with the teacher held within appropriate timelines.

Strengths:

Areas of Improvement:

Teacher's Name_____

Teacher's Signature _____

Date _____

Evaluator's Name _____

Evaluator's Signature _____

Date _____

SAMPLE: TEACHER INTERIM PERFORMANCE REPORT

1. Professional Knowledge

The teacher demonstrates an understanding of the curriculum, subject content, and the developmental needs of students by providing relevant learning experiences.

- Effectively addresses appropriate curriculum standards.

- Integrates key content elements and facilitates students' use of higher-level thinking skills in instruction.

- Demonstrates ability to link present content with past and future learning experiences, other subject areas, and real-world experiences and applications.

- Demonstrates an accurate knowledge of the subject area(s) taught.

- Demonstrates skills relevant to the subject area(s) taught.

- Bases instruction on goals that reflect high expectations and an understanding of the subject.

- Demonstrates an understanding of the intellectual, social, emotional, and physical development of the age group.

- Communicates clearly and checks for understanding.

Comments:

☐ Evident ☐ Not Evident

2. Instructional Planning

The teacher plans using the Virginia Standards of Learning, the school's curriculum, effective strategies, resources, and data to meet the needs of all students.

- Uses student learning data to guide planning.

- Plans time realistically for pacing, content mastery, and transitions.

- Plans for differentiated instruction.

- Aligns lesson objectives to the school's curriculum and student learning needs.

- Develops appropriate long- and short-range plans and adapts plans when needed.

Comments:

☐ Evident ☐ Not Evident

3. Instructional Delivery

The teacher effectively engages students in learning by using a variety of instructional strategies in order to meet individual learning needs.

- Engages and maintains students in active learning.
- Builds upon students' existing knowledge and skills.
- Differentiates instruction to meet students' needs.
- Reinforces learning goals consistently throughout lessons.
- Uses a variety of effective instructional strategies and resources.
- Uses instructional technology to enhance student learning.
- Communicates clearly and checks for understanding.

Comments:

☐ Evident ☐ Not Evident

SAMPLE: TEACHER INTERIM PERFORMANCE REPORT PAGE 2 OF 4

4. Assessment of and for Student Learning

The teacher systematically gathers, analyzes, and uses all relevant data to measure student academic progress, guide instructional content and delivery methods, and provide timely feedback to both students and parents throughout the school year.

- Uses pre-assessment data to develop expectations for students, to differentiate instruction, and to document learning.
- Involves students in setting learning goals and monitoring their own progress.
- Uses a variety of assessment strategies and instruments that are valid and appropriate for the content and for the student population.
- Aligns student assessment with established curriculum standards and benchmarks.
- Uses assessment tools for both formative and summative purposes and uses grading practices that report final mastery in relationship to content goals and objectives.
- Uses assessment tools for both formative and summative purposes to inform, guide, and adjust students' learning.
- Gives constructive and frequent feedback to students on their learning.

Comments:

☐ Evident ☐ Not Evident

SAMPLE: TEACHER INTERIM PERFORMANCE REPORT PAGE 3 OF 4

5. Learning Environment

The teacher uses resources, routines, and procedures to provide a respectful, positive, safe, student-centered environment that is conducive to learning.

- Arranges the classroom to maximize learning while providing a safe environment.
- Establishes clear expectations, with student input, for classroom rules and procedures early in the school year, and enforces them consistently and fairly.
- Maximizes instructional time and minimizes disruptions.
- Establishes a climate of trust and teamwork by being fair, caring, respectful, and enthusiastic.
- Promotes cultural sensitivity.
- Respects students' diversity, including language, culture, race, gender, and special needs.
- Actively listens and pays attention to students' needs and responses.
- Maximizes instructional learning time by working with students individually as well as in small groups or whole groups.

Comments:

☐ Evident ☐ Not Evident

SAMPLE: TEACHER INTERIM PERFORMANCE REPORT PAGE 4 OF 4

6. Professionalism

The teacher maintains a commitment to professional ethics, communicates effectively, and takes responsibility for and participates in professional growth that results in enhanced student learning.

- Collaborates and communicates effectively within the school community to promote students' wellbeing and success.
- Adheres to federal and state laws, school policies, and ethical guidelines.
- Incorporates learning from professional growth opportunities into instructional practice.
- Sets goals for improvement of knowledge and skills.
- Engages in activities outside the classroom intended for school and student enhancement.
- Works in a collegial and collaborative manner with administrators, other school personnel, and the community.
- Builds positive and professional relationships with parents/guardians through frequent and effective communication concerning students' progress.

SAMPLE continues on next page

---

6. Professionalism

The teacher maintains a commitment to professional ethics, communicates effectively, and takes responsibility for and participates in professional growth that results in enhanced student learning.

- Serves as a contributing member of the school's professional learning community through collaboration with teaching colleagues.

- Demonstrates consistent mastery of standard oral and written English in all communication.

Comments:

☐ Evident ☐ Not Evident

---

7. Student Academic Progress

The work of the teacher results in acceptable, measurable, and appropriate student academic progress.

- Sets acceptable, measurable, and appropriate achievement goals for student learning progress based on baseline data.
- Documents the progress of each student throughout the year.
- Provides evidence that achievement goals have been met, including the state-provided growth measure when available as well as other multiple measures of student academic progress.
- Uses available performance outcome data to continually document and communicate student academic progress and develop interim learning targets.

Comments:

☐ Evident ☐ Not Evident

APPENDIX D: GUIDELINES FOR OBSERVING CLASSROOM BEHAVIOR

Student-Teacher Relations

- What is the evidence of organization and clarity in teacher presentations?
- How enthusiastic is the teacher?
- How does the teacher demonstrate care, warmth, and empathy, and how does he or she nurture students?
- How does the teacher motivate students?

- What is the evidence that the teacher listens to and responds to individual students' needs, interests, and concerns?
- How does the teacher encourage respect for other students and their views?
- How does the teacher encourage and build on student discussions?
- What is the evidence that the teacher is concerned with the social-emotional development of students?

The Teaching-Learning Process

- To what extent is the teacher concerned with comprehension and application of knowledge? Analysis, synthesis, and evaluation?
- To what extent does the teacher use inquiry approaches?
- Which instructional methods did the students find most interesting?
- What is the evidence of student learning?
- How does the teacher use real-life examples to stimulate interest, illustrate, and integrate the concepts being taught?
- What instructional techniques are used to motivate divergent thinking?
- How does the teacher integrate different instructional activities?
- How does the teacher prevent frustration and confusion?
- To what extent and how is learning reinforced?
- To what extent and how does the teacher use groups?

Classroom Management

- What student behaviors were acceptable and unacceptable in class?
- How does the teacher effectively use classroom space?
- What did you like and dislike about the physical environment of the classroom?
- How does the teacher enlist student cooperation?
- Are the rules of the classroom known and used by students?
- What activities encourage student engagement? Prevent management problems?
- How is conflict managed?
- What is the evidence that a positive leaning context exists?
- What is the evidence that students are developing responsibly and managing themselves?

(Hoy & Hoy, 2014)

APPENDIX D: DATA COLLECTION FORMS

Classroom Observation Form

Teacher (LName, FName): _____ , _____   Administrator (LName): _____   Start Time/End Time: _____ / _____

Date: __8/31/2010__ Subject: [_____ ▼] Grade Level: [___ ▼] Content: [_____ ▼] School: [_____ ▼]

Lesson Objectives	Observed	Y/N	Comments
Objectives are clear and visible	[▼]	[▼]	[____]
Objectives are appropriate for students	[▼]	[▼]	[____]
Objectives are aligned with curriculum	[▼]	[▼]	[____]
Objectives are achieved	[▼]	[▼]	[____]

Lesson Implementation	Observed	Y/N	Comments
Uses a variety of questioning techniques to check for understanding	[▼]	[▼]	[____]
A variety of strategies are implemented	[▼]	[▼]	[____]
Strategies are appropriate for objectives	[▼]	[▼]	[____]
Instructions are clear	[▼]	[▼]	[____]
Students are engaged	[▼]	[▼]	[____]
Students are on task	[▼]	[▼]	[____]
Time management, transition, and pacing strategies are evident	[▼]	[▼]	[____]
Students are encouraged to ask questions	[▼]	[▼]	[____]
Students' different needs and abilities are accommodated	[▼]	[▼]	[____]

Assessment	Observed	Y/N	Comments
Performance assessment is appropriate for objectives	[▼]	[▼]	[____]
Performance assessment is appropriate for students	[▼]	[▼]	[____]
Students are provided feedback	[▼]	[▼]	[____]
Data from assessments are used to re-teach, clarify or modify instruction as appropriate	[▼]	[▼]	[____]

Classroom Learning Environment	Observed	Y/N	Comments
Teacher fosters an atmosphere of trust and respect	[▼]	[▼]	[____]
Interaction between students and teachers encourages learning	[▼]	[▼]	[____]
Students are encouraged to express a variety of opinions	[▼]	[▼]	[____]
Student learning is the focus of interactions	[▼]	[▼]	[____]

Copyright © 2010 by DCD

Cognitive Levels of Questions and Wait Time

Teacher: _____   Administrator: _____

Date: _____   Observation: Start Time:_____ End Time:_____

Class Observed: _____   Number of Students in the Class:_____

Follow up Dialogue Date:_____

Directions: The purpose of this form is to record the cognitive level of each question the teacher poses during a lesson or lesson segment. For each question, identify the level of the question and count the number of seconds the teacher waits until letting a student respond. Record the number of seconds in the corresponding row in each question's column.

Cognitive Level	Q1	Q2	Q3	Q4	Q5	Q6	Q7	Q8	Q9	Q10	Q11	Total Questions Asked
Remembering												
Understanding												
Applying												
Analyzing												
Evaluating												
Creating												

(Header spanning Q1–Q11: **Wait Time in Seconds**)

Sample Stems

Remembering	Understanding	Applying	Analyzing	Evaluating	Creating
What is the definition for...	Explain what happened after...	What is another instance of...	What steps are important in the process of...	How would you have handled...	Devise your own way to...
What happened after...	Provide a definition of...	Demonstrate the way to...	The solution would be to...	How would you feel if...	Develop a proposal for...
How many...	What is the purpose of...	Which one is most like...	What's the relationship between...	Defend your position about...	How would you deal with...
Who did...	Explain why ___ caused ___	Could this have happened in...	What other conclusions can you reach about...	What do you think should be the outcome?	Can you see a solution to...
When was...	What are some examples?	How would you organize these ideas?	If ___, then ___	What changes would you recommend?	What would happen if...
Define the word...	Who was the key character?	Which factors would you change?	What do you see as other possible outcomes?		How many ways can you...
Which is true or false?	How are these ideas different?				Design a ___ to ___
	What do you think could happen?				

© DCD

INDICATORS OF STUDENT ENGAGEMENT OBSERVATION PROTOCOL

Name_____   School_____Grade/Content_____

Date_____ Time In _____ Time Out _____ Observer _____

The observer uses this tool to record occurrences of high and low-yield practices. Check the middle column only if an item is observed; in a single observation not all items will be observed. Indicators are not checked without evidence. Use the far right column to write specific examples or non-examples for discussion with the teacher.

OBSERVATION "LOOK-FORS"	Observed	SPECIFY EXAMPLES/NON-EXAMPLES
Indicators for High, Active Student Engagement		
1. Engages in setting learning goals		
2. Engages in making choices.		
3. Engages in reading.		
4. Engages in writing.		
5. Engages in discussing text or other input.		
6. Engages in problem solving.		
7. Creates products.		
8. Engages in peer tutoring, cooperative learning, reciprocal teaching, and other cooperative group structures: **Specify**		
9. Applies meta-cognition strategies, ***Specify:*** a) Making connections e) Summarizing b) Inferring/Generating Hypotheses/Predicting f) Visualizing c) Asking/generating questions g) Synthesizing d) Determining importance/big ideas h) Monitoring and clarifying		
10. Creates/uses learning tools, ***indicate:*** a) Concept mapping b) Advance/graphic organizers c) Manipulatives d) Technology e) Other, *Specify*		
11. Engages in self-assessment of their work, what they learn, and how they learn		
12. Engages in asking for and giving specific feedback to peers and to the teacher.		
Lower-Yield Practices for Students		
1. Completes worksheet, homework		
2. Engages in oral turn taking		
3. Responds orally		
4. Engages in listening		
5. Engages in off-task behaviors		

TEACHER BEHAVIORS

A check (√) appears if an item is observed. Note that in a single observation, not all items will be observed. Indicators are not checked without evidence. Observers are to write specific examples or non-examples in the far right column for discussion with the teacher.

THE TEACHER	Observed √	SPECIFY EXAMPLES/NON-EXAMPLES
1. Clarifies and articulates specific learning objectives/learning intentions.		
2. Identifies and communicates challenging success criteria in checklists and rubrics.		
3. Assesses and builds upon students' existing knowledge and skills.		
4. Engages and hooks		
5. Provides input, explains, and models		
6. Guides practice: monitors, coaches and remediates as needed 7.		
8. Provides closure and assesses lesson impact on students, engages students in reflection		
9. Provides time for independent practice		
10. Develops vocabulary and connects concepts and ideas. 11.		
12. Questions for high level thinking and deep learning, responds appropriately to students queries, promotes student questioning.		
13. Uses small group options, **specify a, b, c, d, e:** a) Pairs, c) Cooperative learning, b) Guided reading, d) Reciprocal teaching, e) other		
14. Assigns/uses varied and leveled text, **specify:** a. Nonfiction b. Fiction c. Textbook d. Real world e. Leveled or differentiated text		
15. Integrates student use of technology to enhance learning.		
16. Assesses individual learning to provide specific descriptive feedback at the task, product and process levels; does not mix/confuse praise with feedback.		
17. Differentiates instruction through re-teaching, acceleration, and enrichment, etc.		
18. Uses existing products or samples as models for student products.		
19. Provides choices in assessment products.		
20. Uses a variety of assessment strategies and appropriate instruments.		
19. Arranges classroom configurations to maximize learning.		
20. Uses management strategies to reduce disruptions in learning: clear expectations, rules, procedures, safety, etc.		
21. Maintains and reinforces instructional clarity and alignment across learning goals, lesson organization, explanation, examples, guided practice and assessments.		

Teacher / Student Behavior Observation Form

Teacher: _____   Date: _____

Objective:

	Teacher Behavior	Student Behavior	Specific Examples
Activity / Clock time			
Activity 1 Time:			
Activity 2 Time:			
Activity 3 Time:			
Activity 4 Time:			
Activity 5 Time:			
Activity 6 Time:			
Activity 7 Time:			
Activity 8 Time:			

Teacher Behavior Key
T1. Clarifying learning objective/outcomes
T2. Identifying success criteria/rubric
T3. Engaging & Hooking
T4. Explaining and modeling
T5. Guiding practice
T6. Providing closure
T7. Employing small group options
T8. Listening
T9. Assigning varied & leveled text
T10. Providing descriptive feedback

Student Behavior Key
S1. Setting learning goals
S2. Reading
S3. Writing
S4. Discussing text/input
S5. Problem Solving
S6. Creating a product
S7. Peer tutoring/cooperative learning
S8. Asking questions
S9. Using learning tools
S10. Self-assessing

Teacher/Student Behavior Observation Form

Teacher (Lname, Fname): [＿＿＿] , [＿＿＿]　　**Observer:** John Caggiano

Date: 09/23/13　　**School:** [＿＿＿]　　**Observation** Start Time: [＿＿]　End Time: [＿＿]

Objective: [＿＿＿＿＿＿＿]

Grade Level: [＿＿]　**Subject:** [＿＿＿]　**Content:** [＿＿＿]

Directions: The purpose of this form is to collect information on the behaviors of the teacher and the students in an effort to examine their congruence during a minimum of 20 minutes of continuous instruction. For each phase of the lesson observed, indicate the start time of each activity and use the codes to record what is occurring in the classroom. *Use multiple codes*, if necessary, for each category. Comment or write questions in the space provided as needed.

Activity/Clock Time	Teaching Behavior	Student Behavior	Teaching Strategies	Grouping	Comments/Questions

Teacher Behavior Key

T1 - Presenting	T8 - Listening
T2 - Questioning	T9 - Motivating
T3 - Answering	T10 - Encouraging
T4 - Praising	T11 - Modeling/explicit teaching
T5 - Direction giving	T12 - Monitoring
T6 - Scolding	T13 - Coaching
T6 - Redirecting	

Student Behavior Key

On Task	Off Task
N1 - Listening/Watching	F1 - Inattentive (distracted or daydreaming)
N2 - Doing other work	F2 - Doing other work
N3 - Reading	F3 - Engaged in off-task conversation
N4 - Responding appropriately	F4 - Disturbing others
N5 - Hands-on activity	F5 - Playing
N6 - Questioning	F6 - Other

Teaching Strategies Key

B1 - ID similarities/differences
B2 - Summarize/note taking
B3 - Cooperative learning
B4 - Homework/practice
B5 - Nonlinguistic representations
B6 - Reinforce/provide recognition
B7 - Generating/testing hypotheses
B8 - Questions/cues/advanced organizers
B9 - Set objectives/provide feedback

Grouping Key

G1 - Independent
G2 - Partners
G3 - Small group
G4 - Whole group

Teacher/Student Feedback

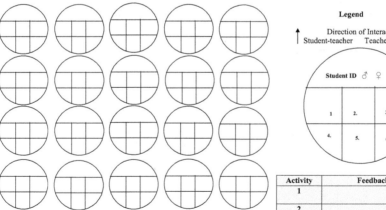

Legend

Direction of Interaction
Student-teacher　Teacher- student

Student ID ♂ ♀

1.	2.	3.
4.	5.	6.

Teacher Provides to Students:

1. Criteria for success
2. Clearly defined learning outcomes
3. Guidance for improvement
4. Timely feedback
5. Corrective feedback
6. Opportunities to Apply Feedback
7. Opportunities for students to improve

Students:

8. Express confusion
9. Ask clarifying questions
10. Demonstrate Comprehension
11. Reflect on their Progress
12. Make connections to prior learning
13. Interact with Peers on Objective
14. Engage in Reciprocal Teaching

Activity	Feedback
1	
2	
3	
4	
5	
6	

Student-Teacher Verbal Interactions

Teacher (Lname, Fname): [   ] , [   ]   Observer: John Caggiano

Date: 09/23/13   School: [   ]   Grade: [   ]

Subject: [   ]   Content: [   ]

Observation Start Time: [   ]   End Time: [   ]

A	B	C	D	E	F

Directions: Each rectangle represents a student in the classroom. The teacher's actions are recorded on the table.

1) In the top third of the rectangle write a student ID (e.g., name, gender, number).

G	H	I	J	K	L

2) Systematically observe the behavior of the teacher as she/he interacts with individual students. Record the code for each verbal interaction from the teacher to a student found in the legend (for example, T2) in one

M	N	O	P	Q	R

of the cells of the student the question is being directed to. Similarly observe the behavior of students as they interact with the teacher. Record the code for that type of interaction in a cell the square representing that individual student (for example, S3). The numbers in the rectangle (right) indicate where to record the teacher and student interaction codes found in the legend.

Student ID
T2	S3

S	T	U	V	W	X

Y	Z	AA	AB	AC	AD

Comments:

For Teacher Interaction with Student use T (+appropriate number from legend below)
For Student Interaction with Teacher use S (+appropriate number from legend below)
1 - Providing Information   6 - Praising
2 - Directing Question   7 - Giving Directions
3 - Responding to Question   8 - Redirecting
4 - Clarifying   9 - Cueing
5 - Encouraging   10 - Soliciting

APPENDIX E: ISLLC STANDARDS

Standard 1

An education leader promotes the success of every student by facilitating the development, articulation, implementation, and stewardship of a vision of learning that is shared and supported by all stakeholders.

Functions

A.   Collaboratively develop and implement a shared vision and mission.

B.   Collect and use data to identify goals, assess organizational effectiveness, and promote organizational learning.

C.   Create and implement plans to achieve goals.

D.   Promote continuous and sustainable improvement.

E.   Monitor and evaluate progress and revise plans.

Standard 2

An education leader promotes the success of every student by advocating, nurturing, and sustaining a school culture and instructional program conducive to student learning and staff professional growth.

Functions

A.   Nurture and sustain a culture of collaboration, trust, learning, and high expectations.

B.   Create a comprehensive, rigorous, and coherent curricular program.

C.   Create a personalized and motivating learning environment for students.

D.   Supervise instruction.

E.   Develop assessment and accountability systems to monitor student progress.

F.   Develop the instructional and leadership capacity of staff.

G.   Maximize time spent on quality instruction.

H.   Promote the use of the most effective and appropriate technologies to support teaching and learning.

I.   Monitor and evaluate the impact of the instructional program.

Standard 3

An education leader promotes the success of every student by ensuring management of the organization, operation, and resources for a safe, efficient, and effective learning environment.

Functions

A.   Monitor and evaluate the management and operational systems.

B.   Obtain, allocate, align, and efficiently utilize human, fiscal, and technological resources.

C.   Promote and protect the welfare and safety of students and staff.

D.   Develop the capacity for distributed leadership.

E.   Ensure teacher and organizational time is focused to support quality instruction and student learning.

Standard 4

An education leader promotes the success of every student by collaborating with faculty and community members, responding to diverse community interests and needs, and mobilizing community resources.

Functions

A. Collect and analyze data and information pertinent to the educational environment.
B. Promote understanding, appreciation, and use of the community's diverse cultural, social, and intellectual resources.
C. Build and sustain positive relationships with families and caregivers.
D. Build and sustain productive relationships with community partners.

INTERSTATE SCHOOL LEADERS LICENSURE CONSORTIUM: STANDARDS FOR SCHOOL LEADERS

Standard 5

An education leader promotes the success of every student by acting with integrity, fairness, and in an ethical manner.

Functions

A. Ensure a system of accountability for every student's academic and social success.
B. Model principles of self-awareness, reflective practice, transparency, and ethical behavior.
C. Safeguard the values of democracy, equity, and diversity.
D. Consider and evaluate the potential moral and legal consequences of decision making.
E. Promote social justice and ensure that individual student needs inform all aspects of schooling.

Standard 6

An education leader promotes the success of every student by understanding, responding to, and influencing the political, social, economic, legal, and cultural context.

Functions

- A. Advocate for children, families, and caregivers.
- B. Act to influence local, district, state, and national decisions affecting student learning.
- C. Assess, analyze, and anticipate emerging trends and initiatives in order to adapt leadership strategies.

REFERENCES

Acheson, K. A., & Gall, M. D. (1997). *Techniques in the clinical supervision of teachers: Preservice and inservice applications* (4th ed.). White Plains, NY: Longman.

Adams, G., & Engelmann, S. (1996). *Research on direct instruction: 25 years beyond DISTAR*. Seattle, WA: Educational Achievement Systems.

Adler, J. S. (1999). Building better bureaucracies. *The Academy of Management Executive, 13*, 36–49.

Adler, P. S., & Borys, B. (1996). Two types of bureaucracy: Enabling and coercive. *Administrative Science Quarterly, 41*, 61–89.

Airasian, P. W. (1994). *Classroom assessment* (2nd ed.). New York, NY: McGraw Hill.

Alexander Hamilton Institute. (1995). *Effective interviews for every situation*. Ramsey, NJ: Modern Business Reports.

Alexander, K., & Alexander, M. D. (2004). *American public school law* (6th ed.). Belmont, CA: Thomson West.

Alig-Mielcarek, J., & Hoy, W. K. (2005). Instructional leadership: Its nature, meaning, and influence. In W. Hoy & C. Miskel (Eds.), *Research and theory in educational administration* (4th ed., pp. 29–51). Greenwich, CT: InfoAge.

Alkin, M. C. (1992). *Techniques in the clinical supervision of teachers: Preservice and inservice applications* (4th ed.). White Plains, NY: Longman.

American Federation of Teachers. (2003). *Setting strong standards*. Washington, DC: Author.

American Recovery and Reinvestment Act. (2009). Public Law 111-5. Washington, DC.

Anderman, L. H. (2013). Academic motivation and achievement in classrooms. In J. Hattie & E. Anderman (Eds.), *International guide to student achievement* (pp. 67–68). New York, NY: Routledge.

Anderson, G. C., & Barnett, J. G. (1987). Characteristics of effective appraisal interviews. *Personnel Review, 16*(4), 18–25.

Anderson, L. W., & Krathwohl, D. R. (Eds.). (2001). *A taxonomy for learning, teaching, and assessing: A revision of Bloom's taxonomy of educational objectives*. New York, NY: Addison, Wesley, Longman.

Andrews, R., & Soder, R. (1987). Principal leadership and student achievement. *Educational Leadership, 44*(6), 9–11.

Andrews, R., Soder, R., & Jacoby, F. (1986, April). *Principal roles, other in-school variables, and academic achievement by ethnicity and SES.* Paper presented at the Annual Meeting of the American Educational Research Association, San Francisco, CA.

Annunziata, J. (1998). Understanding and ensuring due process. *CREATE Newsletter, 1*(1), 3.

Annunziata, J. (1999). Richard Fossey: If a practitioner cleans the windows, will you look in? *Journal of Personnel Evaluation in Education, 13*, 83–92.

Association for Supervision and Curriculum Development. (2012). *Fulfilling the promise of the Common Core State Standards.* Alexandria, VA: Author.

Ball, D. L., Lubienski, S., & Mewborn, D. (2001). Research on teaching mathematics: The unsolved problem of teachers' mathematical knowledge. In V. Richardson (Ed.), *Handbook of research on teaching* (4th ed., pp. 433–456). New York, NY: Macmillan.

Bandura, A. (1993). Perceived self-efficacy in cognitive development and functioning. *Educational Psychologist, 28*, 117–148.

Bandura, A. (1997). *Self-efficacy: The exercise of control.* New York, NY: Freeman.

Bangert-Drowns, R. L., Kulik, C. C., Kulik, J. A., & Morgan, M. (1991). The instructional effect of feedback in test-like events. *Review of Educational Research, 61*, 213–238.

Barker, B. O., & Robinson, K. L. (2001, October). *Effective rural schools and national board professional teaching standards.* Paper presented at the Annual National Rural Education Conference, Albuquerque, NM.

Barnard, C. I. (1938). *The functions of an executive.* Cambridge, MA: Harvard University Press.

Barth, P., Haycock, K., Jackson, H., Mora, K., Ruiz, P., Robinson, S., & Wilkins, A. (1999). *Dispelling the myth: High poverty schools exceeding expectations.* Washington, DC: Education Trust.

Beckham, J. C. (1985). *Legal aspects of employee assessment and selection in public schools.* Topeka, KS: National Organization on Legal Problems of Education.

Bellon, J. J., & Bellon, E. C. (1982). *Classroom supervision and instructional improvement: A synergetic process* (2nd ed.). Dubuque, IA: Kendall/Hunt.

Belzer, A. (2003). Toward broadening the definition of impact in professional development for ABE practitioners. *Adult Basic Education, 13*(1), 44–59.

Berk, R. A. (1988). Fifty reasons why student gain does not mean teacher effectiveness. *Journal of Personnel Evaluation in Education, 1*(4), 345–363.;

Berliner, D. (1987). But do they understand? In V. Richardson-Koehler (Ed.), *Educators' handbook: A research perspective* (pp. 259–293). New York, NY: Longman.

Bernstein, E. (2004). What teacher evaluation should know and be able to do. *NASSP Bulletin, 88*(639), 80–88.

Bill & Melinda Gates Foundation. (2010). *Working with teachers to develop fair and reliable measures of effective teaching.* MET Project White Paper. Seattle, WA: Author.

Bill & Melinda Gates Foundation. (2013). *Ensuring fair and reliable measures of effective teaching: Culminating findings from the MET project's three-year study.* Seattle, WA: Author. Retrieved from http://metproject.org/downloads/MET_Ensuring_Fair_and_Reliable_Measures_Practitioner_Brief.pdf

Blase, J., & Blase, J. (2001). *Empowering teachers: What successful principals do.* Thousand Oaks, CA: Corwin Press.

Blau, P. M., & Scott, W. R. (2003). *Formal organizations: A comparative approach.* San Francisco, CA: Chandler/Stanford: Stanford University Press. (Original work published in 1962)

Bloom, B. S., Engelhart, M. D., Frost, E. J., Hill, W. H., & Krathwohl, D. R. (1956). *Taxonomy of educational objectives. Handbook I: Cognitive domain.* New York, NY: David McKay.

Blumberg, A. (1980). *Supervisors and teachers: A private cold war* (2nd ed.). Berkeley, CA: McCutchan.

Borko, H., & Putnam, R. (1996). Learning to teach. In D. Berliner & R. Calfee (Eds.), *Handbook of educational psychology* (pp. 673–708). New York, NY: Macmillan.

Bottoms, G., & O'Neill, K. (2001). *Preparing a new breed of school principals: It's time for action.* Atlanta, GA: Southern Regional Education Board.

Brewer, D. J., & Stacz, C. (1996). *Enhancing opportunity to learn measures in NCES data.* Santa Monica, CA: RAND.

Brophy, J. E. (1997). Effective teaching. In H. Walberg & G. Heartel (Eds.), *Psychology and educational practice* (pp. 212–232). Berkeley, CA: McCutchan.

Brophy, J. E., & Good, T. L. (1986). Teacher behavior and student achievement. In M.C. Wittrock (Ed.), *Handbook of research on teaching* (pp. 32–376). New York, NY: Macmillan.

Brost, P. (2000). Shared decision making for better schools. *Principal Leadership, 1*(3), 58–63.

Bryk, A. S., Gomez, L. M., & Grunow, A. (2011). Getting ideas into action: Building networked improvement communities in education. In M. Hallinan (Ed.), *Frontiers in sociology of education* (pp. 127–162). New York, NY: Springer. Retrieved from http://www.carnegiefoundation.org/spotlight/webinar-bryk-gomez-building-networked-improvement-communities-in-education

Bryk, A. S., & Schneider, B. (2002). *Trust in schools: A core resource for improvement.* New York, NY: Russell Sage Foundation.

Burris, C., & Garrity, D. (2012). *Opening the Common Core: How to bring all students to college and career readiness.* Thousand Oaks, CA: Corwin Press.

Buzzotta, V. R. (1988). Improve your performance appraisals. *Management Review, 77,* 40A3.

Cain, B. L. (1987). Nonformal teacher discipline. *Dissertation Abstracts International: 48,* 1066–1067.

Calderhead, J. (1996). Teacher: Beliefs and knowledge. In D. Berliner & R. Calfee (Eds.), *Handbook of educational psychology* (pp. 709–725). New York, NY: Macmillan.

Cambron-McCabe, N. H., McCarthy, M. M., & Thomas, S. B. (2004). *Public school law: Teachers' and students' rights* (5th ed.). Boston, MA: Pearson Education.

Cangelosi, J. S. (1990). *Designing tests for evaluating student achievement.* New York, NY: Longman.

Carter, S. C. (2000). *No excuses. Lessons from 21 high-performing, high-poverty schools.* Washington, DC: The Heritage Foundation.

Cawelti, G. (1999). *Portraits of six benchmark schools: Diverse approaches to improving student achievement*. Arlington, VA: Educational Research Service.

Cheng, L., & Couture, J. (2000). Teachers' work in the global culture of performance. *Alberta Journal of Educational Research, 46*(1), 65–74.

Chetty, R., Friedman, J. N., & Rockoff, J. E. (2011). *The long-term impacts of teachers: Teacher value-added and student outcomes in adulthood*. Executive Summary of National Bureau of Economic Research, Working Paper No. 17699. Cambridge, MA: National Bureau of Economic Research.

Chubb, J. E., & Moe, T. M. (1990). *Politics, markets, and America's schools*. Washington, DC: Brookings Institution.

Clarke, S. (2001). *Unlocking formative assessment: Practical strategies for enhancing students' learning in the primary classroom*. London, UK: Hodder and Stoughton Educational.

Clayton, M. K. (2001). *Classroom spaces that work. Strategies for teachers series*. Greenfield, MA: Northeast Foundation for Children.

Clement, M., & Vandenberghe, R. (2001). How school leaders can promote teachers' professional development: An account from the field. *School Leadership & Management, 21*(1), 43–57.

Cogan, M. (1973). *Clinical supervision*. Boston, MA: Houghton Mifflin.

Coleman, J. S., Campbell, E. Q., Hobson, C. J., McPartland, J., Mood, A. M., Weinfeld, F. C., & York, R. I. (1966). *The equality of educational opportunity report*. Washington, DC: U.S. Government Printing Office.

Collingson, V., Killeavy, M., & Stephenson, J. (1999). Exemplary teachers: Practicing an ethic of care in England, Ireland, and the United States. *Journal for a Just and Caring Education, 5*, 349–366.

Comer, J. P. (1997). *Waiting for a miracle: Why schools can't solve our problems—and we can*. New York, VA: Plume, Penguin Group.

Copland, M. A. (2002). *Leadership of inquiry: Building and sustaining capacity for school improvement in the bay area school reform collaborative*. San Francisco, CA: Center for Research on the Context of Teaching.

Cornelius-White, J. (2007). Learner-centered teacher–student relationships are effective: A meta-analysis. *Review of Educational Research, 77*(1), 113–143. doi: 10.3102/003465430298563

Costa, A. L., & Garmston, R. J. (1994). *Cognitive coaching: A foundation for renaissance schools*. Norwood, MA: Christopher-Gordon.

Cotton, K. (1995). *Effective schooling practices: A research synthesis. 1995 update*. School Improvement Research Series. Portland, OR: Northwest Regional Educational Laboratory.

Cotton, K. (2000). *The schooling practices that matter most*. Alexandria, VA: Association for Supervision and Curriculum Development.

Cotton, K. (2003). *Principals and student achievement: What the research says*. Alexandria, VA: Virginia Association for Supervision and Curriculum Development.

Council of Chief School Officers (CCSSO). (2008). *Educational leadership policy standards: ISLLC 2008 as Adopted by the National Policy Board for Educational Administration*. Washington, DC: Author.

Craig, S. D., Sullins, J., Witherspoon, A., & Gholson, B. (2006). The deep-level-reasoning-question effect: The role of dialogue and deep-level-reasoning questions during vicarious learning. *Cognition and Instruction, 24*(4), 565–561.

Cuban, L. (1998, January 28). A tale of two schools. *Education Week, 33*, 48.

Danielson, C. (2001). New trends in teacher evaluation. *Educational Leadership, 58*(5), 12–15.

Danielson, C., & McGreal, T. L. (2005). *Teacher evaluation to enhance professional practice*. Alexandria, VA: Association for Supervision and Curriculum Development.

Daresh, C. J., & Playko, M. A. (1995). *Supervision as effective staff development and inservice education: Supervision as a proactive process concepts and cases* (2nd ed.). Prospect Heights, IL: Waveland Press.

Darling-Hammond, L. (2000). Teacher quality and student achievement: A review of state policy evidence. *Education Policy Analysis Archives, 8(1)*, 1–50. Retrieved from http://epaa.asu.edu/ojs/article/view/392

Darling-Hammond, L. (2006). No Child Left Behind and high school reform. *Harvard Educational Review, 76*(4), 642–667.

Darling-Hammond, L., Amrein-Beardsley, A., Haertel, E., & Rothstein, J. (2012). Evaluating teacher evaluation. *Phi Delta Kappan, 93*(6), 8–15.

Darling-Hammond, L., & Baratz-Snowden, J. (2005). *A good teacher in every classroom: Preparing the highly qualified teachers our children deserve*. San Francisco, CA: Jossey-Bass.

Darling-Hammond, L., Wei, R. C., Andree, A., Richardson, N., & Orphanos, S. (2009). *Professional learning in the learning profession: A status report on teacher development in the united states and abroad*. Oxford, OH: National Staff Development Council.

Derven, M. G. (1990). The paradox of performance appraisals. *Personnel Journal, 69*, 107-111.

DeSander, M. K. (2005). *Tenured teacher dismissal for incompetence and the law:A study of state legislation and judicial decsions, 1983–2003* (Doctoral dissertation). Retrieved from ProQuest. (UMI 3164087)

Desimone, L. M. (2009). Improving impact studies of teachers' professional development: Toward better conceptulaization and measures. *Educational Researcher, 38*(3), 181–199.

Dinham, S. (2007). *Leadership for exceptional educational outcomes*. Teneriffe, Australia: Post Pressed.

DiPaola, M. F., & Hoy, W. K. (2008). *Principals improving instruction: Supervision, evaluation, and professional development*. Boston, MA: Pearson/Allyn and Bacon.

DiPaola, V. M., & DiPaola, M. F. (2007). Increasing student learning: Monitoring and improving instruction through assessment (Instruments). In M. F. DiPaola & W. K. Hoy (Eds.), *Principals improving instruction: Supervision, evaluaion, and professional development* (pp. 201–212). Boston, MA: Allyn & Bacon.

Donovan, S., & Bransford, J. (2005). *How students learn: History in the classroom*. Washington, DC: National Academies Press.

Downey, C., Steffy, B., English, R, Frase, L., & Poston, W. (2004). *The three-minute classroom walk-through*. Thousand Oaks, CA: Corwin Press.

Doyle, W. (1992). Curriculum and pedagogy. In P. W. Jackson (Ed.), *Handbook of research in curriculum* (pp. 486–516). New York, NY: Macmillan.

Drago-Severson, E. (2004). *Helping teachers learn: Principal leadership for adult growth and development*. Thousand Oaks, CA: Corwin.

Dudney, G. M. (2002). *Facilitating teacher development through supervisory class observations*. Retrieved from ERIC database. (ED469715).

DuFour, R. (2002). Beyond instructional leadership: The learning-centered principal. *Educational Leadership, 59*(8), 12–15.

DuFour, R. (2004). The best staff development is in the workplace, not in a workshop. *Journal of Staff Development, 25*(2), 63–64.

DuFour, R., & Eaker, R. (1998). *Professional learning communities at work*. Alexandria, VA: Association of Supervision and Curriculum Development.

Dzubay, D. (2001). *Understanding motivation & supporting teacher renewal*. Portland, OR: Northwest Regional Educational Lab.

Eden, D. (2001). Who controls the teacher? Overt and covert control in schools. *Educational Management & Administration, 29*(1), 97–111.

Eisner, E. W. (2002). The kind of schools we need. *Phi Delta Kappan, 83*(8), 576–583.

Elmore, R. F. (2000). *Building a new structure for school leadership*. Washington, DC: The Albert Shanker Institute.

Emmer, E. T., & Stough, L. M. (2001). Classroom management: A critical part of educational psychology, with implications for teacher education. *Educational Psychology, 36*(2), 103–112.

Erbe, B. M. (2000). *Correlates of school achievement in Chicago elementary chools*. Chicago, IL: Roosevelt University, Department of Education.

Evans, L. (1997). Understanding teacher morale and job satisfaction. *Teaching and Teacher Education, 13*, 831–845.

Evertson, C. M., Emmer, E. T., Clements, B. S., & Worsham, M. E. (2000). *Classroom management for elementary teachers* (5th ed.). Boston, MA: Allyn & Bacon.

Fendick, F. (1990). *The correlation between teacher clarity of communication and student achievement gain: A meta-analysis*. Unpublished doctoral dissertation, University of Florida, Gainesville, FL.

Finkelstein, R. (1998). *The effects of organizational health and pupil control ideology on the achievement and alienation of high school students*. Unpublished doctoral dissertation, St. John's University, Jamaica, NY.

Fleming, G. L. (1999). Principals and teachers: Continuous learners. *Issues About Change, 7*(2).

Forsyth, P. B., Adams, C., & Hoy, W. K. (2011). *Collective trust: Why schools can't improve without it*. New York, NY: Teachers College Press.

Frels, K., Cooper, T. T., & Reagan, B. R. (1984). *Practical aspects of teacher evaluation*. Topeka, KS: National Organization on Legal Problems of Education.

Frels, K., & Horton, J. L. (2003). *A documentation system for teacher improvement or termination* (5th ed.). Dayton, OH: Education Law Association.

Fullan, M. G. (1991). *The new meaning of educational change* (2nd ed.). New York, NY: Teachers College Press.

Fullan, M. G. (1993). *Change forces*. Bristol, PA: The Falmer Press.

Fullan, M. G. (1999). *Change forces: The sequel*. Levittown, PA: Falmer.

Fullan, M. G. (2003). *The moral imperative of school leadership.* Thousand Oaks, CA: Corwin Press.

Fullan, M. G. (2005). *Leadership and sustainability.* Thousand Oaks, CA: Corwin Press.

Fullan, M. G. (2007). *The new meaning of educational change* (4th ed.). New York, NY: Teachers College Press.

Fullan, M. G., Bertani, A., & Quinn, J. (2004). New lessons for district-wide reform. *Educational Leadership, 61*(7).

Gage, N. L. (1975). Can science contribute to the art of teaching? In M. Mohan & R. E. Hull (Eds.), *Teaching effectiveness: Its meaning, assessment, and improvement* (pp. 27–42). Englewood Cliffs, NJ: Educational Technology Publications.

Gall, M. D., & Acheson, K. A. (2011). *Clinical supervision and teacher development: Preservice and inservice applications* (6th ed.). Hoboken, NJ: John Wiley & Sons.

Gardner, H. (2000). *Frames of mind: The theory of multiple intelligences* (3rd ed.). New York, NY: Basic Books.

George, P. S. (2005). A rationale for differentiated instruction in the regular classroom. *Theory Into Practice, 44,* 185–193. doi:10.1207/s15430421tip4403_2

Gess-Newsome, J. (2013). Pedagogical content knowledge. In J. Hattie & E. Anderman (Eds.), *International guide to student achievement* (pp. 257–259). New York, NY: Routledge.

Gessford, J. B. (1997). Evaluation. In *National School Board Association, Termination of school employees: Legal issues and techniques* (pp. 15–30). Alexandria, VA: Association for Supervision and Curriculum.

Getzels, J. W., & Guba, E. G. (1957). Social behavior and the administrative process. *School Review, 65,* 423–441.

Gijbels, D. (2005). *Effects of new learning environments: Taking students' perceptions, approaches to learning and assessment into account.* Maastricht, The Netherlands: University Press.

Gijbels, D., Dochy, F., Van der Bossche, P., & Segers, M. (2005). Effects of problem-based learning: A meta-analysis from the angle of assessment. *Review of Educational Research, 75*(1), 27–61.

Glatthorn, A. A. (1990). *Supervisory leadership: Introduction to instructional supervision.* New York, NY: HarperCollins.

Glatthorn, A. A. (1997). *Differentiated supervision* (2nd ed.). Alexandria, VA: Association for Supervision and Curriculum.

Glickman, C. D. (1981). *Developmental supervision: Alternative practices for helping teachers improve instruction.* Alexandria, VA: Association for Supervision and Curriculum.

Glickman, C. D. (1990). *Supervision of instruction: A development approach* (2nd ed.). Boston, MA: Allyn & Bacon.

Glickman, C. D. (2002). *Leadership for learning: How to help teachers succeed.* Alexandria, VA: Association for Supervision and Curriculum.

Glickman, C. D., Gordon, S. P., & Ross-Gordon, J. M. (2010). *SuperVision and instructional leadership: A developmental approach* (8th ed.). Boston, MA: Allyn & Bacon.

Glickman, C. D., Gordon, S. P., & Ross-Gordon, J. M. (2013). The basic guide to *SuperVision and instructional leadership* (3rd ed.). Boston, MA: Pearson.

Goals 2000: Educate America Act, PL 103-227. (1994).

Goddard, R. D. (2001). Collective efficacy: A neglected construct in the study of schools and student achievement. *Journal of Educational Psychology, 93*(3), 467–476. doi:10.1037//0022-0663.93.3.467

Goddard, R. D. (2002). Collective efficacy and school organization: A multilevel analysis of teacher influence in schools. In W. K. Hoy & C. Miskel (Eds.), *Theory and research in educational administration* (Vol. 1, pp. 169–184). Greenwich, CT: Information Age.

Goddard, R. D., Hoy, W. K., & LoGerfo, L. (2003, April). *Collective efficacy and student achievement in public high school: A path analysis.* Paper presented at the annual meeting of the American Educational Research Association, Chicago, IL.

Goddard, R. D., Hoy, W. K., & Woolfolk Hoy, A. (2000). Collective teacher efficacy: Its meaning, measure and impact on student achievement. *American Educational Research Journal, 37*, 479–507.

Goddard, R. D., Hoy, W. K., & Woolfolk Hoy, A. (2004). Collective efficacy: Theoretical development, empirical evidence, and future directions. *Educational Researcher, 33*, 3–13.

Goddard, R. D., LoGerfo, L., & Hoy, W. K. (2004). High school accountability: The role of collective efficacy. *Educational Policy, 18*(3), 403–425. doi:10.1177/0895904804265066

Goddard, R. D., Sweetland, S. R., & Hoy, W. K. (2000a). *Academic emphasis and student achievement in urban elementary schools.* Annual meeting of the American Educational Association, New Orleans, LA.

Goddard, R. D., Sweetland, S. R., & Hoy, W. K. (2000b). Academic emphasis of urban elementary schools and student achievement: A multi-level analysis. *Educational Administration Quarterly, 36*(5), 683–702. doi:10.1177/00131610021969164

Goddard, R. D., Tschannen-Moran, M., & Hoy, W. K. (2001). A multilevel examination of the distribution and effects of teacher trust in students and parents in urban elementary schools. *Elementary School Journal, 102*(1), 3–17.

Goldhammer, R. (1969). *Clinical supervision: Special methods for the supervision of teachers.* New York, NY: Holt, Rinehart and Winston.

Goldrick, L. (2002). *Improving teacher evaluation to improve teaching quality.* Issue Brief. Washington, DC: National Governors Association Center for Best Practices.

Goldring, E., Porter, A., Murphy, J., Elliott, S. N., & Cravens, X. (2009). Assessing learning-centered leadership: Connections to research, professional standards, and current practices. *Leadership and Policy in Schools, 8*(1), 1–36. doi:10.1080/15700760802014951

Goldstein, H., & Woodhouse, J. (2000). School effectiveness research and educational policy. *Oxford Review of Education, 26*(3), 353–363. doi:10.1080/3054980020001873

Goleman, D. P. (1995). *Emotional intelligence: Why it can matter more than IQ for character, health and lifelong achievement.* New York, NY: Bantam Books.

Good, T. L., & Brophy, J. E. (1997). *Looking in classrooms* (7th ed.). New York, NY: Addison-Wesley.

Goodlad, J. (1994). *Educational renewal: Better teachers, better schools*. San Francisco, CA: Jossey-Bass.

Gregson, J. A., & Sturko, P. A. (2007).Teachers as adult learners: Re-conceptualizing professional development. *Journal of Adult Education*, *36*(1), 1–18.

Gronlund, N. E. (2000). *How to write and use instructional objectives* (6th ed.). Columbus, OH: Merrill.

Gullatt, D. E., & Lofton, B. D. (1996). *The principal's role in promoting academic gain*. Natchitoches, LA: Northwestern State University of Louisiana. Retrieved from ERIC database.

Guskey, T. R. (1995). Professional development in education: In search of the optimal mix. In T. R. Guskey & M. Huberman (Eds.), *Professional development in education* (pp. 114–131). New York, NY: Teachers College Press.

Guskey, T. R. (2000). *Evaluating professional development*. Thousand Oaks, CA: Corwin Press.

Guskey, T. R. (2002). Does it make a difference? Evaluating professional development. *Educational Leadership, 59*(6), 45–51.

Guskey, T. R. (2003). What makes professional development effective? *Phi Delta Kappan, 84*(10), 748–750.

Guskey, T. R., & Sparks, D. (2004). Linking professional development to improvements in student learning. In E. M. Guyton & J. R. Dangel (Eds.), *Research linking teacher preparation and student performance: Teacher education yearbook XII* (pp. 233–247). Dubuque, IA: Kendall/Hunt.

Haas, M. (2005). Teaching methods for secondary Algebra: A meta-analysis of findings. *NASSP Bulletin, 89*(642), 24–46.

Habegger, S. (2008, September/October). The principal's role in successful schools: Creating a positive school culture. *Principal*, pp. 42–46.

Hall G. E., & Hord, S. M. (2010). *Implementing change: Patterns, principles, and potholes* (3rd ed.). Boston, MA: Pearson.

Hallinger, P. (2005). Instructional leadership and the school principal: A passing fancy that refuses to fade away. *Leadership and Policy in Schools, 4*(3), 221–239. doi:10.1080/15700760500244793

Hallinger, P. (2011). Leadership for learning: Lessons from 40 years of empirical research. *Journal of Educational Administration, 49*(2), 125–142. doi:10.1108/09578231111116699

Hallinger, P., & Heck, R. H. (1996). Reassessing the principal's role in school effectiveness. *Educational Administration Quarterly, 32*(1), 5–44. doi:10.1177/0013161X96032001002

Hallinger, P., & Heck, R. H. (2010). Reassessing the principal's role in school effectiveness: A review of the empirical research, 1980–1995. *Educational Administration Quarterly, 38*(6), 654–678.

Hallinger, P., & Murphy, J. (1985). Assessing the instructional management behavior of principals. *Elementary School Journal, 86*(2), 217–247.

Hallinger, P., & Murphy, J. (1986). The social context of effective schools. *American Journal of Education, 94*(3), 328–355.

Halpin, A. W., & Croft, D. B. (1962). *The organizational climate of schools*, Contract SAE 543-8639, US Office of Education Research Project. Washington, DC: USDOE.

Hamre, B. K., & Pianta, R. C. (2001). Early teacher-child relationships and the trajectory of children's school outcomes through eighth grade. *Child Development, 72*, 625–638.

Hanny, R. (1987). Use, but don't abuse, the principles of instructional effectiveness. *The Clearing House, 60*(5), 209–211.

Hansford, B. C., & Hattie, J. A. (1982). The relationship between self and achievement/performance measures. *Review of Educational Research, 52*, 123–142. doi:10.3102/00346543052001123

Harris, B. M. (1975). *Supervisory behavior in education* (2nd ed.). Englewood Cliffs, NJ: Prentice-Hall.

Harvard Family Research Project. (2004). *Promoting quality through professional development: A framework for evaluation*. Cambridge, MA: Author.

Hattie, J. (2009). *Visible learning: A synthesis of over 800 meta-analyses relaing to achievement*. New York, NY: Routledge.

Hattie, J. (2012). *Visible learning for teachers: Maximizing impact on learning*. New York, NY: Routledge.

Hattie J., & Timperley, H. (2007). The power of feedback. *Review of Educational Research, 77*(1), 81–112. doi:10.3102/003465430298487

Hawley, W. D. (1985). Designing and implementing performance-based career ladder plans. *Educational Leadership, 43*(3), 57–61.

Hawley, W. D., & Valli, L. (1999). The essentials of effective professional development: A new consensus. In L. Darling-Hammond & G. Sykes (Eds.), *Teaching as the learning profession: Handbook of policy and practice* (pp. 127–150). San Francisco, CA: Jossey Bass.

Helm, V. M., & St. Maurice, H. (2006). Conducting a successful evaluation conference. In J. Stronge (Ed.), *Evaluating teaching: A guide to current thinking and best practice* (2nd ed., pp. 235–252). Thousand Oaks, CA: Corwin Press.

Henchey, N. (2001). *Schools that make a difference: Final report: Twelve Canadian secondary schools in low income settings*. Kelowna, BC: Society for the Advancement of Excellence in Education.

Herman, J. L., Klein, D. C. D., & Abedi, J. (2000). Assessing students' opportunity to learn: Teacher and student perspectives. *Educational Measurement: Issues and Practice, 19*(4), 16–24. doi:10.1111/j.1745-3992.2000.tb00042.x

Hill, H. C., Rowan, B., & Ball, D. L. (2005). Effects of teachers' mathematical knowledge for teaching on student achievement. *American Educational Research Journal, 42*(2), 371–406. doi:10.3102/00028312042002371

Hines, C. V., Cruickshank, D. R., & Kennedy, J. J. (1982, March). *Measures of teacher clarity and their relationships to student achievement and satisfaction*. Paper presented at the annual meeting of the American Educational Research Association, New York, NY.

Hines, C. V., Cruickshank, D. R., & Kennedy, J. J. (1985). Teacher clarity and its relation to student achievement and satisfaction. *American Educational Research Journal, 22*, 87–99.

Hirschhorn, L. (1997). *Reworking authority: Leading and following in a post-modern organization*. Cambridge, MA: MIT Press.

Holifield, M., & Cline, D. (1997). Clinical supervision and its outcomes: Teachers and principals report. *NASSP Bulletin, 81*(590), 109–113.

Holland, P. A. (2004). Principals as supervisors: A balancing act. *NASSP Bulletin, 88*(639), 3–14.

Homans, G. C. (1950). *The human group.* New York, NY: Harcourt, Brace and World.

Howard, B., & McColskey, W. (2001). Evaluating experienced teachers. *Educational Leaderships, 58*(5), 48–51.

Hoy, W. K. (1972). Some further notes on the OCDQ. *The Journal of Educational Administration, 10.*

Hoy, W. K. (2001). The pupil control studies: A historical, theoretical, and empirical analysis. *Journal of Educational Administration, 39,* 424–441. doi:10.1108/EUM0000000005812

Hoy, W. K. (2002). Faculty trust: A key to student achievement. *Journal of School Public Relations, 23*(2), 88–103.

Hoy, W. K. (2012). School characteristics that make a difference for the achievement of all students: A 40-year academic odyssey. *Journal of Educational Administration, 50,* 76–97.

Hoy, W. K., Blazovsky, R., & Newland, W. (1983). Bureaucracy and alienation: A comparative analysis. *The Journal of Educational Administration, 21,* 109–120.

Hoy, W. K., & Forsyth, P. B. (1986). *Effective supervision: Theory into practice.* New York, NY: Random House.

Hoy, W. K., & Forsyth, P. B. (1987). Beyond clinical supervision: A classroom performance model. *Planning and Changing, 18,* 211–223.

Hoy, W. K., & Hannum, J. (1997). Middle school climate: An empirical assessment of organizational health and student achievement. *Educational Administration Quarterly, 33,* 290–311. doi:10.1177/0013161X97033003003

Hoy, A. W., & Hoy, W. K. (2013). *Instructional leadership: A research-based guide to learning in schools* (4th ed.). Boston, MA: Allyn and Bacon.

Hoy, W. K., & Miskel, C. G. (2005). *Educational administration: Theory, research, and practice* (7th ed.). New York: McGraw-Hill.

Hoy, W. K., & Miskel, C. G. (2013). *Educational administration: Theory, research, and practice* (9th ed.). New York, NY: McGraw Hill.

Hoy, W. K., & Sabo, D. (1998). *Quality middle schools: Open and healthy.* Thousand Oaks, CA: Corwin Press.

Hoy, W. K., Smith, P. A., & Sweetland, S. R. (2002). The development of the organizational climate index for high schools: Its measure and relationship to faculty trust. *The High School Journal, 86*(2), 38–49.

Hoy, W. K., & Sweetland, S. R. (2000). Bureaucracies that work: Enabling not coercive. *Journal of School Leadership, 10,* 525–541.

Hoy, W. K., & Sweetland, S. R. (2001). Designing better schools: The meaning and nature of enabling school structure. *Educational Administration Quarterly, 37,* 296–321.

Hoy, W. K., & Tarter, C. J. (1992). Collaborative decision making: Empowering teachers. *Canadian Administration, 31,* 4–19.

Hoy, W. K., & Tarter, C. J. (1997). *The road to open and healthy schools: A handbook for change* (2nd ed.). Thousand Oaks, CA: Corwin Press.

Hoy, W. K., & Tarter, C. J. (2004). Organizational justice in schools: No justice without trust. *International Journal of Educational Management, 18,* 250–259.

Hoy, W. K., & Tarter, C. J. (2008). *Administrators solving the problems of practice* (3rd ed.). Boston, MA: Pearson.

Hoy, W. K., Tarter, C. J., & Kottkamp, R. (1991). *Open schools/healthy schools: Measuring organizational climate*. Beverly Hills, CA: SAGE.

Hoy, W. K., Tarter, C. J., & Woolfolk Hoy, A. (2006). Academic optimism of schools: A second-order confirmatory factor analysis. In W. K. Hoy & C. Miskel (Eds.), *Contemporary issues in educational policy and school outcomes* (pp. 135–157). Greenwich, CT: Information Age

Hoy, W. K., & Tschannen-Moran, M. (1999). Five faces of trust: An empirical confirmation in urban elementary schools. *Journal of School Leadership, 9,* 184–208.

Hoy, W. K., & Tschannen-Moran, M. (2003). The conceptualization and measurement of faculty trust in schools: The omnibus T-Scale. In W. K. Hoy & C. G. Miskel, *Studies in leading and organizing schools* (pp. 181–208). Greenwich, CT: Information Age.

Hoy, W. K., & Woolfolk, A. E. (1993). Teachers' sense of efficacy and the organizational health of schools. *Elementary School Journal, 93*(4), 355–372.

Hoy, W. K., & Woolfolk Hoy, A. E. (2006). *Instructional leadership: A learning-centered guide* (2nd ed.). Boston, MA: Allyn & Bacon.

Hunter, M. (1982). *Mastery teaching*. El Segundo, CA: TIP Publications.

Interstate School Leaders Licensure Consortium. (2008). *Educational Leadership Policy Standards: ISLLC 2008*. Retrieved from http://www.ccsso.org/Documents/2008/Educational_Leadership_Policy_Standards_2008.pdf

Isherwood, G., & Hoy, W. K. (1973). Bureaucracy reconsidered. *The Journal of Experimental Education*.

Jacobsen, D., Eggen, P., Kauchak, D., & Dulaney, C. (1981). *Methods for teaching: A skills approach*. Columbus, OH: Charles E. Merrill.

Jamentz, K. (2002). *Isolation is the enemy of improvement: Instructional leadership to support standards-based practice*. San Francisco, CA: WestEd.

Johnson, D. W., & Johnson, R. T. (1999). Making cooperative learning work. *Theory into Practice, 38*(2), 67–73. Retrieved from http://www.jstor.org/stable/1477225?origin=JSTOR-pdf

Johnson, J. F., & Asera, R. (1999). *Hope for urban education: A study of nine high-performing, high-poverty, urban elementary schools*. Austin, TX: The University of Texas Charles A. Daria Center.

Joint Committee on Standards for Educational Evaluation. (2013). *The personnel evaluation standards*. Thousand Oaks, CA: Corwin Press. Retrieved from http://www.jcsee.org/personnel-evaluation-standards

Joyce, B. R., & Showers, J. B. (2003). *Student achievement through staff development* (3rd ed.). Alexandria, VA: ASCD.

Kerka, S. (2003). Does adult educator professional development make a difference? *Myths and Realities*, no. 28. Retrieved from http://www.cete.org/acve/docs/mr45.pdf

Killion, J. (2002). *Assessing impact: Evaluating staff development*. Oxford, OH: National Staff Development Council.

King, D. (2002). The changing shape of leadership. *Educational Leadership, 59*(8), 61–63.

Kirby, M. M. & DiPaola, M. F. (2009). Academic optimism and student achievement: A path model. In W. K. Hoy & M. F. DiPaola (Eds.), *Studies in school improvement: Research and theory in educational administration* (pp. 75–92). Charlotte, NC: Information Age Publishing.

Kirkpatrick, D. L. (1998). *Evaluating training programs: The four levels*. San Francisco, CA: Berrett-Koehler.

Klinger, J. K., Ahwee, S., Pilonieta, P., & Menendez, R. (2003). Barriers and facilitators in scaling up research-based practices. *Exceptional Children, 69*(4), 411–429.

Koeppen, K. E. (1998). The experiences of a secondary social studies student teacher: Seeking security by planning for self. *Teaching & Teacher Education, 14*, 401–411.

Krathwohl, D. R., Bloom, B. S., & Masia, B. B. (1964). *Taxonomy of educational objectives. Handbook II: Affective domain*. New York, NY: David McKay.

Krayer, K. J. (1987). Simulation methods for teaching the performance appraisal interview. *Communication Education, 36*, 276–283.

Krein, T. J. (1990). Performance reviews that rate an "A." *Personnel, 67*(5), 38–41.

Lambert, L. (2005). Leadership for lasting reform. *Educational Leadership, 62*(5), 56–59.

La Morte, M. W. (1996). *School law: Cases and concepts* (5th ed.). Needham Heights, MA: Allyn & Bacon.

Land, M. J. (1987). Vagueness and clarity. In M. Dunkin (Ed.), *The international encyclopedia of teaching and teacher education* (pp. 392–397). New York, NY: Pergamon.

Lange, J. T. (1993). Site-based, shared decision making: A resource for restructuring. *NASSP Bulletin, 76*(549), 98–107.

Langer, E. J. (1989). *Mindfullness.* Reading, MA: Merloyd Lawrence Books.

Learning Forward. (2012). *Standards for professional learning*. Retrieved from http://learningforward.org/standards#.UVM-mTfkf3M

Lee, J. O. (2003). Implementing high standards in urban schools: Problems and solutions. *Phi Delta Kappan, 84*(6), 449–455.

Leithwood, K., Harris, A., & Hopkins, D. (2008). Seven strong claims about successful school leadership. *School Leadership & Management, 28*(1), 27–42. doi:10.1080/13632430701800060

Leithwood, K., Louis, K. S., Anderson, S., & Wahlstrom, K. (2004). *How leadership influences student learning*. New York, NY: Wallace Foundation. Retrieved from http://www.wallacefoundation.org/knowledge-center/school-leadership/key-research/Pages/How-Leadership-Influences-Student-Learning.aspx

Levine, E. (2002). One kid at a time. *Educational Leadership, 59*(7), 29–32.

Lezotte, L. W. (1997). *Learning for all*. Okemos, MI: Effective Schools Products, Ltd.

Linn, R. L., & Gronlund, N. E. (2000). *Measurement and assessment in teaching* (8th ed.). Upper Saddle River, NJ: Merrill.

Linn, R. L., & Miller, M. D. (2005). *Measurement and assessment in teaching* (9th ed.). Upper Saddle River, NJ: Merrill/Prentice Hall.

Little, J. W. (1999). Organizing schools for teacher learning. In L. Darling-Hammond & G. Sykes (Eds.), *Teaching as the learning profession: Handbook of policy and practice* (pp. 233–262). San Francisco, CA: Jossey-Bass.

Losyk, B. (1990/1991). Face to face: How to conduct an employee appraisal interview. *Credit Union Executive, 30*(4), 24–26.

Louis, K. S., Kruse, S. D., & Marks, H. (1996). Schoolwide professional community. In F. Newmann and Associates (Eds.), *Authentic achievement: Restructuring schools for intellectual quality* (pp. 179–204). San Francisco, CA: Jossey Bass.

Manatt, R. P. (2000). *Feedback at 360 degree school: Sample feedback report profiles.* Alexandria, VA: Administrator Web Education, American Association of School Administrators.

Mancision, J. (1991). The appraisal interview: Constructive dialogue in action. *Health Care Supervisor, 10*, 41–50.

Mantione, R. D., & Smead, S. (2003). *Weaving through words: Using the arts to teach reading comprehension strategies.* Newark, DE: International Reading Association.

Marsh, H. W., & Seaton, M. (2013). Academic self-concept. In J. Hattie & E. Anderman (Eds.), *International guide to student achievement* (pp. 62–63). New York, NY: Routledge.

Martin, J. (1983). *Mastering instruction.* Boston, MA: Allyn & Bacon.

Marzano, R. J. (2000). *A new era of school reform: Going where the research takes us.* Aurora, CO: Mid-continent Research for Education and Learning. (ERIC Document Reproduction Service No. ED454255).

Marzano, R. J. (2001). *Designing a new taxonomy of educational objectives. Experts in assessment.* Thousand Oaks, CA: Corwin Press.

Marzano, R. J. (2003). *What works in schools: Translating research into action.* Alexandria, VA: Association for Supervision and Curriculum Development.

Marzano, R. J. (2007). *The art and science of teaching: A comprehensive framework for effective instruction.* Alexandria, VA: Association for Supervision and Curriculum Development.

Marzano, R. J. (2011). *Marzano teacher evaluation model.* Retrieved from http://www.marzanoevaluation.com/evaluation/causal_teacher_evaluation_model/

Marzano, R. J., Pickering, D. J., & Pollock, J. E. (2001). *Classroom instruction that works: Research-based strategies for increasing student achievement.* Alexandria, VA: Association of Curriculum and Supervision Development.

Marzano, R. J., Waters, T., & McNulty, B. A. (2005). *School leadership that works: From research to results.* Alexandria, VA: Association of Curriculum and Supervision Development.

Mathis, W. (2012). *Research-based options for education policymaking: Common Core State Standards.* Boulder, CO: National Education Policy Center. Retrieved from http://nepc.colorado.edu

McCloud, S. (2005). From chaos to consistency. *Educational Leadership, 62*(5), 46–49.

McCutcheon, G., & Milner, H. R. (2002). A contemporary study of teacher planning in a high school. *Teachers and Teaching: Theory and Practice, 8*, 81–94.

McDiarmid, G. W., & Clevenger-Bright, M. (2008). Rethinking teacher capacity. In M. Cochran-Smith, S. Feiman-Nemser, & D. J. McIntyre (Eds.), *Handbook* of research on teacher education: Enduring questions and changing contexts (pp. 134–156). Elmsford, NY: Pergamon Press..

McEwan, E. K. (2003). *Seven steps to effective instructional leadership* (2nd ed.). Thousand Oaks, CA: Corwin Press.

McGrath, M. J. (1993). When it's time to dismiss an incompetent teacher. *School Administrator, 50*(3), 30–33.

McGrath, M. J. (2006). Dealing positively with the nonproductive teacher: A legal and ethical perspective on accountability. In J. Stronge (Ed.), *Evaluating teaching: A guide to current thinking and best practice* (2nd ed., pp. 253–267). Thousand Oaks, CA: Corwin Press.

McGreal, T. L. (1983). *Successful teacher evaluation.* Alexandria, VA: Association for Supervision and Curriculum Development.

McGregor, D. M. (1961). The human side of enterprise. In W. G. Bennis, K. D. Benne, & R. Chin (Eds.), *The planning of change* (pp. 422–431). New York, NY: Holt, Rinehart, and Winston.

McGuigan, L. & Hoy, W. K. (2006). Principal leadership: Creating a culture of academic optimism to improve achievement for all students. *Leadership and Policy in Schools, 5,* 203–229.

McLaughlin, M. W. (1990). Embracing contraries: Implementing and sustaining teacher evaluation. In J. Millman & L. Darling-Hammond (Eds.), *The new handbook of teacher evaluation: Assessing elementary and secondary school teachers* (pp. 403–415). Newbury Park, CA: SAGE.

McLaughlin, M. W., & Talbert, J. E. (2006). *Building school-based teacher learning communities: Professional strategies to improve student achievement* (Vol. 45). New York, NY: Teachers College Press.

McMillan, J. H. (2000). *Basic assessment concepts for teachers and administrators.* Thousand Oaks, CA: Corwin Press.

Mendro, R. L. (1998). Student achievement and school and teacher accountability. *Journal of Personnel Evaluation in Education, 12,* 257–267.

Meyer, H. H. (1991). A solution to the performance appraisal feedback enigma. *Academy of Management Executive, 5,* 68–76.

Miles, M. B. (1969). Planned change and organizational health: Figure and ground. In F. D. Carver and T. J. Sergiovanni (Eds.), *Organizations and human behavior* (pp. 375–391). New York, NY: McGraw-Hill.

Mintzberg, H. (1979). *The structuring of organizations.* Englewood Cliffs, NJ: Prentice Hall.

Mintzberg, H. (1989). *Mintzberg on management.* New York, NY: Free Press.

Mosher, R. L., & Purpel, D. E. (1972). *Supervision: The reluctant profession.* Boston, MA: Houghton-Mifflin Company.

Murphy, J. (1990). Principal instructional leadership. *Advances in Educational Administration, 1* (B: Changing perspectives on the school), 163–200.

Murray, H. G. (1983). Low inference classroom teaching behavior and student ratings of college teaching effectiveness. *Journal of Educational Psychology, 75,* 138–149.

National Association of Elementary School Principals (NAESP). (2001). *Leading learning communities: Standards for what principals should know and be able to do.* Alexandria, VA: Author.

National Board for Professional Teaching Standards. (2004). *Why America needs accomplished teachers.* Arlington, VA: Author. Retrieved from http:// www.nbpts.org/edreform/why.cfm

National Board for Professional Teaching Standards. (2005). Examples of education reform. Retrieved from www.wested.org/online_pubs/ RELW_1.2.29_Supp_multistate_appB.pdf

National Commission on Teaching and America's Future. (1996). *What matters most: Teaching for America's future.* Retrieved from *nctaf.org/wp-content/uploads/ 2012/01/WhatMattersMost.pdf*

National Governors Association Center for Best Practices, Council of Chief State School Officers. (2010). *Common Core State Standards.* Washington D.C.: National Governors Association Center for Best Practices, Council of Chief State School Officers.

National Staff Development Council. (2010). *NSDC's definition of professional development.* Retrieved from www.learningforward.org

No Child Left Behind Act of 2001. (2002). Public Law 107-100. Washington, D.C.

Novick, R. (1996). Actual schools, possible practices: New directions in professional development. *Education Policy Analysis Archives, 4*(14), 1–15.

Nuthall, G. A. (2007). *The hidden lives of learners.* Wellington, NZ: New Zealand Council for Educational Research.

Nye, B., Konstantopoulos, S., & Hedges, L. V. (2004). How large are teacher effects? *Educational Evaluation and Policy Analysis, 26*(3), 237–257.

Owen, J., & Davies, P. (2003). *Listening to staff, 2002.* London, UK: Centre for Economic and Social Inclusion, Learning and Skills Development Agency, and Association of Colleges.

Pajak, E. F. (1993). *Approaches to clinical supervision: Alternatives for improving instruction.* Norwood, MA: Christopher-Gordon.

Parsons, T. (1967). Some ingredients of a general theory of formal organization. In Andrew W. Halpin (Ed.), *Administrative theory in education* (pp. 40–72). New York, NY: Macmillan.

Patterson, J. (1993). *Leadership for tomorrow's schools.* Alexandria, VA: Association of Supervision and Curriculum Development.

Péladeau, N., Forget, J., & Gagné, F. (2003). Effect of paced and unpaced practice on skill application and retention: How much is enough? *American Educational Research Journal, 40,* 769–801.

Peltzman, A., Porter, W., Towne, L., & Vranek, J. (2012). *A strong state role in common core state standards implementation: Rubric and self-assessment tool.* Seattle WA: Education First.

Pennock, D. (1992). Effective performance appraisals (really!). *Supervision, 53*(8), 14–16.

Penuel, W. R., Fishman, B. J., Yamaguchi, R., & Gallagher, L. P. (2007). What makes professional development effective? Strategies that foster curriculum implementation. *American Educational Research Journal, 44*(4), 921–958.

Perkins, D. N., Jay, E., & Tishman, S. (1993). Beyond abilities: A dispositional theory of thinking. *Merrill-Palmer Quarterly: Journal of Developmental Psychology, 39*(1), 1–21. Retrieved from http://psycnet.apa.org/psycinfo/1993-20281-001

Peterson, K. D. (1988). Reliability of panel judgments for promotion in a school teacher career ladder system. *Journal of Research and Development in Education*, *21*(4), 95–99.

Peterson, K. D. (1995). *Teacher evaluation: A comprehensive guide to new directions and practices*. Thousand Oaks, CA: Corwin Press.

Peterson, K. D. (2000). *Teacher evaluation: A comprehensive guide to new directions and practices* (2nd ed.). Thousand Oaks, CA: Corwin Press.

Peterson, K. D., & Peterson, C. A. (2006). *Effective teacher evaluation: A guide for principals*. Thousand Oaks, CA: Corwin Press.

Popham, J. (1988). The dysfunctional marriage of formative and summative evaluation. *Journal of Personnel Evaluation in Education*, *1*, 269–273.

Poston, W. K., Jr., Downey, C. J., Steffy, B. E., & English, F. W. (Eds.). (2009). *Advancing the three-minute walk-through: Mastering reflective practice*. Thousand Oaks, CA: Corwin.

Pressley, M., Raphael, L., Gallagher, J. D., & DiBella, J. (2004). Providence-St. Mel School: How a school that works for African American students works. *Journal of Educational Psychology*, *96*(2), 216. doi:10.1037/0022-0663.96.2.216

Race to the Top Act. (2011). Washington, DC. Retrieved from http://www.govtrack.us/congress/bills/112/s844

Rallis, S. F., & Goldring, E. B. (2000). *Principals of dynamic schools: Taking charge of change* (2nd ed.). Thousand Oaks, CA: Corwin Press.

Raudenbush, S., Rowen, B., & Cheong, Y. (1992). Contextual effects on the self-perceived efficacy of high school teachers. *Sociology of Education*, *65*, 150–167.

Reavis, C. A. (1978). *Teacher improvement through clinical supervision*. Bloomington, IN: Phi Delta Kappa Educational Foundation.

Rebore, R. W. (1997). *Personnel administration in education: A management approach* (5th ed.). Needham Heights, MA: Allyn & Bacon.

Reeves, D. B. (2003). *Assessing educational leaders: Evaluating performance for improved individual and organizational results*. Thousand Oaks, CA: Corwin Press.

Reiman, A. J., & Thies-Sprinthall, L. (1998). *Mentoring and supervision for teacher development*. New York, NY: Addison-Wesley Longman.

Reis, S. M., & Renzulli, J. S. (2003). Developing high potentials for innovation in young people through the schoolwide enrichment model. In L. V. Shavinina (Ed.), *International handbook on innovation* (pp. 333–346). London, UK: Pergamon/Elsevier.

Reiss, F., & Hoy, W. K. (1998). Faculty loyalty: An important but neglected concept in the study of schools. *Journal of School Leadership*, *8*, 4–21.

Richards, J. (2003, April). *Principal behaviors that encourage teachers to stay in the profession: Perceptions of k-8 teachers in their second to fifth year of teaching*. Paper presented at the annual meeting of the American Educational Research Association, Chicago, IL.

Rivkin, S. G., Hanushek, E. A., & Kain, J. F. (2001). *Teachers, schools, and academic achievement*. Amherst, MA: Amherst College Press.

Roberts, S. M., & Pruitt, E. Z. (Eds.). (2009). *Schools as professional learning communities: Collaborative activities and strategies for professional development*. Thousand Oaks, CA: Corwin.

Robinson, G. E. (1985). *Effective schools research: A guide to school improvement.* Arlington, VA: Educational Research Service. (ERIC Document Reproduction Service No. ED252970)

Robinson, V. M. J. (2010). From instructional leadership to leadership capabilities: Empirical findings and methodological challenges, *Leadership and Policy in Schools, 9*(1), 1-26. doi:10.1080/15700760903026748

Robinson, V. M. J., Lloyd, C., & Rowe, K. J. (2008). The impact of leadership on student outcomes: An analysis of the differential effects of leadership type. *Educational Administration Quarterly, 44*(5), 635–674. doi:10.1177/0013161X08321509

Robitaille, D. (Ed.). (1993). *Curriculum frameworks for mathematics and science.* Vancouver, Canada: Pacific Educational Press.

Rosenshine, B. (1975). Enthusiastic teaching: A research review. In M. Mohan & R. E. Hull (Eds.), *Teaching effectiveness: Its meaning, assessment, and improvement* (p. 114). Englewood Cliffs, NJ: Educational Technology Publications.

Rosenshine, B., & Furst, N. (1973). The use of direct observation to study teaching. In R. Travers (Ed.), *Second handbook of research on teaching* (pp. 122–183). Chicago, IL: Rand McNally.

Rosenshine, B., & Meister, C. (1994). Reciprocal teaching: A review of the research. *Review of Educational Research, 64*(4), 479–530.

Roseth, C. J., Fang, F., Johnson, D. W., & Johnson, R. T. (2006, April). *Meeting early adolescents' developmental needs: The effects of cooperative, competitive, and individualistic goal structures.* Paper presented at AERA Annual Meeting, San Francisco, CA.

Ross, J. A., Cousins, J. B., & Gadalla, R. (1996). Within-teacher predictors of teacher efficacy. *Teaching and Teacher Education, 12,* 385–400. doi:10.1016/0742-051X(95)00046-M

Rossow, L. F., & Tate, J. O. (2003). *The law of teacher evaluation.* Dayton, OH: Education Law Association.

Rothstein, J. (2011). *Review of learning about teaching: Initial finding from the measures of teaching project.* Boulder, CO: National Education Policy Center. Retrieved from http://nepc.colorado.edu/thinktank/review-learning-about-teaching

Rozzelle, J. (2012). *Classroom observation tool.* Retrieved from http://education.wm.edu/centers/sli/surn/index.php

Ryans, D. G. (1960). *Characteristics of effective teachers, their descriptions, comparisons and appraisal: A research study.* Washington, DC: American Council on Education.

Sacks, P. (1999). *Standardized minds.* Cambridge, MA: Perseus Books.

Sanders, W. L. (1998). Value-added assessment. *School Administrator, 55*(11), 24–27.

Sanders, W. L. & Horn, S. P. (1998). Research findings from the Tennessee value-added assessment system (TVAAS) database: Implications for educational evaluation and research. *Journal of Personnel Evaluation in Education,12*(3), 247–256.

Sawyer, L. (2001). Revamping a teacher evaluation system. *Educational Leadership, 58*(5), 44–47.

Schein, E. H. (1992). *Organizational culture and leadership* (2nd ed.). San Francisco, CA: Jossey-Bass.

Schein, E. H. (2004). *Organizational culture and leadership* (3rd ed.). San Francisco, CA: Jossey-Bass.

Schmidt, W. H., McKnight, C. C., & Raizen, S. A. (1996). *Splintered vision: An investigation of U.S. science and mathematics education: Executive summary.* Lansing, MI: U.S. National Research Center for the Third International Mathematics and Science Study, Michigan State University.

Schmoker, M. L. (1999). *Results: The key to continuous school improvement* (2nd ed.). Alexandria, VA: Association for Supervision and Curriculum Development.

Schunk, D. H., Pintrich, P. R., & Meece, J., L. (2008). *Motivation in education* (3rd ed.). Upper Saddle River, NJ: Pearson Merrill Prentice Hall.

Scriven, M. (1981). Summative teacher evaluation. In J. Millman (Ed.), *Handbook of teacher evaluation* (pp. 244–271). National Council on Measurement in Education series. Beverly Hills, CA: SAGE.

Seidel, T., & Shavelson, R. J. (2007). Teaching effectiveness research in the past decade: The role of theory and research design in disentangling meta-analysis results. *Review of Educational Research, 77*(4), 454–499. doi:10.3102/0034654307310317

Seligman, M. E. P. (1998). *Learned optimism* (2nd ed.). New York, NY: Pocket Books, Simon and Schuster.

Senge, P. (1990). *The fifth discipline: The art and practice of the learning organization.* New York, NY: Currency Doubleday.

Sergiovanni, T. J., & Starratt, R. J. (2010). *Supervision: A re-definition* (8th ed.). Boston, MA: McGraw-Hill.

Shavelson, R. J. (1987). Planning. In M. Dunkin (Ed.), *The international encyclopedia of teaching and teacher education* (pp. 483–486). New York, NY: Pergamon.

Shayer, M. (2003). Not just Piaget; not just Vygotsky, and certainly not Vygotsky as < i> alternative < i> to Piaget. *Learning and Instruction, 13*(5), 465–485.

Shulman, L. S. (1987). Knowledge and teaching: Foundations of the new reform. *Harvard Educational Review, 19*(2), 4–14.

Shute, V. J. (2008). Focus on formative feedback. *Review of Educational Research, 78*(1), 153–189. doi:10.3102/0034654307313795

Sindelar, P. T., Shearer, D. K., Yendol-Hoppey, D., & Liebert, T. W. (2006). The sustainability of inclusive school reform. *Exceptional Children, 72*(3), 317–331.

Sinden, J., Hoy, W. K., & Sweetland, S. R. (2004). Enabling school structures: Principal leadership and organizational commitment of teachers. *Journal of School Leadership, 14,* 195–210.

Smith, P. A., & Hoy, W. K. (2007). Academic optimism and student achievement in urban elementary schools. *Journal of Educational Administration, 45,* 556–568.

Snyder, H. S., Shorey, H. S., Cheavens, J., Pulvers, K. M., Adams III, V. H., & Wiklund, C. (2002). Hope and academic success in college. *Journal of Educational Psychology, 94,* 820–826.

Soar, R. S., & Soar, R. M. (1979). Emotional climate and management. In P. Peterson & H. Walberg (Eds.), *Research on teaching: Concepts, findings, and implications* (pp. 97–119). Berkeley, CA: McCutchan.

Spillane, J. P. (2006). *Distributed leadership.* San Francisco, CA: Jossey-Bass.

Spillane, J. P., Halverson, R., & Diamond, J. B. (2000). *Toward a theory of leadership practice: A distributed perspective.* Evanston, IL: Institute for Policy Research.

Spillane, J. P., Halverson, R., & Diamond, J. B. (2001). Investigating school leadership practice: A distributed perspective. *Educational Researcher, 30*(3), 23–28.

Spillane, J. P., Halverson, R., & Diamond, J. B. (2004). Towards a theory of leadership practice: A distributed perspective. *Journal of Curriculum Studies, 36,* 3–34. doi:10.1080/0022027032000106726

Stein, M., & Spillane, J. (2003, April). *Research on teaching and research on educational administration: Building a bridge.* Paper presented at the annual meeting of the American Education Research Association, Chicago, IL.

Sternberg, R. J. (2000). *Handbook of human intelligence.* New York, NY: Cambridge University Press.

Sternberg, R. J. (2004). Culture and intelligence. *American Psychologist, 59,* 325–338. doi:10.1037/0003-066X.59.5.325

Stodolsky, S. S. (1989). Is teaching really by the book? In P. W. Jackson & S. Haroutunian-Gordon (Eds.), *Eighty-ninth yearbook of the national society for the study of education, Part I* (pp. 159–184). Chicago, IL: University of Chicago Press.

Stronge, J. H. (2002). *Qualities of effective teachers.* Arlington, VA: Association for Supervision and Curriculum Development.

Stronge, J. H. (Ed.). (2006). *Evaluating teaching: A guide to current thinking and best practice* (2nd ed.). Thousand Oaks, CA: Corwin Press.

Stronge, J. H., & Helm, V. M. (1991). *Evaluating professional support personnel in education.* Newbury Park, CA: SAGE.

Stronge, J. H., & Ostrander, L. (2006). Client surveys and teacher evaluation. In J. Stronge (Ed.), *Evaluating teaching: A guide to current thinking and best practice* (2nd ed., pp. 125–151). Thousand Oaks, CA: Corwin Press.

Stronge, J. H., & Tucker, P. D. (2003). *Handbook on teacher evaluation: Assessing and improving performance.* Larchmont, NY: Eye on Education.

Stufflebeam, D. L. (2001). Evaluation checklists: Practical tools for guiding and judging evaluations. *American Journal of Evaluation, 22*(1), 71–79.

Stufflebeam, D. L. (2003). The CIPP model for evaluation. In T. Kellaghan & D. Stufflebeam (Eds.) *International handbook of educational evaluation* (pp. 31–62). Dordrecht, Netherlands: Kluwer. doi:10.1007/978-94-010-0309-4

Sullivan, S., & Glanz, J. (2000). Alternative approaches to supervision: Cases from the field. *Journal of Curriculum and Supervision, 15*(3), 212–235.

Supovitz, J. A., & Poglinco, S. M. (2001). *Instructional leadership in a standards-based reform.* Philadelphia, PA: Consortium for Policy Research in Education, University of Pennsylvania.

Sweetland, S. R., & Hoy, W. K. (2000). School climate, teacher empowerment, and effectiveness. *Educational Administration Quarterly, 36,* 703–729.

Sykes, G. (1999). Teacher and student learning: Strengthening their connection. In L. Darling-Hammond and G. Sykes (Eds.), *Teaching as the learning profession* (pp. 151–180). San Francisco, CA: Jossey-Bass.

Szuminski, K. (2003). *Teacher development in CTE in brief: Fast facts for policy and practice* no. 21. Port Huron, MI: NCCTE Publications.

Teacher Training Center for International Education (TTCIE). (2007). Professional development that makes a difference. *International Education, 22*(2), 33.

Thompson, D. P., McNamara, J. F., & Hoyle, J. R. (1997). Job satisfaction in educational organizations: A synthesis of research findings. *Educational Administration Quarterly, 33*, 7–37. doi:10.1177/0013161X97033001002

Tishman, S., Jay, E., & Perkins, D. N. (1993). Teaching thinking dispositions: From transmission to enculturation. *Theory into Practice, 32*(3), 147–153.

Tobin, K. G. (1980). The effect of an extended teacher wait-time on science achievement. *Journal of Research and Science Teaching, 17*, 469–475.

Togneri, W., & Anderson, S. (2003). *Beyond islands of excellence: What districts can do to improve instruction and achievement in all schools. A leadership brief.* Retrieved from www.learningfirst.org

Tomlinson, C. A. (2001). Standards and the art of teaching: Crafting high-quality classrooms. *NASSP Bulletin, 85*(622), 38–47. doi:10.1177/019263650108562206

Tomlinson, C. A., & Allan, S. D. (2000). *Leadership for differentiating schools and classrooms.* Alexandria, VA: Association for Supervision and Curriculum Development.

Tschannen-Moran, M. (2004). *Trust matters: Leadership for successful schools.* San Francisco, CA: Jossey-Bass.

Tschannen-Moran, M., Woolfolk Hoy, A., & Hoy, W. K. (1998). Teacher efficacy: Its meaning and measure. *Review of Educational Research, 68*(2), 202–248. doi:10.3102/00346543068002202

Tucker, P. D., & DeSander, M. (2006). Legal considerations in designing teacher evaluation systems. In J. H. Stronge (Ed.), *Evaluating teaching: A guide to current thinking and best practice* (2nd ed., pp. 69–97). Thousand Oaks, CA: Corwin Press.

Tucker, P. D., & Stronge, J. H. (2001). Measure for measure: Using student test results in teacher evaluations. *American School Board Journal, 188*(9), 34–37.

Tucker, P. D., & Stronge, J. H. (2005). *Linking Teacher Evaluation and Student Learning.* Alexandria, VA: Association for Supervision and Curriculum Development.

Unruh, A., & Turner, H. E. (1970). *Supervision for change and innovation.* Boston, MA: Houghton-Mifflin Company.

Valente, W. D. (1998). *Law in the schools.* Upper Saddle River, NJ: Prentice Hall.

van Gog, T., Ericsson, K. A., Rikers, R. M. J. P., & Paas, F. (2005). Instructional design for advanced learners: Establishing connections between the theoretical frameworks of cognitive load and deliberate practice. *Educational Technology, Research and Development, 53*(3), 73–81.

Virginia Department of Education. (2011). *Guidelines for uniform performance standards and evaluation criteria for teachers.* Richmond, VA: Author. Retrieved from http://www.doe.virginia.gov/teaching/performance_evaluation/teacher/index.shtml

Wagner, C. A., & DiPaola, M. F. (2011). Academic optimism of high school teachers: Its relationship to organizational citizenship behavior and student achievement. *Journal of School Leadership, 21*, 891–924.

Walker, D., Greenwood, C., Hart, B., & Carta, J. (1994). Prediction of school outcomes based on early language production and socioeconomic factors. *Child Development, 65*(2), 606–621.

Walls, R., Nardi, A., von Minden, A., & Hoffman, N. (2002). The characteristics of effective and ineffective teachers. *Teacher Education Quarterly, 29*, 39–48.

Wang, M. C., Haertel, G. D., & Walberg, H. J. (1993). Toward a knowledge base for school learning. *Review of Educational Research, 63*(3), 249–294.

Wang, M. C., Haertel, G. D., & Walberg, H. J. (1997). Learning influences. In H. Walberg & G. Haertel (Eds.), *Psychology and educational practice* (pp. 199–211). Berkeley, CA: McCutchan.

Waters, J. T., Marzano, R. J., & McNulty, B. A. (2003). *Balanced leadership: What 30 years of research tells us about the effect of leadership on student achievement.* Aurora, CO: Mid-continent Research for Education and Learning.

Webb, C. (1989). Room for improvement: Performance evaluations. *Wilson Library Bulletin, 63*(6), 56–57.

Weber, J. (1996). Leading the instructional program. In S. Smith & P. Piele (Eds.), *School leadership* (pp. 253–278). Eugene, OR: Clearinghouse of Educational Management.

Weber, M. (1947). *The theory of social and economic organizations.* In T. Parsons (Ed.), A. M. Henderson & T. Parsons (Trans.), (pp. 87–423). New York, NY: Free Press.

Weick, K. E., & Sutcliffe, K. M. (2001). *Managing the unexpected: Assuring high performance in an age of complexity.* San Francisco, CA: Jossey Bass.

Weinstein, C. S. (2003). *Secondary classroom management* (2nd ed.). Boston, MA: McGraw-Hill.

Weinstein, C. S., & Mignano, Jr., A. J. (2003). *Elementary classroom management: Lessons from research and practice* (3rd ed.). New York, NY: McGraw-Hill.

Whalan, F. (2012). *Collective responsibility:Redefining what falls between the cracks for school reform.* Rotterdam, The Netherlands: Sense.

Wiggins, G. P., & McTighe, J. (2005). *Understanding by design* (Expanded 2nd ed.). Washington, DC: National Education Association.

Wong, C. S., & Law, K. S. (2002). The effects of leader and follower emotional intelligence on performance and attitude: An exploratory study. *The Leadership Quarterly. 13*, 243–274.

Woolfolk, A. (2014). *Education psychology.* Boston, MA: Pearson.

Woolfolk, A. E., & Brooks, D. (1983). Nonverbal communication in teaching. In E. Gordon (Ed.), *Review of research in education* (Vol. 10, pp. 103–150). Washington, DC: American Educational Research Association.

Woolfolk, A. E., & Hoy, W. K. (1990). Prospective teachers' sense of efficacy and beliefs about control. *Journal of Educational Psychology, 82*, 81–91.

Woolfolk, A. E., Rosoff, B., & Hoy, W. K. (1990). Teachers' sense of efficacy and their beliefs about managing students. *Teaching and Teacher Education, 6*(2), 137–148. doi:10.1016/0742-051X(90)90031-Y

Wright, S. P., Horn, S. P., & Sanders, W. L. (1997). Teacher and classroom context effects on student achievement. Implications for teacher evaluation. *Journal of Personnel Evaluation in Education, 11*, 57–67.

Yamagata-Lynch, L. C. (2003). How a technology professional development program fits into teachers' work life. *Teaching and Teacher Education, 19*(6), 591–607.

Yoon, B., Burstein, L., & Gold, K. (n.d.). *Assessing the content validity of teachers' reports of content coverage and its relationship to student achievement* (CSE Rep. No. 328). Los Angeles, CA: Center for Research in Evaluating Standards and Student Testing, University of California, Los Angeles.

Yoon, K. S., Duncan, T., Lee, S. W.-Y., Scarloss, B., & Shapley, K. (2007). *Reviewing the evidence on how teacher professional development affects student achievement* (Issues & Answers Report, REL 2007–No. 033). Washington, DC: U.S. Department of Education, Institute of Education Sciences, National Center for Education Evaluation and Regional Assistance, Regional Educational Laboratory Southwest. Retrieved from http://ies.ed.gov/ncee/edlabs

Zepada, S. J. (2003). *The principal as instructional leader.* Larchmont, NY: Eye on Education.

Zimmerman, B., & Schunk, D. (Eds.). (2011). *Handbook of self-regulation and performance.* New York, NY: Routledge.

Zirkel, P. A. (1996). *The law of teacher evaluation: A self-assessment handbook.* Bloomington, IN: Phi Delta Kappa Educational Foundation.

ABOUT THE AUTHORS

Michael F. DiPaola is Chancellor Professor in the Educational Policy, Planning & Leadership Program of the School of Education at The College of William & Mary. Dr. DiPaola's career in public education spanned three decades, including a decade of classroom teaching. He served as an assistant principal in a 7-12 school and as principal of a 10-12 senior high school. He received his EdD from Rutgers, The State University of New Jersey. Prior to joining the faculty at William & Mary, he was a school district superintendent for six years. Professor DiPaola is the author or co-author of articles, book chapters, and technical reports on school organizations and the roles and responsibilities of school administrators. He has co-edited five volumes in the series Research and Theory in Educational Administration. Dr. DiPaola is co-author, with Wayne Hoy, of the *Principals Improving Instruction: Supervision Evaluation, and Professional Development.* His teaching and research interests include social processes in school organizations, improving instruction, and building capacity in schools.

Wayne K. Hoy, a former public school mathematics teacher, received his D.Ed. from The Pennsylvania State University. He taught at Oklahoma State University, before moving to Rutgers University in 1968, where he was a distinguished professor, department chair, and Associate Dean for Academic Affairs. In 1994, he was selected as the Fawcett Chair in Educational Administration, an endowed professorship at The Ohio State University. Dr. Hoy is past secretary-treasurer of the National Conference of Professors of Educational Administration (NCPEA), past president of the University Council for Educational Administration (UCEA), a fellow of the American Educational Research Association (AERA) and recipient of the Roald Campbell Lifetime Achievement Award in Educational Administration. He has published more than 130 research articles; he is the author or coauthor of 12 books in the fields of research and theory, educational administration, decision making, leadership, instructional supervision, and research methods as well as editor of another eleven books on educational leadership and policy. Four of his recent books include *Collective Trust: Why Schools Can't Improve Without It* (2011) with Patrick Forsyth and Curt Adams, *Quantitative Research in Educational Administration: A Primer* (2010), *Educational Administration: Theory, Research and Practice* (2013), with Cecil Miskel, and *Instructional Leadership: A Research-based Guide to Learning in Schools* (2013), which he coauthored with his wife, Anita Woolfolk.

INDEX

CPSIA information can be obtained
at www.ICGtesting.com
Printed in the USA
JSHW022032071222
34506JS00006B/168